DILTHEY

Philosopher of the
Human Studies

Rudolf A. Makkreel

DILTHEY

Philosopher of the
Human Studies

PRINCETON UNIVERSITY PRESS

PRINCETON, NEW JERSEY

Copyright © 1975 by Princeton University Press
Published by Princeton University Press
Princeton and London

All Rights Reserved

Library of Congress Cataloging In Publication data
will be found on the last printed page of this book

Composed in Linotype Janson and printed
in the United States of America by Princeton
University Press at Princeton, New Jersey

second printing, 1977

To my Parents

Contents

Preface

Among the major philosophers of the late nineteenth century, none has contributed more to the understanding of historical life than Wilhelm Dilthey (1833–1911). His theory of the *Geisteswissenschaften*, generally acknowledged as a landmark in defining both the historical orientation of the human studies and the limits of the natural sciences, has exerted a profound influence on twentieth-century Continental philosophy. The increasing interest in Dilthey by theorists in various disciplines also attests to the wide-ranging significance of his work. Yet the general recognition of Dilthey's importance has been long in coming, for unlike some of his more strident contemporaries, he produced his effect quietly by suggesting programmatic changes for philosophy. Thus his efforts to provide an experiential grounding for historical understanding first led him to propose a descriptive psychology which Husserl recognized as an important anticipation of phenomenology. Heidegger for his part has characterized his own existential analysis of history as an extension of the interpretive or hermeneutic approach exhibited in Dilthey's late writings. The fact that Dilthey's efficacy can be traced in several, and often divergent, directions has, unfortunately, encouraged fragmentary interpretations of his philosophy.

Contrary to the common tendency to divorce Dilthey's early psychological from his later hermeneutic and historical writings, the present study seeks to show their essential *continuity*. Only by holding together these fundamental aspects of Dilthey's thought can the fruitfulness of his concepts and the overall coherence of his outlook be judged. With this in mind, I argue for the centrality of Dilthey's aesthetic writings and explore their philosophical implications—many of them Kantian—for his theory of history.

In the introductory chapter, the relevant literature on

Dilthey is surveyed by way of contrast to the present approach. Projecting, at the same time, the possibility of a Kantian aesthetic of history, I anticipate some of the conclusions which will be worked out through a gradual explication of Dilthey's concepts and theories. Such a sketch is in accordance with Dilthey's procedure of beginning with a general orientation or an initial sense of the whole in relation to which an understanding of the parts can be obtained.

Chapter 1 gives the historical and theoretical background for the development of Dilthey's mature philosophy. It discusses the theory of the *Geisteswissenschaften* as providing the guiding principles for the subsequent formulation of Dilthey's ideas about psychology, aesthetics, history, and philosophy.

Part Two focuses on Dilthey's aesthetics as a model *Geisteswissenschaft*. In chapter 2, I analyze the concepts of poetic imagination, psychic structure and style, and more generally take note of the aesthetic essays as first steps in working out the problem of relating different methods in the *Geisteswissenschaften*. The next chapter deals with the maturation of the descriptive psychology—the movement from a value-oriented analysis of elementary aesthetic feelings to a more meaning-oriented description of poetic *Erlebnis* (lived experience).

In chapter 4, the epistemological implications of Dilthey's concept of the imagination are considered by relating them to his general critique of synthetic method in the *Geisteswissenschaften*. Ever since Kant, the imagination has been construed as synthetic. But I contend that Dilthey's theory of the imagination involves a concept of articulation which is better able to do justice to poetic technique as well as to the complexities of the historical world.

Part Three covers the much misunderstood transition to the hermeneutic standpoint of Dilthey's late work. In the fifth, and pivotal, chapter, the possibility of more explicitly linking the psychological and the historical is explored by drawing on Dilthey's suggestion for a concept of reflective experience. Here the character of Dilthey's Critique of Historical Reason is disclosed through an interpretation of the role of reflective judgment in Kant's *Critique of Judgment*. Having introduced not merely a reflective component in psychic experience but also a critical framework, Dilthey must, as we show in chapter 6, reconstrue his psychological analysis of *Verstehen* (understanding) from a hermeneutic perspective.

In chapter 7, an exchange of views between Dilthey and Husserl is examined to determine the extent to which Dilthey felt impelled to reformulate his ideas about the psychological description of *Erlebnis* as well. A continuing role for psychology is claimed, not to reduce Dilthey's theories to a psychological level, but to show that even when he developed a more Hegelian approach to history (see chapter 8) many of the insights gained in the earlier psychological and aesthetic writings are preserved to enrich his conceptualization of the human studies.

The two chapters of Part Four are more exploratory in character. Suggestions from Dilthey's final writings on poetry and music are considered in chapter 9 to deal with some of the inadequacies of his *Weltanschauung* theory. They also allow us to formulate some fundamental differences between Dilthey's and Heidegger's positions.

The last chapter applies some of Dilthey's general reflective categories of life to problems of historical and critical interpretation. Special attention is devoted to the concept of style as a way to summarize our theme of the interrelatedness of aesthetic and historical considerations.

Acknowledgments

I WISH to thank the editors of the *Journal of Aesthetics and Art Criticism* for permission to republish parts of an article of mine in vol. 27, Winter 1968, pp. 171–82. I am similarly grateful to the editors of the *Journal of the History of Philosophy* for permission to republish parts of my article "Wilhelm Dilthey and the Neo-Kantians" in vol. 7, October 1969, pp. 423–40, and a review article in vol. 10, April 1972, pp. 232–37.

Throughout my work—especially in attempting to relate aesthetics to historical understanding—I have gained immeasurably from the critical insight of my wife, Frances Tanikawa. Without her editorial comments and criticisms, this book might have been more speedily completed, but it would have appeared without the added understanding drawn from her training and research in history.

I remain grateful to the philosophy department at Columbia University for the encouragement and assistance given me during my studies there, especially to Albert Hofstadter, who first aroused my interest in Dilthey and guided my early work on his aesthetics. A fellowship from the Deutsche Akademische Austauschdienst allowed me to do much of my research on Dilthey through the Freie Universität, West Berlin, and to consult there with Hans-Joachim Lieber.

In the succeeding years, as I expanded my work to show the development of Dilthey's philosophy as a whole, I have benefited greatly from the stimulation and friendship of my students and colleagues. I owe particular thanks to Richard Popkin, Herbert Marcuse, and Jason Saunders, all formerly members of the philosophy department at the University of California, San Diego, and to John Anton and Donald Nilson of Emory University. I wish also to acknowledge the fine assistance given by several graduate students, John

Moore, Fred Gordon, Carlos Botta, Robert Danner, C. Campbell Giddens, Thomas Dorn, and Kenneth Fagan as well as by the departmental staffs of UCSD and Emory, especially Norma Bain and Linda Borkman.

The research grants provided by a University of California Faculty Scholarship and by the University of California Humanities Institute were much appreciated.

Finally, among the many to whom I am indebted for their encouraging interest and support, I would like to thank Herbert Schneider and Edward Mahoney.

Atlanta
December 1974   RUDOLF MAKKREEL

Abbreviations

Aufbau	Dilthey, "Der Aufbau der geschichtlichen Welt in den Geisteswissenschaften"
BT	Heidegger, *Being and Time*, trans. J. Macquarrie and E. Robinson
CJ	Kant, *Critique of Judgment*, trans. J. H. Bernard
CR	Kant, *Critique of Pure Reason*, trans. N. K. Smith
DDM	Dilthey, *Von deutscher Dichtung und Musik*
Die drei Epochen	Dilthey, "Die drei Epochen der modernen Aesthetik und ihre heutige Aufgabe"
ED	Dilthey, *Das Erlebnis und die Dichtung*
Einleitung	Dilthey, *Einleitung in die Geisteswissenschaften*
Entwürfe	Dilthey, "Entwürfe zur Kritik der historischen Vernunft"
GS	Dilthey, *Gesammelte Schriften*
Ideen	Dilthey, "Ideen über eine beschreibende und zergliedernde Psychologie"
Poetik	Dilthey, "Die Einbildungskraft des Dichters: Bausteine für eine Poetik"

DILTHEY

Philosopher of the
Human Studies

Introduction:
Toward an Aesthetic of History

THROUGHOUT his life, Wilhelm Dilthey (1833–1911) identified his philosophical project as the writing of a Critique of
Historical Reason. As a practicing historian of culture and
philosophy, he was at the same time concerned with the
theoretical possibility of justifying historical knowledge. In
1903, he characterized the fundamental issue raised by such
a critical investigation into the nature and conditions of historical knowledge by speaking of an apparently irreconcilable antithesis that

> . . . arises when historical consciousness is followed to
> its last consequences. The finitude of every historical
> phenomenon, . . . the relativity of every kind of human
> apprehension of the totality of things is the last word of
> the historical *Weltanschauung* (world-view). . . . And
> over against this both the demand of thought and the
> striving of philosophy for universal knowledge assert
> themselves. The historical *Weltanschauung* liberates
> the human spirit from the last chains that natural sci-
> ence and philosophy have not yet broken. But where
> are the means to overcome the anarchy of opinions
> which then threatens to befall us? To the solution of the
> long series of problems which are connected with this,
> I have devoted my whole life.[1]

The historical *Weltanschauung* can liberate man from the
last remnants of dogmatism. But if the process of negating

[1] Dilthey, *Gesammelte Schriften* (to be referred to in subsequent
notes as *GS*) 17 vols., Stuttgart: B. G. Teubner, Göttingen: Vandenhoeck & Ruprecht, 1914–1974, V, 9. All translations of Dilthey are
mine unless otherwise noted.

outworn beliefs is not to become totally destructive, it must itself be limited by certain critical standards. Dilthey considered it the task of his Critique of Historical Reason to explore the possibility of such standards or norms. Because he never completed this projected critique, many commentators have viewed it as an abstract ideal set apart from his concrete accomplishments. But as such, it has functioned primarily as a measure for indicating how Dilthey failed to develop an adequate solution to certain ultimate problems he had raised. However, the idea of the critique served Dilthey as the integral guiding perspective in the gradual maturation of his philosophy, and can also be explored to help reveal an inner coherence among his varied works.

Dilthey's inability to complete his planned works, as he himself once pointed out, was connected with the best side of him. It was the result of his conviction that the systematic conclusions of his philosophy should not be arrived at apart from an interdisciplinary investigation of historical experience. Moreover, Dilthey was peculiarly sensitive to the transitional nature of the time in which he lived and the opportunity this opened up for a fundamental re-evaluation of existing philosophical approaches. He felt that German historicists such as Ranke had made great strides in freeing the theory of history from metaphysical speculation. But Dilthey also realized that historicism without a new epistemological grounding was exposed to the dangers of relativism. Just as Kant developed his critical epistemology of the natural sciences by relating the Continental tradition of rationalism to the more sceptical tradition of British empiricism, so Dilthey, a century later, established guidelines for an even more difficult critical perspective for the historical studies. This perspective was to avoid the extremes of a Hegelian idealism and a Comtean positivism.

The Problems of Systematic Unity and Developmental Coherence

It is ironic that Dilthey, whose own historical writings are noted for their concern with the complex and interrelated

facets of the life and work of individuals, should himself
have been denied that kind of consideration. There exist
two aspects to the problem of comprehending the richness
of Dilthey's overall philosophical position. One is the difficulty in relating the many disciplines to which Dilthey contributed and estimating their theoretical implications. The
other involves the historical task of doing justice to the various developmental stages of his thought.

The first or systematic aspect of the problem of understanding Dilthey manifests itself most obviously in the
English-speaking world. Here his general reputation rests
primarily on references to his *Weltanschauung* typology, his
theory of the *Geisteswissenschaften* (human studies), and
certain special methodological problems in the theory of
history.[2]

Because Dilthey contrasts the study of history to that of
nature, he is often confused with Historical Idealists such
as Croce and Collingwood.[3] It is assumed that all three
agree that historians may not make use of general laws in

[2] This failure to realize Dilthey's overall philosophical significance
contrasts sharply to Dilthey's much higher reputation, not only in
Germany, but also in Spain and Latin America. Ortega y Gasset's
claim that Dilthey was "the greatest thinker of the second half of the
nineteenth century" (Ortega y Gasset, José, *Concord and Liberty*,
trans. Helene Weyl, New York: Norton & Co., 1963, p. 131) is undoubtedly responsible for the fact that a large and generally enthusiastic literature now exists on Dilthey in Spanish.

[3] The following works exemplify this pervasive tendency to link
Dilthey with the idealists: Arthur Danto, *Analytical Philosophy of
History*, Cambridge: At the University Press, 1968, p. 205; William
Dray, *Philosophy of History*, Englewood Cliffs: Prentice-Hall, 1964,
p. 3; W. H. Walsh, *An Introduction to Philosophy of History*, London: Hutchinson & Co., 1955, pp. 50, 56. A notable exception is Georg
Henrik von Wright who writes: "The antipositivist philosophy of
science which became prominent towards the end of the nineteenth
century is a much more diversified and heterogeneous trend than positivism. The name 'idealism' which is sometimes used to characterize
it is appropriate only for some of the facets of this trend. A better
name for it seems to me to be *hermeneutics*" (*Explanation and Under-*

their description of an historical event, but must instead provide an empathetic apprehension of the inner workings of the mind of the human agent responsible for that event.[4] In supposedly Diltheyan language this would mean that only natural processes can be "explained" in terms of inductive uniformities and causal laws, whereas history is to be approached in terms of an intuitive process of "understanding" (*Verstehen*) the uniqueness of its events.

This, coupled with the other common account of Dilthey according to which he describes three competing but equally valid *Weltanschauung* types in terms of which Western art and thought can be understood, has contributed to the view that Dilthey supports a subjective, relativistic conception of philosophy.[5] While separate aspects

---

standing, Ithaca: Cornell University Press, 1971, pp. 4–5). See also in this regard Gerard Radnitzky, *Contemporary Schools of Metascience*, 2nd ed. rev., New York: Humanities Press, 1970, II, 21 fn. 22.

[4] See Danto, *Analytical Philosophy of History*, for this kind of statement. Here Ernest Nagel's view that *Verstehen* is a kind of "empathic identification" is upheld (see Ernest Nagel, *The Structure of Science: Problems in the Logic of Scientific Explanation*, New York: Harcourt, Brace and World, 1961, p. 484). Subsequently, however, Danto has acknowledged that "*Verstehen* is a very brilliant notion, utterly misconceived heretofore by crass philosophical critics, myself included" (Arthur Danto, "Causation and Basic Actions," *Inquiry*, 13, 1970, 125). He argues that because *Verstehen* involves the perception of "quite public things" it cannot be a form of empathy. But theorists of empathy like Theodor Lipps quite specifically include public things in their domain. While it is true that *Verstehen* as analyzed by Dilthey does not rely on empathy, this is due, not so much to the objective character of the expressions and actions understood, as to the fact that no identification of subject and object is claimed.

[5] In a sense, the above two stereotypes should cancel each other out. If understanding were really empathetic, then no one would be able to understand anything but other expressions of his own *Weltanschauung* type. However, Dilthey does not so restrict his theory of *Verstehen*. He hardly ever makes use of the term *Einfühlen* (empathy—feeling into) and certainly not to equate it with *Verstehen*. Dilthey more commonly associates the latter with the concept of

6

of his work undeniably lend themselves to such interpretation, Dilthey's thought as a whole is meant to forestall the sceptical consequences of such stereotypes.

Only by studying the interrelations among the several fields in the *Geisteswissenschaften* to which Dilthey made important contributions—principally, psychology, philosophy of history, and aesthetics—can his various conceptual and methodological theories be placed in proper perspective. Most commentators have focused either on Dilthey's method of description as emphasized in his psychology and *Weltanschauungslehre* (theory of world-views), or on the method of *Verstehen* associated with his hermeneutics and theory of historical interpretation. The question to what extent description and understanding limit the role of explanation in the *Geisteswissenschaften* has not been adequately examined. For despite his critique of naturalistic explanation, Dilthey never altogether ruled out its applicability to history. Moreover, in his aesthetics he sought to develop a special method of explanation more appropriate to human productivity by formulating certain laws of the imagination. It is important to consider Dilthey's work in the fields of psychology, aesthetics, and history together if an adequate account of the relation of description, explanation, and understanding is to be obtained. With this, it can be seen that Dilthey does not ground understanding in empathy and intuition, and is aware of the need for a description of structural uniformities. While his conception of the nature and function of explanation changes, its role is never ignored.

These methodological approaches have to be considered in the overall framework of Dilthey's idea of a Critique of

---

Nacherleben (reexperiencing) and its cognate, *Nachfühlen* (refeeling), neither of which refers to a unifying projection of the self into the other. His theory of understanding acknowledges fundamental differences between human beings and historical epochs, while at the same time articulating a common base.

7

Historical Reason. Whatever their sceptical implications in isolation, their ultimate orientation was defined by the question, *How* is *objective* historical understanding possible? To affirm this possibility Dilthey stressed the historicity of *Weltanschauungen* as a way of placing a limit on the speculative claims of metaphysical philosophies of history. And to better characterize what can properly be expected of the study of history, Dilthey undertook an extended inquiry into the concrete nature of our historical experience of life. The transcendental aspect of this inquiry manifests itself in the problem of the interrelation of psychology and epistemology, i.e. the relation of description to norms; the methodological aspect points to a link between aesthetics and history, which will require a comparative analysis of explanation and understanding.

While Kant had separated psychology and epistemology, Dilthey's work in aesthetics and history led him to reopen the question about the extent to which psychological descriptions have a bearing on epistemological theories. This was of especial concern to Dilthey, for in reflecting on his Critique of Historical Reason he found that the categories of the Kantian epistemology were inadequate to cope with historical experience. Dilthey could not, like Kant, appeal to the essentially ahistorical perspective of traditional reason and natural ontology for the categories of his critique, and in grappling with the nature of experience itself, he came to challenge the associationist psychology to which Kant was also still implicitly indebted. With special reference to aesthetic experience, Dilthey formulated a descriptive psychology which stressed the wholeness and continuity of experience. Instead of considering experience as a conceptual ordering of inert sensations, as Kant had defined *Erfahrung*, Dilthey claims that the basic unit of consciousness is itself already experiential, namely, an *Erlebnis* (a lived experience). Whereas *Erfahrung* is a phenomenal construct, Dilthey claims that *Erlebnis* is "real" in that qua consciousness there is nothing more ultimate behind it. Our ability to experience its temporal flow and describe its structure in psychological terms can serve as a guideline for the historical task of bridging the past, present, and future.

Because Dilthey claimed that psychology and epistemology could not be so easily divorced, his philosophy is often presumed to be psychologistic.[6] However, Dilthey's stress on psychology was never meant to question the normative priority of epistemology. Indeed, it could be argued that he wanted a more effective epistemology which could develop meaningful standards by maintaining some form of orientation to experience itself. The Kantian recognition that the transcendental only exists in relation to experience is transformed into the stronger claim that the very meaning of a transcendental principle requires a reference to psychological descriptions of experience. What for Kant remains an

[6] Psychologism is the view that all critical functions of philosophy can be resolved by psychology. Its acceptance would allow the validity of the laws of logic to be derived from natural laws that explain the way human beings think. Similarly, the criteria by which we justify our beliefs as knowledge would be reduced to psychological laws pertaining to the learning process. Dilthey, however, never claimed that the validity of a norm, whether logical, epistemological, or even moral, could be determined by psychology.

Only when the problem of criticism is applied to aesthetics does it become possible to find instances when Dilthey is guilty of a kind of psychologism. Thus in the *Poetik*, he wrote that the reader of a poem should try to reproduce the experience the poet had while creating it. Apparently, Dilthey was willing to grant psychic experience such importance because he was more interested in the value of poetry than in its validity. Later, when Dilthey recognized the inadequacy of a mere value-interpretation of aesthetics and replaced it with a more explicit concern for aesthetic meaning, he himself repudiated the view that the poet's experience is of primary importance for a critical reading of his work.

In general, it can be argued that for Dilthey, psychology determines, not the validity of a norm, but its value. The problem of reconciling the claims both of logical validity and empirical value raised here is similar to that raised by the historical *Weltanschauung*. In chap. 7, we will see how Dilthey avoids the possibility of an ultimate relativism by providing a Husserlian logical grounding for all empirical inquiry.

intra-epistemological relation is fashioned into an extra-epistemological orientation. Dilthey's descriptive psychology represents a body of information which a realistic epistemology must take into account, but must also go beyond.

Our suggestions about the systematic relations between the different areas of Dilthey's work cannot be fully understood apart from a developmental analysis, the other half of the problem of understanding Dilthey. While Herbert A. Hodges in his *Philosophy of Wilhelm Dilthey*[7] has dealt with almost every aspect of Dilthey's thought and has noted its Kantian epistemological framework, his essentially topical organization makes it difficult to grasp the deeper coherence of Dilthey's complex development. Dilthey's Kantianism is discussed as part of a general historical background, and his philosophy as a whole is introduced by an exposition of his final epistemological writings. But to approach Dilthey through his later works can lead to misinterpretation of the earlier works and their role in the growth of the epistemology itself. Nonetheless, Hodges' book remains valuable as one of the most comprehensive accounts of Dilthey and constitutes the starting point, as it were, for all efforts to make Dilthey more accessible to the English-speaking world.

The nature of Dilthey's development has been more of a problem in the German literature on Dilthey. But generally this has produced the belief that sharp discontinuities exist. Whereas Hodges used the final writings to contrast Dilthey's philosophy as a whole with that of his predecessors, in German scholarship these writings are often contrasted with earlier phases of his work in order to better relate him to his successors. Dilthey's immediate students and disciples understandably began their own interpretations of his work by concentrating on those of his final projects which directly influenced them. Subsequently, others have also tended to concentrate on the late works and to view them as antici-

[7] London: Routledge & Kegan Paul, 1952.

pations of contemporary positions and movements. In such selective accounts, Dilthey appears not so much as a philosopher in his own right, but as a precursor of later phenomenology and existentialism. An obvious case in point is Otto Friedrich Bollnow's enthusiastic book, *Dilthey: Eine Einführung in seine Philosophie.*[8] Ostensibly an introduction to Dilthey's philosophy, it reads rather like a prolegomenon to modern existentialism. Another such treatment is Kurt Müller-Vollmer's work on Dilthey's aesthetics, *Towards a Phenomenological Theory of Literature.*[9] Viewing Dilthey as proto-phenomenological, Müller-Vollmer seeks to demonstrate that Dilthey's *Poetik* also can stand the test of a Heideggerian existential analysis. Both interpretations of Dilthey deny the intrinsic significance of the psychological phase of his development. Accepting the general assumption that Dilthey rejected his own psychology through Husserl's influence at the turn of the century, Bollnow ignores the earlier psychological works. Müller-Vollmer similarly notes a radical break between the psychological and phenomenological phases, but claims that it occurred earlier than is usually thought. He argues that Dilthey's psychology of the poetic imagination as formulated in 1887 is in fact already "onto-psychological." The *Poetik* is designated as the "break-through from a positivistic and psychologistic outlook to a new 'phenomenological' way of viewing the human and historical world. . . ." Although Müller-Vollmer takes cognizance of the psychological theories Dilthey offered about the imagination, he in effect discounts them by making them subordinate to an ontological perspective. This interpretation of the *Poetik* leaves unexplained, however, those very aspects of Dilthey's final development which were, by his own acknowledgment, stimulated by Husserl and Hegel. Müller-Vollmer ignores

[8] 2nd ed., Stuttgart: Kohlhammer, 1955.

[9] *Towards a Phenomenological Theory of Literature: A Study of Wilhelm Dilthey's* Poetik, The Hague: Mouton & Co., 1963, pp. 106ff., 45.

11

the problem of change in Dilthey's philosophy by not really dealing with any works written after 1900.

In his recent study of Dilthey's aesthetics, *Morphologie und Hermeneutik*, Frithjof Rodi makes use of an occasionally noted tension between the "morphological" and the "hermeneutical" approaches in Dilthey's methodology to construct a more inclusive framework for interpreting Dilthey's development as a whole.[10] According to Rodi, Dilthey's early works subjected human activities and expressions to a morphological description in terms of a biologically rooted notion of fixed types, while the late works, by contrast, are dominated by the opposing tendencies of the hermeneutical mode of interpretation, which is more open, flexible and historically oriented. His development is thus interpreted as a general movement from schematic typologies with explanative pretensions to an existential mode of understanding. Dilthey's interest in typification is traced back to early Romantic influences from which he never fully escaped, so that even in his late hermeneutical phase his work exhibits some traces of an inconsistent morphology.

Although his formula for comprehending the genesis of Dilthey's work differs from that offered by the other commentators, Rodi nevertheless shares with them a partiality

[10] Frithjof Rodi, *Morphologie und Hermeneutik: Zur Methode von Diltheys Aesthetik*, Stuttgart: Kohlhammer, 1969. *Morphology*, a branch of biology that *explains* differences and changes in animals and plants as variations of certain basic forms or types, provides a naturalistic approach for the study of man. The morphological perspective is quite different from that of *hermeneutics*, which is the theory of *interpretation* originally developed in relation to the peculiar problems that arise in explicating the meaning of divinely inspired scriptures. After hermeneutics was extended by Schleiermacher to deal with any literary text, Dilthey fashioned it into a tool for understanding human history in general (see Rodi, chap. 6).

The contrast between morphology and hermeneutics had already been discerned by Ludwig Landgrebe in his "Wilhelm Diltheys Theorie der Geisteswissenschaften (Analyse ihrer Grundbegriffe)," *Jahrbuch für Philosophie und phänomenologische Forschung*, IX, ed. Edmund Husserl, Halle a.d. S.: Max Niemeyer, 1928, 237–367.

for the final writings at the expense of the earlier—particularly in devaluating the psychology insofar as it is considered to be morphological. While Rodi is more discerning in recognizing that Dilthey never totally rejected psychology, he finds its continuing presence an unfortunate indication of how Dilthey was held back by his own past. However, a closer analysis of Dilthey's theory of the poetic imagination as formulated in 1887 shows that in the psychology itself there is a coalescence of the two approaches. Thus it may be misleading to assume that one developed at the expense of the other: it was in his last years when his hermeneutical reflections were at their peak that Dilthey's idea of type most nearly approximated a morphology in the pejorative sense. Distinctions that may be illuminating in the structural analysis of isolated works by Dilthey become artificial for the understanding of his intellectual development.

The employment of a schematic contrast like Rodi's (itself a morphological device) obscures the more natural continuities in Dilthey's thought, just as its coherence is ignored by focusing on those portions of it most easily identified with his predecessors and successors. What the varying interpretations of Dilthey's development underscore is the fact that his philosophy simply does not fall into any stable epoch in the history of philosophy. To transform someone who was fundamentally a transitional figure into a person divided against himself by two different epochs is to look at Dilthey through a caricature of his own theory of epochs. Although Dilthey considered analyses of epochs crucial in providing contexts for understanding individuals, he refrains from using epochs as determining principles. A person may well reflect changes in his historical situation, or even bridge two epochs, without compromising his own integrity.

Because Dilthey lived in an age of transition, he repeatedly refashioned his point of view in response to the changing issues of the times. His main philosophical concerns

13

would receive varying topical formulations, many of which were never fully executed. What would begin to be explored in terms of one discipline would end as a result for another. What in the early 1890s was expressed in a language of descriptive psychology was transformed into a more phenomenological terminology a decade later. But even here a continuity can be discerned by noting Dilthey's intervening efforts to articulate certain reflective structures of experience which are neither purely introspective in the psychological sense nor purely intentional in the phenomenological sense.

The only serious effort to recount the subtle fabric of Dilthey's intellectual growth has been made by his student and son-in-law, Georg Misch. Written as a preface to the fifth volume of the *Gesammelte Schriften*, it is so compact and allusive that it can be comprehended only by one already thoroughly familiar with Dilthey's work. Misch's later defense of Dilthey's uniqueness vis-à-vis Husserl and Heidegger does go into somewhat greater detail, but many of the contrasts drawn are more esoteric than illuminating.[11]

By analyzing the interrelated aspects of Dilthey's work, the present study will indicate more of a continuity than is usually acknowledged, without, on the other hand, appealing to a schematic unity. To follow the gradual evolution of his thought makes it possible to resist the temptation to contrast an early position to a later, more fashionable standpoint. It can then be shown that many of Dilthey's so-called final discoveries about the hermeneutic circle of interpretation were already sketched out in his earliest work and that some of the ultimate renunciations of psychology are really little more than attacks on the type of explanative psychology he had always opposed. Important changes do occur, but discussion of them must be grounded in a developmental continuum.

[11] Georg Misch, *Lebensphilosophie und Phänomenologie*, 3rd ed., Darmstadt: Wissenschaftliche Buchgesellschaft, 1967.

The Role of Dilthey's Aesthetics

Dilthey never claimed that aesthetics played the foundational role which he claimed first for psychology and then for hermeneutics. Thus his aesthetics was unencumbered by the need to justify its status relative to the other *Geisteswissenschaften*. Not subjected to the vicissitudes of professional controversies and polemics, aesthetics proved to be the domain by means of which Dilthey most often tested as well as exemplified his theoretical reflections. As such, it persisted as a central source of insight for him.

The failure to capitalize on this centrality of aesthetics is undoubtedly another factor that has kept many of Dilthey's commentators from approaching the inner coherence of his work. Hodges, for one, treats the aesthetics as merely another example of Dilthey's theory of the *Geisteswissenschaften*. But to the extent that aesthetics is, in a sense, a "model" *Geisteswissenschaft* for Dilthey, it need not merely confirm what we already know about the *Geisteswissenschaften* from Dilthey's theoretical writings. It can also be suggestive for them in turn. An examination of the progress of Dilthey's aesthetics will prove to be no less than a study of the growth of his thought in general. Dilthey's attempt to do justice to the poetic imagination was a catalyst in the development of the descriptive psychology which then had such important methodological ramifications for his theory of the *Geisteswissenschaften*.

Hodges, however, finds that in contrast to Collingwood's technical use of the concept of the imagination in *The Principles of Art*, Dilthey's use of the term in his *Poetik* is merely popular. "Dilthey overlooks the intuitional level of experience. . . . because he is anxious to emphasize . . . the 'intellectuality' of our experience at a lower level than is often realized."[12] But the fact that Dilthey shows that even at the lowest levels of experience elementary logical operations are involved does not mean that he fails to apprehend

[12] Hodges, *The Philosophy of Wilhelm Dilthey*, pp. 329, 333-34.

15

the theoretical importance of imaginative experience. If his concept of the imagination is not formulated in terms of a doctrine of aesthetic intuition, it is because he relies on a structural rather than a qualitative differentiation from other mental activities.

Hodges and René Wellek after him have minimized the philosophical significance of Dilthey's theory of the poetic imagination by comparing it to that of I. A. Richards. For Hodges, Richards represents "the most obvious parallel to Dilthey's position in aesthetics." They are interpreted as sharing a "fundamentally romantic inspiration, which expresses itself in their psychological theories: Dilthey's dependence on Goethe and Novalis is parallel to the fascination exercised over Richards by Coleridge. Both have foresworn metaphysics, and are trying to keep alive the romantic vision and find adequate expression for it in a positivistic universe. Both seek help from psychology. . . ."[13] Wellek goes further in linking Dilthey and Richards. According to him, Dilthey's views on psychology so closely anticipate those of Richards that "one suspects, if not a direct influence, then some intermediary source in German psychological aesthetics."[14] Given his disapproval of Richards' theory of psychological value, Wellek predictably dismisses Dilthey's aesthetics for also being too psychologistic. But such characterizations are only vaguely helpful, for the likeness breaks down as soon as we specify the nature of the psychology to which each appealed. Both Hodges and Wellek gloss over an important difference in the orientation of the respective psychologies. Richards, in a pseudoscientific accommodation to logical positivism, defined aesthetic feeling physiologically as a balanced state of brain-impulses,[15]

[13] Ibid., p. 107.

[14] René Wellek, "Wilhelm Dilthey's Poetics and Literary Theory," *Wächter und Hüter, Festschrift für Hermann J. Weigand*, New Haven: Yale University Press, 1957, p. 128.

[15] I. A. Richards, *Principles of Literary Criticism*, New York: Harcourt, Brace and World, 1925, pp. 251f.

while Dilthey increasingly regarded aesthetic feeling hermeneutically for the meaning it embodies. In the one case, the imagination is used to cancel out unpleasantly one-sided impulses—our narrowly delimited knowledge of reality is supplemented by an open-ended enjoyment too vague to be really meaningful. In the other, the imagination is a means of distilling a concrete sense of life's meaning. For Richards, art engenders a nonreflective attitude toward life; for Dilthey, a reflective *Weltanschauung*.

Dilthey's theory of the poetic imagination has more far-reaching implications than usually recognized, implications which bear not only on his conception of the historical imagination but also on the more general epistemological project of a Critique of Historical Reason. This project remained unfinished, but its core becomes more clearly visible if Dilthey's ideas concerning a descriptive or structural psychology and his writings on the historical or hermeneutic method are correlated with his aesthetics.

Dilthey and a Kantian Aesthetic of History

To propose the idea of an aesthetic of history has the immediate value of suggesting a reinterpretation of certain epistemological claims of the "Transcendental Aesthetic" of the *Critique of Pure Reason*. Kant conceived of space and time as the formal framework in terms of which our knowledge of nature is constructed. To speak of an aesthetic of nature is to refer to fundamental intuitive conditions necessary for our experience of nature. But whereas relative to nature it may have been adequate to approach time through spatial analogies, for the study of history it is not. Thus an aesthetic of history would involve a consideration of the imaginative conditions that make it possible to have a sense of history as temporal development.

In chapter 5, I will argue that there also exist methodological grounds for attributing an aesthetic of history to Dilthey. I do not thereby imply that his approach to the past

17

was "aesthetical" in the sense that certain Heideggerians have applied it to his theory of history. Their disparaging usage of the term is meant to associate Dilthey with a Rankian kind of historicism. It is suggested that Dilthey cherished the understanding of the past for its own sake and was content to passively reproduce it "as it was" in a history written from the eyewitness perspective. This approach to history is interpreted as deriving its philosophical justification from Kant's conception of aesthetic contemplation.

But it is clearly erroneous to see Dilthey's theory of history as primarily motivated by an antiquarian ideal. Moreover, the Heideggerian suspicion of the Kantian tradition of modern aesthetics is only justified with regard to certain Romantic formulations of it rather than Kant's own. Although Kant emphasizes the subjective and disinterested quality of aesthetic contemplation, he does not reduce it to a passive state. This quiescent stereotype about contemplation derives from Schopenhauer, not Kant. When Kant speaks of either the aesthetic component of experience in general or of the aesthetic judgment of taste in particular, its relation to the productivity of the imagination is stressed. The imagination as discussed in the *Critique of Pure Reason* (1781) constitutes a fundamental epistemological mode of synthesis assuring that the content of our experience is always structured. This activity of the imagination is further brought out in the *Critique of Judgment* (1790). Whereas in the first *Critique* the imagination was strictly subsumable to the laws of the understanding, in the last it becomes a more spontaneous and less determinate mode of representation. As understood by Kant there is a subtle and playful suggestiveness implicit in the enjoyment of beauty which is lost in Schopenhauer's discussion of beauty as providing tranquility and peace. The inner causality that Kant assigns to the aesthetic experience does not relate to a determinate purpose, and yet it is purposive in a reflective or regulative sense.

18

The idea of an aesthetic of history is meant to capture the reflective potential implicit in aesthetic contemplation, thus going beyond the merely visual model which too often keeps the study of aesthetics from exploring broader epistemological issues. In order to provide a basis for understanding how such an approach relates to the fundamental concerns of Dilthey's own theory of history, it will be helpful here to consider certain clues in Kant as to what might constitute an aesthetic of history.

Kant's aesthetic judgment may well be interpreted as purposive precisely in the sense of educating man as a historical creature. The concept of a regulative aesthetic purposiveness serves to ground the central tenet of Kant's historical essays, namely, that man must learn to see his destiny, not in terms of individual happiness, but in terms of shared cultural ideals. The education of his taste implies the ability to move beyond the stage of finding a mere sensuous pleasure in things which appeals to private interest and induces the desire to possess them. The appreciation of beauty presupposes that man can suspend his natural interest in personal pleasure for the sake of a disinterested pleasure that can be shared by all men. When we are able to stand apart from the objects around us and enjoy their form as having educed from us the harmonious play of all our faculties, then we have the right to impute a like pleasure to others. Thus Kant speaks of taste as a kind of *sensus communis* which sets the stage for a "universal feeling of sympathy."[16]

It is important to note that in the *Strife of the Faculties* (1798) Kant grounds his own regulative idea of the moral tendency of the human race in similar terms: a spontaneous "yet disinterested sympathy" widely experienced by those who, like himself, had been "spectators" of the French Revolution. To suggest that Kant exhibited an aesthetic sym-

[16] Immanuel Kant, *Critique of Judgment* (to be referred to in subsequent notes as *CJ*), trans. J. H. Bernard, New York: Hafner Publishing Co., 1951, p. 201.

pathy with the French Revolution while yet a moral disapproval of its actual course is one way to clarify what has been considered his ambiguous position on it. When Kant connects the ideal of history with this "event of our time," the French Revolution does not represent an objective basis for the realization of the cosmopolitan ideal. Instead of considering it as a "cause" of progress in history, he interprets it "only as an intimation, an historical sign. . . ."[17] It is the aesthetic response to the revolution which discloses a moral predisposition in the human race and provides the subjective transcendental ground for positing a cosmopolitan ideal of history. The French Revolution is not a model of how to approach the ideal of history, but disinterested reflection on it does confirm a subjective tendency in that direction.

This is to be understood in the context of Kant's justification of certain imaginative conjectures about the beginning and end of history so long as they are linked to our knowledge of the original predispositions of human nature.[18] Just as in the *Critique of Judgment* it is considered legitimate to speak of beauty *as if* it were a property of the object, so in the writings on history it is made legitimate to speak of nature *as if* she were gradually bringing about a cosmopolitan society. In both cases Kant admits using imaginative fictions to make us aware of certain transcendental conditions of humanity. Although beauty is not an objective trait, to imagine that it is forces us to distinguish it from that which we find merely charming. This attitude is heuristic insofar as it leads us to consider why it is that a subjective feeling need not be just a personal preference. Likewise, the fiction of nature directing us to some moral end is pragmatic only to the extent that it actually activates in man his aesthetically confirmed disposition to use nature toward this end. In the *Critique of Judgment* Kant spoke of how

[17] Immanuel Kant, *On History*, ed. Lewis White Beck, Indianapolis: Bobbs-Merrill, 1963, p. 143.
[18] Ibid., p. 53.

nature can only prepare man for what he himself must achieve historically. Another way of understanding Kant's intention here is to say that if man is the final purpose of nature, we must speak of nature in such a way that it becomes possible to conceive its mechanical operations as compatible with the teleological ideals of moral philosophy. Aesthetic experience makes it possible to imagine nature as a symbol of morality; to so regard it is actually necessary for the meaning and ideal of history to be realized.

Schiller's work helps confirm the relation of aesthetics and history implicit in Kant. His idea of the aesthetic education of man together with his sense of the moral drama of history partly exemplify an aesthetic of history. What this suggests is a possible solution to the problem of how Dilthey's Critique of Historical Reason fits into the tradition established by Kant. Commentators who have dealt with the issue tend to conclude that Dilthey is a Kantian in a Pickwickian sense at best. They cite passages where Dilthey explicitly refutes Kant, and refer to his famous controversies with the Neo-Kantians of his time. Certainly, to claim any direct dependence on Kant or his immediate successors would be appropriate only in relation either to very general features of Dilthey's thought or to some rather special phases of it (for example, around 1894–1895 when he studied the significance of Schiller's historical dramas while exploring the idea of a transcendental or reflective aspect of experience). The Kantian themes here appealed to are not meant to compromise the inherent value of Dilthey's own contributions, but to add to the understanding of them by testing an interpretation of their broader relevance. The first requirement is to understand Dilthey on his own terms. Comparisons with Kant will be offered as a means to consider the different but related ways their respective aesthetic theories have implications for more general philosophical problems still of concern.

Kant's own historical writings were to remain uncritical and as such are rather different in effect from Dilthey's. But if one considers how Kant's historical essays point to an aesthetic of history which could have been intercalated between the transcendental reflections in the "Critique of Aesthetical Judgment" and the descriptive problems of natural history as treated in the "Critique of Teleological Judgment," it makes sense to look more closely at both parts of the *Critique of Judgment* for a possible affinity between Kant and Dilthey.

This affinity has gone unnoticed because all the schools of Neo-Kantianism have emphasized the first two critiques of Kant. They have dwelt on the dualisms of sense and reason and have often ignored Kant's own attempt in the third *Critique* to uncover a harmony between sense and reason in terms of aesthetic feeling. Although the role of the aesthetic imagination is somewhat of an afterthought for Kant, it nevertheless assumes a crucial position in his architectonic.

What is of importance for a comparison with Dilthey's theory of the poetic imagination is the fact that Kant's treatment of the imagination in the *Critique of Judgment* represents an effort to broaden his conception of synthesis so that it refers not only to the specific connection of sense-experience but also to a vaguer harmony of the cognitive faculties. Yet Kant's very success in expanding the concept of synthesis can only help confirm the conclusion to be drawn from Dilthey's work that all interpretations of the imagination as synthetic are ultimately inadequate. To posit a synthetic function means that the original connectedness of life available to *Erlebnis* (lived experience) has been overlooked. According to Dilthey, the poetic and historical imagination draw on this experiential continuum and give it a more explicit and unified structure. Therefore, the imagination should be discussed as a mode of articulation rather than of synthesis.

Dilthey's epistemological reflections about the inadequacy of synthetic conceptions must be related to his methodological distrust of the various synthetic or "constructionist" approaches to the *Geisteswissenschaften*. Hegel's metaphysics of history, Comte's sociology, and even J. S. Mill's psychology are criticized on this score, and Dilthey proposes an analytic approach as more appropriate. That Dilthey attached great importance to analysis is generally ignored by his interpreters. Perhaps one reason for this is that its methodological significance for the theory of the *Geisteswissenschaften* cannot be comprehended without a clarification of how an articulation-perspective serves to transform the function of analysis itself. Analysis need not be restricted to a formal discursive operation, but can be seen to be involved in the processes of imaginative articulation as well. Accordingly, analysis is not so much a mode of explication as a mode of typification. Instead of considering it as a way of dissecting a continuum, Dilthey regards it as a manner of focusing on some part as typical of the whole. Since the imagination is expected to preserve a sense of concreteness in what is analyzed as a type, it becomes possible to argue that the typical should not primarily be considered as a morphological ideal or universal abstracted from the empirical givens, but rather as a product of the historical "condensation" of the real.

Dilthey replaces the traditional notion of historical reason with that of historical understanding and judgment. Whereas Kant's *Critique of Pure Reason* resulted in a concept of understanding (*Verstand*) capable of making determinant judgments about nature, Dilthey's Critique of Historical Reason leads to a concept of understanding (*Verstehen*) more on the order of reflective judgments as explicated in Kant's *Critique of Judgment*. Dilthey's historical understanding might thus be called a reflective mode of understanding.

In a determinant judgment a conceptual predicate is imposed on sense content; a reflective judgment, however, allows the particular content to suggest its own concept. When this distinction is applied to a theory of history, the search for special laws or principles can be seen as an attempt to provide the basis for making determinant judgments about history, while the description of typical structures implicit in the phenomena of history involves the exercise of reflective, historical judgment. The distinction makes possible a shift from the notion of history as a science which establishes explanative laws to that of an interpretive discipline which articulates meaning.

Such a shift is already foreshadowed in Kant when he denies that the course of human history can be predicted by natural laws. Yet refusing to accept the alternatives of either anticipating the future through arbitrary imaginative leaps (*wahrsagern*) or appealing to supernatural prophetic insights (*weissagen*), he explores a third alternative of *wahrsagen* which would remain in the domain of philosophical reflection.[19] According to Kant, philosophical considerations about the beginning and end of history do involve projections of the imagination which go beyond the imaginative interpolations required of the working historian to "fill gaps in the record."[20] However, the imaginative extrapolations are to be reflectively framed by ideas of reason, so that they never lapse into arbitrary fancy. Reflection begets a kind of subjectival perspective on history which then leads to pragmatic judgments whereby history is interpreted as if nature were its providential guide.

Despite Kant's awareness of an affinity between the imagination and reflective judgment, the latter moves beyond the former and becomes rather speculative and abstract. Thus the reflective potentials of aesthetic contemplation and the artistic imagination are not fully brought out in the claims that aesthetic disinterestedness is a sign of human freedom and beauty a symbol of morality. A more intimate connection between the imagination and reflection must be disclosed.

Dilthey's contribution to the interpretive theory of his-

[19] Immanuel Kant, *Der Streit der Fakultäten, Werke in Zehn Bänden*, vol. 9, Darmstadt: Wissenschaftliche Buchgesellschaft, 1968, pp. 351, 356.
[20] Kant, *On History*, p. 53.

tory suggested by Kant was the formulation of historical categories in which the role of the imagination is more thoroughly integrated with reflective judgment. To replace Kant's formal analogues about human nature, Dilthey focuses on concrete historical individuals as centers of reflection. Historical imagination and self-reflection are thus made to intersect: "The first condition for the possibility of a *Geschichtswissenschaft* (history as discipline) lies in the conciousness that I am myself a historical creature, that the one who examines history also makes history" (*GS*,VII,278). Thus the study of history is inseparable from self-inquiry according to Dilthey.

Conceived in this way, the distinction between philosophical history and conventional history becomes questionable. That Kant accepted this distinction can be confirmed by the insignificant role the imagination, and therefore reflection, is assumed to play in conventional history. According to Dilthey, however, even such history based on the records can be understood only through the contributions of the imagination. It is thus no less dependent on epistemological reflection than Kant's philosophical history.

The dualism between abstract speculation and strict scientific method that Kant tolerated is to be overcome. An aesthetic of history need not be interpreted to justify a vague kind of history which gives an impression of the configuration of historical conditions at the same time foreclosing a consideration of how they might be related in terms of causes and grounds. In a review critical of Burckhardt, Dilthey once wrote that an historian should not be satisfied with a loose "aesthetic grouping" of his data apart from a more methodological investigation of their connectedness (*GS*,XI,72). To assume that an aesthetic of history limits history to the art of creating patterns is to overlook a more fundamental sense in which an at least partial continuum of historical life is already accessible to *Erlebnis* and open to disciplined analysis.

We also find Dilthey criticizing the arbitrary nature of

the "aesthetic reflections" of certain German literary critics. To the extent that they are rooted in narrow aesthetic theories they are said to require further orientation in terms of historical understanding.[21] But this involves neither a critique of aesthetics as such nor a rejection of reflection. Reflection is only objectionable if it remains removed from the facts and turns speculative. The term continues to be used by Dilthey in its more neutral epistemological sense, and precisely to designate the task of historical understanding (GS,VII,239,248,327ff.).

The Poetic Imagination and Historical Style

Dilthey explicated the idea of aesthetic reflection in terms of his more specific theory about poetic productivity. Because of this, the expression "poetics of history" might have served equally well to characterize Dilthey's work. The general expression "aesthetic of history" remains more suggestive, however, of the broader theoretical implications opened up by the reflective analysis of *Erlebnis* and its temporal form.

By considering Dilthey's *Poetik* and his historical writings, it can be seen that he treats the poetic imagination and the historical imagination, not merely as parallel, but as basically akin. This points to a concept of style where poetic and historical considerations both come into play. For it is in speaking of the style of a work of art that aesthetic and historical judgments intersect.

The awareness of style presupposes a reflective attitude. If the Kantian transcendental principle that the subject must contribute the general a priori structures to his experience is translated into a more concrete insight about the

---

[21] Dilthey, *Von deutscher Dichtung und Musik: Aus den Studien zur Geschichte des deutschen Geistes* (to be referred to in subsequent notes as *DDM*), 2nd ed., Stuttgart: B. G. Teubner; Göttingen: Vandenhoeck & Ruprecht, 1957, p. 325.

way one reflectively approaches experience in detail, it becomes possible to understand how different styles of apprehension can arise. Kant never pursued this more historically
oriented structural approach to aesthetic problems. For
that we look to Dilthey and his contemporaries.

To aesthetic purists like Susanne K. Langer such an approach may seem like a confusion, for in speaking of understanding poetry she claims that "meanings and motives
which only historical scholarship can supply add nothing
to the poetic events or their poetic significance."[22] Therefore, it must be considered to what extent the psychohistorical context of Dilthey's theory of the imagination is aesthetically relevant.

The role of historical information might be discussed
with reference to an historical drama such as Schiller's *Don
Carlos*. It clearly articulates an historical conflict in terms
of fundamental political principles, so that we need not critically compare the plot with the factual situation on which
it was based. To correct him on details would be to miss
Schiller's poetic intent. Yet, without some knowledge of the
Dutch war of liberation fought against Spain, some of the
minor historical references will be lost to the reader. In
making such references, the author attempts to give a certain richness to his work at the risk of losing the strict unity
of the plot. The ideal is to allow the reader's attention to
move beyond the bounds of the stage and have it rebound
to enrich what is happening on the stage. In *Oedipus Rex*,
too, a good example is found of controlled references outside the plot which serve to give information relevant to the
plot itself. By means of certain narrative devices Sophocles
periodically calls our attention back to a time before the
beginning of the plot, but with the express function of ac-
celerating the forward momentum of the drama. Similarly,
the critic should indulge his historical curiosity only so far

[22] *Feeling and Form*, New York: Charles Scribner's Sons, 1953, p.
219 fn.

as it can ultimately augment the meaning of the work itself. He will explain the significance of allusions only to the extent that they can be integrated back into the stylistic structure established by the work.

Style is a quality that belongs to the work as such. Dilthey writes that it unifies the work and pervades all its parts, e.g. even the lines of the painting (*GS*,VI,271). This suggests that style is not unlike the formal attributes by which Wölfflin distinguishes the Classical and Baroque styles of painting. Yet, for Dilthey, style is not merely formal and does not recur in cycles. What he designates as style is more individual than a form. It is a structural complex pertaining to content as well as form. Such a concept of style renders content and form inseparable.

Those followers of Dilthey who have reduced the historical dimension of a style to what can be reflected in a *Weltanschauung* while using Dilthey's typology of the *Weltanschauungen* to characterize the arts have done him a disservice. They have given the false impression that literature is to be understood as an introduction to the philosophical problems of an age. The formalists are right in rejecting such an approach as abrogating the intrinsic significance of literature. Accordingly, before discussing the question of the complex relation of literature and *Weltanschauung*, some sense of the status of literature must be independently developed.

Others have taken an equally superficial glance at Dilthey's psychological reflections about the arts. They assume that whenever Dilthey introduced psychology into his aesthetics, he was concerned to explain the nature of the artistic in terms of the creative experience of the artist. This was true of only one phase of Dilthey's psychology. On the other hand, the fact that he ultimately minimized the value of reproducing the psychic states of the artist does not betoken a rejection of psychology for understanding art. Even before his so-called phenomenological stage, Dilthey saw

28

that our understanding of art is not to be confined to a knowledge of the artist's intention. He subscribed throughout to Schleiermacher's hermeneutic maxim about aiming to understand an author better than he understood himself.

The New Critics are correct in considering the analysis of the text as crucial in this endeavor. Literary criticism should not be restricted by information about the writer's intentions. Yet we should also recognize that interpretation is always unfinished and haunted by the idea of that intention.

The meaning of a work of literature is not totally intrinsic to it, contrary to the assumptions of Langer and the New Critics. In Dilthey's opinion it is the critic's task to elucidate the work's significance by an understanding of the age and nation in which its creator lived. This need not be interpreted as a complete relativism according to which any work can be justified through an understanding of the context that fostered it. Dilthey would not go as far as the historicist Herder and say that it is unjust to reproach the artist for flaws which in fact can be explained by his milieu, his language, his habits of thought and sensation. Dilthey's contextual analysis does not function to justify works that no longer satisfy a later age but to engender an appreciation of greatness in those that still do.

Works of any period can have universal appeal to the extent that they make use of what Dilthey terms natural symbols or motifs. Dilthey remained convinced that the classical motifs of all great literature can be illuminated by a psychological analysis of experience. Certain motifs stimulate the poet's and the reader's imagination alike. On the other hand, Dilthey agrees with Herder, whom he acknowledges as the founder of historical poetics, when he says that greatness does not demand subservience to fixed rules of poetic composition. What does act as a restraint on the poet is the availability of only a limited number of motifs (GS,VI,236f.). However, the poet is free to employ them in whatever way he chooses, so that to fully appreciate what each poet does with such motifs requires historical sensitivity to style.

Dilthey's concept of style makes possible a kind of criticism that avoids certain problems of other theories of art, particularly those of the expression theory, which has mistakenly been attributed to Dilthey himself.[23] As long as art is defined as an expression of feelings, the issue of sincerity remains all-important and criticism is powerless to do much more than provide hypothetical clues in the search for the author's germinal intuition. At least the imitation theory of art could appeal to natural intuitive norms by which art is to be judged. This theory provided a rationale for a philosophical criticism of the arts which was not, however, always aesthetically relevant. Dilthey's idea of style is meant to encourage an aesthetically fruitful mode of criticism. By defining his concept of the imagination as articulative it may also be possible to overcome the absoluteness that the imitation theory ascribed to intuition. Just as, on the one hand, no intuitive aesthetic standard is immune from historical refinement, so, on the other hand, all poetic and metaphysical truth is subject to analysis in terms of historically conditioned *Weltanschauungen*.

The intuition of a *Weltanschauung* is perspectival and partial, and therefore requires elaboration by the imagination. Thus Dilthey's concept of the imagination plays a key role in his philosophy. Whereas from the standpoint of intuition the *Weltanschauung* types are relatively fixed and thus exclusive, from that of imagination there is no end to the process of analyzing them and possibly arriving at a unifying core. If philosophy is expected to construct an ab-

[23] Although Dilthey does sometimes speak of art as expressive, he cannot be said to subscribe to the theory that expression is a necessary and sufficient condition for defining what is artistic. In chaps. 4, 9, and 10 I shall consider, not only how Dilthey's views diverge from the expression theory of art, but also how they can be used to move beyond it.

30

solute system, Dilthey's *Weltanschauungslehre* must be judged as relativistic, because he sees no way of arriving at a synthetic unity among the three types. However, if philosophy is assigned a more analytic role, there is no reason to despair of our capacity to articulate a typical core common to otherwise relative types.

PART ONE

Theoretical Background

CHAPTER ONE

History and the Theory of the *Geisteswissenschaften*

MORE than anything Wilhelm Dilthey gained his reputation through his contributions to the theory of the *Geisteswissenschaften*. He is considered to have provided the classical formulation of it in 1883 when his *Einleitung in die Geisteswissenschaften (Introduction to the Human Studies)* was published. The theory presented there serves as a framework for understanding Dilthey's conception of philosophy, psychology, literary criticism, and history, as well as his analysis of the relations among them and associated disciplines.

The present study of the development manifested in Dilthey's mature works must determine where the *Einleitung* stands in relation to his subsequent thought. Among other things, the work provides an initial orientation for the study of Dilthey's aesthetics. If our claim about the centrality of aesthetics as a *Geisteswissenschaft* is to be appreciated, an adequate understanding of the general nature of the *Geisteswissenschaften* has to be presupposed.

Before going into an actual analysis of the *Einleitung*, some preliminary discussion of its background will help to introduce what Dilthey means by the *Geisteswissenschaften*. This will involve, first, considering the implications of Dilthey's choice of the term *Geisteswissenschaften* over some of its alternatives, and second, briefly reviewing the development of his interest in the problem.

Meaning of the Term *Geisteswissenschaften*

Although the widely accepted expression "human studies" remains the best translation, there is no really satisfactory

English equivalent for the word *Geisteswissenschaften*. Ironically, the German word received .its first deliberate and generally recognized usage as a translation of John Stuart Mill's term "moral sciences." But the concept of the moral sciences is too limited to characterize that of the *Geisteswissenschaften* as it has come to be used.

Erich Rothacker, a noted scholar on the subject of the *Geisteswissenschaften*, writes that "perhaps the term *Geisteswissenschaften* first appeared in 1849 in Schiel's translation of Mill's *System of Logic*."[1] Strictly speaking, Rothacker's claim is incorrect. In 1843, the historian Johann Gustav Droysen had used the term in the preface to the second volume of his *Geschichte des Hellenismus*. Strangely enough, Rothacker himself had republished Droysen's preface two years before making the claim for Schiel's priority.[2] But the word undoubtedly had no special significance for Droysen, who primarily used the expression *Wissenschaft der Geschichte* (science of history).

Given its commonness today and the long history of its roots *Geist* and *Wissenschaft* in the German philosophical tradition, one would have expected earlier technical usages of the word *Geisteswissenschaft*. Rothacker does cite instances when Hegelians used the related expressions *Wissenschaft des Geistes* and *Geistwissenschaft*. However, it is significant that these are in the singular. These terms can be rendered as "science of spirit" in the metaphysical sense. Krause, for example, employed the latter expression synonymously with "science of reason."[3] For a Hegelian, *Geistwissenschaft* means "philosophy of spirit." There can thus be only one philosophical science of spirit.

Dilthey's conception of the *Geisteswissenschaften* encom-

---

[1] Erich Rothacker, *Logik und Systematik der Geisteswissenschaften*, München: R. Oldenbourg, 1965, p. 6. First published in 1927.

[2] See Johann Gustav Droysen, *Grundriss der Historik*, ed. Erich Rothacker, Halle/a.d.S.: Max Niemeyer, 1925, p. 97.

[3] Rothacker, *Logik und Systematik der Geisteswissenschaften*, pp. 6f.

passes what we would now call the humanities and the social sciences. It covers not only psychology, anthropology, political economy, law, and history, for which Mill's expression "moral sciences" might still have served, but also such disciplines as philology and aesthetics. The various disciplines are conceived as interrelated, although relatively independent. Philosophy is very much involved with the *Geisteswissenschaften*, without, however, being used to place them in any absolute and final perspective. It can never claim to establish *the* system of the *Geisteswissenschaften*. Far from culminating in a Hegelian concept of absolute spirit, the theory of the *Geisteswissenschaften* will lead to an attempt to understand the variety of basic human *Weltanschauungen*.

Dilthey also reveals his break with the idealistic concept of science by insisting on an empirical approach. Dissatisfied with the way that metaphysical systems had distorted and ignored facts, Dilthey stresses that "science" must not sacrifice its responsibility to be empirical in its haste to create a unified order. In France, Comte had already denounced the idea of one grand science. In its stead he established a hierarchical system of the positive sciences leading up to sociology. However, his positivistic system is still too homogeneous according to Dilthey. Comte had refused to consider psychology a science and claimed that all of man's mental functions could be properly and exhaustively studied by biology and sociology. Dilthey considers the positivistic assumption that all of reality need be examined by external observation alone—thus dismissing introspection—to result in a narrowing empiricism. Comte's empiricism he refers to as *Empirismus* in contrast to his own *unbefangene Empirie*, an ideal of an unprejudiced empirical approach which consults the facts of internal experience as well as of external experience (*GS*,I,81). Moreover, Comte's sociological law of historical development, according to which the largely introspective method of the theological and metaphysical stages must give way to positive science, is condemned for being itself a metaphysical remnant (GS,I,107). Dilthey discerns a deterministic and constructionist trait in encyclopedic sociology no less pernicious than that of Hegel's idealistic philosophy of history. Because such speculative disciplines lose sight of the human individuals active in history they do not deserve to be numbered among the Geisteswissenschaften.

Dilthey commends J. S. Mill for having turned his back on Comte's hierarchical system. Mill had assigned psychology an independent status which allowed it to be the basis of a system of the moral and political sciences distinct from the system of the natural sciences. But Dilthey finds fault with the fact that his system of the moral sciences is still modeled on the natural sciences. Dilthey's primary aim is then to argue that the methodology of the Geisteswissenschaften must be different from that of the Naturwissenschaften (natural sciences).

The justification for this methodological claim central to Dilthey's delimitation of the Geisteswissenschaften is to be found in epistemological terms. It is philosophy's task to provide an epistemology that can show that the Geisteswissenschaften, although not as clearly definable in their first principles as the Naturwissenschaften, are no less fundamental, comprehensive, and objective in their results.

In his recent reinterpretation of the concept of the human studies, H. P. Rickman does not list philosophy itself as one of the disciplines to be included. By so doing, he more sharply distinguishes the philosophical question concerning the epistemological foundation of the Geisteswissenschaften from the methodological question about their scientific status. And he writes, "nor . . . is it for the human studies to consider the grounds on which moral principles are held and to ask whether moral judgments have objective validity. This is the subject of philosophy and of ethics in particular. The human studies are, like the physical sciences, concerned with facts; with what is the case, even though the facts . . . are of a special kind."[4]

Though Rickman acknowledges his debt to Dilthey, such sharp distinctions of fact and value were avoided by Dilthey. His distrust of too neat delineations is evidenced in his controversies with the Neo-Kantians of the Baden school, Wilhelm Windelband (1848–1915) and Heinrich Rickert (1863–1936).[5] A brief comparison of Rickert's theory of the *Kulturwissenschaften* with that of the *Geisteswissenschaften* will be helpful here. Rickert's precise logical formulations of the issues will help us to approach Dilthey's less easily defined position.

Rickert asserts that *Geist* is an unsatisfactory idea because it tends to be either hypostatized into a supernatural reality or reduced to the psyche. The term poses the extreme dangers of uncritical idealism on the one hand and psychologism on the other. Although Dilthey comes to see a middle ground here by means of his concept of structural psychology, he did not always fully recognize the pitfalls of psychologism. Rickert's concept of culture (*Kultur*) was intended to be immune to this disease of the late nineteenth century. Thus the concept of the *Kulturwissenschaften*, which does not include psychology, was proposed to replace that of the *Geisteswissenschaften*, which does.

In accordance with the rigorous tenor of Rickert's thought, the translator of his work *Kulturwissenschaft und Naturwissenschaft* has used the term "cultural science" to apply to the study of culture and history.[6] This forces us to call history a science. Since in German and French the con-

---

[4] H. P. Rickman, *Understanding and the Human Studies*, London: Heinemann Educational Books, 1967, pp. 1, 76.

[5] See chap. 5 for a more detailed account of Dilthey's debate with the Neo-Kantians on the status of psychology.

[6] Heinrich Rickert, *Science and History, A Critique of Positivist Epistemology*, trans. George Reisman, Princeton, N.J.: Van Nostrand Co., 1962, p. 14.

cept of science can be applied to any rigorous study or methodology, it is not unusual to call history a science. But this is more problematic in English, due to the general assumption that a science is predictive. Such a view of science rules out history even if, following Mill, one conceives its task to be that of discovering low level empirical generalizations. Though such generalizations might be incorporated into a scientific system by means of the inverse deductive method, they remain too inexact to predict an historical event. Even if they were more exact, the task of determining all the necessary initial conditions would be interminable. Prediction would be more ponderous than the course of events to be predicted.

Recognizing the less exact nature of the *Geisteswissenschaften*, English translators of Dilthey have generally avoided the term "science" and have used phrases like "human studies" and "psychohistorical disciplines." However, to similarly substitute "studies" for "sciences" in translating Rickert's concept of the *Kulturwissenschaften* would be to ignore his epistemological argument that science can be either generalizing or individualizing. Rickert wants to show that the vague material distinction between nature and culture can be replaced by a more precise logical demarcation of generalizing and individualizing concept-formation. The cultural sciences can thus also be referred to as "historical" or "individualizing."

Rickert's argument proceeds roughly as follows: Obviously no science can hope to reproduce reality in detail. Every science must select from the empirical given to create order. To transform reality's "indeterminable heterogeneity into a determinable domain of discrete objects," all the sciences require universal concepts. This is manifestly the case for the natural sciences. Universal concepts are used to select salient features of objects which then allow them to be correlated. Now history deserves the rank of a science because it, too, uses some principle to select the essential from the unessential. What has often been ignored, according to

Rickert, is that universal concepts can be combined to create individual complexes. History employs complexes of universals known as values to select its material. Only those events are reported by a historian which were either positively or negatively efficacious in realizing certain cultural values. Then, to meet the possible objection that a science should not be contaminated with value-judgments, Rickert distinguishes between evaluation and mere reference to values: "valuations must always involve *praise* or *blame*. To refer to values is to do neither." The science of history does not lose its objectivity simply by referring to "hypothetical" cultural values.[7]

However, the claim of objectivity becomes more problematic when attempting to write universal history. For this task, actually held values cannot serve as selective principles because they are too diverse to permit any ordering of history as a whole. According to Rickert, the objectivity of the historian ultimately rests on the presupposition that the cultural values to which he refers his subject matter have objective validity. Values possess a superpersonal validity for Rickert which he does not expect history to actualize, since they are by definition nonsensory. Nevertheless, he believes that historians shall gradually come to agree about the absolute validity of certain cultural values. In this way, the metaphysical postulate that there is a law of progress in history gives way to an epistemological postulate of progress.

Just as Dilthey had rejected the metaphysics of progress in Comte and Hegel, so he objected to the Neo-Kantian postulate as well. He considered the Kantian dualism of existence and value a product of a narrowing formalism. Values are not to be reduced to a series of independent, a priori rational complexes set apart to judge reality. Instead they are to be viewed as immanent in life. Not only do our ideals develop out of life itself but they so intermesh that they can modify each other.

[7] Ibid., pp. 71, 90.

Thus for Dilthey, the historian cannot refer his material to standards of value external to his subject matter. The impersonal standards sought by Rickert are no less external than the personal values used by the moralizing historian to praise or to assign blame. The historian must evaluate on the basis of understanding his subject on its own terms, particularly by discerning the interpersonal values developed out of historical experience.

Perhaps the best reason for translating *Geisteswissenschaften* as "human studies" rather than "cultural studies" is that the concrete human being who embodies values is considered to be central to them. The Neo-Kantian use of *Kultur* shows the danger of losing this concrete individual reference. To render *Geisteswissenschaften* as "cultural studies" incurs the risk that history be understood in the absolute and impersonal manner of the *Kulturwissenschaften*.

Windelband, the founder of the Baden school, had still defined history as individual-oriented or "idiographic," in contrast to the law-oriented "nomothetic" natural sciences,[8] but Rickert, his successor, rejects this definition as he develops the more impersonal and scientific tendencies of *Kulturwissenschaft*. To be sure, Rickert follows his teacher in maintaining that the historical method must deal with unique individuals and cannot establish laws like the nomothetic natural sciences. But insofar as the idiographic does not exclude an artistic approach, he finds it an inappropriate category for history. Rickert is particularly concerned to divorce history from some of the characteristics associated with the arts. The historian should not rely on intuitive perceptions, nor pursue details for their idiosyncratic charms, for in so doing he reduces history to dealing with mere facts which can be considered as surds or remnants that scientists have not yet caught in their net of relations. In effect, the nomothetic-idiographic alternative involves

[8] Wilhelm Windelband, "Geschichte und Naturwissenschaft," reprinted in *Präludien*, vol. 2, Tübingen: J.C.B. Mohr, 1924, p. 145.

an ever shifting a posteriori distinction which needs to be replaced with a more stable a priori distinction between two clearly definable kinds of concept-formation, one for the natural sciences and one for the historical sciences. The laws of the natural sciences involve generalizing concepts, whereas the historical sciences use complexes of those universal concepts to understand differences among phenomena. The function of history as a science is to create individuating concepts, i.e. conceptual composites known as values, rather than to focus on the value of individuality.

By contrast, the differences that Dilthey acknowledges between the natural sciences and the human studies are not to be defined logically in terms of concept-formation as such, but in terms of approach. They are epistemological and methodological in nature and cannot be established on any a priori basis. He also disagrees with Rickert by declaring that a certain amount of artistic sensitivity or tact is important for the human studies. This should not lead us to think that Dilthey conceives history to be idiographic as distinct from nomothetic. His claim that historical individuality can be understood only on the basis of uniformities means that history is not the study of leftover data, but a culminating discipline. Instead of being a study of the merely unique, it searches for typical individuals. The historian must make use of the uniformities of the natural sciences when appropriate, but most of all he must utilize the regularities laid down by more fundamental human studies. His is the most complex of the *Geisteswissenschaften*.

It is sometimes thought that Dilthey gave up the term *Geisteswissenschaften* at the end of his career and adopted that of the *Kulturwissenschaften*.[9] To be sure, Dilthey expresses some final dissatisfaction with the term *Geisteswis-*

[9] Thus Clarence Smith Howe claims that, "in his last writings Dilthey had already come to the conclusion that it would be far better to name these sciences of human nature *Kulturwissenschaften*." See the foreword to his translation of Ernst Cassirer, *The Logic of the Humanities*, New Haven: Yale University Press, 1961, p. xiii.

senschaften at three places in volume VII of the *Gesammelte Schriften*. However, he makes it clear that the alternative of *Kulturwissenschaften* is less acceptable. Whereas the former is not fully adequate (*nicht völlig angemessen*) to convey Dilthey's meaning, the latter "gives rise to some considerable doubts (*erheblichen Bedenken*)."[10] Specifically, Dilthey says that the concept *Kulturwissenschaften* contains ". . . an unproven, one-sided stipulation about the meaning and goal of history. It betrays a too friendly and benevolent view of human existence . . ." (*GS*,VII,323). By stressing abstract cultural ideals, the Neo-Kantians overlook the instinctual aspects of life which lead to real human conflicts and tensions.

Only prior to the *Einleitung in die Geisteswissenschaften* had Dilthey employed alternatives such as moral-political and psychohistorical *Wissenschaften*. But after that he used the term *Geisteswissenschaften* exclusively, even though his definition of their theoretical status did undergo some modifications.

Einleitung as a Bio-bibliographical Reference Point

The *Einleitung in die Geisteswissenschaften* is Dilthey's first major attempt to define the *Geisteswissenschaften*. By the time the first volume of the *Einleitung* was published in 1883, Dilthey was fifty years old and well established in his academic career. The year before, he had been appointed to the prestigious chair of philosophy at the University of Berlin, thus succeeding Hermann Lotze in the position once held by Hegel.

Before the *Einleitung*, Dilthey had already written more than seventy publications,[11] but the great majority of them

[10] *GS*, VII, 323. All translations of Dilthey are mine unless otherwise noted.

[11] Erich Weniger's bibliography lists 71 items. See *GS*, XII, 208–13. Ulrich Herrmann has discovered additional materials. See *GS*, XV, xviii–xxii.

had appeared in lay journals under various pseudonyms. These early writings were mainly reviews and scholarly articles dealing with the life and work of prominent figures in the history of philosophy and literature. Generally, they were more expository than critical.

Although an essay of 1875, entitled "Ueber das Studium der Geschichte der Wissenschaften vom Menschen, der Gesellschaft und dem Staat" (*GS*,V,31–73) had dealt with some of the problems of the *Geisteswissenschaften*, it is rather sketchy and still exploratory. The essay is thus less useful than the *Einleitung* as a reference point for understanding Dilthey's mature writings. As a full-scale theoretical work, the *Einleitung* can be said to mark the beginning of the philosophically significant development of Dilthey's thought.

But Dilthey's philosophical interests grew out of his own earlier historical scholarship. It was with the peculiar problems of history in mind that Dilthey found it necessary to formulate a theory of the *Geisteswissenschaften*. A brief survey of his background should therefore help to indicate the concerns he brought to his theoretical task.

Born and raised in the village of Biebrich on the Rhine, Dilthey was first expected to follow family tradition by eventually succeeding his father as chaplain to the duke of Nassau. However, he was evidently more interested in the study of theology than in going into the ministry. Thus in 1852 he began his university studies by enrolling in the theological faculty of the University of Heidelberg. There he fell under the influence of Kuno Fischer who impressed upon him the importance of a comprehensive study of the history of philosophy. When in 1853 he learned of "Fischer's dismissal by the ministry because of the conservative religious opposition to his pantheism,"[12] Dilthey decided to transfer to the University of Berlin.

[12] William Kluback, *Wilhelm Dilthey's Philosophy of History*, New York: Columbia University Press, 1956, p. 7.

This change had important consequences for his own religious outlook and future studies. Reminiscing on how the countryside around Heidelberg was able to evoke a pantheistic response from him, Dilthey wrote: "Those were unusual moods. But never since have I had such a profound sense of nature. Then came Berlin and my enthusiasm for the arts prevailed over everything."[13] Later Dilthey would associate the loss of this ability to understand nature with the decline of religion as such.

While at the University of Berlin, Dilthey began to find theology too narrowing and became absorbed in historical and philosophical studies as well. He attended the lectures of some of the greatest representatives of German historicism such as Ranke, Jakob Grimm, Böckh, and Mommsen. It was in Ranke and his discourses on universal history that Dilthey discovered the most powerful embodiment of nineteenth-century historical accomplishments. Grimm's more restricted efforts to revive a deeper understanding of the Germanic past also made a strong impression. Dilthey expressed his awe of Grimm by noting how all the students "kept a respectful distance from this imposing figure" (*GS*,V,8). Much more direct contact was possible with Boeckh through his seminar on the Greeks and with the philosopher Friedrich Adolf Trendelenburg, whose seminar on Aristotle inspired a whole generation of historians of ancient philosophy. Finally, Mommsen's masterful work on the Romans sharpened Dilthey's interest in the Stoics and in the Roman political mentality generally.

An entry in his diary shows how Dilthey interpreted the change in his interest that had gradually come about: "My life lay before me today like a series of antecedents, some obscure, others clear, whose consequence is that it is my calling to apprehend the innermost nature of religious life in history and to bring this to the attention of our state- and

---

[13] *Der junge Dilthey: Ein Lebensbild in Briefen und Tagebüchern*, 1852–1870, ed. Clara Misch née Dilthey, 1933, 2nd ed. Stuttgart: B. G. Teubner; Göttingen: Vandenhoeck & Ruprecht, 1960, p. 114.

science-oriented times." Theology came to have a basically historical significance for Dilthey. Its dogmatic claims were nothing more than formulations of religious experience in terms of concepts serving the needs of a particular time.[14]

As a theological student, Dilthey had undertaken a detailed study of the early formulations of the Christian *Welt-anschauung* in Iranaeus, Clement of Alexandria and Origen. He sought to demonstrate how dogma always needed to be criticized and revised in terms of new religious experience. This approach reflects the influence of Schleiermacher's experiential interpretation of Protestantism and his denial of the possibility of a universal, rational religion. In 1860, Dilthey wrote an essay on Schleiermacher's hermeneutics which won him a prize and the regard of Schleiermacher's family. Thereupon he was requested to finish the publication of Schleiermacher's correspondence and commissioned to write Schleiermacher's biography.

Meanwhile, Dilthey's formal theological studies had led up to work on Scholasticism. He was close to obtaining his *Habilitation*,[15] when in 1861, he abruptly transferred to the philosophical faculty. As much as he had looked to religion to illuminate history in general, Dilthey now concluded that religious history by itself constituted a distortion of the true historical perspective.[16] Dilthey's philosophical studies were conducted under the supervision of Trendelenburg. Under his direction Dilthey's interest in medieval thought came to focus more on logical problems. Trendelenburg was especially interested in retracing the development of logical thought since Aristotle as part of an attempt to find an alternative to the Hegelian dialectic. Whereas Hegel had criticized the Aristotelian logic for its abstractness, Trendelenburg found Hegel's dialectic more dynamic, to be sure, but no less abstract. He claimed to find in Aristotle's *De Anima*

---

[14] See *Der junge Dilthey*, pp. 140, 37.

[15] Ibid., p. 105.

[16] Cf. Kluback, *Wilhelm Dilthey's Philosophy of History*, pp. 17, 283.

the basis for a new logic: a "natural-genetic" method as developed in his *Logische Untersuchungen* (1840). Trendelenburg's influence on Dilthey can be measured by Dilthey's own increasing rejection of the Hegelianism he had acquired through Kuno Fischer in Heidelberg. When his two mentors became involved in a polemic, Dilthey not only sided with Trendelenburg, but actually contributed to his essays attacking Fischer. Trendelenburg's strong influence, especially on Dilthey's *Weltanschauung* typology, has been noted in a short study by Joachim Wach.[17]

While engaged in extensive research on nominalism in the tenth and eleventh centuries, Dilthey became plagued with eye troubles. Trendelenburg then suggested that he write on a theme which would require mainly reflection. Because of his close familiarity with Schleiermacher's thought, Dilthey decided to write a critique of Schleiermacher's ethics. In January 1864 he defended his doctoral dissertation entitled "De principiis ethices Schleiermacheri." Later in the same year he completed his *Habilitationsschrift*: "Versuch einer Analyse des moralischen Bewusstseins" (in *GS*,VI,1–55).

In 1867, Dilthey became *ausserordentlicher Professor* in Basel where he met his greatest rival as a cultural historian: Jacob Burckhardt.[18] It was in Basel and in Kiel, where Dilthey received his next appointment, that he was able to devote more of his time to the Schleiermacher biography. This had grown into a tremendous project which involved studying the man's intellectual background, his place in his generation of literary and philosophical contemporaries, the import of his writings and lecture notes, as well as his activities for church and state. As part of the justification of his thesis that Schleiermacher was the Kant of Protestant theology, Dilthey provided a more than fifty-page discussion of Kant's work. Even more impressive is the way that Dilthey

---

[17] *Die Typenlehre Trendelenburgs und ihr Einfluss auf Dilthey*, Tübingen: J.C.B. Mohr, 1926.

[18] *Der junge Dilthey*, pp. 237f.

did a large number of separate studies of literary figures such as Goethe, Tieck, the Schlegel brothers, Novalis, to better characterize Schleiermacher's relation to his Romantic contemporaries. Dilthey finally published the first biographical volume of *Leben Schleiermachers* by 1870, leaving the systematic consideration of Schleiermacher's thought for a later time.

Thirteen years later, in the preface to the *Einleitung in die Geisteswissenschaften*, Dilthey refers to his unfinished work on Schleiermacher. Preparatory studies for the second volume had convinced him that "the exposition and critique of Schleiermacher's system everywhere presupposed deliberations about ultimate philosophical questions" (*GS*,I,xx). The *Einleitung* would make it unnecessary to incorporate such discussions in the biography itself.

The original committee of editors in charge of publishing Dilthey's works no doubt chose the *Einleitung* as the opening volume of the *Gesammelte Schriften* because of its convenience as a theoretical base line. The first volume of the *Einleitung*, which constitutes the main source for this chapter, consists of two books. Book 1 surveys the actual disciplines included among the *Geisteswissenschaften* and examines the nature of their interrelations. Book 2 illustrates how the traditional metaphysical foundations given for these disciplines have proved inadequate, thus clearing the ground for a proper foundation. Such a grounding was to have been the result of a second volume. Had this been published as planned, it would have contained three more books, bringing the total to five.[19] Book 3 was to trace the modern development of the *Geisteswissenschaften* and give a critical evaluation of epistemology up to Dilthey's time.

At least part of what Dilthey had in mind for this third book of the *Einleitung* was executed in some of the admirable historical studies that he published in journals during the 1890s and early 1900s. They were collected posthumous-

[19] See Dilthey's own preface, *GS*, I, xix.

ly in volumes II and III of the *Gesammelte Schriften*. Outstanding among these are the essays studying the flowering of the *Geisteswissenschaften* in the Renaissance, their naturalistic systematization in the seventeenth century, and the growth of historical consciousness in the eighteenth century.[20]

As far as the epistemological critique is concerned, volume V of the *Gesammelte Schriften* contains two essays that deal with the main problems posed about knowledge since Descartes and Kant. One of them is entitled "Beiträge zur Lösung der Frage vom Ursprung unseres Glaubens an die Realität der Aussenwelt und seinem Recht" (1890), and attacks phenomenalism for its solution to the problem of the external world. The other essay to be mentioned in this regard is "Erfahren und Denken" of 1892, a critique of the formal conception of reason inherent in the Kantian epistemology as it had influenced nineteenth-century logicians like Sigwart and Lotze. In subsequent chapters some of the results of these two essays will be discussed because they also develop some of Dilthey's own philosophical views concerning the volitional nature of our belief in the external world and the immanence of reason in experience itself. It is therefore important to note that Misch, Dilthey's literary executor, writes that Dilthey specifically intended the treatise on the problem of the external world to become part of the final systematic books of the *Einleitung*. It was then to have been incorporated in books 4 and 5 where Dilthey planned to give his own epistemological foundation of the *Geisteswissenschaften*.

These concluding books would in effect have constituted the Critique of Historical Reason to which Dilthey refers in dedicating the *Einleitung* to his philosophical friend,

[20] See "Auffassung und Analyse des Menschen im 15. und 16. Jahrhundert" (1891–92), "Das natürliche System der Geisteswissenschaften im 17. Jahrhundert" (1892–93), "Das achtzehnte Jahrhundert und die geschichtliche Welt" (1901).

Count Yorck von Wartenburg. Although all of Dilthey's later work can be seen as addressing itself to the problems involved in this project, Dilthey was unable to begin its overall formulation in a single work until the very end of his life. In volume VII of the *Gesammelte Schriften* we find what the editors have entitled "Entwürfe zur Kritik der historischen Vernunft," a hundred pages of fragments designed to become a part of the second half of the "Aufbau der geschichtlichen Welt in den Geisteswissenschaften" published in 1910. Unfortunately, this manuscript which Dilthey once specifically identified as his Critique of Historical Reason (*GS*,VII,358), was still only a series of sketches when he died the following year. In poor health during his last year, Dilthey had attempted to first finish the Schleiermacher biography. It would be less taxing, he decided, to express his matured theoretical perspective in terms of his actual historical scholarship. Although the second volume of Dilthey's *Leben Schleiermachers* has now been published,[21] it too remained unfinished. Thus Dilthey's two most ambitious projects, the one primarily theoretical, the other primarily historical, suffered similar fates. Around the turn of the century, according to Max Dessoir, Dilthey had already come to be known in Berlin circles as "Mann der ersten Bände"—a man of first volumes.[22] He was never able to rid himself of this reputation. Dilthey's inability to complete his planned works was the result of his conviction that systematic conclusions should not be arrived at in a psychohistorical vacuum. Theories cannot be productive unless thoroughly grounded in historical scholarship, nor is history understandable without critical reflection. The cautious nature of his philosophical reflections led to the publication of works which were usually of a preliminary nature. They would bear titles starting with phrases like

---

[21] *GS*, XIV, in 2 parts, 787 pp.
[22] Cited in Rodi, *Morphologie und Hermeneutik*, p. 11.

"Ideas concerning," "Studies towards," and "Contributions to." It was thus characteristic that the more bold projects, such as the "Introduction to the *Geisteswissenschaften*,"[23] remained unfinished.

Müller-Freienfels reports that Dilthey "was a brilliant teacher and speaker who was more interested in formulating his thoughts in speech than upon paper."[24] His forcefulness as a teacher attracted many disciples who sought to continue his work. Some of these—Misch, Bernhard Groethuysen, and Herman Nohl, to name the most important ones—devoted much effort in gathering, not only Dilthey's scattered publications, but also dictated manuscripts, lecture notes and records of papers delivered publicly, especially at the Prussian Academy of the Sciences where he played such an eminent role. This task of publishing Dilthey's work is itself an unfinished one. Volume 15 of the *Gesammelte Schriften*, which did not appear until 1970, contains in its preface the promise of a further continuation of the collected works. But even apart from these projected volumes, the *Gesammelte Schriften* have made it possible for Dilthey to exert a great influence on modern German intellectual life.[25]

History and Descriptive Psychology

Whereas a theoretical justification for his biographical volume of the *Leben Schleiermachers* could be found in historicism, Dilthey realized that it would be inadequate for

---

[23] Of course "Introduction" here does not denote a work for beginners, but a work which probes what is fundamental for a newly defined set of disciplines.

[24] Richard Müller-Freienfels, *The Evolution of Modern Psychology*, trans. W. Beran Wolfe, New Haven: Yale University Press, 1935, p. 99.

[25] The bibliography shows how gradually Dilthey's writings have become available.

the proposed systematic volume. In the former, Dilthey was primarily concerned to relate the development of Schleiermacher's religious *Weltanschauung* to the artistic and philosophical currents of German Romanticism. However, the concrete nexus of this personal *Weltanschauung* and the historical generation which it represents, does not seem to provide any critical standard for a systematic evaluation of Schleiermacher's work. The ability to compare this *Weltanschauung* with the much broader range of *Weltanschauungen* to which Dilthey had been exposed ever since his theological studies, would be a prerequisite for such an evaluation. One of the functions of the *Einleitung* was to provide a universal framework for such comparative analysis.

The problem of a universal framework had not really been faced by historicism. To be sure, Dilthey acknowledged that the German tradition of historicism had made great strides in ridding history of that insidious kind of universality provided by metaphysical speculation. It had on the one hand liberated the historian from the Enlightenment conception that history can be summed up as the tale of man's progressive conquest of nature, while on the other it had avoided the Hegelian counterpart that history is the dialectical unfolding of world spirit. However, Dilthey recognized that with the rejection of the metaphysics of nature and spirit, historicism needed a new epistemological grounding if it was not to disintegrate into relativism.

The tendency of historicism was to interpret history in terms of seemingly self-sufficient national contexts with the dangerous consequence of reifying the *Volksseele* (the soul of the people of a nation). The philosophical problems inherent in historicism are revealed with Ranke's efforts to revive the eighteenth-century conception of a universal history. How does one evaluate such self-enclosed national histories in relation to each other? Unless some means of transcendental or internal criticism of separate cultures could be uncovered, the traditional appeal to synthetic standards of a transcendent order would have to be reinstituted.[26]

Dilthey is critical of Ranke's claim that to see history objectively one must "efface the self" (*Selbst auslöschen*) (*GS*,I,94). To so suspend the role of reflective judgment is to place an undue burden on the immediacy of intuition as well as to undermine the possibility of a transcendental critique of what is being reported. To the extent that the ultimate eyewitness of Ranke's universal history is God himself, the ideal of self-effacement is not to be interpreted as merely allowing the facts to speak for themselves but as letting God speak through us. Dilthey means to eliminate the transcendent standard still implicit here, when he later states that we can only attain the goal of an objective understanding of history to the degree that we make our inner life universal (*GS*,V,281–82). Instead of extinguishing the notion of the self, Dilthey proposes that we expand it in order to uncover the transcendental conditions of intersubjective understanding.

According to Dilthey, inner experience (*innere Erfahrung*) possesses an initial intelligibility. To suppress this would be to destroy the source from which we derive the meaning of socio-historical, as well as individual, experience. Admittedly, inner experience is limited in scope by personal dispositions and presuppositions. Such individual perspectives need not be denied, but through reflection their horizons of meaning can be shifted so as to be made more and more encompassing. For example, an initial consciousness of how inner experience is bounded by social experience can make it possible for the latter to become incorporated into the former.[27] Dilthey thus anticipates the sociology of

26 This distinction between "transcendental" and "transcendent" follows that existing in post-Kantian philosophy. The transcendental refers to what is presupposed by experience; the transcendent to that which lies beyond experience.

27 See the later discussion of reflective experience in chap. 5.

knowledge according to which one inevitably finds oneself locked in by a particular perspective on reality. The solution is to make the perspective explicit, thereby rendering it less restrictive and more amenable to refinement. Translated back into the terminology of the *Einleitung* this means that all historical understanding presupposes a kind of self-reflection which can do justice to inner experience and explicate its potential.

Psychology is to be the tool that allows our reflective starting point to be generalized and thus become a basis for the comparison and evaluation of other modes of experience. Ranke's desire to see "what actually happened" (*wie es eigentlich gewesen*) would, according to Dilthey, be realizable only " . . . with the scientific knowledge of the psychic unities which make up this historical reality, and of the lasting structures which develop through their interaction and become the carriers of historical progress." The historical past cannot be grasped "by mere seeing, but only by analysis" (*GS*,I,94). It is not a mere spectacle to be perceived from God's transcendent perspective, but a human epic to be understood and continually transcended by successive generations of men. Accordingly, what the historian needs is not some special kind of vision, but an insight into the nature of psychic experience which can help him grasp and analyze the dynamics of the original drama that mere eyewitness reports either veil or ignore.

But having affirmed the importance of psychology for the *Geisteswissenschaften*, Dilthey found the traditional psychologies unable to fulfill the function of illuminating historical experience. They had concerned themselves with experience only to the extent that they could illuminate the process of learning about the external world. And ever since Hobbes, the empirically-minded psychologists had become obsessed with the notion of modeling their field on the natural sciences. Dilthey therefore felt impelled to spend much time formulating ideas for a different kind of psychology—or anthropology as he sometimes called it—

which would be devoted to understanding both the whole-ness and individuality of human experience. It would take into account, not only sense-experience and its relation to the cognitive processes of the psyche, but also the feelings, drives and purposes that combine to constitute a concrete historical person. It was especially important to Dilthey that all these processes not be investigated in a piecemeal fashion but in their interrelations. Only a psychology conceived as part of the *Geisteswissenschaften* could tap the full potential of human experience and thus be of relevance to the writing of history. The historian's sense of the complexity inherent in a momentous decision, and of the richness of the inner experience of a great historical figure cannot be derived from the archives. This sense of life needs to be filled in by the historian's imagination. But if his imagination is not to be arbitrary, it must be guided by a psychology which describes certain regularities discernible in inner experience.

Just as Dilthey's psychology was meant to overcome the tendency of traditional psychology to study introspective phenomena as separate, so it was also meant to overcome the parallel common sense view of the individual as an isolated psychophysical molecule. According to Dilthey, psychology should describe the psychophysical complex in such a way as to preserve it as the basic unit of, while showing it to be inseparable from, social and historical life. The individual is not the hypothetical aggregate of some elementary givens, like his sense impressions. Nor is society the mere aggregate of the individuals that can be located in it. Instead, the individual is the ultimate element of a historical society, and in being conscious he is already an embodiment of that society. He is a self-subsistent whole who in turn points to a larger whole as a microcosm reflects a macrocosm. On the one hand, Dilthey is to be credited, as Husserl put it, for his attempt to have psychology study "not just single experiences, but from the outset the totality

56

of the stream of experience,"[28] and on the other hand, for his ability to incorporate a historical dynamism into his psychological framework, so that appeals to superpersonal subjects are rendered unnecessary. By analyzing national life into that of individuals whose very consciousness could incorporate cultural values and whose very goals are historically oriented, Dilthey was able to reject historicist reifications like the *Volksseele*. Dilthey argues in the *Einleitung* that nations are not special organisms but only "relatively independent centers of culture" (*GS,I,41*), and that the real movers of history are individuals subject to psychological elucidation (*GS,I,53*). Because he is a creative participant in the historical process, the individual is able to identify with and understand his complex socio-historical environment in a way that is impossible for him in studying his natural environment. Whereas nature is the creation of ultimately inscrutable forces, whether natural or divine, society is man's own creation. "Nature is alien to us. She is a mere exterior for us without any inner life. Society is our world. We sympathetically experience (*miterleben*) the interplay of social conditions with the power of our total being. From within we are aware of the states and forces in all their restlessness that constitute the social system" (*GS,I,36–37*).

There is then prima facie nothing behind what we observe in social systems which transcends the human understanding. Precisely because all social systems are historically finite is it possible to reopen the Kantian question of the limits of the understanding. The infinite scope of nature may have justified Kant in distinguishing what we know as a phenomenal world from what it may be in itself. But when it comes to the understanding of the human environment, such a dualism is unnecessary. Thus it may be that the understanding need not always be merely discursive and can be, under certain conditions, intuitive.

[28] Edmund Husserl, *Phänomenologische Psychologie, Husserliana*, vol. IX, 2nd ed., The Hague: Martinus Nijhoff, 1968, p. 355.

The most obvious place to begin investigating this possibility is in the domain of psychology. Kant had assumed that inner experience could only be understood on the model of outer experience. He thus rendered self-knowledge phenomenal and dependent on the explanative power of the natural sciences. The Neo-Kantians, according to Dilthey's criticism, were misguided in appropriating such a naturalistic and derivative conception of psychology. By contrast, Dilthey claims that psychology has certain advantages over the natural sciences. Our inner experience has an initial intelligibility which the data of the physical sciences lack. It is an error to assume that the givens of inner experience are meaningless until explained by some generalization, for as experienced by us they possess a meaningful reality which can be directly described. This is not to deny the difficulty of the task of analyzing and explicating the meaning of human experience. The descriptive sense of psychic life that underlies analysis does not possess the absoluteness usually associated with intuition in that it needs to be filled in. However, it does provide an indubitable experiential starting point. According to Dilthey, a descriptive psychology can provide the *Geisteswissenschaften* with a nonhypothetical conception of the basic elements of socio-historical reality, whereas natural science can only obtain its elements by splitting things into hypothetical particles posited by explanative generalizations: "Natural science constructs matter from small elementary particles which are not capable of any independent existence and are only conceivable as parts of molecules; on the other hand the units which act on each other in the wonderfully complex totality of history and society are individuals, psychophysical wholes each of which differs from every other, each of which constitutes a world. For the world exists nowhere else but in the representations of such an individual" (*GS*,I,29).

As his thought developed, Dilthey would further elaborate his conception of the human psyche. His matured conceptions were to be indicated especially in an essay on the nature of the external world and in two psychological studies of the 1890s, "Ideen über eine beschreibende und zergliedernde Psychologie" and "Ueber vergleichende Psychologie." There Dilthey continues to approach the psyche nonconstructively, although he ceases to speak of it as if it were a simple microcosm which from the beginning harmonizes with other microcosms. In the *Einleitung* of 1883 Dilthey's distrust of hypothetical constructions in the *Geisteswissenschaften* is still rooted in a pantheistic *Weltanschauung* according to which the relation between a microcosm and a macrocosm can be contemplated. However, the notion that man is a microcosm who can fully reflect the cosmos from his perspective will have to be questioned. At this point, we need simply realize that Dilthey is setting up the possibility of a descriptive psychology which differs from traditional psychology in not being explanative.

The Relation of Psychology to the Natural Sciences

In the *Einleitung*, Dilthey asserts that psychology is the most basic *Geisteswissenschaft* (GS,I,32). But, at the same time, he warns that this claim is valid only to the extent that psychology limits itself to describing and analyzing such connections as are present to consciousness. Descriptive psychology may not entangle itself in the traditional disputes over various explanative hypotheses about the physical conditioning of psychic states. Therefore, as a base of the *Geisteswissenschaften* it clearly cannot be exhaustive in its treatment of the psyche (GS,I,29). Dilthey leaves open the possibility of complementing psychological description of inner experience (1) with explanations "from below" using the generalizations of the *Naturwissenschaften*, and (2) with more complex or higher-order descriptive relations which are discernible in the other *Geisteswissenschaften*.

The first alternative of using the results of the natural sciences involves the problem of the relation of consciousness and nature. In the preceding discussion, Dilthey has already been quoted to the effect that the world is in consciousness. From the perspective of consciousness, the natural sciences are more derivative than the human studies. Yet from the standpoint of systematic knowledge the natural sciences have attained an advantage. Although fundamentally more hypothetical than the human studies, they have the means of testing hypotheses about external nature by experimentation and mathematical calculations which are not feasible when dealing with historical life. What was once a mere hypothesis can, in retrospect, become a first principle which leads to knowledge with a degree of systematic clarity that we find lacking in the human studies.

Moreover, the natural scientist can argue that we, as psychophysical creatures, have our place in nature and find ourselves subject to the kind of pervasive causal laws that have been discovered by him. Dilthey does not deny that human beings can be considered as part of nature and to that extent subject to the explanative methods of the natural sciences. But this does not mean that consciousness is derivable from physical phenomena (GS,I,11).

In delimiting the explanative power of the natural sciences, Dilthey indicates how, at a certain point, only a functional correlation can be asserted between the physical and the psychical.

Insofar as the perspective [of natural science] remains conscious of its limits, its results are indisputable. However, these results receive a closer determination of their cognitive value only from the standpoint of inner experience. Natural science analyzes the causal nexus of natural processes. When this analysis has reached the point at which a material state of affairs or a material change is regularly connected with a psychic change without finding any further intermediary, then

only this regularity itself can be established, no connection of cause (*Ursache*) and effect can be applied to
this relation. . . . The mathematical concept of function
is the [appropriate] expression for such a relation.
[*GS*,I,15–16]

Dilthey acknowledges the dependence of psychic life on
material conditions so long as this is not formulated to fore-
close a conception of human purposiveness. To the extent
that consciousness can institute changes, human life cannot
be viewed as totally determined by nature. Thus Dilthey
speaks of the human studies as having a "relative independence" from the natural sciences (*GS*,I,17). Reference to natural laws may be questionable when the specific dependence of psychic processes on physical processes is being
characterized, but is certainly appropriate in the context of
studying what material conditions man reacts to and how
his self-initiated acts produce their results in the world. According to Dilthey, a purpose can only exist for man
through consciousness, yet even to communicate itself spir-
itually to others, it must use means provided in the context
of nature. "How unlikely is the change which the creative
power of spirit has often produced in the external world:
and, nevertheless, in this external world lie the means
whereby alone [humanly] created values exist for others as
well. Thus the few pages which came into the hands of
Copernicus as material remnants of profound mental efforts
by the ancients in the direction towards accepting the motion of the earth, became the starting point of a revolution
in our world view" (*GS*,I,18).

To recognize that the human studies presuppose natural
laws does not mean that they lack their own starting point.
History, as Dilthey referred to it at the beginning of his
work, is a realm ". . . where freedom appears at innumerable points in the midst of the total continuum of objective
necessity characteristic of nature" (*GS*,I,6). There are
points in historical life where the influence exerted is not

comparable to any cause. As will be seen later, this is when the reflex mechanism of the psychophysical organism turns reflective.

Human activity is marked by a certain purposiveness which cannot be accounted for by the natural sciences. Dilthey's refutation of Comte's claim that the inductive findings of sociology can be deduced from the results of biology (GS,I,106f.), reflects his view that it is neither sufficient, nor necessary, to resort to any biological model to account for the purposiveness of society. According to Dilthey, both the origin and understanding of teleology must ultimately be psychological. If we look to the model that inner experience can supply of purposiveness, we will solve the problem of understanding the operations of society long before we can hope to solve the problems of explaining the activities of animal organisms (GS,I,31).

One may ask whether by giving psychology such importance and considering the individual as the agent in history, Dilthey has not embraced what German philosophers like Hegel pejoratively called the "pragmatic history" of the French and English. Dilthey too, however, distances himself from the "viewpoint of the pragmatic historian, for whom the course of history reduces itself to the play of personal forces" (GS,I,53). Such a view finds nothing more than a random interaction of individual interests in society. "But," continues Dilthey, "in reality there comes into being by means of all this mutual determination of individuals, their passions, their vanities, and their interests, the necessary purposive system of the history of humanity" (GS,I,53).

The word "necessary" seems somewhat out of character for Dilthey, but the point is clear. Dilthey wants to locate a middle ground between pragmatic history and a Hegelian philosophy of history. Individuals and their motivations may be the agents of history, but larger transpersonal ends are realized through the social interaction of individuals. We have already noted that psychology deals with only some aspects of the individual. "The object of psychology is at all times merely the individual that has been singled out from the living context of socio-historical reality. It is only through a process of abstraction that psychology can establish the universal characteristics developed by individual creatures in this context" (*GS*,I,30).

But while necessarily abstracting from its context, psychology must preserve the socio-historical nature of the psyche. We cannot posit any isolated psychic processes which are not either conditioned by the socio-historical context or oriented towards it.

Any psychological claims based on so-called natural properties of man are hypothetical. As Dilthey states, "Man as a fact prior to history and society is a fiction of genetic explanation" (*GS*,I,31). To begin with a definition of the "nature" of man is to fix and fill in at the start, what in fact should be left open. What the psychologist points to as fundamental must be so described as to leave room for other characterizations. This is where it becomes necessary to consider the alternate possibility of complementing the psychological description of inner experience with data from the other human studies.

Psychology and the Other Human Studies

The individual, along with being the bearer (*Träger*) of historical development, must also be viewed as the crossing point (*Kreuzungspunkt*) of various systems of social interaction (*GS*,I,37,87). It is to the latter socio-cultural contexts of human activity that the other *Geisteswissenschaften* are more specifically devoted. As noted previously, Dilthey does not separate the humanities from the social sciences, so that, for example, aesthetics as well as economics, are included.

However, in discussing the structures of human interaction, Dilthey makes a significant distinction between (1) cultural systems (*Kultursysteme*) and (2) the external organization of society (*die äussere Organization der Gesell-*

schaft) (*GS*,I,43). The cultural systems are generally spoken of as "purposive systems" (*Zweckzusammenhänge*),[29] in which individuals freely participate, while the external organization of society refers to the institutional arrangements and sanctions that actually bind individuals into specific groups.

The cultural systems—such as the arts, language, science, religion, and economics—are essentially free, cooperative relations serving to fulfill needs and purposes that individuals cannot fulfill by themselves. However, if man's social relations were solely of this functional kind, ". . . each individual would remain an entity for himself. It would be merely their intellect which had created a relation among themselves. They would count on each other, but no living feeling of a community would exist among them" (*GS*,I,47).

Dilthey goes on to assert that man is not just a free, calculating being in abstract harmony with others. He also feels himself subjected to coercive social bonds, which either institutionalize the spiritual functions of cultural systems or satisfy the deep-rooted instinctual needs of human nature. "The impetuous power of his passions as well as his inner need for, and feeling of, community, make man not only a component in the structure of these [cultural] systems, but also a member of the *external organization* of humanity" (*GS*,I,47). In the latter context, individuals are bound by a collective will or the hierarchical relations of power exhibited in the family, the tribe, and the state. The political bond like the family bond is seen as a given necessity and not as a contract between autonomous individuals. One finds oneself already part of a family, a tribe, or a state

[29] This term is sometimes used for the external organization of society as well. But Dilthey specifically states that it denotes an essential quality of cultural systems, not of the external organization of society (*GS*,I,43). In chap. 8, the concept of *Zweckzusammenhang* will be compared to the wider concept of *Wirkungszusammenhang* that Dilthey subsequently substituted for it.

without any rational calculation or justification of its purposes.

By distinguishing the cultural systems from the state-centered external organization of society, Dilthey resists the nationalistic tendencies of the historicists. Thus he writes: "That which our intuition instinctively marks off spatially as a country, a people, and a state, and thus sees as a full reality under the name of Germany or France, is not really the state qua object of the political sciences" (*GS*,I,82). Such an intuition of the nation-state renders it more concrete and ineluctable than it really is, for in fact the "state binds and subjects the individual only partially and relatively" (*GS*,I,82). Although all cultural systems inevitably become institutionalized, only some such as language and religion tend to take on a peculiar national character. Others, like art and science are more cosmopolitan. Thus Dilthey asserts that external organizations do not radically constrain the individual artist or scientist: "The systems of art and science can be developed in their fundamentals, without requiring any reference to the external organization of society. Neither the foundations of aesthetics nor those of the theory of science include the influence of national character on art or science, or the effect of state and professional associations" (*GS*,I,58). Dilthey here appears to be suggesting a kind of separability between cultural system and social organization which neither his own distinction nor reality itself would justify. But Dilthey always assumed that the historian must take both kinds of structure into account so that even the arts would ultimately be discussed in their various local contexts. The real problem for Dilthey is not so much that of ignoring one kind of structure, as allowing one to become an accessory of the other. This danger is especially evident in the study of law, where the subject matter is not easily classifiable. Law can be viewed either as the cultural system of legal theory establishing such doctrines as natural rights, or as the external organization representing the codification and enforcement of positive laws. However, Dilthey reminds us that for any individual there always exists a tension between belief in a higher law and the practical exigency of submitting to positive law, which requires him to constantly compare the two and correlate them as irreducible structures. The theoretical attempts either to deduce positive law from natural law, or to inductively arrive at a higher law by abstracting from different systems of positive law are all misguided (*GS*,I,54f.). Dilthey stresses that both the cultural system of law and its external organization "exist side by side, with each other. To be sure, they are not connected as cause (*Ursache*) and effect, but each has the other as condition for its existence. This relation is one of the most difficult and important forms of the causal (*kausalen*) relation. It can only be explicated in an epistemological . . . foundation of the human studies" (*GS*,I,55).

It is significant that in the above passage Dilthey rejects the substantive *Ursache* and uses the adjective *kausal* in introducing a mode of coexistence particularly important for the human studies. What he may have had in mind is that *Ursache* can be etymologically analyzed into *Ur-sache*, meaning primary fact. It is exactly this aspect of primacy in causation that Dilthey finds inappropriate in the human studies and wants to exclude from his proposed notion of a reciprocity which is *kausal*. Just as causality in the strict explanative sense was not applicable to psychology when correlating neural processes with states of consciousness, so when considering the relation of the ideal and the actual in the other systematic *Geisteswissenschaften*, we cannot simply make one the primary fact (*Ur-sache*) of which the other is the mere effect.

In what sense psychic and cultural systems are causal, and what kinds of lawful connections are possible in them, are problems which will be taken up from time to time as the development of Dilthey's theoretical views is traced. By

66

interpreting the psychophysical connection as a functional relation, Dilthey had granted the human studies a relative methodological independence from the natural sciences. Now he also finds it important to insist on a reciprocal relation between the socio-cultural structures of the human studies themselves in order to leave open the possibility of an epistemological mode of explanation.

Unfortunately, Dilthey never wrote the epistemological section of the *Einleitung* which was to elaborate on this discussion in book 1. For purposes of the immediate issue of the relation of natural law and positive law, it is clear in any case, that Dilthey is alluding to a relation of mutual determination, a sense of interdependence. An understanding of the cultural system of law must take cognizance of the positive codifications of particular states, and vice versa. "Every concept of law thus contains within itself an aspect of the external organization of society. On the other hand, every [political] bond can only be constructed in terms of legal concepts" (*GS*,I,80).

The concrete functional tension that Dilthey discerns between systems of culture and external organizations of society prevents either from being hypostatized. They are to be seen as functional structures activated by individuals rather than autonomous superpersonal entities. If this heuristic principle is kept in mind we can understand why Dilthey expressed strong reservations about the new science of sociology stemming from France and beginning to take root in Germany at the end of the nineteenth century. Dilthey's distrust of synthetic disciplines will be expressed most clearly in terms of a later critique of Kantian synthetic logic. Here in the *Einleitung* it is indicated in his resistance to Lorenz von Stein's *Gesellschaftslehre* for its pretension of creating "a theory intermediary to the studies of the systems of culture and political science" (*GS*,I,85). By conflating the study of systems of culture and external organizations of society into one science of sociology we may

67

gain a more comprehensive perspective on social phenomena, but at the price of losing insight into the individual and his functional relations.[30]

The virtue of Dilthey's approach to society is that cultural systems are partial systems which outlast an individual who participates in them and yet cannot submerge him. No human being is exhausted by any cultural system. He partakes of many different systems at the same time. Even a particular act of an individual can reveal the workings of more than one system. Dilthey cites the example of the publication of a treatise which can be seen under the perspective of its scientific contribution, its economic merits in creating work for printers, its fulfilling a legal contract with a publishing firm, etc. (GS,I,51). The individual is always more than the roles or persona he manifests in the various cultural systems. Far from judging the individual by the values of the systems of culture, Dilthey characterizes him as their "carrier and codeveloper" (GS,I,87). This confirms that the reference to culture here is not Neo-Kantian. Not only does Dilthey relativize the concept of culture into different overlapping systems, but also he supplements it with the external organizations of society. Thus instead of finding the unity of the human studies through a synthetic, comprehensive science like sociology—at least as conceived by Comte or von Stein—Dilthey relates them to the historical individuals in which they intersect.

It is because psychology focuses on individuals that Dilthey argued for the fundamental importance of psychology. However, this does not mean that Dilthey simply substituted psychology for sociology as the synthesizing discipline. Psychology may be the most fundamental of the *Geisteswissenschaften*, but it is not the foundation from which

[30] That Dilthey had only a specific stage of sociology in mind when he rejected it in the *Einleitung* is subsequently acknowledged in a note where he does approve of Simmel's sociology as a mere study of social forms which can be elucidated psychologically. See GS, I, 420–21.

the other disciplines can be derived. This statement will seem less paradoxical if it is recalled that Dilthey could claim a special status for psychology only by limiting it to being descriptive. By itself, its explanative capacity is no greater than that of the other human studies. Only by lending each other mutual support could the human studies develop adequate explanative power. Dilthey's proposed epistemological framework for all the *Geisteswissenschaften* would help clarify the possibility of such explanation.

The System of the *Geisteswissenschaften*

Because Dilthey never completed the second volume of the *Einleitung*, we can only speculate about his proposed epistemology. However, it is clear that it was meant to provide a new explanative method distinct from the hypothetical explanations of the natural sciences (*GS*,I,xvi,95). This would be done by properly relating epistemology to descriptive psychology. As such, an epistemology of the *Geisteswissenschaften* could provide the transcendental ground of explanation worthy of a Critique of Historical Reason.

Significantly enough, it is in the context of his discussion of descriptive psychology in Book 1 of the *Einleitung*, that Dilthey gives some clues to the nature of his new epistemological perspective. They appear in a methodological discussion of the relation of so-called first-order psychological concepts about individuals to second-order psychological concepts necessary to illuminate the operations of systems of culture.

Indeed the studies (*Wissenschaften*) of the systems of culture rest on psychical and psychophysical contents. But to these [studies] correspond concepts which are specifically different from those used in the psychology of individuals. Compared to the latter, these could be called concepts of a second-order in the formative system (*Aufbau*) of the human studies. . . . Thus the psychophysical concepts of need, thrift (*Wirtschaftlich-keit*), work and value, for example, constitute the necessary basis for the analysis to be executed in political economy. [*GS*,I,45–46]

Although the meaning of thrift, for example, can be fully experienced by an individual, it can be characterized as a psychological concept only relative to specific economic ends. Any such second-order psychological concept cannot simply be derived from studying the individual apart from a consideration of concepts of the cultural systems in which he participates.

Descriptive psychology does not establish these second-order concepts and yet from the epistemological standpoint it can be said to anticipate them. Continuing his discussion, Dilthey then addresses himself to the more general problem of how concepts of different orders are to be systematically related:

> The concepts and propositions which make up the base of the knowledge of these [cultural] systems, stand in a relation of dependence to the concepts and propositions developed by psychology. But this relationship is so intricate that only a comprehensive epistemological and logical foundation proceeding from the special position (*Stellung*) that human knowledge has vis-à-vis historical and social reality, can fill the gaps that exist today between the investigation of the psychophysical on the one hand and that of political economy, law, religion, etc. on the other hand. This gap is felt by every scientist. The philosophy of science in England and France, which sees here again nothing more than a relation of deductive and inductive operations and believes it can solve this difficult problem in a merely logical way by investigating the relative scope of these two operations, has nowhere shown its fruitlessness more clearly than in these extensive debates. [*GS*,I,46]

Elsewhere a similar complaint is registered with reference to the monotonous clatter (*Geklapper*) of the words "induction" and "deduction" in Mill's writings (*GS*,I,108). For Dilthey, it is beside the point whether or not the moral or social sciences first obtain their generalizations inductively from experience and then confirm them deductively from the principles of some more fundamental science. Such discussions mistakenly presuppose that the human studies are systematically related to each other on the schema of the natural sciences. It is evident that Dilthey considers the influential Cartesian system of axiomatic and deductive science an inadequate model for the human studies. In contrast to the natural sciences, there is no one-sided dependence and hierarchical stratification in the system of the human studies. In differentiating the natural sciences from the human studies, Dilthey suggests how they may be contrasted in terms of their respective ideals of a constructionist system (*Konstruktion*) and a developmental or formative system (*Aufbau*) (*GS*,I,30f.). The constructionist system of the natural sciences is hypothetical from the ground up. The more fundamental its hypotheses, the greater their explanative power. In the developmental system of the human studies, hypotheses may be ventured only in the late stages of investigation. The possibility of explanation develops out of a cumulative process in which the different disciplines supplement each other.

In effect, the developmental system of the *Geisteswissenschaften* culminates in historical explanation. As at once the most concrete and the most complex of the human studies, history constitutes the ultimate testing ground of their explanative potential. Even though the system of the human studies is not logically integrated, the insights and analyses of the various disciplines must be drawn upon to explain any concrete historical reality. However specific its subject matter, history can be said to reflect all the issues and intricacies of the more generalizing human studies which

71

have previously been discussed. This "reflective" role of history can be illustrated through Dilthey's claim that "the position of biography within the general study of history corresponds to that of psychology within the theoretical studies of socio-historical reality" (GS,I,33).

To understand this analogy concerning the roles of biography and psychology for history and the human studies, biography as the history of the individual must not be misinterpreted as merely filling in the content of an ego-schema established by psychology. The point is rather that in their respective contexts, both biography and psychology are fundamental, because they deal with the individual as a focal point of more general systems. Biography is not merely concerned with the unique as such. Even to the extent that in its fundamental bio-graphical form, history is an art, it is not idio-graphic. For Dilthey, history is comparable to art, "because in it, as in the imagination of the artist, the universal is intuited in the particular and not . . . as in theory, abstracted from the particular and presented for its own sake" (GS,I,40).

To explain the history of an individual is to render his life an embodiment of much more general features of historical reality. It is in fulfilling this task that the biographer exemplifies how the concepts of psychology, the cultural systems and the external organization of society are to be related.

Dilthey's own interest in biography, it should be noted here, centered on cultural rather than political figures. Thus in his historical analyses the political bonds of the external organization of society are often transmuted into the more comprehensive conditioning factors defined by a Zeitgeist (spirit of an age) or the intellectual climate of an historical epoch. A short section in the Einleitung on the nature of the study of literature and literary figures is indicative of how this shift might be understood. Although this discussion does not focus as much on the concrete social structures that condition literature as one would at first have expected from his theory of the Geisteswissenschaften, nevertheless,

72

it shows that if the *Zeitgeist* or *Weltansicht* (world-view) of an epoch is to be a relevant literary context it will need to be structured around the "social reality of the time" (*GS*,I,88).

Dilthey's brief discussion of the study of literature provides the most concrete model of how psychological, cultural, and socio-historical concepts are to intersect systematically within a specific human study. The ease with which Dilthey cites the kind of historical conditions and literary ideals in relation to which the productivity of the poet can be studied psychologically, suggests that a poetics, or aesthetics in general, can be considered a model *Geisteswissenschaft*. If psychology is the most fundamental human study and history the most complex, then it seems that aesthetics can be singled out as the most illuminating. Dilthey does not execute his ideas about aesthetics in the *Einleitung*. But in the following decade he was to devote two major essays to these ideas.

PART TWO

The Concept of the Imagination

CHAPTER TWO

Psychology and the Poetic Imagination

IN 1887, four years after the *Einleitung in die Geisteswissenschaften*, Dilthey published a major treatise on aesthetics entitled "Die Einbildungskraft des Dichters: Bausteine für eine Poetik" ("The Imagination of the Poet: Elements for a Poetics"). In this work, often simply referred to as his *Poetik*,[1] Dilthey affirms the important role that his aesthetic interests have played in the development of his thought as a whole. He notes that his "philosophical view of history unfolded through a study of literary history," and that, "perhaps a poetics will have a similar significance for the systematic study of historical expressions of life' (*GS*,VI,109).

Dilthey's first point, that it was through his literary studies that he had developed some of his views on history as formulated in the first volume of the *Einleitung*, has been widely recognized. However, commentators have generally overlooked Dilthey's second point, which reveals his expectation that a poetics could make an analogous contribution to the proposed systematic portions of the *Einleitung*. Misch has remarked in passing that Dilthey's *Poetik*, together with his theory of history, constitutes, "the nuclear cell (*Keimzelle*) of his idea of life" (*GS*,V,ix), but he neither documented nor developed this claim. Otherwise the *Poetik* is considered to be mainly of interest for the particular field of aesthetics. But it does have the broader rele-

---

[1] This convention will be followed here. The treatise, written for a *Festschrift* honoring Eduard Zeller's seventieth birthday, is reprinted in *GS*, VI, 103–241. Dilthey's efforts to rewrite it, thereby producing a more complete *Poetik*, were not fulfilled. Notes towards a revision have been published in *GS*, VI, 307–20, and will be referred to in subsequent chapters.

vance envisioned by Dilthey and will be analyzed in this and the next two chapters as representing a crucial step towards the solution of certain larger methodological and theoretical problems left unresolved by the *Einleitung*.

With his concept of the imagination Dilthey made certain central contributions to both aesthetics and the epistemology of the *Geisteswissenschaften*. The full significance of the poetic imagination and the aesthetic principles arrived at in the *Poetik* cannot be understood apart from the general theoretical approach developed at the same time. To provide a better overview, certain general psychological laws of the poetic imagination are examined in this chapter, with the more concrete characterization of the poetic imagination reserved for the one following.

It was in his *Poetik* that Dilthey felt able to formulate the kinds of explanative laws appropriate to the human studies— a fact that lends support to an interpretation of his aesthetics as a model *Geisteswissenschaft*. "The hope arises," Dilthey wrote, "that through a poetics the efficacy (*Wirken*) of psychical processes in historical products could be elucidated (*aufgeklärt*) in an unusually exact manner" (*GS*, VI,109). Whereas ordinarily psychology can only *describe* the operations of mind, in the context of a poetics psychology seems able to *explain* the processes of imaginative metamorphosis. Dilthey asserts that this is largely due to the special nature of its subject and materials.

As distinct from the theories of religion or ethics for instance, a poetics has perhaps a great advantage with respect to the study of the basic fact of the human studies, which is the historicity (*Geschichtlichkeit*) of free human nature. In no other domain, with the exception of science, have the products of human activities been so fully preserved. The products are stratified in historical order (*aufeinandergeschichtet*) in the literary tradition. Active powers seem still to pulsate in such historical products. . . . The poet lives before our eyes; evidence about his creativity exists. Thus the poetic formative process, its psychological structure and its historical variability can be studied especially well. [*GS*,VI,108–9]

In the *Einleitung*, Dilthey had claimed that of all the cultural systems science and art are the most pure in their relative freedom from the external organization of society. Because there is a minimum of tension between cultural ideals and social institutions in these two systems they provide the clearest insight into the relation of individual freedom and historical determination. Of these two cultural systems, art is now asserted to possess an added distinction through the richness of its materials. Artists, especially writers, have left us many accounts of their creative processes, while scientists, who are primarily concerned with the confirmation of their conclusions by other scientists, seldom report on their experiences of discovery. Because poets and writers prize uniqueness, they reflect more on the mysterious workings of their creative processes. Sometimes this very self-consciousness becomes thematized in subsequent literary works. A poetics, according to Dilthey, can and should exploit the wealth of autobiographical data that writers have given us.

Since psychological considerations about the poetic imagination are predominant in the *Poetik*, it has been criticized as psychologistic. Certainly Dilthey's tendency to consider the work of art in terms of the experience of the artist and the spectator would lead to an insufficient definition of the nature of art, and he himself later admitted the need to place more emphasis on the objective status of the work itself (*GS*,VI,311). However, Dilthey never denied the legitimacy of his efforts to bring psychology to bear on the problem of gaining an objective understanding of the function of the arts, as he had always been aware that an over-exploitation of psycho-biographical data would lead away from the real solution. Personal testimony of artists and psychological insights into their creative intentions should serve, not as a substitute for, but as a confirmation of, aesthetic understanding obtained independently. It is just this special opportunity of testing aesthetic principles that makes Dilthey's claim for the importance of aesthetics convincing.

In 1878, Dilthey published a long review essay of Herman Grimm's *Vorlesungen* on the life and work of Goethe. Entitled "Ueber die Einbildungskraft der Dichter," this sixty-two page essay contains Dilthey's own account of the nature of Goethe's poetic imagination as well as some of the first formulations of the problems to be dealt with in the *Poetik*. In it, he asserts the ". . . impossibility of simply explaining the products of the poet's imagination from the available data concerning his life. This is because all kinds of suggestions for the motifs, characters and plots of his works are already in the air." Noting that it is the appreciation of the work of an artist that involuntarily leads to inferences about his imagination, Dilthey argues that such inferences need to be ". . . regulated by the hermeneutic theory of understanding (unfortunately neglected ever since Schleiermacher and Böckh) and complemented by direct biographical investigation."[2]

It is significant to observe here that the regulative role of hermeneutic understanding is to be considered as an aspect of Dilthey's early conception of historical explanation. As his thought matured, Dilthey would narrow his definition of explanation and attach an increasing importance to understanding as the definitive method of the *Geisteswissenschaften*. Regardless of whether explanation or understanding is posited as the ultimate goal of Dilthey's theory of the poetic imagination, it is clear from this early essay that psycho-biographical data can only be useful in terms of a larger context.

The *Einleitung* subsequently explicated this context in

[2] See *Zeitschrift für Völkerpsychologie*, X, 1878, pp. 49, 64.

terms of possible socio-historical conditions on the one hand, and the purposes of a cultural system on the other. In that work, Dilthey was especially concerned with the possibility of comprehensive historical explanations. Nevertheless, his discussions there of the ideals of the cultural system of art are relevant as a framework for developing rules of aesthetic understanding and critical evaluation.

By the time Dilthey wrote his *Poetik* he had thus already established the point that a poem is not merely an expression of the private experience of the poet, but equally a socio-cultural product. However, it is precisely because literature constitutes a cultural system where public institutions are of minimal importance that the individual writer is required to play a pivotal public role. Dilthey's psychology of the poetic imagination may be expected to give a more specific explanation of a poem than an historical explanation. But the theory of the imagination is conceived broadly enough to deal with the wider cultural significance of the individual artist's activity and must accordingly include second-order psychological concepts.

The Three Tasks of a Poetics

In the *Einleitung* it is claimed that "the *Geisteswissenschaften* consist of three classes of propositions formulating (1) facts, (2) theorems, and (3) value-judgments and rules" (*GS*,I,26). Applied to the sphere of aesthetics, this means that a poetics must encompass (1) an *historical* study of the influences of a literary tradition and a particular social context on a work of literature, (2) a *theoretical* investigation of the creative poetic processes, and (3) a *normative* consideration of rules for the production and evaluation of poetic works (*GS*,I,88f.). These three tasks of a poetics would seem to establish three separate subdisciplines, each having a totally different methodological character: (1) literary history which is descriptive, (2) a psychology which, although descriptive in its roots, is also instrumental in explaining creativity, and (3) a study of the rules of technique which allow poetic creativity to become publicly understandable as part of a cultural system. However, Dilthey's goal was to view them in their connectedness within one system of poetics.

From the perspective of the *Einleitung*, the problem of the systematic unity of the three approaches of factual description, theoretical explanation, and normative understanding had revealed the need for a new epistemology. In the *Poetik*, Dilthey broaches this same problem of relating the three approaches as he develops a psychology of the poetic imagination. To see how his theory of the imagination stands as a model for the ultimate systematic task of his philosophy, it will be helpful to also briefly consider Dilthey's other major essay on aesthetics, "Die drei Epochen der modernen Aesthetik und ihre heutige Aufgabe" ("The Three Epochs of Modern Aesthetics and Its Present Task").[3] In this more programmatic work, published in 1892, Dilthey further explicates the task he had undertaken in the *Poetik* by comparing it to traditional conceptions of the overall tasks of aesthetics.

Dilthey finds that modern aesthetics, as it had developed up to the time of his own youth, can be divided into three epochs. By considering Dilthey's discussion of these epochs in terms of the theoretical perspective of the *Einleitung*, each epoch can be seen to stress one of the three methodological approaches analyzed above. Each represents an attempt to fashion one such approach into a systematic foundation of aesthetics from which its total task can be derived. Dilthey's criticism of the one-sidedness of these systems similarly reflects his demand in the *Einleitung* that his epistemology encompass all three kinds of propositions characteristic of the *Geisteswissenschaften* without reducing any one to the others.

[3] Published in *Die Deutsche Rundschau* XVIII, 1892 and reprinted in *GS*, VI, 242–87. Subsequently referred to as *Die drei Epochen*.

Viewed in this light, *Die drei Epochen* can clarify how Dilthey's psychology of the poetic imagination was meant to develop a more inclusive approach to aesthetics. The following discussion will also pursue certain suggestions from his analysis of past aesthetic systems to indicate why they had been unable to provide an adequate theory of the imagination.

According to Dilthey, the first epoch of modern aesthetics represents the rationalistic approach to art which "understands beauty as a manifestation of the logical in the sensuous" (*GS*,VI,253). This Cartesian approach is characteristic of the seventeenth century, but only received systematic formulation through Baumgarten, who also introduced the term "aesthetics" in his *Reflections on Poetry* (1735) to designate a new science of sensory cognition. Dilthey shows how this rational system of aesthetics was largely indebted to Leibniz's conception of a harmonious universe and his parallel intuition of the human soul as a creative nexus of powers. For Leibniz the source of aesthetic pleasure lay in the logical character of the form of things. The general ideal of unity in a manifold led to a conception of the artist as willfully imposing an architectonic order on matter.

In his evaluation of rationalist aesthetics, Dilthey makes it clear that "even the freest expression of the imagination is regulated by rules. . . . And all these rules are finally grounded in the rational order of the universe" (*GS*,VI,253). This aesthetic system is one-sided in subsuming sense to logic, feeling to will. Spontaneity of impulse is sacrificed to the will-for-perfect-order. Not only is such an aesthetics primarily *normative* in stressing the ideals of the cultural system of art at the expense of psychohistorical factors, but its norms receive a metaphysical grounding which endow them with absoluteness. Thus the ideals of the cultural system of art provide a rationale for translating general norms into fixed rules of technique—a fixity similar to that imposed on artists by the external organization of an institutional counterpart like an art academy. Due to its predominantly normative character, the rationalist aesthetics results in the denial of any real autonomy to the imagination of the individual artist. To find such autonomy we must turn to the second epoch of modern aesthetics.

The system of the second epoch is fundamentally *theoretical* or explanative in nature. Dilthey finds it especially characteristic of eighteenth-century Britain, where the idea of beauty was analyzed in terms of subjective sense impressions. Prepared for by Hutcheson and Harris, executed by Kames, and then later perfected by Fechner in his *Vorschule der Aesthetik*, this mode of analysis is psychological in nature and tends to model aesthetics on the experimental sciences (*GS*,VI,257). Its aim is to explain general agreement about taste by analyzing the work of art into its components, each of which could be tested for its "lawful" effect on the observer. Aesthetics thereby becomes a part of what Dilthey calls "spectator psychology"—a fitting name for the sense-oriented psychology criticized in the *Einleitung*.

The inadequacy of this theoretical approach lies in the fact that the aesthetic nature of the work of art is reduced to separate impressions produced on the spectator, especially as direct effects on his feeling. It is naive to think that the several parts into which a work of art can be analyzed will have an isolated and immediate pleasurable effect. Dilthey points out that many of the apparently natural responses of feeling are, in fact, historically conditioned, and that the atomistic nature of spectator psychology makes it incapable of explaining the contextual aspects of aesthetic experience (*GS*,VI,264f.).

The implications of Dilthey's analysis for a possible critique of this epoch's concept of the imagination can be developed by considering what role the imagination played in the aesthetic and epistemological theories of the time. Whereas the Cartesians tended to be suspicious of the imagination, and made no real distinction between it and sense, from the time of Bacon and Hobbes, the British had exhibited a more positive attitude towards the imagination. For Addison, as Dilthey notes in the *Poetik*, the imagination is to be conceived as an extended sense of sight (*GS*,VI,115). It is distinguished from both sense and understanding: "The Pleasures of the Imagination, taken in their full Extent, are not so gross as those of Sense, nor so refined as those of the Understanding."[4] Instead of stressing the pathological side of the imagination, Addison connected it with the appreciation of greatness, the uncommon, and the beautiful.

Looking briefly at Hume we find a more technical conception of the imagination within eighteenth-century British psychology. Far from being only a source of error, Hume considers the imagination an indispensable factor in our belief in a stable reality. We are led, he wrote, "by the natural propensity of the imagination, to ascribe a continu'd existence to . . . perceptions, which we find to resemble each other in their interrupted appearance."[5] However, when analyzed, the notion of the permanence of perceived objects shows nothing more substantial than associations of our perceptual impressions. The function of the imagination to ascribe permanence to objects is only practically, not theoretically, justifiable.

While for Hume the imagination is not to be controlled by rules as it is for the rationalists, he still restricted it to working only with the elementary images posited by associationist psychology. As such, the imagination could be seen to operate either as reproducing past associations of ideas or producing new associations. The reproductive function is described by Hume in the *Inquiry*: "Whenever any object is presented to the memory or senses, it immediately, by the force of custom, carries the imagination to con-

---

[4] *The Spectator*, 411, cited from *Addison and Steele: Selections from the Tatler and the Spectator*, ed. Robert J. Allen, New York: Holt, Rinehart & Winston, 1966, p. 207.

[5] David Hume, *A Treatise of Human Nature*. Oxford: Oxford University Press, 1968, p. 210.

ceive that object, which is usually conjoined to it."[6] Here the imagination remains tied to the habitual order of experience, whereas in the following statement its freedom to vary the associations of experience is stressed: "Nothing is more free than the imagination of man; and though it cannot exceed that original stock of ideas furnished by the internal and external senses, it has unlimited power of mixing, compounding, separating, and dividing these ideas."[7] It is in this relatively more free mode that the imagination is spoken of as fancy. Although more free, fancy still only plays with the fixed ideas that constitute the unalterable elements of sensory experience. It is impossible for fancy to add anything to the givens of sense.

Generally during this period, the artist's imagination was conceived in terms of the fanciful play of images. Insofar as the aesthetic theory of the eighteenth century relied on associationist psychology, the essential creativity of the imagination could not be recognized. The artist's freedom was thought to only manifest itself in making different combinations of his impressions, rearranging them to produce new complex ideas.

Because Dilthey was critical of the spectator psychology used in the second epoch of aesthetics, Müller-Vollmer assumes he rejected the psychological approach as such.[8] If this were the case, Die drei Epochen would constitute a repudiation of the psychology of the imagination developed in the Poetik, rather than a retrospective justification of it. However, it is clear that Dilthey only rejected a specific kind of psychology, and even then acknowledged certain of its contributions. As applied to aesthetic impressions, spectator psychology had initiated a much needed analysis

[6] David Hume, An Inquiry Concerning Human Understanding. Indianapolis: Bobbs-Merrill, 1955, p. 61.

[7] Ibid.

[8] Müller-Vollmer, Towards a Phenomenological Theory of Literature, p. 65. It will be seen later that this misinterpretation has led Müller-Vollmer to a false evaluation of Dilthey's final philosophical position.

86

of feeling. Moreover, Dilthey recognized that the uniformities about impressions and feelings discovered by experimental psychologists should be included in a consideration of artistic technique because they can help in the explanation of certain details of aesthetic experience. Yet they cannot account for the overall meaning which characterizes a work of art and sets it apart.

For a more adequate appreciation of the concrete meaning of works of art, Dilthey turns to the *historical* approach prevalent in Germany since the late eighteenth century. It is only in this third epoch of aesthetics that the classical ideal of universal standards is challenged. The British psychologists had been sceptical of the first epoch's metaphysical foundation for classical norms of art, but not of the universality of norms as such. They sought empirical explanations of agreement in taste to replace rational justification of norms. The German Romantic movement, however, stressed the existence of fundamental, historically conditioned deviations in taste which reflected differences of national genius.

According to the historicists, transgressions of sacred classical rules in works of art are justified as long as the works remain true to their local context and express the spirit of their particular epoch of national development. For Herder, a poem should not be an artificial construction based on abstract rules, but a characteristic growth from the soil of a nation. Once the critic has adequately described its peculiar context, a work can be properly appreciated by people of other nations and other times.

We have here the makings of a theory which recognized the historical base of the artist's imagination. However, the artist is ultimately pictured as merely re-creating what is already unconsciously developed by the spirit of a people. By contrast, it will be seen that when Dilthey relates the artist to a *Zeitgeist*, he conceives the artist's imagination not so much as reflecting its time as creating a unity for it.

Hegel, who is also to be considered in this third historical epoch, made the artist even less creative by interpreting his art as the product of Absolute Spirit. Yet Hegel's peculiar contribution might be said to reside in his attempt to combine the normative approach of the first epoch with the historical concerns of the third.[9] Although, like the Romantics, Hegel denied the validity of universal rules of technique or form, he insisted that art be judged by the rationality of its content. The history of art was to be interpreted as reflecting the dialectic of Reason. But assuming that the time had passed for Absolute Spirit to reveal itself in art, Hegel found it unnecessary to extrapolate from the artistic principles determinant for past epochs to predict future developments as well. He was thus willing to assign historical limits to the prescriptive power of the philosophy of art without qualifying its absolutist perspective.

Hegel's ambitious synthesis of rationalism and historical consciousness was not appreciated by Dilthey, since it exemplified the closed philosophy of history already criticized in the *Einleitung*. In particular, Dilthey was convinced that aesthetics still had a task relative to the future, for he considered the arts to be as vital as ever in satisfying man's need for expressing his *Weltanschauung*. An awareness of this continuing, psychologically rooted function of the arts led Dilthey to undertake a re-evaluation of the nature of psychology as part of his own attempt to overcome the one-sidedness of each of the three modern aesthetic systems.

By broadening the conception of psychology characteristic of the intermediate epoch, psychological theory could be made to overlap with the normative and historical considerations of the other two epochs. The normative, in turn, had to be redefined so that it no longer referred to what is metaphysically valid in an absolute sense, but to methodological rules for evaluating what from past aesthetic systems was still relevant for establishing aesthetic principles.

---

[9] This is not suggested here by Dilthey, for it was not until later that he came to reassess his negative opinion of Hegel. See "Die Jugendgeschichte Hegels" (1905), *GS*, IV, 1–187.

This evaluative approach opened the way for a historical consideration of traditional norms, while at the same time allowing for their confirmation through psychology. Thus Dilthey introduced certain psychological criteria for testing classical norms with his claim that "a work of art is a *classic* if it satisfies our senses and expands our soul, i.e. if it produces a lasting and total satisfaction in people of different nationalities and times" (*GS*,VI,272–73). The suggestion of a possible inner connection between the normative and psychological approaches of the first two epochs presupposes that psychology can be developed to make such a total response intelligible. But this is a reasonable expectation only if the approaches of the last two epochs are allowed to intersect more closely.

Dilthey hoped to overcome the deficiencies of the second and third epochs by applying the historico-descriptive method of the latter to the theoretical psychological explanations of the former. What was wrong with eighteenth-century psychological analysis was that it assumed every individual to be alike; it was oriented towards the spectator rather than towards the creator and his historically conditioned genius. On the other hand, despite the admirable appreciation of creativity that marks nineteenth-century German aesthetics, neither the historicist conception of it as a product of national genius, nor the philosophical conception of it as a transcendental power, properly took into account the artist as an individual. To the extent that the importance of the individual was recognized at all, it led to the Romantic notion of the artist as abnormal, or even insane. One of the tasks set for Dilthey's psychology was to develop a sense of individuality which would not tend to lapse into eccentricity. The idea of the normal would thus have to be reconsidered to distinguish it from that of sameness. According to Dilthey, the idealist aestheticians had ". . . all stopped short of the decisive point: the psychological analysis of the creative process in a particular art" (*GS*,VI,268). Because German idealism had no real use for psychology, Fichte's idea of the transcendental imagination was too easily transformed into Schelling's concept of unconscious creation. As such, transcendental creativity becomes a mere counterpart to a deterministic concept of historical genius. Only if the creativity of the imagination is ascribed to psychological individuals can historical determinism be resisted.

Dilthey was sure that the psychology proposed in the *Einleitung* could be developed to do justice, not only to the ability of the poet to freely transform images, but also to the historically conditioned cultural system within which this process takes place. But the *Einleitung* had provided only a preliminary sketch of his views, and it was not until 1894 when he published his treatise "Ideen über eine beschreibende und zergliedernde Psychologie" ("Ideas Concerning a Descriptive and Analytic Psychology")[10] that Dilthey fully formulated his main ideas concerning psychology. However, in the intervening years many of these ideas were first developed in the context of the task of creating a theory of the poetic imagination. The fact that this theory played an influential role in relation to the *Ideen* makes it important to note some of Dilthey's more general observations about the nature of psychic life in the *Poetik* as well as the laws of imaginative metamorphosis to which they lead.

The Laws of Imaginative Metamorphosis

In the *Einleitung*, Dilthey had spoken primarily of the need for a descriptive psychology. Critical of the traditional ways in which psychology had tried to explain mental phenomena, he had pointed out many areas where causal explanations are not necessary. Although he had reserved the task of a comprehensive explanation of psychic life for the

10 This work, usually referred to as the *Ideen*, was first printed in the *Sitzungsberichte der Berliner Akademie der Wissenschaften*, 1894, pp. 1309-1407. Reprinted in *GS*, V, 139-237.

second epistemological volume, he introduced a special type of psychological explanation in the *Poetik* of 1887. There he speaks of a "psychological method" which by appropriating already existent insights into the artist's creative processes would be able to provide a causal explanation of literary products. "Poetics seems to stand under conditions which perhaps make it possible for it to provide for the first time an inner explanation of a total historico-spiritual (*geistig-geschichtlichen*) product according to causal methods" (*GS*,VI,125). This will be, Dilthey hopes, an improvement over the explanations of traditional psychology which accounted for how a phenomenon stands in lawful relations to its antecedents and consequents. Whereas such relations are external and hypothetical, Dilthey developed the idea of a nonhypothetical, or inner, connectedness in his psychology. What an "inner explanation" would render intelligible is how psychic life as a whole, or any phenomenon in it, preserves itself in time and develops its own character.

Past psychological explanations of the imagination were also of an external kind in that they appealed to hypothetical associative relations between distinct representations or ideas. According to Hume, a given idea can reproduce another if the two resemble each other or if they were once associated in terms of a spatial or temporal contiguity. Association so conceived is based on rather loose, if not arbitrary, connections which Dilthey finds inadequate for discussing psychic life. In an attempt to reformulate the idea of association, Dilthey asserts that it presupposes a fusion that can be described to exist among the constituents of psychic processes:

> Perceptions and representations which are similar or alike, fuse into each other (*treten ineinander*) independently of the position they take in the psychic context. They form a content, which is as a rule connected with a consciousness of the different acts that constitute it and which can incorporate distinctions among its

91

component contents insofar as they are not simply ignored. In contradistinction to the causal nexus of the external world, all representations involved in this psychic process are equally close and equally distant from each other. [GS,VI,140–41]

Dilthey admits that figures of speech taken from the external world inevitably crop up in discussions about psychic processes and explains this by the fact that our knowledge of nature has advanced more rapidly than our knowledge of ourselves (GS,VI,140). But if we do continue to speak of the representations of psychic life as physical points having location, it must be with certain negative qualifications. Accordingly, when in the above passage Dilthey speaks of the equidistance of all representations, this constitutes his attempt to neutralize spatial relations into what might be called symbolic relations. The figure of equidistance can serve to counteract the notion of association by contiguity. There must be more than a merely mechanical reason why one representation should call up another. The principle of association as Dilthey reinterprets it, derives its intelligibility only in relation to a larger mental framework. "Perceptions and representations or their components, which were connected in the unity of a process of consciousness, can," Dilthey wrote, "mutually reproduce each other under given conditions of interest and attention" (GS,VI,141).

Since interest in what we perceive is a function of the feelings through which we attach value to things, and since attentiveness presupposes an additional contribution of the will (GS,VI,139), Dilthey claims that the standard consideration of associative relations amongst representations must also take into account the activities of feeling and will. Although Dilthey grants representations a fundamental status, he refuses to consider them as the basic elements of psychic life and thereby reduce feeling and volition to mere relations of representations. The assumption that representations generally produce certain feelings which in turn may lead to certain dispositions to act, is only superficially correct. A more intimate connection of these three components of psychic life becomes conceivable when it is recognized that representations themselves receive certain retroactive changes from our feelings and volitions. Feelings and acts of will are not simply reactions to the representational base of the psyche, but can in turn have an influence on it. Once again we find that special relationship discussed in chapter 1 of something secondary which is not simply derivable from something more primary. There the relation of interdependence was methodological, here it is more purely dynamic.

With the introduction of such psychological reciprocity, it is no longer possible to consider representations as isolated constants and to speak of their reproduction in the strict sense. The same representation ". . . can no more return than the same leaf can grow back on a tree the following spring" (*GS*,VI,172). This is not just due to some natural process of representational decay on the one hand, or the continual accumulation of new sensory stimuli on the other hand, but reflects a more important sense in which perception is a process inseparable from the dynamism of the feelings and impulses.[11] In another section of the *Poetik*,

[11] A similarly dynamic conception of psychic life is formulated in the writings of William James, especially in *The Principles of Psychology* of 1890. His chapter "The Stream of Thought" convincingly refutes the associationist "assumption of 'simple ideas of sensation' recurring in immutable shape" by focusing as much on the "transitive parts" as on the "substantive parts" of the stream of consciousness. (See *The Principles of Psychology*, vol. I, New York: Dover Publications, 1950, pp. 233, 243.) In the *Ideen* of 1894, when Dilthey reiterates his view that the theory of the mechanical reproduction of images is untenable, he does so by noting that his leaf metaphor of the *Poetik* "has in the meantime been thoroughly grounded by [William] James with his amazingly realistic power to perceive inner experience" (*GS*, V, 177). Anticipations of phenomenology have been seen in the writings of both; for James see among others: Hans Lin-

Dilthey went so far as to claim that "perceptions or representations as they appear in the real nexus (*Zusammenhang*) of psychic life, are penetrated, colored and animated by feelings; . . . efforts of attentiveness that stem from feeling, but are also forms of volitional activity, impart an impulsive energy to individual images or permit them to sink away again. Therefore, every representation in the real psyche is a *process*; the sensations themselves which are connected in an image as well as their relations, are subject to *inner changes*" (*GS*,VI,139).

Having affirmed these "inner changes" against the associationists, Dilthey turned to the problem of describing the fundamental ways in which representations undergo internal transformations. The laws of association, even when reformulated to show the fluidity and interconnectedness of psychic life, can only deal with relations *between* representations and are by their very nature unable to explain changes *within* an image.

When applied to the discussion of the poetic imagination, Dilthey speaks of such inner changes as "the metamorphosis of images (*Metamorphose der Bilder*)" (*GS*,VI,171). In this context, he establishes a distinct set of three laws of imaginative metamorphosis. He does not specifically label these laws, but the way he characterizes their artistic consequences suggests that they might be called: (1) the law of exclusion (*Ausschaltung*), (2) the law of change in intensity (*Intensität*), and (3) the law of completion (*Ergänzung*) (*GS*,VI,172–75).

These three laws were meant to provide an inner explanation of the productivity of the poetic imagination. However, they describe imaginative processes in general, and it is only the third which is discussed exclusively in terms of the artist and the poet. Although the third law would

schoten, *Op weg naar een fenomenologische psychologie*, Utrecht: Erven J. Bijleveld, 1959; John Wild, *The Radical Empiricism of William James*, Garden City, N.Y.: Anchor Books, 1970.

seem to establish some distinguishing qualities of the imaginative process, the first two are clearly not special to the imagination as such, but hold for all representational processes (including the so-called reproductive processes of memory). To bring out the continuity that Dilthey finds in psychic life, according to which almost every process is in some way formative (a process of *Bildung* if not of *Einbildung*), these two laws will be interpreted here as a further development of the preceding analysis of the interest of feeling. The third law will be discussed following a fuller account of the general psychological framework necessary to elucidate its meaning.

Dilthey formulates the first law (of exclusion) very simply: "Images transform themselves because components either drop out (*ausfallen*) or are eliminated or excluded (*ausgeschaltet*)" (*GS*,VI,172). Although Dilthey does not make it explicit, this law can be seen to reflect the effect that attentiveness has on representational processes. We fail to attend to aspects of the given which do not interest us. As we focus on what is central in an image, more and more will tend to drop out. Memory processes exhibit the same exclusion principle. We ordinarily remember our original impressions only in rough outline because most of their content no longer matches our direct interest. The poet, however, will often actively or intentionally exclude some aspects of things, even if he vividly remembers them, in order to produce a more unified image. Thus a dramatist will find it significant to eliminate certain refractory features or qualities of a person he has chosen to portray, for the sake of creating a character possessing what Dilthey calls "a clarity and harmony of parts" (*GS*,VI,173). From this and other examples that Dilthey uses, we can conclude that law 1 makes it possible to account for *qualitative* (albeit negative) changes within an image. However, this law does not explain much about literary productivity. If other laws were not also operative, imaginative metamorphosis would lead only to "the shallow harmony of an empty ideal" (*GS*,VI,173).

The second law (of change in intensity) reads as follows: "Images change in that they expand or shrink, in that the intensity (*Intensität*) of the sensations of which they are composed is increased or decreased" (*GS*,VI,173). Here interest does not serve as a mere formal selective principle for deciding whether or not something is worth attending to. Rather, the concrete interest of feeling actually colors the resultant image. Again, ordinary processes of memory can illustrate what is meant here. The same event can take on a different dimension as we remember it at different times under diverse emotional conditions. Thus if we happen to remember a childhood event when in a melancholy mood, then its vividness tends to be dampened, and the people involved in it seem to diminish in their liveliness. However, in a nostalgic state of mind that event can be enlarged and made more lively than it really had been. With reference to the poetic imagination the latter tendency is especially operative. Poets have the gift of intensifying their actual experiences and enlarging life. In fact, Dilthey claims that the adjective "poetic" can be applied to the non-linguistic arts too insofar as they heighten our experience by enlivening reality and thus create a fuller, more meaningful world (*GS*,VI,131).

Although anything that heightens life may be called poetic, poetry itself is expected to do more. The question is whether laws 1 and 2 suffice to account for the productivity of the poetic imagination. Dilthey himself sums up the value of these two laws for understanding the poetic imagination, commenting that "exclusion and intensification serve to provide art with idealized images," but even together they are "not sufficient to fill a poem with satisfying life. . . ." (*GS*,VI,174). As Dilthey had characterized it, the product of law 1 was an empty ideal. Since it turns out that law 2 only introduces the possibility of a *quantitative* change of degree, it cannot move beyond the ideality of law 1.[12] To select from reality and then expand what remains may still only produce a caricature of reality.

These two laws point to the essential lifelike nature of the image, but are unable to explain how a poet creates an image so full and "satisfying" as to actually embody his sense of life. This will require a third law of metamorphosis which deals more specifically with the nature of the poetic imagination as well as the broader implications of Dilthey's psychology.

Having asserted that images change in the course of time according to fluctuations of interest and attention, Dilthey still had to explain these fluctuations. The first two laws constitute theoretically pregnant descriptions which suggest, but do not provide, the controlling conditions of metamorphosis. The descriptions of the varying temporal contexts of interest and attentiveness to which such changes as the exclusion, intensification and impoverishment of parts of an image are referred, possess no more than a general psychohistorical value. Unless some more comprehensive context for the life of feeling and willing can be located, the inner explanations of these laws of imaginative metamorphosis will lack real explanative power.

With the addition of the third law (of the completion of images) Dilthey expected his theory of the poetic imagination to become explanative. Formulated in terms of his conception of an integral psychic structure, the third law may be said to deal with *structural* changes in images.[13] In order to prepare for a proper interpretation of this law the discus-

---

[12] The fact that Dilthey judges intensification merely to produce an idealization indicates that it is not considered in relation to a total image, but only to some parts selected in accordance with law 1. Dilthey's essential interest is in the *cumulative* effects of the laws of metamorphosis.

[13] The full significance of this claim will become more evident in chap. 3.

sion must be broadened to include the normative aspects of Dilthey's psychology.

The reconciliation of the psychological and historical approaches was only half of Dilthey's methodological task, the other half being the exploration of psychological theory in relation to the problem of norms. What Dilthey's enthusiasm about inner causal explanation indicates is that he had developed a way to incorporate a normative structure into his psychological description. Such a breakthrough was accomplished through his conception of a controlling psychic structure or system to be found in normal experience.[14]

This idea of a psychic system was introduced in a lecture on "Dichterische Einbildungskraft und Wahnsinn" ("Poetic Imagination and Insanity").[15] There Dilthey stressed how the fundamental interrelatedness of all of a person's experience can be explained by what he called the "acquired psychic nexus" (erworbener seelischer Zusammenhang). The term "acquired" indicates that the nexus or structuring of our experience is not abstract and inferred, but concretely "possessed" through the individual's life history. The nexus is thus a system which is historically acquired and reveals the structural ordering of past experience.

It is interesting to note that in German, the word Geschichte (history) has as one of its roots the word Schichte (stratum). This reflects a kind of archeological conception of history which makes history more than a chronological narrative. The past must have some structure if it is to constitute history and not be an amorphous background blindly conditioning the future. Stressing that the acquired psychic nexus is not just a storehouse of separable data, Dilthey notes that, "It consists not merely of contents, but also of connections that have been produced among those con-

14 The relation of the normative and the normal will be explored more in the following chapter.
15 Reprinted in GS, VI, 90–102.

tents. The connections are just as real as the contents" (*GS*,VI,143).

Therefore, the acquired psychic nexus does not so much stand over against experience as it articulates the connectedness that normally exists within experience. As part of the experience-continuum, it serves as a controlling influence on individual processes, while at the same time being shaped by them. This is evident in Dilthey's statement that apperception ". . . constitutes the simplest case in which the total psychic nexus (*Zusammenhang des Seelenlebens*) acts on an individual process and receives a retroactive influence" (*GS*,VI,144).

However, the acquired psychic nexus is more than the sum of our conscious representations with which earlier theories of apperception were concerned. According to the theory as developed by Herbart, ordinary perception involves seeing present givens in terms of an "apperceptive mass" of representations accumulated through past experience. Apperception renders present experience conscious and in turn assimilates it to the totality of our conscious representations.[16] For Dilthey, the acquired psychic nexus is an essential condition of consciousness, but is not by that token sharply focused within it. "The particular components of this nexus are not clearly (*klar*) conceived and not distinctly (*deutlich*) delineated," he writes, "nor are the relations between them raised to bright consciousness. Yet we are in possession of this acquired nexus and it is active. That which is present in consciousness is oriented towards it, as well as bounded, determined, and grounded by it" (*GS*,VI,143).

The distinction between the conscious and the unconscious is not fully applicable in Dilthey's theory. We are aware of the psychic nexus, so that it is not really unconscious. But we are not conscious of it in such a way that

[16] Edwin G. Boring, *A History of Experimental Psychology*, 2nd ed., New York: Appleton-Century-Crofts, 1950, pp. 256f.

clear and distinct elements can be discerned in it. Here we find Dilthey anticipating Husserl's critique of the Cartesian assumption that apodictic evidence for the existence of the self must be clear and distinct. The indubitability of inner experience does not also possess the mathematical attribute of precision.

A further reason for not considering the acquired psychic nexus fully definable stems from the fact that Dilthey considers it to ". . . encompass not only our representations, but also determinations of value arising from our feelings and ideas of purposes deriving from acts of will—to wit, the habits of feeling and will" (GS,VI,143). By so interrelating representation, feeling, and volition, the concept of the acquired psychic nexus serves to counteract the notion of separate faculties. As irreducible as representation, feeling, and volition may be, no psychic act can be simply of one kind. Every act involves at least some activity of representation, feeling and willing. It is the peculiar proportion of these three aspects that characterizes the nature of the act. Only if representation is dominant, is the act to be treated as representational.

The central role that feeling has been asserted to play in psychic life is confirmed by Dilthey's description of the acquired psychic nexus as an essentially *evaluative* structure. As it develops, this inclusive nexus shields us from having to react to every stimulus of our milieu and allows us to act on it reflectively. Instead of having our interest determined by the various feelings arbitrarily aroused by changing life-situations, our feelings are ordered into an evaluative structure which assures an increasing coherence in our attitudes towards the world.

Thus in speaking of the efficacy of the acquired psychic nexus, Dilthey insists that ". . . despite its highly composite nature, it works as a whole (*er wirkt als ein Ganzes*) on the representations or states which exist in the spotlight of our attentiveness" (GS,VI,143). Its evaluative structure constitutes the basis for focusing our interest of feeling in practical life. When feelings are objectified in terms of values, attention becomes ever more refined in its selectivity. As it stands in the service of the will, our actions can become increasingly meaningful and deliberate.

It is important to note that the values embodied in the acquired psychic nexus are interpreted to include public cultural ideals as well as the more personal values of the individual, for with the addition of the cultural-normative to the psychological and socio-historical dimensions of the acquired psychic nexus, Dilthey has in effect satisfied the conditions of explanation set forth in the *Einleitung*. In sum, the acquired psychic nexus can serve as an appropriate framework for explanation in the human studies. Given such a context, what Dilthey refers to as psychological explanations obviously go beyond strictly psychological considerations.

Turning now to the third law of the imaginative metamorphosis we can see the special link between the poetic imagination and the acquired psychic nexus. Insofar as the law of completion may be interpreted as dealing with structural changes in images, metamorphosis reflects a development or elaboration of the structure of the acquired psychic nexus. But, in turn, Dilthey's discussion of the third law provides a further description and analysis of how the acquired psychic nexus functions in our experiences, for the poetic imagination can best articulate its feeling-oriented, evaluative nature.

Whereas laws 1 and 2 of metamorphosis dealt with relatively simple qualitative and quantitative changes within an image, law 3 (of completion) concerns the structural transformation of an image made possible by its relation to other representations. The danger that metamorphosis produces a thin psychological caricature of reality is overcome through the process of completion in which the image comes to embody its overall context. Completion brings a fullness or concreteness to imagery by representing its rela-

101

tion to the acquired psychic nexus. Dilthey's ideal of poetic typification is anticipated here, for it is through this process that Dilthey claims that an image can become typical of reality.

In the third law of metamorphosis, Dilthey introduces the idea of a nucleus or core (*Kern*) of an image which can be interpreted to sum up the concentrating power of the first two laws. Once metamorphosis has located the central core in someone's image, his general representational consciousness must be related to the way it further unfolds. For Dilthey, the full "unfolding of the nucleus (*kernhafte Entfaltung*) of an image" (*GS*,VI,175), will involve the incorporation of new components, allowing what is at the fringe of consciousness to be brought into focus in a completed image. Thus he formulates the third law: "Images and their connections transform themselves in that new components and connections penetrate into their innermost core (*innersten Kern*) and thus supplement or complete (*ergänzen*) them" (*GS*,VI,174).

It should be realized that the completion under consideration here does not constitute a mere external addition to the original image such as was exhibited in the discussion of association and fusion. Association covers images entering into a relation of mutual signification; fusion involves images combining into a large complex unity of meaning. In both cases, the images can preserve their original identity despite being incorporated into a larger context. What is proposed in law 3, on the other hand, is that when new components deriving from a larger context enter into the very nucleus of a particular image, their identity is "absorbed" in the symbolic core of this image. These added components are, as it were, compressed into a single image, so that it can unfold to typify them.

Completion is a mode of elaboration which is at once external and internal. The third law in effect articulates what was already implicit in the earlier discussions of association and metamorphosis: When images enter into changed relationships with each other, they may simultaneously undergo inner changes; yet, inner changes set off by feelings, occur "not in a vacuum, but in the midst of all the psychic processes which incessantly affect our sphere of experience . . ." (*GS*,VI,185). Thus Dilthey explicates law 3 as follows: "*Only when the whole acquired psychic nexus becomes active*, can images transform themselves on the basis of it: *innumerable, immeasurable, almost imperceptible changes* occur in their nucleus. Thus the completion or elaboration of the particular derives from the fullness of psychic life" (*GS*,VI,175).

While clearly summarizing much of what has been said about completion, this quote is, however, in one respect misleading, for by saying, "only when the whole acquired psychic nexus becomes active," in the context of a discussion of the third law, Dilthey suggests that the nexus is not normally active in the first two. However, according to Dilthey's general assurance that this overall psychic nexus actively influences *all* normal processes, it must be assumed as operative in all three modes of metamorphosis.

Yet, without implying that the acquired psychic nexus is otherwise inactive, a case can be made for a special relation between it and the law of completion, for the process of completion alone can allow an image to embody or symbolize the structure of the acquired psychic nexus. Many processes controlled by the acquired psychic nexus do not manifest or help to represent its structural influence. This is due to the fact that the controlling framework of psychic life is often obscured by more immediate conditioning factors that are also operative. Thus external stimuli which impinge on our senses, and the problematic situations in which we find ourselves, distract from the apprehension of more fundamental structures of mental life.

Such limiting conditions can most readily be illustrated in terms of processes of memory. Usually a memory sequence involves an intentionally delimited mode of metamorphosis because of the need to be truthful to an original experience. Here image transformation occurs primarily for the sake of focusing on some isolated aspects of an original experience which are relevant to a present need. By contrast, when through a kind of instantaneous recall, a sense of the entire experience is revived, it tends to not be focused at all. For its part, the law of imaginative completion should be able to preserve a sense of the wholeness of an experience while at the same time articulating it.

Ordinarily, external conditions deter images from being fully completed, and help to explain why exclusion and intensification often fail to contribute to the process of making an image representative. When Dilthey spoke of the entire psychic nexus as first active in the process of completion, he may have meant to suggest that this constitutes the rare case where local conditions or special requirements do not obscure the way the acquired psychic nexus itself regulates the imagination.

If, as Dilthey says in *Die drei Epochen,* "the imagination does not aim at the imitation of a particular given entity, then its processes of excluding, expanding, and shrinking in the service of producing a powerful image are only bound to those conditions which result from the total order of reality (*Zusammenhang des Wirklichen*) within which the freely created image should be possible" (*GS*,VI,283). The imagination can thus expand the images of our experience to make them typical of reality as such. Yet in dealing with the relation of the imagination to reality, Dilthey distinguished three main types of imagination according to whether they refer to reality in terms of representation, feeling, or volition. These three subdomains of the acquired psychic nexus respectively define what Dilthey calls the "scientific," "artistic," and "practical" imagination. Since in such a scheme, the artistic imagination appears tied to only one of the three aspects of the psychic structure, this raises the question whether it can by itself represent the whole. Similarly, it must be asked if the poetic imagination has a special "artistic" function that might stand in the way of its typifying the fullness of reality.

All three types of imagination transcend the given of experience, but for different reasons. In the scientific imagination, images are transformed for the sake of representation or knowledge of the external world. Its ultimate product is a hypothesis which goes beyond the description of observed data in order to arrive at a possible explanation of them.

The practical imagination transcends our experience of reality for the sake of what is willed. The natural impulse of the will is to directly mold reality according to personal desires, i.e. to act externally to control and adapt our environment. However, Dilthey points out that our religious and moral consciousness requires that we not always act impulsively, but pause to order our impulses and goals in terms of priorities. Here Dilthey speaks specifically of a practical imagination constituted by "inner activities of will which guide the course of our representations, feelings and passions" in light of "ideals" (GS,VI,146f.). Whereas the representation that dominates an external act of the will may be a simple imaginary representation of something no longer or not yet present, an ideal that guides our inner life presupposes a self-conscious process of constant reevaluation. It is undeniable that feelings play an important role in the fashioning of moral ideals. Yet Dilthey distinguishes the practical mode of the imagination from the more purely feeling-oriented, artistic, or poetic imagination.

The artistic imagination presupposes an aesthetic contemplation of reality which occurs in moments when the process of the mutual adaptation of self and environment is suspended. Dilthey indicates that such an aesthetic suspension can derive either from temporary conditions when "an equilibrium of feeling is attained in which life takes a holiday, as it were" (GS,VI,147), or from moments of tension when "unnerving and ineradicable facts impart their

105

dark colors to all things . . ." (GS,VI,147). In the former situation one feels in harmony with reality, so that adaptive action is unnecessary; in the latter, one senses a fundamental tension which cannot possibly be removed by any external or internal act of will. Such states force one to consider, not just the significance of specific aspects or projects of life, but the sense of life itself. Since the artistic, poetic imagination is influenced by the feelings associated with these extreme human situations, all its imagery can be expanded in terms of the reflective framework they make possible.[17]

Of these three ways in which the imagination transcends the given of experience, that of the artistic, poetic imagination is least restricted by specific purposes and considerations. Scientific hypotheses must always remain testable by empirical data, and practical ideals cannot long stay divorced from considerations about available resources for action. The scientific and practical imagination work within a more determinate framework of criteria of verification and applicability to conduct, whereas the poetic imagination, being free from descriptive and pragmatic responsibility, allows images to unfold in a much more spontaneous and comprehensive fashion. The poet lets a certain pregnant image of reality develop naturally in accordance with his feelings, so that poetic images ". . . unfold freely beyond the limits of the real" (GS,VI,137).

If one correlates the above statement that the artistic imagination transcends reality with Dilthey's claim that

[17] Although Dilthey is rather cryptic in the passages quoted, the process of expanding images through the aesthetic feelings associated with these two extreme conditions suggests a basis for the distinction between beauty and sublimity respectively. The former state might be considered as the source of the positive appreciation of life often expressed in lyrical poetry; the latter of a more comprehensive vision where life is related to death, as in tragedy. See *Das Erlebnis und die Dichtung: Lessing, Goethe, Novalis, Hölderlin*, 13th ed., Stuttgart: B. G. Teubner; Göttingen: Vandenhoeck & Ruprecht, 1957, p. 146. Hereafter cited as *ED*.

image transformation ". . . never consists in the creation of new contents which have nowhere been experienced . . ." (*GS*,VI,142), the result might seem to be little more than a reformulation of the Humean conception of fancy, arbitrarily rearranging the given ideas of experience. The imagination would remain bound by the material of our experience and yet fancifully transgress the order of reality.[18] In her criticism of Dilthey's *Poetik*, Anneliese Liebe has, in effect, suggested such an interpretation. Equating the transcendence of reality, as Dilthey defines it, with the indulgence of fantasies, she sees the poet as basically inclined to pass over reality and yet wise enough to curb this tendency. According to her interpretation of Dilthey, it is the desire to be understood by normal people that restrains the poet from indulging himself through his imagination, so that technical considerations about the aesthetic impression to be produced on the spectator constitute the prime safeguard against poetic license.[19]

But to suppose that the poetic imagination needs external checks is to misunderstand the whole tenor of Dilthey's account. The very formulation of poetic metamorphosis in terms of laws indicates that the imagination is inherently bounded in its freedom. Moreover, it is Dilthey's prime con-

[18] To be sure, Dilthey's denial of new content rules out all but the subtractive qualitative changes characteristic of the first law of metamorphosis. Accordingly, when Dilthey speaks of the introduction of new components in the third law he must mean relatively new components deriving from other experiences. So far, he would agree with Hume. However, there is no reason to also assume that when the imagination transcends the "limits of the real," it must arbitrarily combine images so as to also negate what Dilthey has already referred to as the total order of reality (*Zusammenhang des Wirklichen*).

[19] "So setzen also auch die Notwendigkeiten des asthetischen Eindrucks der Ueberschreitung der Wirklichkeit eine feste Grenze." Anneliese Liebe, "Die Aesthetik Wilhelm Diltheys," Dissertation, Halle a.d.S.: Bleicherode i. Harz, 1938, p. 36.

cern to show that the poetic imagination transcends reality precisely for the sake of uncovering the typical in reality. "The typical, the ideal in poetry," he writes, "is of such a kind as to transcend reality by means of experience so that it can nevertheless be felt more powerfully and understood more profoundly than in the most faithful copies of reality" (*GS*,VI,172). Literature can create a fundamental understanding of reality, not despite the fact that the poetic imagination transcends reality, but because of it. For the more spontaneously feelings transform images, the more they disclose the normative structure of the acquired psychic nexus. This paradox forces us to further reflect on the important role that has been ascribed to the acquired psychic nexus vis-à-vis the structural changes involved in the law of poetic completion.

In its evaluation of reality, the acquired psychic nexus is not especially concerned with individual representations, yet it first makes possible a total perspective on the world in relation to which individual representations are meaningful. So likewise, a poetic image which unfolds under the sole guidance of the acquired psychic nexus may not be true to individual details of reality. However, by being representative or typical of the totality of the psychic nexus, it can in turn give a sense of a world, although not necessarily knowledge of it.

It is through the law of completion that reality can be felt more powerfully and related to inner sense. Conversely, completion can create an appropriate intuitive content for a state of feeling. External experience is animated by inner experience and inner life given visibility through outer manifestations (*GS*,VI,175). These two modes of completion are central to poetic metamorphosis, and Dilthey grounds them in the fact that the acquired psychic nexus is itself a systematic intersection of inner and outer, the psychical and the historical. It is neither totally subjective nor totally objective just as the labels "consciousness" and "unconsciousness" were not really applicable. It constitutes our evaluation of life, our *Weltanschauung*, in which feeling and intuition intertwine.

When the psychic nexus, conceived as an inner-outer complex, regulates the poetic imagination, it cannot really be said to impose anything on it from without. Once new components are incorporated by the unfolding image, they come to have an inner necessity. What from the perspective of the original image may at first seem an external addition, receives an inner necessity from the perspective of the psychic nexus. The intersection of the inner-outer in the psychic nexus allows us to interpret this process of metamorphosis as the self-completion of the original image, rather than as a mere mode of external combination of images.

The Imagination and the Apprehension of Style

We have seen Dilthey move away from the views of the imagination that characterized the spectator psychology of aesthetic impressions. Taking the already executed work of art as their point of departure, and considering it an external form only, the psychological aestheticians of the eighteenth century found it perfectly adequate to conceive of the imagination as producing external combinations of images. But by being so easily satisfied, they reduced their discipline to an analytic by-product of a technical conception of art. With Dilthey, the theory of the imagination is not derived from a theory of technique, but provides the framework for it. What he calls the "inner form" or "style" of a literary work, should be considered as the imaginative unity of its technical components.[20] Law 3 of poetic metamorphosis will thus be used as a model in chapter 4 for understanding how Dilthey describes the way different technical aspects of a work of literature such as motif, plot,

[20] The concepts of inner form and style will be more fully discussed in chaps. 4 and 10.

109

characters, action, diction, etc., "unfold" from each other.

Because such concepts as the unfolding of images and inner form readily suggest an organic conception of creativity, Frithjof Rodi, for instance, dismisses Dilthey's theory of the imagination as "morphological" and therefore incapable of dealing with the "hermeneutical" tasks of interpreting the historical ramifications of art. According to Rodi, Dilthey conceived of imaginative metamorphosis as a gradual plantlike development which can be described according to its type of pattern (*morphe*). He notes that Dilthey gave perhaps the best example of such metamorphosis by citing Goethe's description of the workings of his imagination: "When I closed my eyes I had the gift of being able to imagine a flower . . . which never retained its original shape for any moment. Instead, it would display itself in different aspects and from its core new flowers would unfold from colored petals or even from green leaves" (*GS*,VI,178). In addition, Rodi elaborately documents how Goethe's organicist influence on Dilthey was in fact mediated and furthered through the work of the physiologist Johannes Müller.[21] Rodi attaches particular significance to Müller's organic notion of the unfolding of images as from a seed (*Keim*), and the idea that this occurs by means of a "rhythmic process of contraction (*Beschränken*) and expansion (*Erweitern*) . . .—a thought whose affinity with the concepts of polarity and the interplay of the systole and diastole is evident."[22]

However, Dilthey quotes many sources other than Goethe and Müller which do not specifically invoke their particular conception of imaginative metamorphosis. After all, metamorphosis need not be conceived organically, and could be interpreted through various other images of transformation. Thus in Ovid's mythical sense, metamorphosis refers to a sudden, inexplicable transformation lacking any transitional passage, rather than a steady plant-like growth which can readily be described.

[21] See Rodi, *Morphologie und Hermeneutik*, p. 62.
[22] Ibid., p. 68.

While Rodi is correct in pointing out that Dilthey's laws of the imagination bear the mark of Müller's ideas, this applies essentially to the first two laws. He neglects to mention that in the *Poetik*, Dilthey developed a third law which shatters the very morphological framework of Goethe and Müller. Instead of referring to a seed (*Keim*) which unfolds on its own, Dilthey speaks of a nucleus (*Kern*) which is subject to completion from without. Müller had conceived the imaginative processes of contracting and expanding on the order of Goethe's *Urpflanze* (an archetypal plant of which all other plants would be merely variations). Dilthey, however, does not posit any initially fixed form which merely unfolds from within. Rather, as noted above, he speaks of the "unfolding" of an image as a process of completion where the incorporation of new components into its very core enables it to symbolize more than itself. This third law is therefore not susceptible to morphological analysis. It involves a change which is neither simply *between* images, as in the laws of association, nor simply *within* images, as in laws 1 and 2 of metamorphosis, but both *within* and *without*.

Rodi does admit that the *Poetik* as a work is not totally morphological, and that the organic conception of creativity is supplemented by a more meaning-oriented or hermeneutical conception. But this interest in meaning is explained through Dilthey's category of *Erlebnis* (lived experience), and is assumed to stand in unresolved conflict with the theory of the imagination (which is totally compromised by the *morphe* of metamorphosis). In viewing the hermeneutical and psychological theories as contrasting elements of the *Poetik*, Rodi reflects the widespread failure to recognize Dilthey's concern with meaning in the psychology of the imagination itself.

Yet, in the *Poetik*, Dilthey explicitly connects the third law of imaginative metamorphosis to a principle of meaning. "The law of completion," he writes, "corresponds to a principle of the articulation (*Herausbildung*) of what is essential and meaningful (*Bedeutenden*) . . ." (*GS*,VI,196). More specifically, this articulated meaning is the product of the imaginative metamorphosis of particular images into something typical. This link has created considerable confusion, for it has been most commonly assumed that the imaginative process of typification is nothing but a means for arriving at certain general types. But a general type is really more the inverse of imaginative typicality than its elaboration. Abstract types are classificatory devices which define contrasts on a basis of unity. Thus Dilthey himself distinguished three types of imagination—scientific, practical and poetic—as different modes of transcending experience, on the underlying assumption that any mode of imagination at least transcends the given. Such an abstract classification is indeed "morphological" and does characterize Dilthey's overall approach to the *Weltanschauungslehre*. However, Dilthey's theory of imaginative typicality has a very different concern, namely, to discern unity in diversity. The typical as produced by the imagination is an image which has developed from a concrete experiential context and relates to that context alone. It is representative of an individual psychic nexus which is historically determined, and does not establish an abstract type as part of a hypothetical universal scheme. While general types are fixed forms and fundamentally ahistorical, typicality can be explicated in terms of Dilthey's historical concept of style, where style is interpreted to be an inner form which articulates a unified meaning in what might seem like a mere manifold from an external perspective.

One of Dilthey's chief gains in developing a psychology of the poetic imagination was to be able to illuminate such a concept of style and combat the fixed "morphological" concept of style of the first normative system of aesthetics. Dilthey also criticized the application of traditional spectator psychology to aesthetics for its failure to cope with the descriptive sense of a stylistic continuum so central to aesthetic experience:

Experimental aesthetics is unable to explain how the work of art is more than a heap of impressions. Through the analysis of aesthetic impressions, it attains only an aggregate of effective components. The unity of the work of art is, for it, merely one operative factor beside others. If this unity is lacking, then there is just one less element that arouses pleasure. However, it is thought as a matter of course that this deficiency can be overcome by adding other elements. The style of a work of art and its peculiar effects can accordingly not really be made comprehensible by this experimental aesthetics. [*GS*,VI,270]

The total stylistic meaning of a work is not just an additive effect of the elements into which it can be analyzed. The inability of experimental aesthetics to interpret style had by Dilthey's time found its counterpart in the incapacity of naturalistic artists to create a style of their own.

For Dilthey, realistic trends in art, such as naturalism, were but transitional stages which recur between fully developed epochs. Naturalism offers no proper aesthetic system, for it leads to the confusion of art and science. Dilthey was critical of naturalists like Zola precisely because he felt they were not aware of the difference between the descriptive analysis of science and imaginative typification. Although Dilthey appreciated the forthrightness of the naturalists in preferring truthfulness to beauty, he could not approve of the way they conceived their search for truth. He sums up his own attitude towards the naturalistic motto of truth as follows: "We have shown how an estimable feeling for truth here nevertheless leads literature down the wrong path. To be sure, the poet has real life as his theme and accordingly the truth. But for him everything that exists is understandable through the point around which it revolves in action and feeling, never through the abstraction of the conceptual attitude" (*GS*,VI,286).

As convincing as the naturalist may be in his efforts to

113

give a point by point description of reality, he does not provide the reader with that typical point in terms of which it can be adequately interpreted. His scientific pretensions allow him to reduce man's ability to apprehend the meaning of reality to the separate impressions a camera can record. To counteract a mere concern with the impressionistic as such, Dilthey applies his own psychological approach to argue that the aesthetic concern for stylistic unity is already implicit in the way that normal perception tends to be organized around a dominant impression.

In a section of the *Die drei Epochen* that leads up to a discussion of how the stylistic unity of a great portrait is to be understood, Dilthey first speaks more generally of how we ordinarily apprehend a face when it makes a powerful impression on us:

> I perceive a face . . . an aggregate of colors, spatial relations. . . . The unity of my consciousness is active in their apprehension by means of a great number of imperceptible acts that elapse quickly. Thus image-components are united and completed (*ergänzt*) by my inner life. My own psychic life is in resonance. The structure (*Zusammenhang*) of what is perceived is acquired (*erworben*) from a point which is especially impressive—I call it the aesthetic point of impression (*ästhetischen Eindruckspunkt*). [*GS*,VI,282]

The idea of a unifying point of impression is introduced in language reminiscent of law 3 of the poetic imagination. The continuation of the above quote reveals a similar reference to the other two laws of imaginative metamorphosis:

> Every carefully apprehended face is understood from such a dominant impression. The overall features are constructed from it as a starting point. Under the influence of this impression . . . indifferent features are excluded, speaking traits are emphasized and refractory ones de-emphasized. Thus the remaining whole

(*Zusammenhang*) is united ever more decisively. [*GS*,VI,282]

In illuminating the spectator response by laws of metamorphosis (which can most easily be exemplified in a description of the poetic imagination), Dilthey at the same time re-enforces the link that exists between his psychological theory of the imagination and his meaning-oriented concern for style. The idea of a dominant point of impression is then exploited to suggest the genesis of the overall stylistic unity expected of the portrait painter. The "genius" of such an artist involves being able to choose that point of impression from which the depths of a person's character can be disclosed.

This focusing of the laws of imaginative metamorphosis in terms of a perceptual point of impression can produce the realization that there exists neither an absolute nuclear starting point for the imagination nor a final context. The point of impression is a function of the various traits that converge on it and can in turn continually refine the context that it serves to unify.

The possibility of relating the creativity of the imagination and the apprehension of style suggests that the process of completion is not as unique to poetic or artistic image transformation as was at first claimed. What the third law of metamorphosis explained as the culmination of the different activities of the poet is now interpreted to be the initial guiding framework for the other two laws of metamorphosis as they govern the operations of ordinary perception. In the *Poetik*, law 3 referred to the ultimate control of the acquired psychic nexus in augmenting the scope and power of an image. Now in the explication of style it functions more as an organizational principle which helps to redefine the meaning and delimit the totality of what is imaginatively perceived around an originally powerful impression. The relation of the poetic imagination to ordinary experience and understanding will be further examined in the following chapter. In the meanwhile, it can be pointed out that the emphasis in the ordinary process of apprehending reality is to attain an ever tighter unity of meaning. The artist, on the other hand, must combine such unification with the attempt to encompass more and more of the character of what is portrayed.

CHAPTER THREE

Aesthetic Norms and Poetic *Erlebnis*

DILTHEY'S PSYCHOLOGY of the imagination was conceived in terms of the problem of meaning in poetry and we were able to underscore this by relating the *Poetik* to the discussion of style in *Die drei Epochen*. But because the overall approach of the *Poetik* is value-oriented, concern for the interpretation of meaning becomes part of a more pervasive interest in norms of evaluation.[1] Accordingly, Dilthey proposes his aesthetic psychology not just to explain the poet's creativity, but also to provide a basis for describing the reader's response.

Together with the general psychological framework developed for his theory of the imagination, Dilthey formulates specific aesthetic principles to demonstrate the normative potential of his poetics. He arrives at these norms through an examination of feeling. Although feeling is ultimately a function of the acquired psychic nexus, it can present as foreground what was established as mere explanative background by the psychic nexus. By declaring that a descriptive analysis of feeling must underlie the explanation of imaginative metamorphosis (*GS*,VI,148), Dilthey seems at the same time to be laying the basis for a more concrete account of the poetic imagination.

When we examine the ways in which Dilthey specifically works out the normative considerations initially introduced in the last chapter, a real tension within the *Poetik* becomes

[1] In chap. 9 we will find that Dilthey reverses his view about the relative importance of interpretation and evaluation by arguing that the interpretation of the meaning of experience produces a more coherent understanding of life than the appreciation of the value of things.

evident however. This is not the alleged tension between psychological and hermeneutical goals, but one pertaining to the aims and methodological assumptions of psychology itself. Dilthey's general psycho-cultural framework makes possible an "inner explanation" of the poetic imagination as well as a descriptive analysis of aesthetic feeling. Both description and inner explanation can be interpreted as ways of overcoming the hypothetical constructions of ordinary explanation. Nevertheless, in formulating certain higher aesthetic principles, Dilthey himself lapses into constructionist explanation and thereby vitiates his effort to develop appropriate inner explanations in the *Poetik*. To more effectively dispel constructionist tendencies from his approach, Dilthey subsequently replaces the concept of inner explanation with that of understanding in his treatise "Ideen über eine beschreibende und zergliedernde Psychologie." By taking note of the *Ideen*, both for this methodological revision and for the more fully developed ideas about *Erlebnis* and the structural development of the individual, we can more thoroughly draw out the implications in the *Poetik* for a possible definition of the poetic imagination.

Spheres of Feeling and Aesthetic Principles

While the role of feeling in aesthetic experience had always been assumed, Dilthey considered previous discussions of feeling inadequate for dealing with aesthetic norms. In providing his own descriptive analysis of certain aesthetically relevant spheres of feeling (*Gefühlskreise*), Dilthey sought to avoid the overly subjective conception of aesthetic feeling as simply a mode of pleasure—whether interpreted in the crude hedonistic sense of gratification or in the purely formal sense of a disinterested pleasure.

The spheres of feeling analyzed by Dilthey help to define aesthetic principles only to the extent that they are mediated by representations of the work of art. The aesthetically significant spheres of feeling are thus not simply subjective.

They are described in the *Poetik* as evaluative responses to objective correlatives. As a general consequence, Dilthey allows the more objective concept of value to be coordinated with feeling. "For value," he writes, "is nothing more than the representational expression for the fact which is experienced in feeling . . . In pleasure we in part enjoy the condition of objects—their beauty and meaning (*Bedeutung*)—and in part the intensification of our own existence—personal states that provide value (*Wert*) to our own existence" (*GS*,VI,150). Through feeling so conceived, aesthetic experience contains intrinsic values which can be articulated into normative aesthetic principles.

Of the six spheres of feeling described by Dilthey, only the first refers to the mere subjective sensations of pain and pleasure. This first sphere is treated as marginal because all differences can be understood in terms of gradations of intensity and need involve no qualitative distinctions in feeling. Physiological in origin, sensations of pain and pleasure do not presuppose any contribution of consciousness. Since these feelings result without the intervention of representations (*GS*,VI,150), they are of no poetic significance to Dilthey.

The other five spheres, with their representational correlates, permit qualitative distinctions, and it is Dilthey's description of the latter that has led some to view the *Poetik* as having a certain phenomenological value.[2] In introducing these spheres, Dilthey makes clear his intention to suspend hypothetical speculation: "For the time being, the question whether these qualitative differences derive exclusively from the content of representation and the attentiveness of the will, or whether they exist independently in the functions of the life of feeling . . . is insoluble. . . . Nor can we say whether the function of the feeling process considered for itself might consist of a mere monotonous gradation of pleasure and pain" (*GS*,VI,149).

[2] Müller-Vollmer, *Towards a Phenomenological Theory of Literature*, p. 44.

119

Although dependent on representation, aesthetic feeling is not to be considered a mere by-product of it. Changes in feeling may be induced by representations, but the nature of feeling qua feeling is not derivable from representation. As Dilthey was to write later in the *Ideen*: "There lies no sufficient ground in representations for them to go over into feelings; one could conceive of a merely representational creature who being in the midst of a battle would look on his own destruction as an indifferent and will-less spectator. . . . The relation between these different components, not derivable from one another, is sui generis" (*GS*,V,213).

Just as the concept of causality was deemed inadequate to characterize the psychophysical link, so here, too, simple causal explanative conceptions appear inappropriate when dealing with the relations between the representational, the feeling, and the volitional levels of consciousness. If psychic life is to be interpreted, not only in terms of linear processes, but also in terms of levels of consciousness, then a causal analysis of how one state is sufficient to produce another, must be supplemented with a hierarchical analysis of necessary conditions which need have no corresponding effect at all. Moreover, if a state of one level does produce an effect on another level, it does not pass away or become absorbed by the latter, but remains to be affected in turn. A representation which has produced a feeling can be preserved historically in memory, and as such it will in turn be subject to retroactive influence from this feeling. The representational stratum of psychic life is thus not the *Urschichte* which determines all others. It is merely that stratum which is presupposed by the others.

Although this discussion anticipates the phenomenological notion of genetic strata that are to be distinguished from genetic processes interpreted causally, Dilthey, unlike Husserl, does not systematically separate them as transcendental and natural realms respectively. But he does rid feeling of its simple subjectivity and arbitrariness by phenomenologically describing certain spheres in terms of intentional correlates.

Dilthey characterizes the second sphere of feelings as "constituted by the elementary feelings which arise from the contents of sensation under the condition of a concentrated interest" (*GS*,VI,150). This sphere is close to the first in dealing with pleasure and pain, but the concentration of interest provides consciousness with a mediating role.

Dilthey starts his discussion of the second sphere by asserting that the intensity of sensation already stands in a regular relation to pleasure and pain, so that sounds having too low or too high an intensity will be unpleasant. But the effect of intensity is so direct as to seem an inappropriate example for the dynamics of the second sphere, which leads us to think that in this opening discussion, Dilthey is referring back to the first sphere for the sake of contrast. If this is the case, then sphere 2 would properly focus on aesthetic discriminations such as between the soothing quality of certain sounds and the harshness of others. It is in this context that Dilthey speaks of an aesthetic principle of sensuous charm.

If sounds are to be considered aesthetically they must not be present merely through their effects—as they would be if considered in sphere 1—but as tones which create those effects. Because he is mainly concerned with poetics, Dilthey's comments are directed to the tonal qualities of this sphere of feeling: "In poetry, these feelings condition the aesthetic effects insofar as the mere stress on soft sounds in the diction (*Tonmaterial*) of many a lyrical poem, especially those of Goethe, provide an unexpected charm. We can designate the aesthetic principle according to which the simple sensory elements used in art are fit to produce such an effect, the *principle of sensuous charm (Prinzip des sinnlichen Reizes)*" (*GS*,VI,151). The second sphere has already brought us to the point where feeling and representation are inseparable and not blindly associated. Through the ac-

121

,tivity of consciousness, sensations come to embody feelings. It is here that it becomes appropriate to speak of certain tones, colors, or lines (like the smooth curve) as intrinsically pleasant or charming.

Dilthey's very first principle of sensuous charm sets his aesthetics in conflict with Kant's transcendental aesthetics. Kant had based his hope for agreement in matters of taste on the possibility of defining aesthetic pleasure as a disinterested pleasure disassociated from the sensuous effects of charm and emotion (*Reiz und Rührung*).[3] Disinterested pleasure is understood as a pure feeling (*Gefühl*) pertaining to the *form* of our representations. It is to be differentiated from our emotional response to the *content* of representation. Any agreeable emotion aroused by the charm of sense is thought to appeal exclusively to private sensuous interest. This appeal to our sensuous interest results in the desire to possess the object that produces such pleasure and a concern for that object's continued existence. The inclinations so aroused by the contents of sense may put us at odds with one another; at best they will allow us to tolerate each other, but never will they lead to agreement about taste. By contrast, aesthetic feeling, as defined by Kant, can be shared because it suspends all private existential concerns about the object of our representation. Although subjective, aesthetic feeling is communicable in that it abstracts a pure form from the sensuous content of representation. The disinterested pleasure of aesthetic feeling is, as we will see, ultimately explained as a formal subjective pleasure in the harmony of our cognitive faculties considered in their transcendental abstractness.

For Dilthey, however, all feelings reflect a mode of interest, but this may manifest itself in a free-floating kind of interestedness which is not specifically channeled in terms of particular ends. Thus in speaking of a sensuous charm which is "unexpected" or unsought, he affirms that it need

[3] Immanuel Kant, *Kritik der Urteilskraft, Werke in Zehn Bänden,* 8, 303.

not be connected to any *private* interest at all. Against Kant, Dilthey argued that it is neither necessary nor possible to divorce sensuous content from form in order to assure an appropriate aesthetic response.

But Dilthey also disagreed with those of the British empiricists who had sought to derive aesthetic pleasure from sensuous interest. Against them, he pointed out that observations about natural qualities having specific emotive effects on the spectator are not aesthetically illuminating apart from our consciousness or awareness that these qualities are fit (*geeignet*) to have an aesthetic effect. This suggests Rudolf Arnheim's *Gestalt* conception of the physiognomics of nature, which by attributing expressive qualities to nature herself obviates the hypothesis of empathetic projection to account for the fact that we perceive a willow as sad. However, given the claim in the *Einleitung* that modern man can no longer conceive of nature mythically, it is clear that Dilthey would not ascribe such anthropomorphic expressiveness to nature. With his refusal to consider the pleasantness of soft consonants as merely the function of human projection, Dilthey can be said to hold in effect a middle position between Theodor Lipps' theory of empathy and Arnheim's theory of embodiment.

Moving to the next sphere, Dilthey describes its essential features as follows: "The *third stratum of feelings* comprehends those feelings which arise in perception and are called forth by the relations of sensuous contents to each other. In this way, harmony and contrast manifest themselves in tone and color. Pleasure in symmetry is the most pervasive of the spatial feelings; pleasure in rhythm, of the temporal feelings" (*GS*,VI,151).

Rhythm seems so fundamental to our psychological response to art that aestheticians like Susanne Langer consider it a biologically rooted feeling of form. Although Dilthey himself took note of the rhythmical aspects of such bodily functions as our heartbeat, inhalation and exhalation, waking and sleeping, he refused to derive a psychological theory of rhythm from them. According to Dilthey, the fact that rhythm allows us to apprehend a uniformity or consistency within the overall patterns established by sensation, is not explicable in terms of the immediate bodily effect of rhythmical sensations. The claim that the aesthetic sense of rhythm is a higher form of a biological reflex is characterized as a "hypothesis which is at least for the time being undemonstrable" (*GS*,VI,151).

The aesthetic principle established on the basis of Dilthey's analysis of the third sphere of feeling is that of the *pleasurable proportion among sensations* (*GS*,VI,152). In poetry this means that we can derive a certain pleasure from the metrical aspects of the diction regardless of the meaning of the individual words employed. The pleasure is in what might be termed the "sensuous form" of the sounds. It is thus possible to distinguish a sense of verbal significance apart from any conceptual meaning. Here Dilthey exhibits the more affirmative aspect of his phenomenological approach to feeling. Not content to merely question proposed reductive explanations of our aesthetic response, he is concerned to open up and explore as many levels of aesthetic appreciation as possible.

According to Dilthey, "The *fourth feeling-sphere* is made up of the great variety of feelings which spring from the reflective connection of our representational and thought processes without taking into account the relation of their [artistic or poetic] content (*ihres Gehaltes*) to our being" (*GS*,VI,152). Whereas the relations involved in sphere 3 were claimed to be apprehended through the senses, Dilthey here introduces more explicit connections made possible by thought in which sensuous representations could be said to be understood in a more unified manner. From this he derives an aesthetic "*principle of pleasure in the reflective* (denkende) *connection of representations*" (*GS*, VI,153).

Because the traditional formal principles of unity in variety and unity of interests are contained in the fourth sphere of feeling, Müller-Vollmer sees it as the locus of Dilthey's concern with artistic form. However, this fourth sphere is not distinguished from the others in terms of form as such. Although the third sphere was not directly discussed in terms of form, it clearly already involved formal relationships.

In making a transition from sphere 4 to sphere 5, Dilthey does discuss the relation of form to content and thereby might appear to be identifying form with this fourth sphere and content with the fifth. But just as the latter is not the only sphere dealing with content (the sixth is explicitly asserted to also apply to the content of literature), so form is not merely to be located in the fourth sphere.

To be sure, Dilthey stresses that the feelings of the fourth sphere are aroused by the mere forms of the processes of representation and thought. But this does not imply a total independence from what has been analyzed in the second and third spheres. Müller-Vollmer's claim that the feelings of form ". . . do not originate from the contents of the representations"[4] is unjustified, but can be explained by the ambiguity of the word "content." Content (*Inhalt*) may be interpreted to denote either sensuous content (*Sinnesinhalt*) or subject matter in the sense of meaning-content (*Gehalt*). An analysis of the language used by Dilthey in the relevant passages indicates that he is not contrasting form to the contents of sensation (*Sinnesinhalten*) already discussed in the second and third spheres, but is instead concerned about distinguishing it from the subsequent treatment of the poetic or meaning content (*Gehalt der Dichtung*). A precedent for such projecting ahead was found in analyzing the third sphere where Dilthey defined the pleasure in metrical relations as independent from the understanding of the meaning of the words used. Again, the question of the full meaning or *Gehalt* of the work is intentionally kept in abeyance.

---

[4] Müller-Vollmer, *Towards a Phenomenological Theory of Literature*, p. 121.

Dilthey holds no monolithic conception of form which can be located exclusively in sphere 4 and contrasted to either sense of content in the other spheres. The whole tenor of Dilthey's philosophy is to challenge Kant's form-content dualism. Dilthey sees form as everywhere implicit in content. To abruptly introduce form in the fourth sphere and to separate it from sensuous content, would involve making the kind of leap that Dilthey objects to in a priori theorizing.

The kind of form that is explored in this fourth sphere of feeling appears to be what was referred to in the previous chapter as inner form. Rather than being an executed form, it is mental or imaginative form. Although primarily suggestive, it is not as abstract as Kant's feeling of form which ultimately involves no more than the playful harmony of the faculties. Inner form is able to incorporate the sensuous elements discussed in the earlier spheres of feeling. Similarly, Dilthey's principle of reflective pleasure in form is not intended to cancel the already mentioned principle of sensuous charm. All that the reflective pleasure provides is a temporary reprieve from the inevitable tendencies of the content (*Gehalt*) of a work to be referred to our personal existence and appeal to our practical interest in life.

The "purity" of form here recognized by Dilthey constitutes a disinterested pleasure only to the extent that we momentarily dwell on one aspect of the totality of the art work before proceeding to comprehend the work in its totality. Thus form is not first disclosed in sphere 4, nor is its significance exhausted until we understand the meaning-content of the work. The total form of the work in all its details can be dealt with only after the problem of the artistic content has been broached. It is in fact reserved for the investigation into artistic technique to be discussed in the following chapter.

We now turn to spheres 5 and 6 of feeling to consider how their respective aesthetic principles judge the content of art for its human relevance, i.e. how adequately art deals with man's involvement in life. Dilthey claims that "the *fifth sphere of feeling* results from the individual material impulses which pervade the whole of life and which we can fully penetrate in feeling" (*GS*,VI,154). These feelings constitute emotions aroused when our basic life-preserving drives are either obstructed or furthered by our environment. All emotions of self-consciousness like pride, self-respect, shame, and fear are more or less refined ways of estimating how successful we are in preserving and furthering our existence. Yet our emotions are not rooted in personal existence alone. Equally strong social emotions exist ". . . through which the pain and pleasure of others is felt as ours. In the case of sympathy, pity, and love it is as if we incorporated the life of others into our own" (*GS*,VI,154).

The more truthfully a poet can relate human situations and actions to the way our emotions are actually rooted in the varied aspects of life, the more powerful will his effect be on the reader, according to Dilthey. The poetic principle here designated is that of *truthfulness* (*Wahrhaftigkeit*) (*GS*,VI,155). This sphere provides the core material (*Stoff*) of poetry as well as the criterion for determining whether the imagery elaborated by the poetic imagination is sufficiently faithful to psychohistorical reality. The naturalist would see this as an ultimate concern and transform it into a principle of truth as such (*Wahrheit*). But for Dilthey, the content of poetry must satisfy another equally strong requirement which is related to a sixth sphere of feeling. "The *last sphere of feeling* arises when we become conscious of the general properties of impulses of the will and experience their value" (*GS*,VI,155). Here feelings do not merely judge a human action or deed for its naturalness, but for its moral worth. Thus we find a special joy in being able to abide by our decisions despite difficult circumstances. More generally, we admire moral resoluteness of character and acts of loving sacrifice. Such emotions are linked to the aesthetic *principle of ideality* which requires that the poetic content of great literature be not merely true to life, but present an ideal of life (*GS*,VI,156).

Of the six spheres of feeling, the first had no special aesthetic significance. The remaining five aesthetic principles are undeniably a somewhat limited, and therefore arbitrary, beginning for a theory of poetic technique. However, they do bear on central aesthetic issues and clearly take cognizance of traditional standards. Dilthey's main concern here is to demonstrate that if any traditional aesthetic norms are to be justified as universally valid they must be "grounded" in an analysis of general psychological uniformities. Thus Dilthey writes, "The state of consciousness of a people at a given time conditions or determines poetic technique," thus subjecting it to ". . . rules whose validity is . . . historically circumscribed; but from human nature there arise principles which govern taste and creativity just as universally and necessarily as logical principles control thought and science" (*GS*,VI,157).

Although Dilthey claims that his aesthetic principles are universally valid, they are not meant to be exhaustive. The aesthetic impression could have been analyzed differently, for as he says, "The number of these principles, norms or laws is indefinite (*unbestimmt*). They are merely formulas which designate the conditions of particular aesthetical operational elements. The number of such elements is unbounded (*unbegrenzt*) because of the infinite divisibility of the total aesthetic effect" (*GS*,VI,157).

Yet the very notion of an infinite divisibility of elements and an indefinite number of principles implies that any one aesthetic principle could explain no more than a particular kind of effect produced by a work of art, never its total effect. So in his discussion of a small set of principles, Dilthey was evidently concerned with only some partial aspects of a whole work.

However, in the following section, Dilthey begins to

explain the effect of the work as a whole by certain higher aesthetic principles linked to complexes of feeling. In this section, he formulates a *principle of a total effect* (*Total-wirkung*) according to which a new pleasurable feeling will arise when several instances of an elementary aesthetic feeling are considered together. This new feeling will render the total effect greater than the sum of the separate effects (*GS*,VI,158f.). Another higher principle discussed is that of the *relativity of feeling* whereby different ways of ordering a series of pleasurable stimuli can make the result more or less pleasurable. Thus Dilthey asserts that when we proceed from smaller to greater pleasures (or from greater to smaller pains) the total pleasurable result will be more intense than if the sequence is reversed (*GS*,VI,159). This is then related to a *principle of reconciliation* according to which pain can ultimately be compensated for by pleasure, and dissonance resolved by harmony.

It is in Dilthey's treatment of these and several other higher aesthetic principles that an implicit constructionist tendency, which had been overcome in dealing with the elementary principles, becomes most apparent. In his analysis of the spheres of feeling, Dilthey had, to be sure, generally followed Fechner in his method of proceeding "from the bottom up." The spheres could thus be interpreted as strata gradually extending upwards from feelings aroused by purely sensory elements to those appropriate to moral ideals. Nevertheless, in his descriptive analysis, Dilthey carefully avoided any explanatory hypotheses that would link the spheres into a constructive system. He dismissed the attempt to derive one sphere from another by calling them all elementary and emphasizing their uniqueness.

All the higher principles, however, are primarily concerned with ways of increasing the intensity, not the qualitative distinctness, of pleasurable feelings. When applied to the relation of feelings from various spheres, this means that the elementary, qualitative distinctions are allowed to dissolve. The higher principles really only presuppose the naturalistic sense of pleasure of the first sphere of feeling. The abstractness that is once again assigned to feeling allows Dilthey to introduce complex constructs of feeling.

If traditional psychologists were wrong to see images as fixed atoms, it is surely inappropriate for Dilthey to regard aesthetic responses and feelings as building blocks whose additive effects intensify pleasure. We cannot simply consider the overall values of a work of art as cumulative values. Although feelings from different strata may reenforce each other, it is also possible to conceive of conflicts existing between them. A particular color like green may be soothing in itself, but as the coloring of a particular object it may come to have such strong negative associations for us that our natural reaction to it is canceled out. Even without being incompatible, two different aspects of the total aesthetic impression of a work of art may detract from each other when simultaneously in consciousness. This is because in any given reading of the work we cannot be equally conscious of all its aspects. We apprehend the whole only while making certain strands thematic.

The section on higher aesthetic principles is especially dependent on Fechner's *Vorschule der Aesthetik*, and Dilthey succumbs to its constructionist scheme in which elementary feelings combine to produce the overall effect of a work. Although Dilthey is more cautious than Fechner in his formulations of higher or second-order principles, Dilthey nevertheless leaves himself open to his own criticisms of Fechner and the British psychologists made in *Die drei Epochen*. His awareness of this appears in later efforts to rewrite the *Poetik* in 1907 and 1908 when he notes that this section was to be reworked to "cut out the explanative psychology" (*GS*,VI,312). However, it would not have been enough to excise isolated passages from the original *Poetik*. The very subtitle "Building Blocks (*Bausteine*) for a Poetics" indicates that there is a constructionist intent running through a work which is on the whole different in emphasis. To the extent that feelings are studied not merely dynamically for their effect on images, but also as constants combining into more complex feelings, there arises a conflict between the explanative power of his aesthetic principles on the one hand, and that of the acquired psychic nexus on the other.

It was not until 1894, when Dilthey worked out the methodological issues of his psychology in the *Ideen*, that he further exploited the theoretical resources of his concept of the acquired psychic nexus (*erworbener seelischer Zusammenhang*). Its full consequences are there drawn to clearly establish the primacy of normative structural influences over discrete feeling elements in psychology. Thus Dilthey demonstrates that to construct a totality from psychical elements is to ignore the priority of this totality in our actual experience. In the *Poetik*, the acquired psychic nexus functioned primarily as the framework for the third law of the poetic imagination, but had not yet been made the proper basis for claiming anything definitive and individualizing about the poetic imagination as such. The lingering tendency of that work to treat elements as "building blocks" accounts for this failure. A consideration of the *Ideen* at this point can help to develop the potential of the other, more fruitful, structural trend of the *Poetik*, and show that what is normal from the standpoint of elementary processes can be understood as being unique from the standpoint of structure. Moreover, it can serve to justify Dilthey's claim that the poet is an extraordinary individual without being abnormal, or even insane as the Romantics tended to think.

The Primacy of Structure and the Possibility of Defining Individuality

In the *Einleitung* of 1883, Dilthey had been mainly concerned with establishing the wholeness of the psyche, and by so doing assumed he would provide an adequate starting point for his theory of the *Geisteswissenschaften*. The individual psyche conceived as a directly given microcosm of the human world was to be the elementary unit of the *Geisteswissenschaften*. However, the *Ideen* reveals that Dilthey had moved beyond his earlier views towards a more sophisticated conception of individuality which drew on the developmental and structural implications of the acquired psychic nexus. Here the psyche is described as an inner continuum or nexus (*Zusammenhang*) from which individuality is to be acquired through socio-historical development. As indicated by the plan of the *Ideen*, a full conception of the individual can be broached only after the psyche has been carefully considered in a cross section of its structural components and then followed in terms of its developmental axis. Thus the work is organized into three parts: (1) a descriptive study establishing the comprehensive structures of representation, feeling, and will to be found in the psyche, together with an analysis of their elements; (2) an account of psychic development; and (3) an examination of individuality in terms of the articulated structure of the acquired psychic nexus.[5]

While it has been generally noted that Dilthey's concern with defining individuality led him to develop his method of understanding, what has been overlooked is how the new emphasis in the *Ideen* on the acquired nature of individuality proved significant enough to entail modifications of the initial distinction of the *Naturwissenschaften* and *Geisteswissenschaften* laid down in the *Einleitung*. There it was claimed that in the human studies the elements are given, whereas in the natural sciences they are a product of hypothesis (*GS*,1,29). Two kinds of elementary units were thus opposed: (1) human individuals as the complex or microcosmic elements of the *Geisteswissenschaften*, and (2) atoms as the simple elements of the *Naturwissenschaften*. According to the standpoint of the *Ideen*, however, there is no longer any basis for such a distinction, because the assumption that individuality is an elementary concept has been rejected. What is described as given in the

[5] *Ideen*, chaps. 7, 8, and 9, in *GS*, V, 200–237.

psyche is a structure from which, on the one hand, elements can be analyzed and on the other, individuality developed.

Dilthey now accepts a neutral concept of the elemental, according to which elements are always a product of analysis and never directly given. If the natural sciences are still distinguished as hypothetical this is because they limit the number of elements by which to make the processes of nature intelligible. The human studies may not similarly place an initial delimitation on what is elemental. The dynamic nature of psychic life can be analyzed into an indefinite variety of elements, with the consequence that any particular element tends to be unimportant. Only when few elements are posited can generalizations about them be of moment and hypotheses connecting them bold. Such boldness is permissible in the natural sciences because in them alone can extensive use be made of mathematically exact experiments to confirm, reject, or modify hypotheses.

According to Dilthey, the adequacy of hypothetical explanations presupposes that the elements appealed to be not only limited in number, but also univocally definable (*GS*,V,139). Since the natural scientist isolates atomic elements out of the already discontinuous phenomenal complexes provided by the experience of the external world, these elements can legitimately be regarded as more definite and fundamental than any general connections. Speaking of psychic life, however, Dilthey warns that it is not to be regarded as ". . . constituting itself from elements; it is not a composition . . .: it is originally and always an encompassing unity. From this unity psychic functions have differentiated themselves, but remain bound to their context. This fact, whose highest expression is unity of consciousness and the unity of the person, entirely distinguishes psychic life from the whole physical world" (*GS*,V,211). The supposedly elementary functions of psychic life are thus not fundamental in that they are susceptible to indefinite transformation as the identity of the person develops.

Having reformulated the distinction between the *Natur-*

wissenschaften and *Geisteswissenschaften* in terms of the roles of what is elemental, Dilthey summarizes the respective basis for asserting connectedness: In the *Naturwissenschaften*, "the continuum of nature is given only through inference, by means of the connection of hypotheses. For the *Geisteswissenschaften*, on the other hand, . . . a continuum of psychic life is given as primary and fundamental" (*GS*,V,143–44). Clearly no general hypotheses are necessary in the *Geisteswissenschaften*. Moreover, the fact that psychic life appears to be infinitely divisible rules out any overall hypothetical explanation of the psychic continuum, for this would require an unlimited series of hypothetical connections. Because this places an impossible demand on psychology, Dilthey concludes that it must seek for understanding, not explanation: "We *explain* nature, but we *understand* (*verstehen*) psychic life" (*GS*,V,144, italics added).

This motto serves to redefine the problematic of the *Geisteswissenschaften* by making the process of understanding more fundamental to them than it had previously been. The ideal of explaining a phenomenon—both in the naturalistic sense of finding its causal conditions and in Dilthey's modified terms of inner explanation appropriate to the human studies—is now replaced by the ideal of understanding that phenomenon in relation to its specific context and without the use of hypotheses.

The contrast between understanding and explanation has proven difficult to characterize; it is certainly *not* reducible to the simple form of immediate versus mediate knowledge so often suggested. When Dilthey writes in the *Ideen* that "We explain through purely intellectual processes, but we understand through the cooperation of all our psychic powers (*Gemütskräfte*) . . ." it is apparent that intellectual operations are not excluded from the process of understanding. Although a direct sense of the whole is appealed to, Dilthey describes how that which is understood is mediated by it. "In understanding we proceed from the context of the whole (*Zusammenhang des Ganzen*) as given in its vitality, in order to make the parts comprehensible on the basis of it. . . . All psychological thought contains the basic feature that the apprehension of the whole makes possible and determines the interpretation of the individual" (*GS*, V,172).

In the *Ideen*, Dilthey was especially concerned with understanding as it applied to psychology. Broadly, it could be said that explanation involves subsuming the particular data or elements that can be abstracted from our experience to general laws, whereas understanding is more concerned with focusing on the concrete contents of individual processes of experience to consider how they function as part of a larger continuum. Dilthey discusses the general problem more fully in later writings, so that the relation between the two methods will be further developed and gradually clarified.[6]

As long as Dilthey countenanced fundamental elements, however specially defined, in the human studies, he could not dispense with all aspects of the explanative ideal, for the proper connection of these elements still required some mode of explanation. What was anticipated in the *Einleitung* as a new type of explanation, and worked out in the *Poetik* as laws of the poetic imagination, will have to be rethought in terms of the concept of understanding.

Yet for all the new emphasis on understanding, explanative hypotheses are not banished from psychology altogether. Dilthey is willing to grant certain hypotheses from traditional explanative psychology a subordinate role in his descriptive psychology. "It can," he acknowledges, "incorporate those hypotheses which explanative psychology arrived at with respect to single groups of phenomena (*die einzelnen Erscheinungsgruppen*)" (*GS*,V,173). If hypotheses are restricted to questions of detail, they are able to fill in

[6] See below, especially chaps. 6 and 8.

the overall structures provided by descriptive psychology. The extent to which Dilthey allowed hypotheses to continue to play a role can be measured in that part of the *Ideen* dealing with development in psychic life. Through this discussion we can discern three kinds of teleology and the gradual relevance of hypotheses to them.

Dilthey's first response to the problem of development is to claim that inner experience is teleological; it provides us with a sense of purposiveness (*Zweckmässigkeit*) which is *subjective* and *immanent*. "It is subjective," says Dilthey, "because it is directly given in inner experience. It is immanent because it is not grounded in any conceived end outside of itself" (*GS*,V,215). The purposiveness initially experienced in psychic life is therefore not hypothetical.

Dilthey also recognizes a second kind of teleology which is *immanent* and *objective* (*GS*,V,216). It is immanent since it does not refer to a nonpsychological goal, but objective in that its significance is not immediately evident from experience. He notes here how hypotheses about human nature are introduced, for example, in claims that our tendency to maintain pleasure and avoid pain serves the end of self-preservation. Although this second type of teleology is inferred from external behavior, it must be confirmed by inner experience. The hypotheses implicit here about human nature must therefore be distinguished from those involved in a third kind of teleology which is *external* (*GS*,V,215). It is clear from Dilthey's discussion that the latter is the sort of external, "objective" purposiveness referred to in hypotheses about organic development and biological adaptation.

As we have seen, Dilthey has been most critical of those who base the psychological sense of purposiveness on this third or biological form of teleology. Yet because Dilthey himself makes use of examples of biological growth in his descriptions of psychic development, some have contended that Dilthey's own psychology is too biologistic. Anna Tumarkin makes this objection, especially with regard to Dilthey's willingness to call psychic life adaptive.[7]

In an appendix to the *Ideen*, Dilthey had commented that his reference to animal responses was only meant to lead into (*überleiten*) the description of inner processes and not to argue for the interpretation of psychic processes through organic processes (*GS*,V,239). However, his assurances do not really clarify his position, for it is puzzling that a purposiveness "directly given" and immanent to inner experience should need to be introduced by another kind of teleology.

In the text of the *Ideen*, Dilthey had spoken of the fact that psychic connections can be ". . . confirmed by a survey about its presence and function in the entire animal kingdom" (*GS*,V,210–11). Although such a procedure of confirming psychological insights runs the risk of contaminating them with naturalistic hypotheses, it could be interpreted as merely an attempt to provide structural clarification for what is experienced rather vaguely. Because, as noted before, psychic life is undeniably vague, Dilthey sometimes found analogies with the more exactly definable processes of the natural sciences useful. This did not mean, however, that the starting point of the human studies is any the less certain or in need of explanation by the natural sciences.

It is indeed a general rule with Dilthey that an analysis of inner processes needs to be supplemented with an analysis of related external processes. In his ethical writings, he

[7] Anna Tumarkin, *Die Methoden der psychologischen Forschung*, Leipzig: B. G. Teubner, 1929, pp. 51–52. Similar shortcomings are found by Hans-Joachim Lieber in "Die psychische Struktur. Untersuchungen zum Begriff einer Struktur des Seelenlebens bei Dilthey," Inaugural Dissertation, Universität Berlin, 1945, pp. 62, 66. Some of the socio-historical ramifications of Dilthey's reliance on biology are criticized from a Marxist perspective in a more recent study by Lieber: "Geschichte und Gesellschaft im Denken Diltheys," *Kölner Zeitschrift für Soziologie und Sozialpsychologie*, 17, 1965, 703–42.

asserts that a complete ethics must incorporate not only a scrutiny of human motivation, deliberation, and decision but also an analysis of deeds performed. The former study investigates the lived moral sense of the participant; the latter the disinterested view of the spectator. Although any conception of moral freedom is impossible without the first, the perspective of the other is necessary to gain the requisite conceptual purity to deal with the problems of value-relations (*GS*,X,27f.). The same claim is made for aesthetics when Dilthey correlates the productivity of the poetic imagination with the receptivity of the spectator (*GS*,VI,190f.). The distance of the spectator can provide the theory of the imagination with the kind of critical exactness that is necessary for the establishment of poetic technique.

However, these very analogies show that inner experience should properly be compared with human behavior, not organic life as such. A study of the modes of human behavior was to be more specifically included in Dilthey's proposed comparative psychology, and any uniformities about development so introduced would only involve hypotheses associated with the second kind of teleology. In summary, it can be said that the third kind of teleology may at most confirm certain derivative aspects of the first kind, while the latter in turn must ultimately be able to confirm teleology of the second, intermediary sort.

In the last part of the *Ideen*, on individuality, we can see that Dilthey makes use of the intermediary kind of hypotheses described in the section on human development. Much of his discussion of individuality proceeds from what must be considered hypotheses about human nature, although relative to his own use, Dilthey formulates them as normative pronouncements. Thus he declares, "The uniformity (*Gleichförmigkeit*) of human nature expresses itself in the fact that the same qualitative determinations and combinatory forms appear in all men (where abnormal defects do not exist)" (*GS*,V,229). For Dilthey to postulate the abnormality of a person who does not possess any given attribute or combination of attributes is rather presumptuous, especially if the number of elementary qualities that can be analyzed is infinite. Nevertheless, Dilthey's claims about human nature may be treated as useful hypotheses about normality that attempt to establish a basis of common properties out of which individualizing character-traits develop.

After asserting that "individuals do not differ from each other by qualitative determinations or connections that might be present in one and not in another" (*GS*,V,229), Dilthey admits that the intensity of each quality may vary from person to person. Sometimes qualities are present to such a small extent as to be, in effect, unnoticeable. Thus he writes that "the *quantitative relations* in which they manifest themselves are very different from each other; these differences combine into ever new combinations, and on this [first of all] rest the *differences of individuality*."[8]

But individuality cannot be explained in terms of mere differences of degree. To compare two persons directly by measuring the intensity of innumerable attributes is to assume that these attributes are independent variables and can be juxtaposed. Dilthey's structural psychology denies this and orders qualities hierarchically as part of an overall nexus. Accordingly, he explicitly states that "individuality is . . . not already contained in [qualitative] differences, but arises only when such differences are connected into a purposive whole. Individuality is not innate, as Schleiermacher and Humboldt assume, but is first formed (*gestaltet*) through development" (*GS*,V,236–37).

What has to be understood is how certain prominent qualities tend to render related qualities prominent as well. If

[8] *GS*, V, 229. Italics in the text. The qualification contained in the brackets was taken by Misch from Dilthey's handwritten additions to the text.

a particular quality is strong it will reinforce other qualities and prevent still others from developing. Each individual is thus a structural configuration of certain dominant qualities in tension with a base of subordinate qualities. This tension may be unresolved for much of a person's life until finally a functional unity or *Gestalt* is achieved. Dilthey gives the example of ambition leading someone to gradually overcome his shyness in public (*GS*,V,232).

Here we have the basis for understanding the genesis of a concrete structural type. The *Gestalt* that Dilthey refers to is a final articulation of the acquired psychic nexus by which we can define a person's character (*GS*,V,225f.). But once this is used to type a person it almost inevitably leads us to forget the recalcitrant traits that were only gradually subdued. Dilthey points out that, ordinarily, we type people superficially by assuming that only similar qualities can be related into a dominant complex. Thus it is commonly thought that great piety would make a person rather reliable and loyal. However, such common sense expectations about consistency of character are not always true to experience. Not only can stereotypes lead to artificial puzzlement about human behavior, but they can also divert us from seeking the more deeply embedded structures of the mutual interdependence of properties. "How properties presuppose each other and exclude each other lies so deep that it is invisible to the view of the ordinary observer" (*GS*,V,231). A properly grounded structural theory of what is typical (as distinct from a morphology of types) is not only compatible with, but also conducive to, the understanding of individuality. Even when no qualitative differences exist, superficial quantitative variations can be articulated into basic structural deviations.

These reflections about the relationship of individuality and typicality serve to further our understanding of Dilthey's effort to define the poetic imagination by comparing certain of its attributes with those of other processes of psychic life.

Poetic Imagination Structurally Defined in Terms of *Erlebnis*

In an early section of the *Poetik*, Dilthey describes some of the more noticeable strengths or abilities of the poet, none of which, however, may be regarded as unique to him. Dilthey introduces a list of five main functions or achievements of the poetic imagination by saying that "the same processes which appear in every psyche are operative here, but in special proportions of intensity" (*GS*,VI,131).

The first trait by which Dilthey characterizes the poet is that his perceptual impressions are more intense, exact, and manifold than usual. An acute interest in the rich details of reality may also be reflected in his possession of an especially large vocabulary (*GS*,VI,132f.). Secondly, the poet can revive memory images possessing unusual ". . . clarity of outline, strength of sense, and energy of projection" (*GS*,VI,133). It is interesting to note how Dilthey admits that such imagery can be projected into space, that it need not be a two-dimensional "shadow" in an inner space. Yet he does not rule out the possibility that the shadow images are more usual.[9] Thirdly, Dilthey notes that the energy with which the poet can reproduce psychic states, either his own or those of others, presupposes an unusual intensity of feeling (*GS*,VI,134f.). Fourthly, the poet is said to be especially gifted in charging images with life, in finding "satisfaction in intuition saturated with feeling" (*GS*,VI,136). Finally, the poet distinguishes himself by "freely unfolding images beyond the bounds of reality" (*GS*,VI,137).

Considered distributively, each mark or trait of the poetic imagination indicates a rather superficial or external difference of degree between creative and other processes. When viewed together and in context, however, we discov-

---

[9] The extent to which Dilthey is guilty of what Sartre calls the phenomenalistic illusion of immanence will have to be determined after we have dealt with Dilthey's theories of *Erlebnis* and introspection (see chap. 9).

er that although all five differences are formulated relative to ordinary processes, the last also introduces a comparison with abnormal processes. Thus, just as the poet begins to appear more unusual in his freedom, he comes in danger of being classified with psychopaths. Yet Dilthey insists that the poet differs from *all* other classes of people ". . . and to a much higher degree than is assumed as a rule" (*GS*,VI,132). This fifth trait of the poetic imagination must be so conceived as to allow for a *tertium quid* between the ordinary and the abnormal. But before attempting any comparative definition of the poetic imagination, we must first explore the more integral or unifying perspective that the acquired psychic nexus provides for all five traits. As developed in the *Ideen*, the notion of articulating individuality structurally helps to discern an inner link among the different traits which can elucidate the nature of the poetic imagination.

What may appear to be rather divergent traits—consider, for example, the tension between accuracy of vision (1) and free transformation (5); between the clarity of outline of images (1, 2) and the vagueness inherent in reproducing feeling (3)—are in fact held together by Dilthey's underlying concept of *Erlebnis* (lived or felt experience). To the extent that the concept of *Erlebnis* can illuminate the way images are charged with feeling, and feelings are formulated in terms of images, it must be recognized as central to an understanding of the poetic imagination. But since *Erlebnis* as used in the *Poetik* (1887) refers especially to what is felt in experience, it remained necessary to designate the representational content of experience separately. Accordingly, Dilthey was unable to resist the commonplace of conceiving the imagination in terms of images. The idea of a point of impression that we found in *Die drei Epochen* (1892) does indicate that imagery may not only be transformed by feeling, but can also itself be felt in terms of its impact. Yet such language is still misleadingly physicalistic and atomistic. Not until in the *Ideen* (1894) does *Erlebnis* become sufficiently defined to be able to encompass both the concept of the nuclear image used in the third law of metamorphosis and that of the point of impression used in style analysis. Described as the unit of experience ". . . in which the processes of the entire mind or psyche (*Gemüt*) cooperate and in which totality is given, as distinct from the senses which only offer a manifold of details" (*GS*,V,172), *Erlebnis* can overcome the elemental associations that still cling to the concepts of image and point of impression.

Dilthey's plans for revising the *Poetik* in 1907 and 1908 show that ultimately the imagination was to have been directly defined through *Erlebnis* rather than in terms of imagery and feeling. He there acknowledges that by having referred images so prominently to feeling in the *Poetik*, he gave the false impression that his aesthetics was hedonistic. He proposes to reformulate his analysis of the spheres of feeling in a new chapter entitled "Spheres of *Erlebnis* (*Erlebniskreise*)" (*GS*,VI,310f.). This more specific appeal to *Erlebnis* allows such phrases as "enjoyed in feeling," "transformed in feeling," to be excised and replaced with less hedonistic expressions such as "seen in its significance," "transformed according to its meaning" (*GS*,VI,312).

Before the less explicitly conceived but aesthetically important role of *Erlebnis* in the original *Poetik* can be assessed, it will be necessary to clear away some of the confusions that have arisen from Dilthey's use of the term in his more popular essays on literary criticism.

Urged by his students to republish some of his early writings in literary criticism, Dilthey revised and rewrote his essays on Lessing, Goethe, Novalis, and Hölderlin, and brought them together under the title *Das Erlebnis und die Dichtung*. Published in 1906, it was immediately praised for exhibiting both unusual scholarship and sensitivity. Ferdinand Schmidt acclaimed it as one of those rare critical works comparable to Goethe's essay on Winckelmann.[10]

[10] Ferdinand Schmidt, "Das Erlebnis und die Dichtung," *Preussische Jahrbücher*, CXXIII, Berlin, 1906, 201.

Hans-Georg Gadamer ascribed to the fame of this single volume the fact that *Erlebnis* became so fashionable a word in early twentieth-century literary criticism, and that it has since been incorporated into other European languages.[11]

The lasting value of *Das Erlebnis und die Dichtung* can be accounted for by the fine understanding that Dilthey reveals, not only of individual works, but also of the whole attitude or *Weltanschauung* of a poet and his generation. Its direct influence was manifested in the rise of the so-called *geistesgeschichtliche* school of literary history. Some of its adherents—Rudolf Unger, Emil Ermatinger, and Julius Petersen, for example—came to interpret the history of literature as one possible way to deal with philosophical problems. Unfortunately, literary history gradually became the victim of a sterile typology and the subtlety of Dilthey's approach evaporated. This is in no small part due to a misunderstanding of Dilthey's concept of *Erlebnis*.

As Müller-Vollmer has shown, Dilthey's followers had not so much ignored the concept of *Erlebnis* as misused it.[12] The literary theory of Julius Petersen is a good case in point. By cataloguing twelve kinds of *Erlebnis* as worked out by Müller-Freienfels and then classifying them according to Dilthey's three abstract *Weltanschauung* types, Petersen stripped the term *Erlebnis* of any potential structural or philosophical import for a poetic theory. His compendium of the usages of *Erlebnis* is so eclectic that it even included "those repressed *Erlebnisse* derived from psychoanalysis, which have been pushed from consciousness into the subconscious (*Unterbewusstsein*) . . ."[13] This is in conflict with Dilthey's own characterization of *Erlebnis* as a

---

[11] Hans-Georg Gadamer, *Wahrheit und Methode*. 2nd ed. Tübingen: J.C.B. Mohr, 1965, pp. 57ff.

[12] Müller-Vollmer, *Towards a Phenomenological Theory of Literature*, pp. 35-38.

[13] Julius Petersen, *Die Wissenschaft von der Dichtung; System und Methodenlehre der Literaturwissenschaft*, 2nd ed., Berlin: Junker und Dünnhaupt, 1944, p. 364.

unit of experience which is immediately recognizable as manifesting a meaningful relation to human life (*GS*,VI, 314). Dilthey clearly rules out any kind of *Erlebnis* located in the subconscious.

Müller-Vollmer expresses an appropriate disdain of Petersen's encyclopedic catalog by exclaiming, ". . . in vain do we search for a philosophically sound definition of what is meant here by *Erlebnis*."[14] Yet he is not altogether just in his claim that Petersen's "usage of the *Erlebnis* concept implied the notion of a fundamental dichotomy between an ego and a world, a dichotomy which Dilthey had striven to overcome," for Petersen makes some explicit statements to the contrary. Whereas another representative of the *geistesgeschichtliche* school, the noted Oskar Walzel, does separate *Erlebnis* and reflection—the chaotic, raw material of intuition provided by the world as opposed to the form created by the artist's mental powers—Petersen is obviously aware that *Erlebnis* can itself be formed:

> Goethe himself pointed the way to this conclusion when he separated experience from life (*Erleben vom Leben*) and already conceived of the former as a process of productive formation. *Erleben* comes about through the artistic apprehension of life by means of the imagination . . . The true artist . . . cannot experience without the impulsion and compulsion to shape. . . . *Erlebnis* is only completed in the execution [of the literary work]. The poem brings the *Erlebnis* to its conclusion.[15]

So far Petersen is not untrue to Dilthey's view that *Erlebnis* and expression can only be distinguished in terms of the degree of formedness. Yet he senses the need for an inter-

---

[14] Müller-Vollmer, *Towards a Phenomenological Theory of Literature*, pp. 37, 38.

[15] Petersen, *Die Wissenschaft von der Dichtung*, pp. 352–53, 370. *Erleben* as used here with reference to Goethe is roughly equivalent to experience. It is less technical than Dilthey's concept of *Erlebnis*.

mediary function between *Erlebnis* and poetic expression. Allegedly following Dilthey, Petersen assigns this mediating role to feeling: "When, in accordance with Dilthey, the key to the explanation of poetic creation is seen in the analysis of feeling, this involves no contradiction with the key position which was previously assigned to *Erlebnis* and then to the imagination. Rather, emotional and affective stirrings assume a mediating role between *Erlebnis* and imagination."[16]

To be sure, Dilthey attributes a key role to feelings in the imaginative process, but never as separate from *Erlebnis*. When Dilthey wrote the *Poetik*, he was content to use the concept of *Erlebnis* rather sparingly and it could even be argued that at that stage *Erlebnis* was employed almost synonymously with "feeling." There exists then no basis in Dilthey's philosophy for assigning feelings a mediating function between *Erlebnis* and imagination.

Even further removed from Dilthey is a passage in which Petersen attributes the ultimate task of imaginative transformation to the poet's *Weltbild* (world-picture): "No single *Erlebnis* turns into poetry without its form being born from the womb of a *Weltbild* which the poet carries in himself as the order of all impressions of life."[17] A *Weltbild*, however, is but one aspect of a *Weltanschauung*; it constitutes the specifically cognitive factor and is therefore less suitable to illuminate the study of literature than Dilthey's concept of *Weltanschauung*.[18] What is more objectionable here than any possible dualism between *Erlebnis* as subjective and imagination as objective, is the supposition that an abstract *Weltbild* can categorize *Erlebnis*, thereby filtering out all its concrete personal vitality. A too impersonal interpretation of literature is indeed not uncommon in the *geistesgeschichtliche* school of literary history.

The problems inherent in viewing *Erlebnis* as the mani-

---

[16] Ibid., p. 403.   [17] Ibid., p. 372.
[18] Dilthey's own restrictions on the applicability of his *Weltanschauungslehre* to literature will be considered in chap. 9.

festation of something more fundamental than itself are indeed rooted in Dilthey's own account of *Erlebnis*. Thus Dilthey himself claimed that "in *Erlebnis*, the individual process is borne by the total system of psychic life. Its connectedness, both in terms of itself and in relation to the whole of psychic life, belongs to immediate experience" (*GS*,V,172). However, it is at the same time quite obvious that *Erlebnis*, instead of being a mere product of the acquired psychic nexus, is its active counterpart in full consciousness. Neither an isolated element of consciousness, nor a simple reflection of the dispositional structure of psychic life, *Erlebnis* constitutes an integral intersection of all its powers.

What in our first discussions of the poetic imagination was conceptualized as the completion of an image whose nucleus must be penetrated by other components reflecting the evaluative structure of the acquired psychic nexus, can now be more directly and dynamically described in terms of the focusing potential of *Erlebnis*. Just as an understanding of the acquired psychic nexus was found necessary for defining human character, so the fact that *Erlebnis* concretely embodies the psychic nexus allows it to structurally individuate the products of the mind.

Erlebnis is often translated as "lived experience" to distinguish it from the more ordinary experience designated by *Erfahrung*. The most obvious contrast that can be made here is between *Erlebnis* and our ordinary experience of the external world (*äussere Erfahrung*): *Erlebnis* is in possession of its givens, but external experience confronts its givens (*GS*,V,197). The phenomena of *Erlebnis* are given with certainty, whereas the objects of external experience are at least partly products of inference. Because Dilthey uses the term *Innewerden* to designate the intimate mode in which we appropriate *Erlebnis*, nothing would seem simpler than to oppose it to external experience and call it "inner experience" (*innere Erfahrung*). Dilthey does indeed often treat *Erlebnis* and *innere Erfahrung* as if they re-

147

ferred to the same thing. He even uses the combined form *inneres Erlebnis* in the *Poetik* (*GS*,VI,137). To be sure, the phrase *ausseres Erlebnis* is a contradiction in terms while *inneres Erlebnis* is not. However, the fact that Dilthey uses the latter phrase at all, indicates that *Erlebnis* is not to be simply defined as inner experience. If it were, *inneres Erlebnis* would amount to a redundancy.

As long as *Erlebnis* is understood only in the usual sense of inner experience (*innere Erfahrung*) the subtle thread that Dilthey weaves among the five listed accomplishments of the poetic imagination will not be discerned. To grasp the significance of Dilthey's claim in the *Poetik* that "the poet . . . teaches us . . . to enjoy the whole world as *Erlebnis*" (*GS*,VI,131), it must be realized that *Erlebnis* and external experience do not exclude each other as inner versus outer. Lived experience is not restricted to a consciousness of our state of mind, but also involves our attitude to, and thus awareness of, external reality. *Erlebnis* can come to incorporate contents of outer sense whereas *innere Erfahrung* cannot (*GS*,V,247). A more detailed discussion of the relation of *Erlebnis* and external experience will be given in chapter 5 where Dilthey's concept of reflective experience will be introduced. But even in the *Poetik* itself, it is made clear at certain crucial points that *Erlebnis*, as ". . . the real nucleus of poetry, contains a relation of inner and outer" (*GS*,VI,226). This allows us to understand why Dilthey would say of intense perceptual imagery that it is the first component of the poet's *Erlebnis* (*GS*,VI,132), despite the fact that he often speaks of *Erlebnis* as an inner process.

If we relate the five achievements of the poetic imagination to this underlying notion of *Erlebnis*, they no longer need be seen as five disparate factors, but as five moments of *Erlebnis*. The apparent tensions among them[19] resolve into the following conception of the various genetic moments in the development of *Erlebnis*. All *Erlebnis* has (1) a perceptual core which (2) must be supplemented with

[19] See above, p. 142.

148

images of past experience to attain fullness. Past events are dead to us unless we can (3) reproduce the feelings that they evoked initially. Once this background is appropriated, we can (4) properly view reality as embodied with feeling and (5) unfold an ideal of reality as a consequence.

Accuracy of vision can now be viewed as a presupposition for free transformation, if the latter is conceived as the unfolding of *Erlebnis*. Moreover, the clarity of the outer and the vagueness of the inner can now be seen to intersect in the fourth attribute of the poet, or what Dilthey calls his ability to have "intuition saturated with feeling" (*GS*,VI,136). All these moments combine to articulate the special structure of the poetic imagination.

Two Types of Poetic Imagination

Ever since his essay on Goethe, first published in 1878, Dilthey had distinguished two main types of poetic imagination of which Shakespeare and Rousseau can be considered the best representatives. Shakespeare saw everything as an actor able to project himself imaginatively into various roles. The richness of nature, society, and history was the inspiration of his imagination (*ED*,132f.). Dilthey calls this kind of imagination objective. At the other extreme is the subjective type represented by Rousseau, whose imagination seems to have turned totally inward. From childhood memories he extrapolated an ideal of happiness which compensated for the unhappiness of his actual outer existence (*ED*,138f.). Goethe is regarded as unusual for having struck a balance between the inner and outer, the subjective and objective modes of the imagination. Dilthey expresses his awe of Goethe's great imaginative capacity for understanding life: "He was able to understand by putting what was alien in relation to his own life. Once understood it became a moment of his own development. So rich was his nature, so strong his need to give his existence an unbounded scope and his insights objectivity, that he even

149

incorporated the religious, scientific, and philosophical movements of his time in his *Erlebnis*" (*ED*,151).

This same distinction of the types of poetic imagination is made in the *Poetik*. One might have expected Dilthey to have discussed the objective imagination in relation to the perceptual and memorial powers of the poet (achievements 1 and 2), and the subjective imagination in relation to the energy which poets tend to reproduce and project feelings (achievements 3 and 4). Instead they are both discussed as part of a corollary to Dilthey's description of the fourth achievement. It is here that the notion of images needing to be animated by feelings is allowed to imperceptibly lead into the more fundamental concept of *Erlebnis* as the interpenetration of image and feeling.

This suggests that on a closer examination the division among the two types of poetic imagination may not be as sharp as it at first appears, and that Goethe's reconciliation is not so unusual. To be sure, certain writers who are endowed with an objective imagination disclose how suddenly they find themselves confronted with a vision. Jean Paul, for example, wrote in one of his letters: "The real poet when he writes is merely the spectator of his characters rather than their prompter. He watches them live, as in a dream, and listens to them" (quoted in *GS*,VI,181). Yet it seems permissible to speculate that such seemingly involuntary, dreamlike creation is based on emotional preparation. What suddenly reveals itself to a writer like Goncharov, who similarly speaks of the independent existence of his characters, was undoubtedly anticipated by feeling. Moreover, Dickens, who would have to be classified as having an objective imagination, reveals a great emotional involvement with his characters. Insofar as he identifies with Mr. Pickwick, he cannot be deceived by the character as if this were a stranger confronting him. Even so-called objective poets infuse their feelings into their subject matter.

One thing is clear: Only to the extent that a poet has been able to enliven his images with feeling and give visible form to his feeling can genuine imaginative metamorphosis be instituted. This has already been discussed as an aspect of the law of completion, and can now be seen to focus in *Erlebnis* itself. The interdependence of inner and outer characteristic of the acquired psychic nexus must be tested in terms of *Erlebnis*. Reformulating this interdependence as one of feeling and form, we find it expressed in certain natural symbols of language and myth (*GS*,VI,227), which can in turn be more self-consciously developed through imaginative metamorphosis. The parallel here created between *Erlebnis* and poetic imagination is of course best disclosed in Dilthey's description of Goethe's creative process: "For an inner *Erlebnis* a generally interesting incident is found. With one stroke a fusion takes place through inspiration. Then a process of slow metamorphosis and completion of the discovered symbol begins" (*GS*,VI,212). This description can be taken as Dilthey's normative ideal of the poetic imagination. Only the initial conditions of the *Erlebnis* vary.

It is not the scope of *Erlebnis* alone that assures greatness in poetry. Still more essential is the balance of the felt and the seen which can make even lyrical poetry more than personal. Although literature is said to have its origin in the *Erlebnis* of the poet, it is not meant to be autobiographical in the narrow sense nor to arouse the reader's idle curiosity about the author's life. Taken in this way, biographical considerations can only distract from the poetic understanding. But great poetry cannot fail to be biographical in a more authentic sense. It does not arise from the experience of the poet without also being transformed under the guidance of his historically acquired psychic nexus. Esoteric poetry inspired by chance experience or produced in a sudden act of discharge may lead to speculation about the poet's private life, but such poetry is of no interest to Dilthey.

In his *Leben Schleiermachers*, Dilthey most definitively revealed his ideal of the proper role of biographical information by contrasting it to a Romantic misuse of the autobiographical. Especially noteworthy is Dilthey's treatment of the friendship and collaboration of Schleiermacher and Friedrich Schlegel. By displaying their common concerns, he was able to delineate the individuality of each. For instance, Dilthey contrasted the two men with reference to Schlegel's *Luzinde*, which caused a scandal through its thinly disguised representation of their Berlin circle and disclosures of the author's relations with the married daughter of Moses Mendelssohn. Even though Schleiermacher thought it unwise to write such a novel, he did publish some anonymous letters in its defense. Led by a sense of loyalty, he sought to justify his friend by again raising some of the ethical objections to the conventional conception of marriage that he had earlier formulated in his *Soliloquies*.

Dilthey traces the different kinds of personal statements involved in Schlegel's confessional novel and Schleiermacher's reflective soliloquies back to their respective modes of experiencing reality: "If it were natural for Friedrich [Schlegel] to immediately yield himself to a new phenomenon with intense vigor in order to completely master it in one leap, so it followed from the steady harmony of Schleiermacher's nature that he would connect everything new to what he possessed in a calm but constant process of appropriation. He advanced only slowly, but put his personal stamp on everything that he accepted and fused it with his whole being."[20]

Because Schlegel tended to lose himself in his experience of the world, he could not but trivialize the biographical aspect of his art by projecting interesting details about his life into his works. Not allowing his experience to unfold into *Erlebnis*, he could never be a good poet, whereas Schleiermacher, despite his lack of artistic pretensions, is characterized by Dilthey as having a profoundly poetic disposition similar to Goethe's. To the extent that great poetry is biographical, it is so not in the sense of manifesting per-

[20] *Leben Schleiermachers*, ed. H. Mulert, vol. 1, 2nd ed., Berlin: W. de Gruyter, 1922, p. 503.

sonal mannerisms, but of revealing a unity of style which derives from the total being of the poet—a being that comprehends more than private states of mind.

Erlebnis can unfold poetically only if guided by the acquired psychic nexus. It is essential that the implicit sense of totality in *Erlebnis* be explicated, and that this be done in a nonarbitrary way. However, it was precisely in this process of transcending the givens of experience that the Romantics had located an affinity between genius and insanity, thereby posing the problem of discerning the boundary between the normal and the abnormal.

The True Sanity of the Poet

At the time Dilthey developed his theory of the poetic imagination, the Romantic theory of poetic madness had been revived in terms of more "scientific" and naturalistic claims that genius was allied with moral and intellectual degeneracy. In his lecture, "Dichterische Einbildungskraft und Wahnsinn," where he introduced his concept of the acquired psychic nexus in an effort to separate the poetic imagination from insanity, Dilthey remarks:

> Schopenhauer established his theory of the pathological constitution of genius with the approval of all who believed themselves to be suffering from their own genius. According to him, an overly powerful cerebral life burdens the genial person with an abnormal irritability. . . . In France this point of view has been dressed up with the rhetoric of psychiatric theory. France has been the center of psychiatry ever since the great Pinel. However, it has also been the source of many psychiatric fantasies, which, because they are comparable to the fantasies of *Naturphilosophie* in Germany, point to a "Romanticism of the materialists." [*GS*,VI,91]

Dilthey then notes that Renaudin attached more importance to hallucination than genius and that Moreau reduced genius to a state of exaltation which lies beyond the bounds of mental health.

Despite the fact that the poet describing his own creative processes sometimes speaks of dream-like powers, hallucinations, and melancholy, Dilthey claims that he is not to be considered as psychopathic. Although the poet differs from ordinary practical men in his relative lack of concern for adapting his creative activities to directly given reality, he never loses his sense of reality. Dilthey insists that the poet could not transcend reality and still disclose the typical in it without the guidance of a rich, well-integrated, acquired psychic nexus. Thus the free transformation of poetic *Erlebnis* argues for the true sanity and health of the poet and the fullest functioning of the normative or evaluative structure of the acquired psychic nexus. The poetic image can only have as much unity and richness as is possessed by the acquired psychic nexus.

We can assume that the ordinary practical person will have a unified but rather limited acquired psychic nexus. He has narrowed his main values to the realm of the attainable. The content of his life is determined by his practical goals, and he sees only as much of the road he travels as is necessary to arrive at his destination efficiently. The affective transformation of perceptual impressions is restricted by the particular task to be performed. It is not that the acquired psychic nexus is inactive, for Dilthey has defined it to influence all ordinary psychic processes; but its operation is confined by the function of having to adapt to reality (*GS*,VI,168f.). In the poet, too, the acquired psychic nexus can be reduced to a background for more specific impulses when, for example, he finds himself forced to cope with the world and the practical necessities of selling his work for sustenance.

However, the significance of his poetry presupposes his acquired psychic nexus to be greater in scope and less restricted by special adaptive functions than that of the ordinary person. The fund of past experience which usually decays into a blind conditioning factor for future behavior must be preserved historically and made conscious in the structure of the poet's *Erlebnis*. While the influence of the acquired psychic nexus is ordinarily deflected into a narrow channel, it is embodied in its integrity by the poetic imagination.

In the case of the pathological imagination, however, the acquired psychic nexus is claimed to be inoperative. As Dilthey notes in "Dichterische Einbildungskraft und Wahnsinn," its control "... breaks down in dream and insanity, so that the regulative apparatus which keeps impressions, representations, and feelings adapted to reality disappears, as it were" (*GS*,VI,94). Contrasting the pathological and poetic imagination, Dilthey suggests that the availability of cerebral energy accounts for the difference. In referring to the acquired psychic nexus, he declares that, "only the highest energy of cerebral life can make possible the broad efficacy of this entire apparatus, so that the most remote representations can come into contact and be used" (*GS*,VI,168). The vitality of the acquired psychic nexus in the poetic imagination exhibits this "highest energy," while in the pathological there is an actual deficiency.

But for Dilthey to claim that much cerebral energy is necessary for the activity of the acquired psychic nexus is to indulge in a psychophysical hypothesis. Equally hypothetical is his apparent acceptance of the then current theories that mental illness stems from physiological disorders caused by an inadequate supply of blood to the brain (*GS*,VI,96,170). It might be suggested in a less hypothetical vein that mental disturbances arise when more representations, values, or impulses exist than can be incorporated by the acquired psychic nexus. This would imply that the acquired psychic nexus breaks down either because it is (1) inactive, or (2) rich in scope, but not articulated, or (3) articulated, but too limited in scope to deal with the richness of the life in which one is actively involved. Whereas the ordinary person is able to balance his limited control over reality by restricting his needs, the abnormal person is not able to compensate by such self-renunciation.

In case (1) we imagine a person constitutionally at the mercy of the stimuli to which he is exposed. No selective or screening mechanism exists whereby impressions can be evaluated and confirmed. Nothing can therefore prevent a stimulus from having a hallucinatory effect. In case (2) there is only a partial articulation of a wide range of impressions, that is, they are structured, but only in a disjointed manner. An interesting example from Dilthey's literary criticism can be found in the following remarks about Ludwig Tieck, another, not totally successful Romantic poet:

> Nature gave him an unusual ability to experience or live through (*durchleben*) moods with the most turbulent participation of all his powers, and from them to produce forms by means of an easily and spontaneously constructive imagination. It is not infrequently the case that such an extraordinary power burns up as mere material all elements of life which approach it. Thus the true and profound personal development, which constitutes the greatness of poets as well as thinkers, does not come about in the very midst of the fullness and wealth of life and thought. If I am not mistaken, this was the case with Tieck.[21]

Tieck's experience may have been broad in scope, but it was not fully structured as *Erlebnis*. Reality was intensely *durchlebt*, but not *erlebt*. Whereas Schlegel's interests were characterized as overly centrifugal, Dilthey considers Tieck's to be so centripetal as to overagitate his imagination. Having been critical of the author of *Luzinde* for lacking inventiveness, Dilthey now finds fault with Tieck for having an arbitrary imagination.

> With the highest flights of his imagination there is mixed an indomitable tendency for the absurd. The

[21] *Leben Schleiermachers*, 1, 307.

most fearful fate does not seem tragic in his work. From the most subtle, one would like to say "crafty," observations of people there does not result the formation of a significant, fully rounded character. Moreover, his persistent form-studies do not lead him to that true inner form which is the very expression of a positive poetic content.[22]

That inner form or style which only a united psychic nexus can unfold is sadly lacking in Tieck's poetry. Clinically considered, such richness of experience lacking any unity of form can lead to schizophrenia where the acquired psychic nexus is split into several partial systems.

In case (3) too much is demanded of a limited acquired psychic nexus. This can occur when suddenly a person is confronted with experience which is too diverse or complex to fit into his framework of reality. Such experiences can lead to the breakdown of a stunted acquired psychic nexus. The old framework for reality may have been perfectly adequate. It may even continue to be applied logically. But because the fund of acquired representations is limited, the conclusions based on it are too one-sided and inadequate to guide behavior.

Dilthey was himself keen to point out that even the most mentally imbalanced person may have an acute logical sense. He argues that logical reasoning can only be esteemed as the highest attainment of psychic life if it mediates propositions while under the control of the acquired psychic nexus. In the case of a madman whose conclusions are logically valid but false, Dilthey assumes that it is because his acquired psychic nexus is inactive (*GS*,VI,169f.). Rather than make such an assumption, we have suggested that it may be active but inadequate. The unity of the acquired psychic nexus may itself be logical or abstract only.

If the unity of the acquired psychic nexus is to be flexible enough to cope with reality and yet transcend it, it must be

22 Ibid., see pp. 537, 308.

157

a concrete, felt unity. The poet is that rare individual who can balance the richness of his imagery with a unity of feeling. That is, he must be able to articulate his psychic nexus in such a manner so as to create a comprehensive evaluative structuring of reality. His imagination is definable insofar as it develops in accordance with the original unity of inner and outer experience that Dilthey ascribes to *Erlebnis*. Seeing that the poet more fully explores the potentials of experience than is ordinarily done, and therefore more directly embodies the acquired psychic nexus, Dilthey recognizes that he is able to tap a fundamental, normative core of human experience. Thus while the poet's imagination stands apart as a special type, its products are such as to be typical of mankind.

Paradoxically, the sense in which the poet seems to be extraordinary is that he is more normal than ordinary men, rather than that he is abnormal. The stereotype that creativity comes at the price of abnormality is at least in part due to a tendency to confuse the normal with the ordinary, the abnormal with the extraordinary. A distinction between what is normal and ordinary is suggested by Dilthey's own use of the idea of being "more normal" when speaking of the artistic imagination in *Die drei Epochen*: "The more rich, normal, and deep the acquired psychic nexus is, and the more completely it relates to the images to fill and saturate them, the more the artistic product will constitute a representation of reality in its true meaning" (*GS*,VI,278). The poetic imagination is then normal in the extra-ordinary sense of being normative, but not, however, in the Nietzschean sense of being super-normal.

Although Dilthey and Nietzsche were contemporaries and shared a distrust of the Romantic myth of the mad genius as divinely inspired, Nietzsche's conception of the artist still retained much more of the elitism associated with Romanticism. Like Dilthey, he was critical of the decadent, self-indulgent, escapist tendencies that recurrently plagued art movements in the nineteenth century, and tried to revalidate the life-serving process of art with the aid of his own psychological insights. But whereas Dilthey transformed the naturalistic demand that art be truthful about life into a normative theory of typification, Nietzsche created an antithesis between artistic illusion and the search for truth. Dilthey claimed that the heightened consciousness of the poet renders his illusions incapable of deluding him, but Nietzsche explains artistic illusion as a product of the will to delude and deceive. For Nietzsche, a creative relation to life presupposes having negated the positivistic value of truth according to which the given is the norm, for the sake of a higher kind of value. The artist's superiority to reality manifests itself in illusions which are of more value than truth. Thus in *The Will to Power* Nietzsche recounts the viewpoint of his *Birth of Tragedy* as follows: "The will to appearance, to illusion, to deception, to becoming and change (to objectified deception) here counts as more profound, primeval, 'metaphysical' than the will to truth, to reality. . . ."[23]

Care must thus be exercised in comparing these two contemporaries. For Nietzsche to assume that Apollonian illusion is the artifice by which the tragedian can reconcile us with the creative-destructive Dionysian principle of reality is to make reconciliation a utilitarian process whereby we are put into an affirmative relation to life. Dilthey, however, does not expect art to help us adapt to life, but to make a balanced reflection about life possible. One might suggest the different veins of the respective philosophies of life of Nietzsche and Dilthey by stating that one willfully affirms life even to the extent of using falsehoods, whereas the other reflectively accepts it. In the one case art is an antinormative manifestation of human willpower, in the other a normative expression of human experience.

[23] Friedrich Nietzsche, *The Will to Power*, trans. Walter Kaufmann and R. J. Hollingdale, New York: Random House, 1967, p. 453.

CHAPTER FOUR

From Synthesis to Articulation

SINCE Kant, most philosophers have assigned the imagination a synthetic task. By showing that the usual synthetic functions that have been attributed to the imagination, whether conceived empirically or transcendentally, are inadequate from Dilthey's standpoint, we can further underline the methodological significance of the *Poetik*. The critique of synthesis formulated in the present chapter is fundamental to both Dilthey's psychology and epistemology. As such this chapter can also serve as a transition to part III where the development of Dilthey's broader philosophical and historical theories will be examined.

Dilthey does not help us in establishing a philosophical perspective on his theory of the imagination by making any traditional distinctions like that between imagination and fancy. The words *Phantasie, Einbildungskraft*, and *Imagination* are used interchangeably and never defined in relation to standard philosophical usages.[1] This may have given commentators such as Hodges the impression that Dilthey employs the notion of imagination in a merely "popular sense," without attributing any special theoretical significance to it.[2] But the fact that Dilthey seems to be rather indiscriminate in his terminology and that he does not clearly delineate his concept of imagination with reference to other technical formulations should not lead us to deny its philosophical implications.

[1] Thus in chap. 2 we could only conclude from the tenor of his approach that Dilthey would find Hume's theory of fancy inadequate.
[2] Hodges, *The Philosophy of Wilhelm Dilthey*, p. 329.

Yet even those who have realized the importance of Dilthey's concept of the imagination are not always free from misconceptions about it. Müller-Vollmer, who is one of the few to have dealt with his theory of the poetic imagination, assumes that its philosophical import can only be realized by discounting its psychological basis. Thus he writes: "Dilthey was able to overcome the limitations inherent in the psychological approach by attributing especial importance to the poet's creative imagination." And he contrasts him on this score with Wilhelm Wundt's purely psychological theory: "Wundt in his *Völkerpsychologie* defined this kind of imagination merely as a capacity to arrange and rearrange given elements of experience into new combinations. Nothing new was ever added to them. For Dilthey, however, the poet is capable of producing images 'which unfold freely beyond the limits of reality.' "[3]

The contrast Müller-Vollmer offers, however, is totally misleading in picturing Wundt's theory as merely a late nineteenth-century version of Hume's theory of fancy. Although it is true that Wundt stands in both the British associationist and the German experimentalist traditions, he is important for having recognized that the laws of association are simply not adequate to define the imagination. Wundt, like John Stuart Mill, represents an effort within the empirical tradition to develop a notion of "creative synthesis" in order to overcome the disintegrative aspects of the Humean psychology without, however, embracing the Kantian transcendental standpoint and its synthetic a priori categories. An oversimplified version of Wundt's theory can only obscure the more important differences between him and Dilthey, especially with regard to the role of synthesis.

Wundt developed a *Völkerpsychologie*, a constructionist system, which can be regarded as a brilliant application of the approach to psychology that proceeds from the bottom up. He starts with elementary acts that operate in isolation

[3] Müller-Vollmer, *Towards a Phenomenological Theory of Literature*, p. 103.

and gradually builds up more and more complex levels of psychological activity to account for the cultural life of *Völker* (nations or peoples). He even goes so far as to construct a synthetic *Volksseele* (soul of a nation): "Thus the *Volksseele* is a product of individual psyches from which it is composed; but the individual psyches are not any the less products of the *Volksseele* in which they participate."[4]

Dilthey had already dismissed concepts like *Volksseele* and *Volksgeist* (spirit of a nation) in his *Einleitung* by saying, "These concepts are as useless for history as that of vital impulse in physiology. What the expression *Volk* means can only be explicated analytically. . . ."[5] Similarly, a careful examination of the *Poetik* and *Ideen* can show that Dilthey would be equally suspicious of Wundt's theory of the imagination as a creative synthesis. And this is not because it is a psychological theory of the imagination, but because it is a product of a particular constructionist approach to psychology which distorts the nature of creativity by first positing artificial contrasts.

While underestimating the emergent synthetic functions that Wundt was able to introduce into his associationist psychology, Müller-Vollmer at the same time overestimates the importance of Dilthey's claim that images can unfold beyond the limits of reality. What Dilthey means by imagery transcending reality does not involve any "synthetic" transcendence of the psychological conditions of experience. By claiming that for Dilthey the creative imagination must ". . . add to the original components of experience," Müller-Vollmer ignores Dilthey's own counterclaims in the *Poetik*

[4] Wilhelm Wundt, *Völkerpsychologie: Eine Untersuchung der Entwicklungsgesetze von Sprache, Mythus und Sitte*, vol. I, part 1, Leipzig: Wilhelm Engelmann, 1900, p. 10.

[5] *GS*, I, 41. When Dilthey later relaxes some of his scruples against such synthetic concepts, it is only the concept of *Volksgeist* that can hold any attraction for him. This is because a view that takes the concept of *Volksseele* seriously falsely reduces the dialectic of history to the dimension of a psychological construction. See below chap. 8.

itself.[6] Dilthey explicitly denies the "new creation of contents (*Neuschöpfung von Inhalten*) which were nowhere experienced" (*GS*,VI,142). When the process of completion of the third law of imaginative metamorphosis is said to involve "new" elements entering into a poetic image, it is to be assumed that they stem from past experience. This is actually confirmed by Dilthey's later essay "Goethe und die dichterische Phantasie" where the process of completion is more directly related to memory (*ED*,116).

Walter Heynen has presented an account of Dilthey's theory of the poetic imagination which is completely at odds with Müller-Vollmer's. Demonstrating how circumspect Dilthey was in his treatment of the imagination, Heynen concludes that the imagination differs from perception only in degree.[7] But to consider Dilthey's theory of imagination a mode of perception is just as unfounded as to regard Wundt's theory of the imagination merely a mode of fancy.

In fact, by looking more closely at the *Poetik* and Wundt's *Völkerpsychologie*, we will find a parallel concern to distinguish the imaginative processes from ordinary perceptual processes on the basis of certain common functions. Neither Dilthey nor Wundt wishes to conceive of the imagination as a peculiar faculty of the mind. But where Dilthey distinguishes the imagination structurally, Wundt projects a qualitative difference. He asserts in the *Völkerpsychologie*: "It is self-evident that this creative activity is not concerned with a specific faculty, but with a peculiar result in which the general mental functions unite."[8] Wundt thinks of the creative imagination as a climactic process in which many common functions of the psyche finally cooperate to form

[6] Müller-Vollmer, *Towards a Phenomenological Theory of Literature*, p. 135.

[7] Walter Heynen, *Diltheys Psychologie des dichterischen Schaffens*, *Abhandlungen zur Philosophie und ihre Geschichte*, vol. 48, ed. B. Erdmann, Halle a.d.S.: Max Niemeyer, 1916, pp. 4f.

[8] Wundt, *Völkerpsychologie*, vol. III, 1908, p. 53.

a most complex activity. The creative imagination is *qualitatively* different from other representational activities in that it presupposes the operation of all psychic processes.

According to Dilthey, however, the total psyche is active in every normal psychic process, so that Wundt's appeal to totality cannot be the basis for any qualitative peculiarity of the imagination. For Dilthey the imagination differs *structurally* from other mental processes in that the control of the acquired psychic nexus is unimpeded by any physiological conditioning or theoretical and practical ideals of adaptation.

In the *Ideen*, Dilthey refers to Wundt's definition of creative synthesis as found in the *Vorlesungen über die Menschen-und Thierseele* (1863) without, however, specifically criticizing it. He quotes Wundt as follows:

> . . . psychic connections can be explained through the causal interaction of psychic elements, but nevertheless, these connections possess *new qualitative* properties which were not contained in the elements. At the same time, special value determinations, not anticipated in the elements, will attach themselves to these new properties. Insofar as in all such cases psychic synthesis produces something novel, I will designate it as a *creative synthesis*. [*GS*,V,167, italics added]

Although Dilthey had praised Wundt for giving up the principle of *causa aequat effectum* in his psychology, there is no reason to suppose that he would agree with the way Wundt formulated his position in the above quotation. Instead, the fact that terms like "creative synthesis" and "qualitative novelty" were conspicuously avoided in the *Poetik* leads one to suspect that Dilthey might have some reservations. This is confirmed by taking note of the immediate context in which Wundt is discussed in the *Ideen*. He is chosen as one of several representatives of the explanative psychology that Dilthey proposes to replace with a descriptive psychology. Although Hodges is correct to point out that Dilthey means to show how Wundt has ". . . moved away from the crude sensationalist position and recognized the synthetic and creative character of mental processes,"[9] Dilthey nevertheless regards him as one who refined the sensationalist approach as part of an unjustified attempt to preserve it.

Wundt's concept of creative synthesis should therefore be related to an earlier discussion in the same chapter where Dilthey explicitly attacked John Stuart Mill's theory of psychic chemistry. In the *System of Logic*, Mill had spoken of certain psychological combinations as analogous to chemical reactions, and referred to them as "cases of mental chemistry: in which it is proper to say that the simple ideas generate, rather than that they compose, the complex ones."[10] Dilthey interprets such an appeal to chemical synthesis as a subterfuge to preserve the presuppositions of traditional associationist psychology, thus ignoring the need for a descriptive psychology which alone can do justice to the overall fundamental structures of the psyche.

Having begun his analysis of Mill's explanative psychology by noting how he assumes a psychic chemistry, Dilthey writes that "when simple ideas or feelings are compounded, they can produce a state which is simple for inner perception and at the same time completely different qualitatively from the components. . . . The laws of psychic life are at times deemed comparable to mechanical laws and at times to chemical laws" (GS,V,160). Mechanical explanations on the order of association are preserved as far as is feasible and then conveniently supplemented with the axiom that sometimes certain synthetic qualitative changes comparable to chemical changes take place. Dilthey continues his evaluation of Mill as follows: "It is clear that the acceptance of such a completely general and indefinite axiom, which contrasts curiously with the exactness of real natural laws, must

[9] Hodges, *The Philosophy of Wilhelm Dilthey*, p. 204.

[10] John Stuart Mill, *A System of Logic*, vol. 2, 7th ed. London: Longmans, Green, Reader, and Dryer, 1868, p. 438.

exceedingly facilitate the task of the explanative psychologist. For he hides the lack of true derivation. He allows himself to hold on to certain uniform antecedents and fill up the gap between them and the succeeding state by a psychic chemistry" (GS,V,160–61).

Dilthey leaves no doubt that he means to use the phrase "psychic chemistry" in an exclusively pejorative sense. Given his suspicion of chemical synthesis as an ad hoc defense of the constructionist method, it is clear that Wundt's theory of creative synthesis cannot be exempted from similar doubts. Although Wundt saw much more acutely than his predecessors the need to correct traditional associationism, he nevertheless did not question the validity of its essential principles. Thus, Wundt is aware that such elementary operations as the rearrangement of representational contents do not suffice to define the imagination. Yet the very attempt to establish the simpler processes as the basis for explaining the higher operations of the imagination necessitated an appeal to the kind of sudden, mysterious, qualitative novelty that Dilthey's theory of imaginative metamorphosis was intended to obviate. It is precisely because Wundt preserves a discrete, associationist base that he has to account for creativity in terms of a special synthesis.

In the *Ideen*, Dilthey uses the idea of creative synthesis to refer only to scientific productivity, not to artistic creativity. Given its constructionist ideal of deriving as much as possible from a limited number of elements, science may have to resort to a chemical model of compounding them. But such synthesis can never account for anything more than artificial novelty, while in all life processes, those of psychic life in particular, there is real novelty which can be articulated structurally. "I make use of the concept of articulation (*Artikulation*)," writes Dilthey, "to express how a living context is the basis of all development. All differentiations and the more clear and fine relations develop from this structure. . . . The acts in which this development takes place *create* what could not yet be manifested in earlier states. They bring out new values. Yet how different these acts can be! In addition to the creative syntheses of science, there exists the artistic process of the formation of symbols for the stirrings of inner life . . ." (*GS*,V,217–18).

A psychology modeled on the natural sciences will try to explain psychological growth in terms of synthesis. But no matter how useful the chemical analogy of synthesis may be as a tool for explanative psychology, it cannot, according to Dilthey, do justice to the dynamism of psychic processes. Nor can it characterize the way the formative processes of the imagination symbolically articulate the acquired psychic nexus. Thus the concept of the creative synthesis of qualitatively new content has to be interpreted as a fiction within the context of an articulative life-process where values become more and more differentiated in relation to an original continuum.

Dilthey's psychology describes an experienced continuity of psychic life and therefore need fill no gaps. Individual components can be abstracted from this continuum, but always preserve their orientation towards it. It is on this basis that the fusion of representations discussed in chapter 2 can be understood as inherent in the life of representations as such. To enter into specific relations is merely a particular outgrowth of the fundamental relatedness of representations in *Erlebnis*. The advantage of not relying on combinations to explain the psychic continuum is that it renders unnecessary the assumption that in connecting representations they become swallowed up in a higher unity as chemical elements are submerged in a compound. As early as 1875, in the essay "Ueber das Studium der Geschichte der Wissenschaften vom Menschen, der Gesellschaft und dem Staat," Dilthey had been wary of confusing psychical and chemical modes of complexity: "The combination of two sensations still shows the attributes that we perceived in them singly, whereas in the combination of two substances, qualities change in a manner no longer explicable"

(*GS*,V,45). A chemical compound does not permit us to directly recognize the elements that were synthesized. On the other hand, the principle of fusion that Dilthey establishes as basic to psychic life does permit us to recognize elements in complex representations. Whether or not we actually discern them is a function of our interest and attentiveness, i.e. a function of our acquired psychic nexus (*erworbener seelischer Zusammenhang*).

It is interesting to note that Dilthey uses the word *Verschmelzung* rather than *Synthese* to label what we have discussed as fusion. This suggests that synthesis has a purely naturalistic meaning, which is to be avoided when describing psychic life. Perhaps Dilthey hesitated to use the term "synthesis" in both the *Poetik* and the *Ideen* because so many psychologists had used it to try to explain what are at bottom meaning-relations which can only be understood. The fact that Dilthey tried to minimize the use of organic terminology in his psychology, would also make sense in terms of this distinction, for it is in organic theories that the difference between natural synthesis and mental fusion is hardest to defend.

An organic mode of synthesis had proved appealing to many Romantic thinkers precisely as a way of mediating the natural and the ideal. Coleridge, in his *Biographia Literaria*, provides an illuminating model for such an approach. Although the task of the imagination is broached in post-Kantian terms by positing a metaphysical identity of the ideal and the real, its operations are still conceived in natural terms.[11] The actual description of the imagination discloses certain analogies between it and organic growth. These analogies are fostered by a fundamental distinction that Coleridge wishes to institute between imagination and fancy. A new ideal of a creative *imagination*, which spontaneously fuses images, is opposed to the Humean ideal of *fancy*, whose only freedom lies in rearranging them. The

[11] Samuel T. Coleridge, *Biographia Literaria*, vol. 1, ed. by John Shawcross, London: Oxford University Press, 1958, pp. 178, 202.

dynamic possibility of synthesizing images is contrasted to the mechanical conception of combining them by association.

Coleridge rightfully scorns fancy for having "no other counters to play with, but fixities and definites. The Fancy is indeed no other than a mode of Memory emancipated from the order of time and space; . . . [It] must receive all its materials ready made from the law of association. . . ." To this he contrasts the imagination or what he calls the esemplastic power. "It dissolves, diffuses, dissipates, in order to re-create; or where this process is rendered impossible, yet still at all events it struggles to idealize and to unify. It is essentially *vital*, even as all objects (*as* objects) are essentially fixed and dead."[12]

M. H. Abrams conveniently elaborates Coleridge's "aesthetics of organism" in the following simile: "As a plant assimilates the most diverse materials of earth and air, so the synthetic power of imagination 'reveals itself,' in Coleridge's famous phrase, 'in the balance or reconciliation of *opposites* or discordant qualities.' "[13] The very force of this graphic comparison can bring us to the realization, however, that synthesis itself is not conceived as an organic process, but as a chemical process. Whereas the way that the imagination feeds on a multifarious experience may be compared to the way a plant absorbs and filters whatever it can obtain from the soil, the final stage of assimilation seems to be an exclusively chemical process.

The unfavorable connotations of mechanical explanation have led many aestheticians to appeal to a biological model when in fact a purely chemical model probably would have sufficed to express how they conceived the imaginative process. Since in Coleridge's case, the elements which the imagination fuses or unites are said to be originally discordant, they cannot be parts of an organic continuum, for that

[12] Ibid., p. 202.
[13] M. H. Abrams, *The Mirror and the Lamp: Romantic Theory and the Critical Tradition*, New York: Norton, 1958, p. 220.

would have placed them in a relation of mutual dependence from the beginning. Again, for Coleridge to assert that the imagination has the power to dissolve indicates that he assumed for its elements a certain initial discreteness as of disparate chemical elements before synthesis into a compound. The opposition between fancying and creating can now be interpreted as follows: fancy must be content to *play* with fixities; imagination can go on to dissolve them into a unity.

If this is the case, then Coleridge has not really questioned the assumption that images are fixed elements. They are not basically vital for him. Only a special power can make one image fuse into another, just as special conditions may be necessary for two chemical elements to fuse into a compound. Synthesis is applied to the elements of the psyche as a form externally imposed on content. Such a formalistic, chemical conception of synthesis does allow Coleridge to transcend associationist psychology, but at the price of creating a dualism which leaves unquestioned the initial assumptions implicit in it. Coleridge's main concern is to separate will, thought, and attention from the control of the blind mechanism of association. He does not, however, deny association the role of supplying "to all other faculties their objects, to all thought the elements of its materials."[14]

Already we have seen how Dilthey proceeds much more radically in his descriptive psychology by making fusion the condition of the laws of association. Only thus could he challenge the very presupposition of traditional psychology that representations are the atomic units of mental life.

A proper precedent for considering fusion the basis for association can be found by turning to the Subjective Deduction of Kant's *Critique of Pure Reason*. This section, where Kant confronts the problem of relating the imagination to sense while nevertheless distinguishing them on

[14] Coleridge, *Biographia Literaria*, p. 73.

transcendental grounds, is worth examining because it contains epistemological notions about synthesis and synopsis which Kant never adequately explicated and which Dilthey helped to reconsider and reevaluate. Even though Dilthey does not expressly discuss Kant's theory of the imagination, an extended account of it is crucial to bring out the philosophical implications of Dilthey's own theory.

The Subjective Deduction characterizes the imagination as a subjective source that makes experience possible as an empirical product of the understanding (*CR*,A97f.). Kant claims that the imagination exhibits one of three modes of synthesis necessary for experience. All three are referred back to what he describes as a synopsis of sense. From a Diltheyan perspective, the way Kant introduces this synopsis is of the utmost importance, for here he claims that "knowledge is [essentially] a whole in which representations stand compared and connected. As sense contains a manifold in its intuition, I ascribe to it a synopsis."[15] Kant immediately adds that without synthesis this synopsis could not constitute knowledge of any sort. Nevertheless, synopsis remains presupposed by all modes of synthesis. Although Kant does not further explore this idea of synopsis, it could be compared in function to Dilthey's idea of *Erlebnis*. It constitutes a kind of original togetherness which then needs to be explicated. But because Kant characterizes the synopsis of sense as totally passive it can have no status in consciousness.

Only through the contribution of acts of synthesis can sense become intelligible. The most fundamental form of synthesis that Kant discusses is necessary for apprehending the manifold of sense in an intuition. A sense of the continuity of time is essential in relating different components of an intuition, for without the form of time the individual sensuous components of an intuition would stand apart as isolated moments. What would otherwise be a mere diversity

[15] Immanuel Kant, *Critique of Pure Reason*, trans. Norman Kemp Smith, New York: St. Martin's Press, 1961, A97.

171

of elements must be "run through" (*CR*,A99) successively in our inner sense so that they can be held together.[16] A formless diversity becomes a manifold relatedness of parts in a whole through what Kant calls the *synthesis of apprehension*. This synthesis seems to come closest to what Dilthey means by fusion. It is the least objectionable way of sketching out what Kant had called a "synopsis of sense."

Kant proceeds from his discussion of synopsis and the synthesis of apprehension to point out that representations acquire a more specific relatedness by having frequently accompanied each other, so that finally one can produce another even in the absence of the object of the latter. This reproductive relation is associative, but presupposes a special *synthesis of imagination*. Whereas Dilthey would consider the original unity of apprehension a sufficient synthetic condition for the possibility of laws of association and experience in general, Kant claims that we must also ". . . assume a pure transcendental synthesis of imagination as conditioning the very possibility of all experience. For experience as such necessarily presupposes the reproducibility of appearances" (*CR*,A101–2). It seems that for Kant the synthesis of apprehension cannot be considered to encompass anything but an indefinite totality, for in discussing the possibility of representing something complex, he says that "obviously the various manifold representations that are involved must be apprehended by me in thought one after the other. But if I . . . did not reproduce them while advancing to those that follow, a complete representation would never be obtained . . ." (*CR*,A102). A definite totality can only be represented by supplementing the synthesis of apprehension with the synthesis of reproduction. For as I proceed to focus on new representational components, I

[16] Immanuel Kant, *Kritik der reinen Vernunft*, *Werke in Zehn Bänden*, vols. 3 and 4, ed. Wilhelm Weischedel, Darmstadt: Wissenschaftliche Buchgesellschaft, 1968, 3, 163. *Durchlaufen* means not only "running through," but also "perusing hastily" or "surveying at a glance."

must link them with those previously attended to. The imagination thus has the transcendental task of reproducing the immediate past and linking it to the present.

Kant's use of the imagination to ground the synthesis of reproduction does not, however, exhaust his conception of the imagination. The imagination also serves as an intermediary between sense and reason. Its cognitive contribution cannot be fully assessed until it is related to the third kind of synthesis which Kant calls the *synthesis of recognition* (*CR*,A103ff.). This is a conceptual synthesis which allows us to account for the duration of a representation in time, so that something can be recognized as identical despite having been reproduced by the imagination. Such a synthesis is necessary if the vague totality of the synthesis of apprehension is to acquire, not only definiteness in terms of parts, but also a coherent unity. The recognition of an overall identity requires conceptualization, which according to Kant, "combines what is manifold, what is successively intuited (*nach und nach Angeschaute*), and what is thereupon also reproduced, into one representation."[17] Conceptual recognition involves not just a higher mode of synthesis, but actually encompasses the results of the other two modes.

Although the three forms of synthesis are developed "from the bottom up" (*von unten auf*),[18] the last is already presupposed by the first. Even the mere relation of parts apprehended in synthesis 1 is impossible without a special mode of the synthesis of recognition, namely, what Kant terms *unity of apperception*. This synthesis of apperception involves the transcendental consciousness of the cognitive subject's identity. As the most fundamental mode of synthesis of recognition, it is not to be confused with self-knowledge through inner sense and can only be expressed in terms of an abstract "I think." Kant transforms the Car-

[17]A103. I have here modified the NKS translation. Cf. *Werke in Zehn Bänden*, 3, 165.

[18] Cf. *CR*, A119 and *Werke in Zehn Bänden*, 3, 176.

173

tesian *cogito* into the transcendental principle of all knowledge. "The abiding and unchanging 'I' (pure apperception) forms the correlate of all our representations in so far as it is to be at all possible that we should become conscious of them" (*CR*,A123). Just as recognition presupposes apprehension, so apprehension presupposes pure apperception or self-recognition.

There thus exists a circularity in the Subjective Deduction which Dilthey came to accept as inescapable for his epistemology of the *Geisteswissenschaften*. Dilthey's claim that the understanding of psychohistorical reality involves a circle according to which no element can be understood apart from the whole of which it is part and no whole apart from its elements, is another way of questioning the validity of the constructionist approach in the *Geisteswissenschaften*. Specifically, it repudiates the idea of a presuppositionless philosophical starting point on the order of a mathematical axiom. From Dilthey's point of view, Kant was somewhat extreme in reducing the *cogito* from its Cartesian status as a metaphysical axiom to that of a transcendental epistemological presupposition. Abstract conditions of consciousness constitute equally inadequate starting points as far as Dilthey is concerned, so that instead, he begins with a more concrete sense of experience while freely admitting that its presuppositions need to be analyzed and refined. Thus the understanding of even the most simple human *Erlebnis* already presupposes some sense of its context, and that too will require illumination from other *Erlebnisse* and eventually the idea of an ordering self. Notwithstanding the abstractness of Kant's approach in the Subjective Deduction, the synthesis of apprehension does seem to provide the kind of contextual point of departure that Dilthey seeks. Although Kant describes his approach here as proceeding from the bottom up, it is not constructionist. The synthesis of recognition is not derived from the other two modes, but only loosely grounded in them.

The circularity that has been discerned in the analysis of

the subjective conditions of knowledge will be seen to involve a tension which Kant wants to resolve in the *Critique of Pure Reason* as a whole. But for the time being we are not interested in how Kant proceeded to unify his conception of synthesis by making the synthesis of recognition all-determinant from the objective standpoint. Instead, we will link Kant's three epistemological modes of synthesis to three kinds of synthesis that Dilthey analyzed in the context of his moral theory. By mutually illuminating theoretical and practical conceptions of synthesis, the different possible meanings of synthesis can be tested for their relevance to Dilthey's aesthetic concerns.

Three Kinds of Synthesis

In Dilthey's inaugural dissertation, "Versuch einer Analyse des moralischen Bewusstseins," written in 1864, three kinds of synthesis are distinguished to account for the variety of ways in which moral judgments make claims on us (*GS*,VI,25–28). We find here an elaboration or reinterpretation of Kant's synthetic a priori categorical imperative in terms of Dilthey's own attempt to approach the problem of moral consciousness from a psychohistorical perspective. The fact that this section on synthesis was repeated verbatim in Dilthey's lectures on a "System der Ethik"—delivered in 1890—means that it cannot be discounted as a youthful aberration. Although we have seen that the concept of synthesis is avoided in certain psychological contexts, it is not systematically rejected. Dilthey's lectures on ethics show that he does not simply dismiss synthesis as a chemical or organic concept, but considers it to have a heuristic philosophical value, at least when used in a specified sense.

Dilthey writes that, "something synthetic underlies our moral consciousness. This can be conceived as a unity (*Einheit*), as an unsurveyable plurality (*Vielheit*), or as a structured totality (*aus verschiedenen Gliedern bestehende Mehrheit*) . . ." (*GS*,X,108). Synthesis is thus conceived in

175

terms of the Kantian categories of (1) unity, (2) plurality, and (3) totality. Dilthey's subsequent characterization of various traditional moral theories indicates that these alternatives can be further explicated into the following more specific conceptions of synthesis: (1) *a strict unifying bond*, (2) *a harmonious grouping*, and (3) *a comprehensive totality* (*GS*,X,108ff.). Accordingly, they roughly resemble the three modes of synthesis of Kant's Subjective Deduction, if taken in reverse order: the synthesis of recognition involves a strict bond; the synthesis of reproduction a harmonious plurality; and because what Kant calls "apprehension" is for Dilthey an initial mode of understanding, the synthesis of apprehension can already be referred to as a comprehensive totality.

In terms of ethical obligation, the three modes of synthesis manifest themselves in what Dilthey distinguishes as (1) a bond of duty, (2) a sense of sympathy with others, and (3) a consciousness of ideals (*GS*,X,109f.). Kant's own interpretation of the moral claim was in terms of the first kind of synthesis. But for Dilthey the bond of duty imposed on the individual by a law of reason is too abstract to do justice to our moral experience. The second kind of synthesis which reduces the moral order to a kind of harmony is treated no less critically. Once again J. S. Mill becomes Dilthey's target. Mill's utilitarian faith in a harmony of private interests is exposed as involving a conception of man's social nature which is too liberal or too loose to serve as the sole base of morality (*GS*,X,39). His appeal to sympathy ". . . already presupposes a consciousness of some bond, some sense of community that supports it" (*GS*,X,80).

What characterizes the third mode of ethical synthesis is the claim that an ideal exerts on an individual. Compared to the abstract and negative demands of duty, an ideal provides a concrete and positive goal for action. Dilthey's constant reference here to the perfection of the moral organization of man is reminiscent of the concept of the external organization of society discussed in chapter 1, and suggests that these ideals are communal. Nevertheless, the occurrence of the expression "creative synthesis" in this context is puzzling. Is it meant to apply to the ideals of individuals or to those of the community at large? We have already pointed to the pejorative use of the concept of creative synthesis in the *Ideen* which was published four years after the "System der Ethik" was written. It is possible that Dilthey changed his mind about creative synthesis during those four years. Or we could suppose that he was willing to consider the concept appropriate in ethical theory which discusses values and not in a fundamental *Geisteswissenschaft* like psychology which studies individual processes having representational content. Finally, it might be argued that in his lectures on ethics Dilthey was willing to borrow certain phrases from the idealists in order to acknowledge the sources for this particular ethical approach without, however, endorsing the concepts involved.

In any case, it is clear that this third kind of synthesis could not form the sole basis for moral action either. Just as Kant and Mill were the respective representatives of the first two moral approaches, Hegel's attempt to overcome the abstract morality (*Moralität*) of the Kantian categorical imperative in terms of a more concrete and affirmative ethical system (*Sittlichkeit*) could be interpreted as typical of the third approach. However, Hegel's mode of synthesis is not allowed to predominate over the others. Accordingly, Dilthey continues to use the more neutral concept of moral theory while referring to ethical problems.

True to his general method, Dilthey proclaims that only by preserving all three synthetic approaches can one do justice to our moral experience. "All these forms intersect (*kreuzen sich*): in life by supporting each other, in moral theory by competing for dominance" (*GS*,X,110). There is then no way in which these three modes of synthesis can themselves be synthesized. No grand synthetic system of ethics, no overall constructionist approach to the problems of morality is possible. There exist three disparate synthetic

177

methods each of which has only a limited application. Any attempt to generalize them into a comprehensive method arouses Dilthey's suspicion.

Dilthey's own methodological concerns were on the whole negative, i.e. to show that no single method can do justice to reality, that the *Naturwissenschaften* and *Geisteswissenschaften* must stress different methods. Thus psychic chemistry needed to be refuted because it appealed to a special synthesis as a general ad hoc device which served nicely to keep intact the constructionist ideals erroneously adopted in psychology from the natural sciences.

Dilthey's methodological ideal for a system of the human studies independent of the natural sciences is summarized in the following remarks about psychology:

> Psychology must take the opposite path to that taken by the representatives of the constructionist method. . . . She must start with developed psychic life, not derive it from elementary processes. Certainly, analysis and synthesis and, subordinate to them, induction and deduction, cannot be sundered totally in psychology. They condition each other in the living process of knowledge like inhaling and exhaling, to use Goethe's beautiful phrase. . . . But it is crucial that the course of psychology be exclusively descriptive and analytic, even though synthetic acts of thought are necessary in the service of this procedure. [*GS*,V,168–69]

Synthesis is not denied its role, even in psychology. However, because psychology is not a natural science, synthesis must be kept subservient to analysis. Psychic life is too subtle to be reproduced by any artificial conceptual devices. Once we analyze a psychic process into its parts it is hopeless to try to completely reconstruct the original totality. What is even more important, according to Dilthey, is that we never needed to construct this totality in the first place. It was possible to experience it and it is possible to recollect it.

Synthesis is kept subordinate in Dilthey's methodological considerations because synopsis is presupposed as a fundamental trait of psychic life. This still leaves open the question of the relationship between the imagination and synthesis. It is especially useful to consider the feasibility of defining the imagination in terms of the three kinds of synthesis we have just discussed. In fact, most theories of the imagination have reduced it to (1) a mode of objective or unifying synthesis or (2) a subjective or harmonizing synthesis or (3) a kind of ideal projective or expressive synthesis. All three senses of imaginative synthesis are exhibited in Kant's works, the first in the *Critique of Pure Reason*, the other two in the *Critique of Judgment*.

The following attempt to illustrate ways in which Dilthey's theory of the imagination provides alternatives to Kant's special conceptions of the imagination, is at the same time intended to lay the basis for understanding the fundamental context established for Dilthey's theoretical approach by Kant's aesthetic reflections. Although none of the three senses of synthesis could satisfy Dilthey in his description of the poetic imagination, such differences do not preclude our exploring his underlying affinities with Kant in the following chapter.[19]

[19] It is thus important to challenge Hugo Krakauer's thesis that Dilthey was fundamentally opposed to Kant's philosophy: "In seinem ganzen Wesen fühlte sich Dilthey Kant entgegengesetzt, wenn er auch an vielen Stellen mit höchster Achtung von Kants Kritizismus spricht. . . . So möchten wir auf Dilthey selber den Satz anwenden, mit dem er Hegels Gesinnung Kant gegenüber charakterisiert hat! 'Er hat Kant gegenüber eine Stimmung, die eigen gemischt ist aus Ehrfurcht und aus tiefer Abneigung.'" Hugo Krakauer, *Diltheys Stellung zur theoretischen Philosophie Kants*, Breslau: Koebner'sche Verlagsbuchhandlung, 1913, p. 34. Some citations from Dilthey's *Antrittsvorlesung in Basel* of 1867 can show a basically favorable attitude towards Kant: "Denn mir scheint das Grundproblem der Philosophie von Kant für alle Zeiten festgestellt zu sein. . . . Und ebenso unantastbar in seinem grossen Zügen, obwohl mancher Reform im einzelnen bedürftig, erscheint mir Kants Resultat." *GS*, V, 12. This more than just "respectful" evaluation is confirmed by the way Dilthey characterized

Imagination as Synthetic and as Analytic

The classical locus of a concept of the imagination defined as synthetic in the first sense of producing a strict objective unity is Kant's chapter on the schematism in the *Critique of Pure Reason*. Whereas the Subjective Deduction had pointed to the autonomy of the imagination, Kant's overall epistemological concern with the objectivity of empirical knowledge led him to stress the determinant role of the transcendental unity of apperception in relation to the synthesis of imagination. Thus towards the end of the Transcendental Deduction, Kant draws the following conclusion: "The objective unity of all empirical consciousness in one consciousness, that of original apperception, is thus the necessary condition of all possible perception; and [this being recognized we can prove that] the affinity of all appearances, near or remote, is a necessary consequence of a synthesis in imagination which is grounded *a priori* on rules" (*CR*,A123). It is evident from the context that the a priori rules on which the synthesis of the imagination is based are rules of the understanding. Whereas in the earlier subjective part of the Transcendental Deduction Kant had spoken of the imagination reproducing according to rules which nevertheless are not formulable in conceptual terms in that they precede the synthesis of recognition in a concept, now rules as such are defined as products of the understanding. By characterizing the understanding as the *faculty of rules* (*CR*,A126), Kant can justify his claim that "in the under-

---

his task as a Critique of Historical Reason throughout his life. Again, if he had really found Kant as repugnant as Krakauer suggests, he surely would not have been the one to conceive of the definitive *Akademieausgabe* of Kant's works, negotiate its support, and then agree to accept the time-consuming task of chairing the committee of editors responsible for it. See *Briefwechsel zwischen Wilhelm Dilthey und dem Grafen Paul Yorck von Wartenburg, 1877–1897*. Ed. Sigrid von der Schulenburg Halle a.d.S.: Max Niemeyer, 1923, pp. 170, 181, 186.

standing there are then pure *a priori* modes of knowledge which contain the necessary unity of the pure synthesis of imagination in respect of all possible appearances" (*CR*,A119).

One could argue that the confusion about the autonomy of the imagination can be dispelled by considering the principle of apperception as the necessary condition for the *possibility* of objective knowledge, and the imagination as the necessary but subjective form for the *actualization* of this knowledge. However, it cannot be denied that the attempt to proceed genetically from a loose synthesis of apprehension to the strict unity of recognition by way of the synthesis of the imagination is compromised by the need to subsume the transcendental function of the imagination under the categories of the understanding. To the extent that the synthesis of imagination produces an objective affinity of representations, it loses its autonomy.

This tension between subjective and objective considerations is avoided in the Transcendental Deduction of the second edition. In this revised version no attempt is made to proceed genetically from the subjective sources of knowledge to the objective justification of its products. On the contrary, Kant reverses the order in which he treats these three modes of synthesis. The synthesis of apprehension is discussed last and is derived from the synthesis of apperception as an empirical application (*CR*,B160,B164). Only the synthesis of apperception and the synthesis of imagination are still described as transcendental activities (*CR*,B151). But Kant retains the transcendental function of the synthesis of the imagination by reducing it to a figurative mode of the synthesis of apperception. To the extent that the imagination is acknowledged to be spontaneous at all, it is defined as "a faculty which determines the sensibility *a priori*; and its synthesis of intuitions, conforming as it does to the *categories* . . . is an action of the understanding on the sensibility . . ." (*CR*,B152).

There is really just one mode of transcendental synthesis,

of which the *productive* synthesis of the imagination is a mere application. What was distinguished in the first edition as a *transcendental* imaginative synthesis of *reproduction* is now discussed only in terms of the psychological or empirical realm of association. The productive imagination is no more autonomous than the reproductive imagination. Both apply rules imposed by the understanding: the former in a pure manner, the latter empirically. Any semblance of spontaneity that the imagination may have had in the first edition vanishes in the second. It is clear now that the imagination cannot function as an independent intermediary between sense and understanding. Whether or not Kant dropped the Subjective Deduction only for the tactical reasons he gives in the preface to the second edition, it has had the effect of stressing a dualism of intellect and sense, form and content that Dilthey finds objectionable and in need of reform.

Everything that Dilthey considers questionable about Kant can be located in his doctrine of the "*epigenesis* of pure reason" as formulated in the revised Transcendental Deduction (*CR*,B167). The relationship of this notion of the self-determination of reason to the already discussed idea of spontaneous genesis can be more clearly understood from Kant's discussion of the naturalistic mode of epigenesis in the "Critique of Teleological Judgment." Epigenesis is there characterized as a mitigated form of the preformation theory according to which the development of life is not merely the unravelling of an explicit natural scheme, but is "self-generating" (*selbst-hervorbringend*) in the sense of adding something to an implicit scheme.[20] Applied to the problems of reason, epigenesis shows that the categories of the understanding are not a priori in the sense of necessary dispositions implanted in us, but in the sense of being self-generated or "self-thought" (*CR*,B167). The notion of the a priori is saved by dropping the appendage of innateness. Kant realizes that if the categories were innate

[20] *CJ*, 273; and *Werke in Zehn Bänden*, 8, 545.

ideas implanted in us, then our objective knowledge would be just as much determined from without as the empiricists claim and just as much subject to doubt.

Kant's genetic account of synthesis assumed something as given at each stage. But according to the a priori perspective of epigenesis, the given itself presupposes the synthetic activity of the understanding. Thus even the synopsis of sense can have no objective significance apart from conceptual synthesis.

In 1892, Dilthey presented his paper "Erfahren und Denken" ("Experience and Thought") to the Prussian Academy of the Sciences. It is an explicit attack on the Kantian dualism of sense and reason, according to which all form of sense is determined by the conceptual activity of the understanding. Dilthey proposes a conception of form that can be analyzed from the sense-content of experience, instead of being synthetically imposed on experience by thought. He claims that certain formal aspects of experience are already implicit in its psychological description, and do not require a higher transcendental justification.

In particular, Dilthey takes note of some inherent formal differences in the way the various senses present their manifold; thus he says that we can be aware of, or ". . . possess several tones at the same time and perceive their distinctness without juxtaposing them. On the other hand, in the domain of the senses of touch and sight only a juxtaposition exists. It is evident that the nature of the contents of sense . . . conditions the form of their connection" (GS,V,77). No epistemology can be adequate if it ignores such nonhypothetical empirical truths. According to Dilthey, it is one of the tasks of epistemology to clarify certain basic regularities provided by a descriptive psychology. This is not to deny, however, that as soon as psychology begins to incorporate hypotheses it becomes subordinate to epistemology.

Precisely because Kant considered himself to be above psychological considerations did his epistemology become powerless to criticize eighteenth-century psychological assumptions about representational elements and faculties. One of the purposes of Dilthey's descriptive psychology as a prolegomenon to any epistemology would be to weed out such historically conditioned assumptions as much as possible. Dilthey found such an empirical testing of epistemological presuppositions to be also lacking (and less excusably so) in the writings of some Kantian logicians of his own time such as Lotze and Christoph Sigwart. Dilthey agrees with them that synthesis is not given in experience as such. Yet this does not require us to go to the extreme of deriving it from thought. Instead of limiting himself to the Kantian alternatives of a *transcendental* logic which posits synthesis as a formal condition rendering sensibility possible, or a *synthetic* logic which actually binds the empirical contents of sense, Dilthey proposes an *analytic* logic. Rather than subordinate sense to reason, experience to thought, an analytic logic ". . . must seek a genetic relation here. It is clear then that experience is to be demonstrated as the primary phenomenon and thought as secondary" (*GS*,V,86). Or, as Dilthey said somewhat earlier in the same paper: ". . . we are led by the facts themselves to the postulate of an immanence of order or form in the material of our experiences" (*GS*,V,79).

Dilthey's call for a genetic account of immanent form has brought us back to Kant's notion of the synopsis of sense. But this could at best provide an implicit order which then required synthesis to become explicit. It is clear that whatever connectedness synopsis implied, it was not susceptible to analysis for Kant until mediated by synthesis, for he claimed that, "only as having been combined *by the understanding* can anything that allows of analysis be given to the faculty of representation" (*CR*,B130). For Dilthey, however, acts of synthesis are not possible until the original continuum has been analyzed. The question then arises whether the descriptive continuity to which Dilthey appeals should be characterized as synthetic at all. Here Husserl's conception of synthesis as a passive trait of consciousness suggests itself. Thus Husserl uses the passive synthesis involved in the consciousness of internal time as the framework for all particular acts of consciousness.[21] Passive synthesis is that kind of synthesis which must already be presupposed if any objectivity is to be constituted. However, Husserl puts just as much stress on active synthesis. In fact, he follows Kant by considering the imagination as a mode of active synthesis. It constructs possible objects of consciousness.

For Dilthey, on the other hand, connectedness is not merely the transcendental phenomenological background of experience, but is implicit in the foreground of ordinary experience itself. To make these connections definite does not require active synthesis, but analysis of the given.

Dilthey's critique of synthesis has now been carried from the scientific to the more general epistemological level affecting the imagination itself. The peculiar accomplishment of the imagination as Dilthey sees it is not so much synthetic as analytic. Analysis is ordinarily conceived as a mode of immediate inference that isolates a part from its general context. Naturally, we must rethink this discursive notion of analysis if we are to make sense of Dilthey's expectation that an analytic logic can discover "genetic" relations. Dilthey aims at a mode of analysis that can explicate without simply reducing scope. Instead of separating parts from their context, it must bring out their relationship to their context. Analysis as Dilthey develops it in the *Geisteswissenschaften* is much more a focusing on certain parts as central to a context than an isolated scrutiny of parts. Laws 1 and 2 of the poetic imagination can thus be called analytic insofar as they abstract from certain components and focus on others. Those remaining components are intensified to constitute a tighter, more complex model of the original image. It is law 3 which guides this process so that the sense

[21] Edmund Husserl, *Cartesian Meditations: An Introduction to Phenomenology*, trans. Dorion Cairns, The Hague: Martinus Nijhoff, 1960, pp. 41ff.

of the whole is never lost, but made more explicit. One way of understanding how genesis could be involved in such an analytic process is to conceive the need for relocating what at first sight may have been the dominant point in a complex impression. Many a point of impression can unify and condense what is immediately apprehended as meaningful. However, a shift to some special focal point may be necessary if we are to articulate what is typical in this complex. We have here a case of imaginative analysis that leads to something concretely typical and must be kept distinct from analytic abstraction in the service of concept formation.

Imagination as Harmonizing and as Intersecting

Kant, too, recognized that the imagination as an aesthetic faculty cannot stand in the service of concept-formation. Thus, in the *Critique of Judgment* he considers the possibility of a harmony between the imagination and the understanding, again allowing the imagination a certain independence. This is the most subtle of Kant's critiques because he rethinks some of the theoretical assumptions of the *Critique of Pure Reason* without abrogating them. He refines them in such a way as to give himself more room for human spontaneity without suspending the validity of the rules of the understanding. He grants the imagination its own spontaneous activity (*Selbsttätigkeit*), if not its own law (*Autonomie*).[22]

In terms of content, the imagination is always determined by the understanding, but considered as a faculty it can be granted a degree of independence. Whereas an objective judgment of experience requires that the content of sense be subsumed under definite concepts of the understanding, an aesthetic judgment, being subjective, only presupposes a general harmony of the faculties involved, namely, the imagination and the understanding. The aesthetic judgment does not evaluate beauty by means of conceptual rules es-

[22] *CJ*, 77–78; *Werke in Zehn Bänden*, 8, 324.

tablished by the understanding and therefore cannot be demonstrated to be universal. Yet such a judgment does indirectly lay claim to a subjective universality because the representation of the "mutual agreement" of the imagina-tion and the understanding on which it is based is also a transcendental condition for the possibility of knowledge in general. Referring to this agreement, Kant says that "this subjective relation, suitable for cognition in general, must be valid for everyone, and thus must be universally communicable . . ." (*CJ*,52). Although too indeterminate to be conceptualized or formulated by rules, this general condition of knowledge is felt in terms of the pleasure of the free play of all our cognitive powers.

Thus Kant posits a vague synthesis of harmony, not strong enough to bind the contents of sense presented by the work of art, but sufficient to refer the forms of representation to our feeling. When we make a judgment of taste we are primarily legislating to our feeling. This self-legislation or "heautonomy" (*CJ*,22) of the imagination reflects what Kant calls a synthetic a priori principle of feeling. However, in speaking of actual judgments of taste that pronounce something to be beautiful, Kant says that they merely *impute* to everyone the same feeling of pleasure relative to the same object (*CJ*,50f.). Because the judgment of taste cannot demand or "postulate the agreement of everyone" (*CJ*,50), it is not strictly speaking a priori. Kant is explicit about this consequence in the *First Introduction to the Critique of Judgment*: "Although a priori aesthetic judgments are not possible, a priori principles nonetheless exist in the necessary idea [*Idee*] of the systematic unity of experience. . . ."[23]

However, in the *Critique of Judgment* itself, Kant does make a case for considering the judgment of taste in terms of ". . . the general problem of transcendental philosophy:

[23] Trans. James Haden. Indianapolis: Bobbs-Merrill, 1965, p. 37. An aesthetic ordering of experience is suggested here and will be investigated in the next chapter.

how are synthetical *a priori* judgments possible?" (*CJ*,131). He points out that the judgments ". . . are *a priori*, or desire to be regarded as such," and that they are synthetic because they add to the intuition of an object ". . . something that is not a cognition, viz. a feeling of pleasure (or pain)" (*CJ*,131). Yet such a synthesis is not objective as in the first two *Critiques*. Kant does not claim that beauty is a property of objects, but simply speaks *as if* it were a property of objects (*CJ*,46f.). Our sense of beauty is thus fundamentally subjective.

This same subjectivity applies to the productive imagination, for Kant ascribes to it a suggestivity which allows it to go beyond the available concepts of the understanding and create aesthetical ideas. An aesthetical idea is defined by Kant as ". . . that representation of the imagination which occasions much thought, without however any definite thought, i.e. any *concept*, being capable of being adequate to it . . ." (*CJ*,157). With the aid of his theory of genius, Kant is able to counter the view that the productivity of the imagination is necessarily arbitrary. Although there exist no conceptual rules to guide the artist's imagination, if his work is to be considered art and not just nonsensical fantasy, it must still in some way be bound by rules. For Kant, these are rules of genius. The production of art requires genius which Kant asserts to be ". . . the innate (*angeborne*) mental disposition (*ingenium*) whereby nature gives the rule to art."[24]

By appealing to an innate rule of genius, Kant revives the problem of an implicit or preconceptual rule of the imagination which was discovered earlier in the Subjective Deduction of the *Critique of Pure Reason*. The following passage from the *Critique of Judgment* speaks of the impossibility of learning the rules of art and makes a distinction between *copying* and *imitating* a master artist which is reminiscent of the distinction between mere *associ-*

[24] *CJ*, 150; *Werke in Zehn Bänden*, 8, 405–6.

ative reproduction and *transcendental reproduction* made in the first edition of the *Critique of Pure Reason*:

> If now it is a natural gift which must prescribe its rule to art (as beautiful art), of what kind is this rule? It cannot be reduced to a formula and serve as a precept, for then the judgment upon the beautiful would be determinable according to concepts; but the rule must be abstracted from the fact, i.e. from the product, on which others may try their own talent by using it as a model, not to be *copied* but to be *imitated*. How this is possible is hard to explain. The ideas of the artist excite like ideas in his pupils if nature has endowed them with a like proportion of their mental powers. [*CJ*,152]

An artistic imitation is to be distinguished from a copy in that only the former goes beyond the original model of beauty. An imitation may seem like an analytical abstract, but in Kantian terms it is nevertheless comparable to a transcendental synthesis of reproduction which requires special mental conditions to make it possible.

In the case of scientific knowledge, Kant had disputed the theory of innate ideas because it would make the objective validity of knowledge an empirical hypothesis. But in the case of artistic productivity, special innate dispositions are accepted precisely as a way of marking off certain individuals with the capacity to produce aesthetic ideas. What is special about a genius is that his ideas transcend the specific conceptual limits of the understanding, and yet do not contradict its general legislative principles. In fact, far from running into conflict with the understanding, aesthetic ideas can come to contribute to its stock of concepts.

The imagination in its aesthetic roles is thus synthetic in the subjective senses of creating harmony and being suggestive. More generally, it serves Kant in establishing a harmony between sense and reason which at the same time anticipates a possible underlying transcendental unity for what is dualistically formulated in the first two *Critiques*. But unless these subjective aspects of imaginative synthesis are specifiable in more objective terms, they will not help to define the nature of the artistic imagination.

From the Diltheyan perspective, Kant would have to be criticized for allowing his concern with the role of the imagination in the architectonic of his philosophy to override considerations of how the imagination can itself create more concrete modes of order. If a pervasive sense of harmony and underlying unity is to be artistically fruitful, it must be possible for the imagination to also locate specific unifying points of impression in which comparatively different structures of experience intersect. Only as such can a suggestive harmony produce a more objective sense of order, for example, an apprehension of how the parts of a work of art create a unity of *interdependence*. Whereas an appeal to synthetic harmony tends to dissolve objective differences, the ideas of intersection and interdependence that have been discussed in Dilthey's writings allow comparative differences to be preserved.

Imagination as Expressive and as Articulating Poetic Technique

In order to overcome the indeterminacy of his aesthetic theory, Kant also added a discussion of artistic expression. Aesthetic creativity, or genius is thought to require special assistance from spirit (*Geist*) to be able to express itself (*CJ*,160f.). Alfred Baeumler has brought out the relation of *Geist* to *Witz* (wit), and this more colloquial term will often be used in the place of "spirit."[25] Because Kant defined spirit or wit as the "faculty of seizing the quickly passing play of imagination [characteristic of genius] and of

[25] Alfred Baeumler, *Das Irrationalitätsproblem in der Aesthetik und Logik des 18. Jahrhunderts bis zur Kritik der Urteilskraft.* Darmstadt: Wissenschaftliche Buchgesellschaft, 1967, p. 159.

unifying it in a concept" (*CJ*,161), what was termed a dependence of genius on spirit can be interpreted as a search for a determinate synthesis. Whereas genius suggestively goes beyond any existing concepts of the discursive understanding, wit actually projects new concepts to communicate what would otherwise remain ineffable. It must be considered as the synthetic power of expressing the aesthetic ideas of genius. What is suggested by the play of imagination must be comprehended and connected by wit. Once again, Kant is forced to impose a form from without, for the expressive power of wit is external to the creative power of genius. That a genius be able to express himself and communicate his ideas to others is left to chance, so to speak. The power of artistic expression is called a talent which must ultimately call rules of skill to its aid.

Dilthey's concept of inner form can be contrasted to Kant's concept of form, just as previously Dilthey's demand for an analytic logic was opposed to the synthetic logic of the Kantians. Analytic logic as conceived by Dilthey was intended to discover the limits of sense from within, rather than by subordinating it to transcendent standards of reason. Similarly, the concept of inner form allows form to develop from within the poetic image or *Erlebnis*. It is through the contribution of poetic technique that, to use Dilthey's own words, "the meaning of *Erlebnis* receives its articulation (*Artikulation*)" (*GS*,VI,217). Just as he had shown in the *Ideen* that the *Gestalt* of the acquired psychic nexus is articulated from a fundamental psychic structure (*Struktur*) through a process of development, so it seems appropriate to speak of the relation of inner and outer form as articulative, rather than as expressive.

If the *Erlebnis* is seen in connection with the total psyche, one can interpret the articulative process of the poetic imagination as a special mode of analysis. As indicated earlier, analysis need not be restricted to the abstractive and focusing aspects of the first two laws of metamorphosis. It may even be genetic as in the third law, but it should be realized that we are then only speaking of the unfolding of inner form, namely, of a meaning relation.

Although law 3 of the poetic imagination is called the law of completion, it does not involve the imposition of an external form on *Erlebnis*. The components added to the original image satisfy an inner demand. They are not synthetically added on, but articulated from the acquired psychic nexus which constitutes the guiding framework of imaginative metamorphosis.

Before considering the way in which the poetic imagination delimits itself analytically for Dilthey, it is important to examine the feasibility of improving on Kant's synthetic conception of the imagination by collapsing his distinction between aesthetic suggestivity and artistic expression. Whereas Kant had conceived of expression as a technical mode of externalizing aesthetic ideas, the exponents of the modern expression theory do not consider expression a technical term, but a properly aesthetic concept. They argue that the imagination must be viewed as inherently expressive and formative. Thus in Dewey's theory of art, expression does not merely unify and fix objectively what was first vaguely conceived by the imagination, but characterizes the imagination from the start.

Dewey's treatment of the imagination in *Art as Experience* has the virtue of taking the nature of the artistic medium seriously. He declares that the artist's imagery is not just free-floating, but already anticipates "the objective medium undergoing development." This does not mean that the artist must imaginatively project a work in all its details before actually executing it in terms of his medium. Expression is defined as the counterpart of a process of compression whereby what is imaginatively pressed outwards also receives a retroactive influence. Seeing what happens to one's medium can actually modify one's initial conception, and is not a secondary affair as in Kant. This gives the imaginative synthesis between inner and outer a new openness: ". . . the physical process develops imagination, while imagination is conceived in terms of concrete material. Only by progressive organization of 'inner' and 'outer' material in organic connection with each other can anything be produced that is not a learned document or an illustration of something familiar."[26] Because art will always evolve with man and his environment according to Dewey, technical rules can be assumed to be futile attempts to fix the expressive process.

Kant was willing to consider the synthesis of expression in terms of problems of technique because of its usefulness for classifying the arts in a comprehensive system. But such a closed synthetic scheme is dismissed as unilluminating from the perspective of expression theory. Thus Dewey tries to preserve the openness of the imaginative synthesis by speaking of expression in organic terms. He assures us that the artist's inner vision ". . . remains as the organ by which outer vision is controlled, and it takes on structure as the latter is absorbed within it."[27] The artistic expression may be imaginatively anticipated, but it can in no way be prescribed by technical rules.

Despite differences in the way Kant and Dewey conceived the relation between expression and technique, it should be clear that they both discounted the importance of technique. Kant acknowledged its artificiality by making it secondary to the imagination, Dewey by having the imagination preempt its formative role. Dilthey, however, does not consider the theory of poetic technique an artificial constituent of his *Poetik*. This is because he emphasizes the specifically historical character of technique in a way that Kant, the traditionalist, and Dewey, the natural evolutionist, could not. According to Dilthey, artistic form is unintelligible apart from technical considerations. An examination of the history of the rules of technique explicates what is already contained in the laws of the imagination, but always

[26] John Dewey, *Art as Experience*. New York: Capricorn, 1958, p. 75.
[27] Ibid., p. 268.

in an unexpected manner. "Only out of the historically obtained content of drama," says Dilthey, "is it possible to make its appropriate form understandable. Form is not universally valid, but relative and historical" (*GS*,VI,204). Outer form cannot be synthetically projected by inner form, but may be derivable from it in retrospect. This means that the relation of inner form and outer form is to be approached analytically, not synthetically—through retrospective articulation, not projective expression. Only when outer form has been realized can its meaning be analyzed in terms of inner form. There are thus certain aspects of poetic metamorphosis that should be articulated in light of the finished poetic product.

Dilthey's approach to the psychological development of individuality in the *Ideen* revealed a similar circularity. Although development leads to the acquired psychic nexus, certain aspects of development can only be understood by means of the final *Gestalt* or articulation of this nexus. Whereas any psychological description or explanation must go forward with the processes involved, Dilthey said in the *Ideen* that "knowledge itself can only go back analytically from the acquired psychic nexus to the conditions and factors of its development" (*GS*,V,214). Although developmental hypotheses were permitted, it can now be seen why their explanative scope was severely curtailed. Similar restrictions on explanation exist in the theory of technique developed in the *Poetik*.

The seven moments of poetic technique that Dilthey lists —"subject matter, poetic mood, motif, plot (*Fabel*), characters, action, and means of representation" (*GS*,VI,216)—do not constitute a set of independent conditions which if incorporated into the laws of the imagination allow anything to be predicted. We have already seen that an unbounded number of aesthetic principles were possible by analyzing feeling. Similarly, the number of technical considerations that could be opened up is indeterminate (*GS*,VI,202). As a consequence, any finite set of technical moments can at best point to a typical significance.

Each aspect of the executed work may undoubtedly be explained in terms of some technical rule derivable from a general aesthetic norm. But no matter how many universally valid technical rules a work may exemplify, as a totality it receives its meaning from the way they intersect. The work as an historical complex is not rule-bound. No artistic product can be explained in its entirety because its form is more concrete than the synthesis of its parts. Moreover, it is clear that there can be no synthesis of an unbounded number of aspects or qualities, but only a structural articulation where some become dominant and others submerged. This genetic structural relationship provides the key to Dilthey's conception of the historicity of technique.

The psychological concept of the articulation of individuality in terms of typical patterns finds its historical counterpart in the attempt to define a specific artistic style in relation to more general literary style-forms (*Stilformen*). Just as one can speak of certain natural phases in the development of an individual in his environment, so ". . . there exists a lawful sequence (*gesetzmässige Abfolge*) of style-forms within a nation" (*GS*,VI,236). There is a sense in which technological progress allows certain general technical aspects of style-forms to develop autonomously. However, this assures no corresponding stylistic or aesthetic progress. Indeed, as the style-forms available become more specialized and refined, it becomes all the more difficult for stylistic integrity to assert itself. Separate formal accomplishments only obtain aesthetic importance if incorporated in the overarching laws of poetic imagination, i.e. if they are more than means calculated to arouse specific effects. The predictable development of style-forms must be seen in relation to the unpredictable genesis of the inner form or individuating style of a specific work.

This genesis of inner form in terms of poetic technique

is sketched out in Dilthey's detailed discussion of the seven factors listed above. Of these, subject matter alone is never mentioned as a moment of inner form (*GS*,VI,202,228). This may be because in this respect the artist is at the mercy of the world and the data it provides in a purely external sense. The role of subject matter is analogous to that of the first sphere of feeling analyzed in the previous chapter: it supplies a necessary condition.

Moods are the subjective states that give the poet his first sense of control over his subject matter. They allow the poet to select from objective reality and intensify certain of its components. In this process, moods exhibit the working of laws 1 and 2 of the poetic imagination. Dilthey's treatment of moods raises the question of their technical value, for no really important correlations between them and poetry seem feasible until we see the third law of the imagination exemplified as well.

Only in the section on poetic motifs (*Motive*) does the *Poetik* itself refer to a unity of inner and outer that goes beyond the purely personal. There Dilthey admits that the "transformation of the subject matter under the influence of the various and contrasting moods it can arouse is further dependent on the ability to grasp the significance (*Bedeutsamkeit*) of the life situations contained in the subject matter" (*GS*,VI,216). The motifs in terms of which this significance is to be discerned are much less arbitrary than moods. A motif is at once more impersonal and more powerful in producing poetic metamorphosis. It is technically ". . . a motive power (*Triebkraft*) through which the material of reality is transformed into something that is poetically moving or effective (*das poetisch Bewegende*). . . . In a more comprehensive poetic work a number of motifs cooperate. Among them one dominant motif must have the impulse to produce the unity of the entire work" (*GS*,VI,216). This passage is reminiscent of the image-transforming powers ascribed to feeling and recalls our earlier discussion of the point of impression (see chapter

2). Whereas ordinary perception may suggest more than one point of impression, the artistic imagination must unfold the one fundamental point among them.

Dilthey claims that there are only a limited number of recurring motifs in literature. Unfortunately, he only provides one rather strange example: the fascination exerted by water of which Undine is the embodiment. A kind of natural symbolism possessing mythical significance is suggested by this, and will be confirmed in Dilthey's subsequent treatment of the means of representation. But first he moves on to a discussion of plot, characters, and action: "When all the genetic moments cooperate, a structure of the work arises through continuous transformation. This structure stands before the poet's eyes, as it were, before he can begin the detailed execution. Aristotle's *Poetics* designates this as the *mythos.* The German word for plot (*Fabel*) derives from the Roman *Fabula.* In it characters and actions are interwoven" (*GS*,VI,218). The structure of the plot in which characters and their actions are related is comparable to poetic *Erlebnis* and its capacity to structurally focus the cooperating powers of the psyche. The metamorphosis whereby an inner form unfolds in accordance with the acquired psychic nexus finds its technical embodiment in the plot.

At this point Dilthey comments on the importance of an historical study of literary structures. Literary history can confirm certain fundamental distinctions of genre which have threatened to become meaningless from the standpoint of expression. Thus Dilthey notes that epic poets do not need to structure the action as carefully as dramatists, but their plots seem to undergo more transformation during the actual execution of the work. Again, where theory can demonstrate that character and action are both necessary components of the plot, history shows that the Latin countries have concentrated on the play and counterplay implicit in action; the Germanic countries on the psychological reflection that goes into character portrayal (*GS*,VI,219).

It is in his remarks on poetic language that Dilthey most fully conveys his views on the inner-outer relation by making it clear that the words in which a poem is expressed must not be interpreted as a mere externalization. Dilthey reports Goethe's view that the image, the simile, and the trope are not added to what is felt, as a garment is slipped over the body, but instead should be compared to its natural skin. From this it is concluded that, "symbolic activity, which is the soul of the poetic process, extends throughout the body of the literary work up to personification and metaphor, synecdoche, and metonymy" (GS,VI,227).

Symbolic activity is recognized to be more fundamental than diction as such. It has its roots in the fundamental unity of inner and outer in *Erlebnis* where representation is symbolic of feeling. "If one understands by a natural symbol a representational content that stands in a steady, regular relation to an inner state, then a comparative consideration shows that on the basis of our psychophysical nature there exists a sphere of natural symbols for dream and insanity, as for language, myth, and poetry" (GS,VI,227). Dilthey speaks again of a limited number of basic myths, as before he spoke of a limited number of possible motifs. The symbolic refinements of poetic technique are rooted in the fundamental impulse of apprehending significance.

Dilthey maintains his principle of poetic continuity even when dealing with the final stages of the execution. "The nature of poetic creativity which shapes the motifs, the plot, characters, and action out of the subject matter," is according to him ". . . also the specific means of representation, even in the individual sounds of the latter. The style-forms enumerated by classical rhetoric and poetics must be interpreted from that standpoint" (GS,VI,226).

Therefore, problems of diction should not be examined in a study of rhetoric exclusively concerned with the effectiveness of language, and separate from poetics. The figures of speech used by the poet are not merely to be judged by the rhetorical concern of communicating the poet's vision to his public, but must also be judged as an integral aspect of the articulation of the poet's meaning. Style is designated as ". . . the inner form of a work from the initial process of extricating motifs from the material to the working out of tropes, figures, meter, and language . . ." (GS,VI,228).

The concept of inner form or individuating style encompasses the entire process of poetic metamorphosis including the very considerations of the sensuous effects of the work on the audience. However, when the means of representation are calculated with reference to the spectator, Dilthey reminds us that they must be referred to his imagination: "It is decisive . . . that the medium [of literature] may not be regarded simply as linguistic expression, as a succession of words. . . . The other moment of the means of representation, in which the total image develops and exists as a whole, is the connection of processes in the imagination of the hearer or reader made possible by memory" (GS,VI,209).

By means of this comment, Dilthey is able to free literature from certain of the restrictions that Lessing had placed on it through his analysis of its medium. According to Lessing's famous distinction between painting and poetry, they employ wholly different signs and means of imitation. The one uses forms and colors in space, the other articulates sounds in time. Lessing concludes from this that "signs arranged side by side can represent only objects existing side by side, or whose parts so exist, while consecutive signs can express only objects which succeed each other, in time."[28] Thus the poet encroaches on the proper domain of the painter when he describes a scene in any detail. What can be surveyed at a glance of the eye as existing in conjunction requires a long succession of words in order to be described according to Lessing. For the epic poet to depict more than those few aspects of a scene necessary for orienting the movement of the action is to expect of the listener "a great

[28] Gotthold E. Lessing, *Laocoon: An Essay upon the Limits of Painting and Poetry*, trans. Ellen Frothingham, Boston: Little, Brown, 1898, pp. 91.

effort of the imagination to very little purpose."[29] Poets should realize that there exists an inherent difficulty of recalling auditory "impressions in the proper order and with even the moderate degree of rapidity necessary to the obtaining of a tolerable idea of the whole."[30]

Such limitations on description in poetry stem from a proper desire not to have poets spend their ingenuity achieving effects that the visual arts could more easily produce. However, Lessing overstates his case. The fact that a poet is unable to evoke as graphic and accurate a picture of a scene as a painter, does not prevent him from evoking a stronger impression of such a scene. A powerful sense of the whole can often be better conveyed in the poet's words than by the painter's brushstrokes. Or as Dilthey says, alluding to Lessing's pronouncement: "From the fact that words succeed each other in time, it does not follow that the imaginative nexus arising in the mind is to be limited to a mere succession of images" (GS,VI,210). Poetic images can sum up prior images and anticipate others. Dilthey admits that a long series of descriptive passages is tiring for the reader if they only lead up to something else. Therefore, a dramatist or novelist should describe things that are of inherent interest and at the same time capable of evoking an imaginative context for the action portrayed. Implicit in Dilthey's prescription is the realization that the poet's skill with language serves to create pregnant images in which a whole scene is embodied. A certain part of a whole can be so metamorphosed as to become typical of the whole.

With his concept of *Erlebnis*, Dilthey is not faced with the dilemma that Lessing found insoluble. Even in its most technical elaborations, the poetic imagination remains a dynamic function whereby parts of experience are sensed in their living relation to the entirety of experience. The question of how the imagination can synthesize all the successive images evoked by words in a total image is no longer a problem. Once a fundamental continuity of images, of sense

[29] Ibid., p. 109.   [30] Ibid., pp. 102–3.

and reason, of imaginative unfolding and technical execution is granted, it is possible to dispense with the concept of synthesis in defining the imagination. The imagination does not possess the function of synthesizing in any of the three senses of synthesis discussed: (1) it does not need to produce a bond between separate images; (2) it does more than provide a harmony between sense and reason; and (3) it is not necessary for it to project an ideal totality.

In rejecting the imagination as synthetic, Dilthey does not fall into the usual analytic-synthetic antithesis. Accordingly, analysis is not meant so much to divide up a whole into isolated parts as to discriminate the parts in relation to the whole. For this particular mode of analysis, which keeps the whole sense of totality constantly in mind, the term "articulation" is probably most appropriate. Articulation produces no synthetic or projective leaps, but can provide a gradual, creative explication of how an *Erlebnis* relates to the acquired psychic nexus of which it is a part. Considering its ability to create a concrete unity for a continuum of images by focusing on a central or dominant image, we will henceforth call the imagination "articulative."

The introduction of the concept of articulation may also be helpful in reformulating the methodological results of chapter 1. We recall how the individual subject was interpreted by Dilthey as the intersection of cultural systems and the external organization of society, and how systematic attempts to create a grand socio-historical synthesis for the human studies were criticized for having overlooked the unity of perspective that is possible through psychological analysis. The ability of the poet to unfold a typical point of impression has therefore more than just an aesthetic import. In that the poetic imagination can be seen as a way of focusing on certain images as intersections of the cooperating functions of the acquired psychic nexus, the poetic articulation of inner form can stand as a model for the general process of understanding complex interdependence. Applied to the historian's task, it can help to articulate the particular

201

point of intersection which is constituted by a great individual. To the extent that it is possible for historical understanding to disclose that which is representative of an age in the biographical account of an individual, the power of the poetic imagination to articulate typicality amidst ordinary experience becomes a basic tool for human understanding.

PART THREE

A Hermeneutic Critique of
Historical Reason

CHAPTER FIVE

Reflective Experience and Historical Judgment

IN 1894, Windelband delivered a lecture entitled "Geschichte und Naturwissenschaft" ("History and Natural Science") in which he claimed that psychology has no intrinsic relevance to the historical sciences and should be considered a natural science instead.[1] Thus Windelband was one of the first of many who have denied that Dilthey's psychology could be legitimately related to historical knowledge or, more broadly, serve as the foundation for the human studies. To meet the objection that psychic experience is too narrow a base for human understanding, Dilthey suggests how a reflective mode of experience and a comparative method would allow his psychology to deal more adequately with the understanding of others.

The concept of reflective experience discussed in chapters 5 and 6 will be interpreted as a transitional link between Dilthey's early psychological aesthetics and his later historical theory. Although little noticed, Dilthey's remarks on reflective experience are significant in suggesting that his projected Critique of Historical Reason might be more properly interpreted as a Critique of Historical Judgment. Accordingly, Dilthey's rejection of the determinant claims of reason and his efforts to cope with the problem of intersubjectivity will be examined in light of Kant's discussion of aesthetic and reflective judgment. By thus referring back to the *Critique of Judgment* we can arrive at a Kantian mediation between Dilthey's psychological theory of the imagination and his historical hermeneutics.

[1] Windelband, *Präludien*, 2, 136–60.

Comparative Psychology: From Reflex to Reflection

After the publication of the *Ideen* in 1894, Dilthey intended to continue his psychological program with a comparative psychology which would further develop the understanding of individuality given in the descriptive psychology.[2] Recognizing that the self-understanding of an individual will remain incomplete until supplemented by the understanding of others, Dilthey hoped to explicate our knowledge of others through their objective expressions and a comparison and classification of character types. However, this project became bogged down in controversy because Dilthey found it necessary to defend his descriptive psychology, not only against Neo-Kantians like Windelband, but also against the strong criticisms of some experimental psychologists. Its complicated history provides an interesting point of departure for defining Dilthey's position vis-à-vis his contemporaries.

In 1895 Dilthey sent an essay entitled "Ueber vergleichende Psychologie" ("Concerning Comparative Psychology") to the printer. This was meant to be the beginning of a larger treatise on comparative psychology. The first part of the essay contains an extended reply to Windelband in which Dilthey defends his general distinction between the *Geisteswissenschaften* and the *Naturwissenschaften* and reaffirms the status of psychology as a human study. This is followed by sections on the importance of the problem of individuality in the human studies and on the significance of the arts in providing "the first representation of the human-historical world in its individuality." The last part reviews the history of the comparative method in various disciplines as a background for its possible application to his psychology.

However, Dilthey withdrew the manuscript before it

[2] See above, pp. 138–40.

206

went to press.[3] The following year, he published under the more modest title "Beiträge zum Studium der Individualität" ("Contributions to the Study of Individuality"), those portions dealing mainly with the contribution of artists to the understanding of human individuality.[4] He thus dropped the final exploratory section on comparative method as a way of classifying such artistic insights, as well as his opening response to Windelband. Instead, Dilthey prefaced the "Beiträge" with a summary of the main principles of his descriptive psychology and a response to a highly critical review of the *Ideen* by Hermann Ebbinghaus, a prominent experimental psychologist.[5]

Dilthey apparently felt that before raising additional problems about the nature of comparative psychology, it would be better to clarify the particular way in which his descriptive psychology differs from the naturalistically conceived psychology of the experimentalists. Moreover, as Misch has suggested, Dilthey did not wish to elaborate on his disagreements with the Neo-Kantians at a time when even more serious conflicts with professional psychologists had arisen (*GS*,V,423). Although the Neo-Kantians differed from Dilthey in not wanting to reform naturalistic psychology, they at least saw its limits. While they denied the feasibility of psychology as a human study, they at least were equally aware that psychology as a natural science could not provide an adequate understanding of human individuality.

In his critique of the *Ideen*, Ebbinghaus argued that psychology as a natural science was already beginning to accomplish what Dilthey had set forth in his program for a

[3] The essay was first printed in *GS*, V, 241–316.

[4] Printed in the *Sitzungsberichte der preussischen Akademie der Wissenschaften*, 1896, pp. 295–335. Reprinted in *GS*, V, 265–303 as part of "Ueber vergleichende Psychologie." See *GS*, V, 242 fn. for further details.

[5] Ebbinghaus' attack can be found in *Zeitschrift für Psychologie*, IX, 1895, pp. 161–205. For Dilthey's response see *GS*, V, 237–40.

descriptive psychology as a *Geisteswissenschaft*. Only ignorance of the recent advances in experimental psychology could have led him to seek such an unnecessary substitute. Moreover, Ebbinghaus charged that Dilthey had been unable to keep to his own ideal of a purely descriptive psychology that would dispense with all hypotheses. For example, Dilthey claimed to have nonhypothetical access to the totality of psychic life, but his description showed that it is actually experienced in a piecemeal fashion. And since Dilthey himself admitted that the overall structure of the psyche is not directly apprehended through intuition, Ebbinghaus concluded that it was as much a construction or a product of inductive hypotheses for Dilthey as for explanative psychologists.

In his rebuttal, Dilthey rejects as a misinterpretation Ebbinghaus' assumption that he had meant to do away with hypotheses altogether. He had only limited their position and scope. However, he strongly denies that structure, a central concept in his psychology, is hypothetical. He refers back to the *Ideen* where he had stated that because consciousness cannot simultaneously encompass all the structures of the psyche, our sense of totality has to be articulated in terms of partial experiences of it. Such articulation involves elementary logical operations that are part of our experience as distinct from the discursive logical operations that go beyond it. Thus the elementary logical operation of abstraction transforms what is initially a concrete, but vague, sense of *connectedness* or purposiveness into a more definite functional *connection* where x is related to y as its purpose. Dilthey writes that "Only through abstraction do we lift out a function or a specific mode of connection from a concrete continuum. And only through a generalization (*Verallgemeinerung*) do we establish the ever recurring form of a function . . ." (*GS*,V,171). If functional relations are thereby rendered a product of logical operations, all this, nevertheless, "possesses its guideline in the immediate consciousness of the value of an individual function for the whole, which natural knowledge does not possess" (*GS*,V,173).

Elementary logical operations, such as abstracting and apprehending differences and resemblances, are inseparable from our experience and refine it without distorting it. Thus while psychic structure is not an immediate given, it is not by that token necessarily hypothetical, for it is possible to transcend the given without inference. The idea of mediation without inference is never fully articulated by Dilthey, yet it is central to his claim that in psychology, and the *Geisteswissenschaften* in general, connectedness or order is not a product of hypothesis as in the case of the *Naturwissenschaften*.

A hypothesis is never fully justified by the available data —it thus involves conjecture. As in all cases of inductive argument there is a nondemonstrable leap, a discontinuity between the generalization affirmed and the evidence for it. The elementary operations that Dilthey speaks of also go beyond the givens of experience, but in such a way that the resultant clarification is still continuous with the experience. Instead of creating an *inductive* ordering for experience, these operations might be said to *educe* an order that is already latent in experience. On this interpretation, the elementary logical operations assumed by Dilthey's descriptive psychology anticipate Husserl's program of phenomenological explication where an implicit sense of the overall structures of consciousness becomes gradually specified.

Part of Dilthey's difficulty in defending his own psychological method against Ebbinghaus is that he did not propose one of the usual alternatives to the inductive method of the experimentalists. He does not justify the idea of psychic connectedness either by another mode of inference (deduction) or by introspection (understood as immediate intuition), although he shows some affinities with the exponents of both. It is therefore simpler to grasp the way Bergson criticizes experimental psychology from the intuitionist perspective defined in his *Essai sur les données im-*

médiates de la conscience, or even the way the Neo-Kantians, from the perspective of a transcendental deduction of the unity of consciousness, ask the "critical" question how experimental psychology is possible. To clarify Dilthey's position it is necessary to challenge the assumption of both Bergson and the Neo-Kantians that any approach critical of the experimental study of external behavior must appeal to some antithetically defined touchstone, whether introspective or transcendental.

A brief comparison with Bergson will be useful at this point to show that Dilthey is not substituting a pure introspective psychology for experimental psychology, but rather proposing a reflective framework that can come to terms with both. Moreover, it can prepare the ground for delineating Dilthey's relation to the Neo-Kantians, who in rejecting both introspection and external observation as epistemological starting points, sought for a pure transcendental foundation. The concept of reflective experience will suggest a kind of intermediate standpoint in which aspects of both the introspective and transcendental approaches remain in contact with the empirical study of outer experience. The task of reflection is to discover a continuity between the inner and the outer as well as between the intuitive and the intellectual.

In his celebrated critique of the modern mathematical conception of time, Bergson (1859–1941) asserts that the natural sciences have distorted the experienced reality of time. Our intuition of duration has been corrupted by the effort to comprehend time through spatial analogies. The scientist measures time by analyzing it into a series of points. But once this is done, he is no longer operating with real parts of time, but with artificially fixed elements created by his conceptual analysis. From such abstract elements the original continuity and movement of time can never be reconstructed:

We can, no doubt, by an effort of the imagination, so-
lidify this duration once it has passed by, divide it into
pieces set side by side and count all the pieces. . . . Undoubtedly a continuity of elements prolonged into one
another partakes of unity as much as it does of multiplicity. . . . Are we to conclude from this that duration
must be defined by both unity and multiplicity at the
same time? But curiously enough, no matter how I
manipulate the two concepts, apportion them in various ways, practice on them the most delicate operations of mental chemistry, I shall never obtain anything
which resembles the simple intuition I have of
duration.[6]

We find here, as in Dilthey, an appeal to an original
wholeness of experience which no amount of imaginative
synthesis can re-create. However, Bergson extends this into
a critique of science which is so extreme as to involve the
rejection of all intellectual mediation and symbolic activity.
Because science analyzes intuition into fixed images, which
are then described in terms of artificial symbols, it can at
best relate them into partial systems by means of conceptual
synthesis. While Bergson allows that these specific scientific
systems have a certain practical value, they nevertheless
represent distortions of reality. Thus the attempt of traditional metaphysics to complete the sciences by further syntheses is misguided. Only a metaphysics which is recon-
strued as intuitive can encompass reality in its entirety:

If there exists a means of possessing a reality absolutely,
instead of knowing it relatively, of placing oneself within it instead of adopting points of view toward it, of
having the intuition of it instead of making the analysis
of it, in short, of grasping it over and above all expres-

[6] Quotations are from Henri Bergson, "Introduction to Metaphysics" (1903), in *The Creative Mind*, trans. Mabelle L. Andison, New
York: Philosophical Library, 1946, pp. 198–99.

sion, translation or symbolical representation, meta-physics is that very means. *Metaphysics is therefore the science which claims to dispense with symbols.*[7]

While equally distrustful of intellectual or metaphysical synthesis, Dilthey would find Bergson's creation of an abso-lute division between immediate intuition and all modes of scientific mediation unacceptable. Bergson regards analysis as a necessary counterpart of synthesis and dismisses it as well, thus ruling out Dilthey's redefinition of imagination whereby the continuum of experience can be articulated into an *analytic* unity.

When Bergson claims that, "description, history, and analysis . . . leave me in the relative,"[8] he is in effect chal-lenging the way Dilthey had attempted to provide a meth-odological foundation for the *Geisteswissenschaften.* From Bergson's perspective, the descriptive and analytical meth-ods of Dilthey's psychology can only provide a symbolic approximation of psychic reality—not the absolute intui-tion of it. However, Dilthey was convinced that descrip-tion and analysis could be developed as scientific methods of inquiry which would be able to do justice to life without imposing artificial forms on it.

Dilthey differs from Bergson in recognizing that intellec-tual operations are implicit even in what the latter calls "deep introspection."[9] In the *Ideen,* he had argued that the certainty of inner experience need not be compromised by the acts of mediation involved in elementary operations. Like Bergson, Dilthey points to the advantages of inner ex-perience or inner perception (*innere Wahrnehmung*) over against external perception of objects: "When I feel sad, this feeling of sadness is *not my object,* but while this state is conscious for me it is there for me (*ist er für mich da*) as

[7] Ibid., 191.   [8] Ibid., p. 189.
[9] See Bergson, *Time and Free Will,* trans. F. L. Pogson, New York: Harper Torchbooks, 1960, p. 231.

the one to whom it is conscious. I possess it in the mode of having full access to it (*Ich werde seiner inne*)" (*GS*,V,197). But this *Innewerden* through which we possess inner experience is not yet tantamount to introspective knowledge. Although *Erlebnis* is not phenomenal like external experience of nature, and nothing exists behind it as a thing-in-itself, its richness cannot be immediately grasped through intuition.

For Dilthey, a full knowledge of psychic life has to be mediated by acts of attentive perception or "observation" (*Beobachten*). In discussing the need for such introspective activity, Dilthey was aware that he must contend with the argument that the observation of one's own states is impossible. "To be sure, it would be impossible," he noted, "if it were bound to the distinction of the observing subject and his object. . . . [but] we must guard against transferring what takes place in the observation of external objects to the observant apprehension of inner states" (*GS*,V,197–98).

Introspection should not be interpreted as ordinary perception which has been turned inward. Just as *Erlebnis* is not simply a counterpart of external experience, so introspection is not necessarily subject to the limits of perspectival perception. The observation of one's own states can be distinguished from their immediate lived presence by the stronger activity of will necessary for attentiveness. Because this heightened awareness involves a mere difference of degree, Dilthey concludes that the original sense of being in possession of one's states (*Innewerden*) need not be lost in introspection. In neither case is there a subject-object distinction.

There is, however, one clear limitation inherent in introspection. Attentiveness cancels all states of confusion and arbitrary playfulness. "We can never," according to Dilthey, "observe the play of our representations or attentively apprehend the thought-act itself. We only know of such processes through memory. But the latter is a much more

213

reliable aid than is usually assumed. In particular, we can still seize a just interrupted process in memory like the last threads of a web that has been torn" (*GS*,V,198).

In cases when introspection may stop the flow of *Erlebnis*, retrospection has the advantage of leaving its original structure intact. But retrospection would seem to introduce the perspectival problem of distance. Dilthey did not go into this problem in the *Ideen*, nor did he seriously deal with the referred-to limitations of introspection. In his later writings he would express stronger doubts about its contributions (see chapter 7). But his claims for it had always been moderate. Although he defended introspection against those who would altogether deny its role, he never justified it as being a self-sufficient source of knowledge.

On the whole, Dilthey's general tendency is first to revise rather than to reject what he criticized. And it is precisely because he tried to retain what is of value in the old that his work appears tentative, even inconsistent, when compared with that of younger contemporaries like Bergson and Husserl, who more confidently announced radical new beginnings for philosophy.[10] In many ways Bergson was able to more sharply delineate his position, since he set aside certain traditional epistemological problems which Dilthey still thought worthy of serious consideration. This difference discloses itself in their respective philosophies of life and in the way they conceive the relation of the self to the world.

Both Bergson and Dilthey consider the concept of nature, as constructed by the natural sciences, an inadequate context for comprehending man, and replace it with the idea of life. They differ, however, in that for Bergson this means reinterpreting nature in terms of organic life forces, while for Dilthey it involves turning to the psychohistorical world instead. Vital impulse (*élan vital*) makes possible an im-

[10] Both were born in 1859, and thus were twenty-six years younger than Dilthey. Relations between Dilthey and Husserl will be discussed in chap. 7.

mediate contact with nature and allows Bergson to dismiss the epistemological problem of the external world. But for Dilthey, no matter how much man may view himself as part of life and his impulses expressions of it, there will always be something external about life's reality, and man's knowledge of it will always remain problematic. Man may be able to understand the historical aspects of life, but its natural aspects he can only explain by means of hypotheses.[11] The vital impulses are not in themselves measures of reality, for only through a recognition of a resistance to these impulses can reality come to be defined.

This thesis was explicitly argued in an essay on the origin of our belief in the external world.[12] Psychic impulses as discussed there are not grasped as an uninterrupted flow, but described in terms of the resisting pressure they meet. For such pressure to be recognized as a force independent from any vital impulse of ours, we must be able to preserve an initial volitional intention in consciousness and compare it to the actual outcome. This fundamental act of comparison is interpreted by Dilthey to be the source of the distinction between an ego and the world. To the extent that a consciousness of resistance as limitation arises, experience ceases to be a mere reflex mechanism of stimulus-response. Through reflective comparison it becomes defined in terms of an ego-world structure.

Although the external world is not directly intuited as for Bergson, neither is it a postulate of the intellect as for Descartes. Thus Dilthey writes that "the theory of the immediate givenness of the reality of the external world does not ... prove valid. On the other hand, we would like to establish that the reality of the external world is *not inferred* from the data of consciousness, i.e. derived by mere thought processes" (*GS*,V,104). The reason that our belief in the

---

[11] See above, pp. 56–57, 134.

[12] Dilthey, "Beiträge zur Lösung der Frage vom Ursprung unseres Glaubens an die Realität der Aussenwelt und seinem Recht" (1890), reprinted in *GS*, V, 90–138.

existence of the external world comes with a sense of immediacy is that the process of comparing the ego and world is more elementary than ordinary discursive logical operations. Although the act of comparison involves a mediating process, it is already implicit in experience and requires no hypothetical inference such as would be necessary to give our belief in the external world the status of actual knowledge of nature. Fundamentally then, relating the psyche to the world is not to be seen as "throwing a bridge" from a primary ego to a hypothetical world in the Cartesian manner.[13]

Dilthey's position here represents a partial reform of the phenomenalist approach to the problem of the external world. According to Dilthey, *phenomenalism* constitutes an unwarranted intellectualization of an insight which he himself accepts as the first axiom of philosophy. This axiom of *phenomenality* (*Phänomenalität*), as Dilthey calls it, affirms that everything existing for me must be a fact of my consciousness (*GS*,V,90). Phenomenalism goes beyond this valid axiom by considering everything as synthetic constructs of mental representations or ideas. Although critical of phenomenalism, Dilthey is careful to distinguish it from *solipsism*, which is an even more extreme interpretation of phenomenality. The solipsist maintains that nothing exists independent of the constituting power of consciousness. In other words, he considers all of reality a product of his ego (*GS*,V,91f.). Just as Dilthey's position differs from phenomenalism by not considering the existence of the external world an intellectual hypothesis, so it differs from solipsism by not considering the world dependent on the will of the ego. Although solipsists may be credited for acknowledging the role that the will plays in our belief in the external world, they use the concept of the will inappropriately to create an egocentric epistemology.

[13] Dilthey, *Briefwechsel zwischen Wilhelm Dilthey und dem Grafen Paul Yorck von Wartenburg, 1877–1897*, p. 55.

The fundamental reason why the mediation required to disclose the external world involves no leap of inference, no "bridge-building," is that Dilthey does not start with an ego. The psychological description of the continuum of consciousness does not require us to posit any a priori ego as the carrier of the processes involved. The ego is differentiated out of consciousness as the correlate of the world. It is the recognition of resistance as limitation of impulse that produces a consciousness of self as distinct from the other. In that the mediation requisite for the belief in an external world distinguishes rather than connects, it is analytic. It involves fixing a certain intentional impulse and holding it up for comparison with a state of nonfulfillment. Discerning such an unexpected contrast is an essential condition for being able to articulate the distinction of self and world, inner and outer. It leads then to what has been described as an acquired psychic nexus which serves both as a storehouse of experience and as a guide to action in our surrounding world.

Individuality for Dilthey is neither ready-made nor merely a product of conditioning by the milieu, but must be articulated through consciousness as an acquired selfhood. Biologically, we are endowed with certain impulses with which to react to stimuli so that we can adapt to our milieu and survive in it. However, the psychic creature is such as to be able to differentiate his feelings from his intentional impulses. Once feelings come to constitute a separate structure within the psychic domain, sense-impressions no longer produce automatic *reflexes* but can be *reflected* upon and evaluated before we act on them (*GS*,X,48f.). It is the acquired psychic nexus that can help us to respond to our milieu rationally, adapting it to ourselves as far as possible and adapting ourselves to it as far as necessary.

Even though Bergson does not restrict the vital impulses to that which is biologically determined, they are nevertheless insufficient for dealing with the complexities of psychic structure and the historical world. Dilthey's theory of ex-

217

perience has already been shown to take both psychic and historical factors into account. However, the possibility of objective historical knowledge could not really be justified until after Dilthey expanded his concept of experience in his debate with Windelband to suggest a third mode—neither inner nor outer—which we will call "reflective experience."

Psychology, Historical Understanding, and Reflective Experience

Windelband's lecture of 1894 marked the opening of a long controversy between Dilthey and the Neo-Kantians over the theory of the *Geisteswissenschaften*. Dilthey's distinction between the *Geisteswissenschaften* and *Naturwissenschaften* founders, Windelband claimed, when applied to psychology, a discipline where a classification based on subject matter proves totally inadequate. He grants that, "according to its subject matter, it can only be characterized as a *Geisteswissenschaft* and, in a certain sense, as the foundation of all the others. However, according to its procedure or method, psychology is from beginning to end a *Naturwissenschaft*."[14]

Windelband suggests that any subject-matter distinction between the natural sciences and the human studies should be dropped, and proposes in its place his formal or methodological distinction between the nomothetic and idiographic sciences. The nomothetic sciences establish lawful uniformities, while the idiographic sciences describe unique historical patterns. In this schema, psychology would be grouped among the *Naturwissenschaften* because it aims at laws. Most of the remaining so-called *Geisteswissenschaften* would be listed as historical sciences because of their interest in individual *Gestalten*.[15]

Although he had not been specifically named, Dilthey

14 Windelband, *Präludien*, 2, 143.
15 Ibid., pp. 143–44.

218

recognized the importance of meeting this challenge to his distinction between the *Geisteswissenschaften* and *Naturwissenschaften* if his psychological program were to remain relevant to the problem of historical understanding. Thus he incorporated a timely response to Windelband in the original 1895 essay on comparative psychology. In addition to restating some of his own principles, he counters by exposing weaknesses in Windelband's methodological distinction. All the *Naturwissenschaften* cannot be simply classified as nomothetic, for such generally accepted natural sciences as astronomy and biology are also idiographic in their descriptions and classifications. More importantly, Dilthey objects to the use of the nomothetic-idiographic distinction to single out and separate psychology from the other *Geisteswissenschaften*. If Windelband is to be consistent, economics, linguistics, and aesthetics should also be considered natural sciences, because they too arrive at generalizations (*GS*,V,257).

It should be noted, however, that in this particular line of argument Dilthey is oversimplifying Windelband's approach. For Windelband recognized that economics contains certain generalizations but did not disqualify it as a historical science because he thought its primary concern was to describe economic systems in their concrete workings. On the other hand, he classified psychology as a natural science because he viewed it as aiming exclusively at general laws. It is precisely this assumption about the nomothetic nature of psychology that Dilthey had rightly brought into question. His effort to describe inner experience and articulate the development of individuality allows his psychology to approximate Windelband's idiographic ideal as much as does economics. Moreover, it seems clear that in economics, description of concrete patterns is for the sake of generalization, whereas in Dilthey's psychology generalizations are used for understanding the historical uniqueness of individuals. Speaking specifically of comparative psychology, Dilthey points out that it shares many of the same concerns with history; both are interested in understanding the singular through a sense of contrast (*GS*,V,256).

If the full consequences of Windelband's proposal were to be drawn, each of the *Geisteswissenschaften*, including psychology, would have to be sundered into a nomothetic and an idiographic part. But Dilthey warns that this kind of separation would strip all the human studies of their significance, for historical data only become meaningful if understood in the framework of regularities: "What is most characteristic of the systematic human studies is their consideration of individuation in connection with general theories . . . To elucidate this connection in psychology as well, is the very goal of the present treatise [on comparative psychology]" (*GS*,V,258).

Aware of the flaws of Windelband's methodological distinction, Rickert would in 1899 put forward more fundamental epistemological reasons why the Neo-Kantians consider psychology as inherently a natural science. He admits that because psychology relies on inner experience as opposed to outer experience, it is different from the other natural sciences in being nonphysical. This is due to the fact that inner and outer experience are exclusive and must be systematized separately. According to Rickert, such a division of labor necessitated by differences of content is of no logical or epistemological significance. Psychology is still a generalizing science which constructs a natural system of inner causality paralleling that of physical causality.

As an empirical science it is incapable of defining individuality, for it can study mental objects and processes but it cannot provide the grounds for the unity of the subject. "Because concept-formation in psychology refers exclusively to the *content* of psychical life, the logical unity of consciousness can never become its object. Indeed, *no* empirical science concerns itself with this form which properly belongs to the logical *presuppositions* of every empirical inquiry (*Empirie*)."[16] For Rickert, the concept of the ego must be grounded in an a priori epistemology, just as in his theory of history the concept of personality needed to be derived from certain ideal cultural values.[17] Here we find the strict separation of inner and outer, content and form, empirical and a priori that Dilthey's psychological and epistemological writings had endeavored to overcome.

Perhaps the main reason why the Neo-Kantians found psychology irrelevant to historical understanding, was that in divorcing outer from inner experience, they made psychic experience reducible to inner sense or perception. Thus in charging that "inner perception" is an inadequate basis for the *Geisteswissenschaften*,[18] Windelband revealed what Dilthey considered a too narrow interpretation of psychology, i.e. one that makes it too introspective. Always having been interested in exploring the relation between inner and outer experience, Dilthey now, in his essay on comparative psychology, points to a type of experience through which the two are more explicitly connected. He notes how in reflection, outer experience is related to the context of inner experience, without being totally dissolved into the latter. "The experiences that thus arise constitute a third class. They are analogous to inner experience (*innere Erfahrung*) and serve to extend our knowledge beyond the context of psychic life, beyond the horizon of inner experience" (*GS*,V,247).

Although Dilthey seems to present this third or reflective mode of experience as part of a review of his descriptive psychology, it represents an important advance in his efforts to include external reference in psychic experience. In his psychological aesthetics the objects of external percep-

---

[16] Rickert, *Science and History*, trans. Reisman, p. 49. Translation modified in accordance with the third edition of *Kulturwissenschaft und Naturwissenschaft*, Tübingen: J.C.B. Mohr, 1915, p. 53.

[17] See above, pp. 41–43.

[18] Windelband, *Präludien*, pp. 142f.

tion were incorporated by the psychic nexus in what was to a large extent an unconscious absorption into the structure of the self. Reflective experience, however, involves conscious comparison and, because the objects of external perception do not lose their identity, points beyond itself.

The concept of a reflective mode of experience will become important in showing how historical data can acquire a spiritual significance without being reduced to inner experience or losing their reference to the external world. Against the Neo-Kantian contention that his theory of the *Geisteswissenschaften* involved a material distinction of spiritual and natural entities, Dilthey emphasizes that reflection does not presuppose a special kind of spiritual object. Rather, this third mode of experience allows us to recognize any historical or natural product as having a possible human significance. As Dilthey says, "obviously the difference between the *Naturwissenschaften* and *Geisteswissenschaften* is not grounded in differentiating two classes of *objects* (*Objekten*). A distinction of natural objects and spiritual objects does not exist" (*GS*,V,248, italics added). Instead, he draws a contrast between physical and spiritual *facts* (*Tatsachen*) that does not require us to posit a material distinction between kinds of entities. Thus, the same data of sense may be interpreted as physical facts if they are placed only in the context of outer experience and as spiritual facts if they are either directly or indirectly related to the context of inner experience.

In extending experience to include reflection, Dilthey did not wish to arbitrarily stretch the meaning of inner experience. Although the historical world gains its significance through being related to inner experience, it is only accessible through the senses. "I assume that no sense-perception could take on the character of an inner experience," Dilthey asserts. "Thus it appears questionable whether the concept of inner experience can be expanded beyond its normal bounds so as to encompass this third domain of experience . . ." (*GS*,V,247). Instead, Dilthey indicates that he is only broadening the concept of psychic experience in a transcendental sense, for he claims to draw the inspiration for a third mode of experience from Kant's transcendental method.

Here we can see Dilthey undercutting the objections of the Neo-Kantians by developing some of the insights of their own master. Indeed much of Dilthey's work is best interpreted as an effort to establish a psychological analogue to the Kantian notion of legislating an order to the external world by means of a transcendental framework. Thereby Dilthey hoped to overcome Kant's dualism between the psychological and epistemological which the Neo-Kantians had so exaggerated. But Dilthey makes no claims for any fixed a priori categories which provide the spiritual or historical world its order, so that it was not without hesitation that he labeled his third kind of experience "transcendental."

Because Kant spoke of the transcendental as a condition of experience, it may seem perverse for Dilthey to call *any* type of experience "transcendental." However, he also uses the word "reflection" in this context, showing how inner experience naturally leads to reflectivity, or an "expansion of its horizons" (*GS*,V,246). Therefore it is less misleading to call this third kind of experience "reflective experience." In any case, Dilthey indicates that he uses the term "transcendental" only to mark a point of departure: "I will let this expression stand here at first, although it receives a more comprehensive meaning . . . since today transcendental reflection must naturally be related to psychology . . ." (*GS*,V,246).

If we look ahead to his later discussions of transcendental philosophy, we find that he uses the word in two senses. Thus at one point Dilthey identifies as transcendental, "every determination which has its basis in something trans-individual" (*GS*,VII,289), but then proceeds to attack transcendental *philosophy* for positing unconditional norms and transcendental egos from which everything empirical can

223

be deduced. Dilthey objects to the constructionist character that Fichte in particular gave the transcendental approach. In using the word "transcendental" Dilthey appears to distinguish a more general Kantian sense from a more specific Fichtean sense. As far as Dilthey is concerned, the Neo-Kantians of the Baden school—Windelband and Rickert— are really Neo-Fichteans.

Any suggestion that Dilthey is in some respects more faithful to the original Kant than the Neo-Kantians themselves needs some clarification, for Dilthey's relation to Kant is far from obvious.[19] Yet in speaking of the possibility of a more comprehensive meaning of "transcendental reflection" when related to descriptive psychology, Dilthey has suggested a real basis for claiming an affinity with Kant: the Kant who wrote the introductions to the *Critique of Judgment*.

Kant drafted two introductions to the *Critique of Judgment*. The one appearing with the *Critique* itself is a second, shorter version of the original introduction which was posthumously published (in 1922) under the title *First Introduction to the Critique of Judgment*. The *First Introduction* is especially interesting, for it indicates that the principle of transcendental reflection is incompatible with the ideals of explanative psychology, but not with the contributions of a descriptive psychology.[20] There are also some suggestive comments about the technique (*Technik*) of nature which were deleted from the second version.

Although the complete text of the *First Introduction* was not published during Dilthey's lifetime, he probably read the original manuscript since in 1889 he referred to its existence.[21] Having urged that Kant's scattered manuscript and

[19] See above, chap. 4, fn. 19.

[20] *First Introduction to the Critique of Judgment*, trans. James Haden, Indianapolis: Bobbs-Merrill, 1965, pp. 41f. Hereafter cited as *First Introduction*.

[21] Haden has noted in his foreword to the *First Introduction* that the manuscript was known to exist among a group of papers at the

letters be gathered together in a national archive, and a definitive collection be brought out by the Prussian Academy of the Sciences, Dilthey himself took a first step by publishing the correspondence between Kant and Jakob Sigismund Beck. In one of these letters Kant explained that he had withheld the *First Introduction* only because of its excessive length, and recommended it as "containing still much that will contribute to a more complete insight into the concept of a teleology of nature" (*GS*,IV,341).

We could well speculate that the *First Introduction* led Dilthey to claim in his lectures on the critical system that Kant's epistemology contained the seeds of a descriptive psychology.[22] But no direct influence is being argued here, for it is less important to establish that Dilthey was specifically inspired by Kant's introductions than to gain some cross-illumination by recognizing a continuity of concerns and insights.

Precisely because Dilthey did not himself explicate his idea of reflective experience fully, it is important to explore its relation to Kant's conception of reflective judgment. In addition to underscoring some of the differences between the Neo-Kantians and Dilthey, the following interpretation of Kant will provide an orientation in developing the implications of reflective experience for Dilthey's system of the *Geisteswissenschaften*. We will then be able to argue that reflective judgment is as essential for understanding the historical order of the human studies as it was for Kant's conception of the systematic order of the natural sciences.

University of Rostock "as early as 1889" (p. viii). That was the year that Dilthey wrote his essay "Archive der Literatur in ihrer Bedeutung für das Studium der Geschichte der Philosophie," in which he describes how the manuscript passed into the possession of the University of Rostock. See *GS*, IV, 567f.

[22] "Diltheys Kant-Darstellung in seiner letzten Vorlesung Ueber das System der Philosophie," in Dietrich W. Bischoff, *Wilhelm Diltheys geschichtliche Lebensphilosophie*. Leipzig: B. G. Teubner, 1935, pp. 55–59.

Reflective Judgment and Systematic
Order in Kant

In the introductions to the third *Critique*, Kant developed into an integral part of his philosophy the concept of transcendental reflection which had been only briefly discussed in an appendix to the Analytic of the *Critique of Pure Reason*. Whereas in 1781 Kant had spoken of reflection as a mere prerequisite for judgment which distinguished whether a representation belongs to sense or to understanding (*CR*,A261–B317), in 1790 he treated it as a mode of judgment itself. As such, reflection assumed a more general role, not just distinguishing the components of the cognitive faculty, but relating all the faculties to each other. Reflection then is used not to delineate the dualism between sense and reason, which Dilthey attacked, but to outline their possible unity. The introductions to the *Critique of Judgment* show Kant to be most acutely conscious of the limitations of a constructionist approach whereby reason determines sense, and we can also compare this aspect of Kant to Dilthey.

By including reflection in his concept of judgment, Kant was able to reconsider the problem of systematic knowledge that had been left as a task for pure reason in the first *Critique*. He had always been aware that the a priori categories of the understanding make possible the search for causal laws, but do not help to integrate such causal generalizations into any intelligible order. These categories do not offer us any scientific principles by which to unify empirical laws.

To know that all natural phenomena are subsumable to laws does not give any assurance that these laws themselves are knowable. Here Hume's problem of induction must again be faced, for Kant's claim that the cause-effect relation is a priori is not meant to exclude the inductive use of experience in discovering specific causal laws. If there exist an infinite number of laws, how can we expect to know them all and discover any order among them to render them more comprehensible?

But while Kant admits the need for empirical generalizations, he does not consider our overall systematic knowledge of nature to be purely inductive and hypothetical. His attempt to find alternatives to induction on the systematic level is of special relevance to Dilthey's own efforts to elucidate the way in which historical consciousness involves a sense of overall connectedness that is not hypothetical. Although Kant at first merely supplements natural hypotheses by a "hypothetical employment of reason"—a solution which could hardly be acceptable to Dilthey—in his last *Critique* we find a more adequate approach to the problem of relating the inductive claims of experience and an a priori need for order.

In the first *Critique*, the overall order of our knowledge is interpreted in terms of the architectonic of reason. The task of judgment in relation to the deductive ideals of reason is merely to apply this architectonic: "If reason is a faculty of deducing the particular from the universal, and if the universal is already *certain in itself* and given, only *judgment* is required to execute the process of subsumption, and the particular is thereby determined in a necessary manner" (*CR*,A646–B674).

When the universal is problematic, however, and only the particular certain, reason cannot provide us with any *constitutive* concepts for creating systematic order. Nevertheless, it at least must create certain *regulative* guidelines through what Kant calls a hypothetical use of reason. "The hypothetical employment of reason, based upon ideas viewed as problematic concepts, is not properly speaking *constitutive*, that is, it is not of such a character that, judging in all strictness, we can regard it as proving the truth of the universal rule which we have adopted as hypothesis. . . . The hypothetical employment of reason is regulative only; its sole aim is, so far as may be possible, to bring unity into the body of our detailed knowledge, and thereby to *approximate* the rule to universality" (*CR*,A647–B675). From the architectonic standpoint, the search for the concrete systematic unity of the knowledge of the understanding involves such a hypothetical use of reason. Here reason regulates the ordering of scientific data or laws in terms of what is only a projected ideal.

Kant points out, for example, that in practice the scientist must assume that, despite the infinite manifold of empirical data of nature, it is possible to devise certain heuristic principles of classification. He lists three such principles of ordering phenomena: (1) the *homogeneity* of a manifold under higher genera, (2) the *specification* of subspecies, and (3) the *continuity* of species (*CR*,A657–B685f.). Kant warns that if they are regarded as giving objective insight, irreconcilable conflicts in their application will arise.

> Thus one thinker may be more particularly interested in *manifoldness* (in accordance with the principle of specification), another thinker in *unity* (in accordance with the principle of aggregation). Each believes that his judgment has been arrived at through insight into the object, whereas it really rests entirely on the greater or lesser attachment to one of the two principles. And since neither of these principles is based on objective grounds, but solely on the interest of reason, the title "principles" is not strictly applicable, they may more fittingly be entitled "maxims." [*CR*,A666–B694ff.]

Strictly considered, these three principles are only relative and subjective maxims of reason, but Kant continues to ascribe an "objective but indeterminate validity" to them (*CR*,A663–B691). Insofar as they are unavoidable presuppositions for the systematic knowledge of nature, Kant speaks of the transcendental deduction of all the regulative ideas of speculative reason (*CR*,A671–B699). Yet none in particular seems to be capable of a transcendental deduction (*CR*,A664–B692). As such, the regulative ideas are subjective maxims and only indirectly receive their justification by being oriented towards an objective ideal of reason.

In the *Critique of Judgment*, the expansion of the concept of judgment to include reflection served Kant in effecting a more direct justification for such regulative ideas. The first *Critique* had dealt only with a determinant judgment according to which particulars are determined by universals. Even when we do not know the appropriate universal under which to subsume a particular, reason forces the determinant judgment to assume a hypothetical universal which can be applied to particulars. But once, as in the introductions to the *Critique of Judgment*, the faculty of judgment is considered in relation, not to the dialectical demands of reason, but to the empirical needs of the understanding, it should no longer be viewed as exclusively determinant.

We have already seen how in aesthetic experience, a determinant judgment is avoided by referring the representation of sense to the faculty of understanding in general, rather than subsuming it under an already existent concept of the understanding. An aesthetic harmony between sense and understanding is felt which focuses only on the form of the representation. Given such a play of the faculties, it becomes possible to consider whether the content of such a representation cannot sometimes suggest a new concept to the understanding—even if that would destroy the aesthetic experience qua aesthetic experience.

Since the understanding has only a limited number of concepts at its disposal, it must be supplemented by more universals. To meet this need, Kant introduces the idea of a reflective judgment which proceeds from particulars to universals as yet unknown (*CJ*,15). In the theory of reflective judgment the problem of inductive generalization is reevaluated in light of the nature of aesthetic judgment. Just as any particular liking of an art work is referred in aesthetic judgment to a subjective universality of taste, so reflective judgment points to principles having a subjective

229

ground. The universals aimed at by reflective judgment possess something like a hypothetical character; and yet if the activity itself is to have any justification it must, according to Kant, receive a transcendental deduction. Consequently, the regulative ideas that remained problematic and hypothetical from the objective standpoint of the architectonic of reason, become justified as subjectively necessary from the standpoint of reflective judgment. Kant speaks of the principle of transcendental reflection as self-justifying in the *Critique of Judgment*:

> The reflective judgment, which is obliged to ascend from the particular in nature to the universal, requires on that account a principle that it cannot borrow from experience, because its function is to establish the unity of all empirical principles under higher ones, and hence to establish the possibility of their systematic subordination. Such a transcendental principle, then, the reflective judgment can only give as a law from and to itself. It cannot derive it from outside (because then it would be the determinant judgment); nor can it prescribe it to nature, because reflection upon the laws of nature *adjusts itself by (nach) nature*, and not nature by the conditions according to which we attempt to arrive at a concept of it which is quite *contingent in respect of nature*. [*CJ*,16, italics added]

The supposition in the first *Critique* that "objects must conform to our knowledge" (*CR*,Bxvi), clearly does not suffice here in the third *Critique* when it comes to comprehending nature in its concrete totality. Reflection having now been defined as adjusting itself to (*nach*) nature, its a priori principle cannot be anything but subjectively binding. The transcendental deduction of order in the *Critique of Judgment* no longer appeals to an objective ideal, but to a subjective sense of the necessary cooperation of the cognitive faculties. The empirical unity sought for is not derived from any hypothetical idea, because such an idea would be "con-

tingent in respect of nature." Moreover, Kant seems to reduce the three heuristic principles discussed in the *Critique
of Pure Reason* to one "law of the specification of nature"
(*CJ*,22), which would mean that this law is itself capable
of a transcendental deduction. Kant no longer advances the
hypothesis that systematic order must be derived from a
fixed objective idea but suggests in the *First Introduction*
(p. 19) that the general concept by which one orders nature needs to be continually specified, i.e. revised in terms
of experience.

The centrality of aesthetic experience in the *Critique of
Judgment* thus gives a different character to the problem
of systematizing our knowledge. The systematic order, at
first derived from rational ideas, is now empirical and inspired by aesthetic ideas. In an aesthetic idea we have no
concept adequate to intuition. It is the converse of the rational idea where there is no intuition adequate to concepts
(*CJ*,157). In neither case is there knowledge. But rational
ideas never produce knowledge because they transcend experience, while aesthetic ideas can suggest new knowledge.
Through reflection new concepts may be created to express
what has been felt aesthetically. Although strictly speaking
the experience of beauty merely shows a certain representation to have a form which is purposive in relation to our
faculties, i.e. puts them in harmony, it is also interpreted as
encouraging our faith in the overall order of nature.

Establishing too direct a relation between aesthetic and
rational ideas would involve an uncritical synthesis of intuition and reason. Yet in the *Critique of Judgment*, Kant suggests certain parallels between aesthetic order and a rational architectonic that allow for at least indirect relations
between intuition and reason. Whereas the understanding
and judgment are merely concerned with the conceptual
problems of the particular-universal relation, intuition and
reason both operate basically in terms of the part-whole
relation. In the *Critique of Pure Reason* Kant overlooked
how the synthesis of intuitive apprehension as discussed in

the Subjective Deduction might have some affinity with the task of pure reason to comprehend the totality of knowledge. In the *Critique of Judgment*, however, Kant is willing to consider certain aesthetic analogues in human experience which make up for the limits of our discursive intellect.

Although in projecting the form of a system the whole must precede its parts, our discursive intellect can only construct a concrete system by proceeding from its parts. This is in contrast to an intuitive intellect for which an immediate knowledge of the whole is "the ground of the possibility of the connection of the parts" (*CJ*,256). Without denying his original claim that an intuitive intellect is a human impossibility, Kant now finds it possible to point to aesthetic apprehension as its approximation. In an aesthetic judgment we do not construct an object from representational components as we do in ordinary perception. Aesthetic judgment is more immediate than that. But the price we pay for this immediate apprehension of harmonious order or the inner purposiveness of a whole in intuition is that we cannot verify it by the agreement of others. Strictly speaking, the aesthetic judgment which declares an object to be beautiful does not provide knowledge. We only apprehend the harmony of the parts of the representation *as if* it were an objective quality.

But more than being an analogue of intuitive knowledge, the aesthetic judgment can be of indirect value in relating aesthetic and rational ideas in terms of what Kant calls "symbolical knowledge." Whereas discursive knowledge was defined in the *Critique of Pure Reason* so that a correspondent schematic representation is required for a concept, in the *Critique of Judgment* the possibility of a symbolical or indirect presentation of a rational idea is opened up. Thus concepts which have no direct intuitive counterpart can yet be granted a symbolical intuitive content by means of analogy. In such an analogy ". . . judgment exercises a double function, first applying the concept to the object of a sensible intuition, and then applying the mere rule

232

of reflection made upon that intuition to a quite different object of which the first is only the symbol" (*CJ*,197–98). The possibility of transferring reflection about an empirical object to an ideal object allows Kant to speak of a symbolical knowledge of God. If we choose a sublime but human experience as symbolic of divinity then our reflection on the former can in turn be transferred to the rational idea of the latter. Because we can never find a concrete representation of God in experience, theoretical knowledge of him is still denied. Nevertheless, we may find certain formal, aesthetic analogues in experience that will produce symbolical knowledge of him (*CJ*,198).

Symbolical knowledge of God as an ideal of systematic order presupposes reflective judgment on what lies within experience. Here there is no a priori conceptual schema or transcendent architectonic for judgment to execute determinantly. Perhaps this contrast between order derived from within experience and from without is best summed up in the *First Introduction* when Kant asserts that, "a basic distinction must be made between the determining judgment and the reflective judgment, only the second of which has its own a priori principles. The former proceeds only *schematically*, under the laws of another faculty (the understanding); the latter, however, proceeds purely *technically* under its own laws. Fundamental to this activity is a principle of the technique (*Technik*) of nature, hence the concept of a purposiveness necessarily presupposed a priori in it" (p. 52).

It would have been incongruous to speak of such an a priori technical principle or a technique of nature in the *Critique of Pure Reason*. From the absolute perspective of the architectonic unity of reason, "technical unity" had been described as merely a "contingently occasioned" order (*CR*,A833–B861). In the *First Introduction*, by contrast, technique is no longer construed as simply the mechanical execution of some architectural master-plan, but is conceived in terms of the creativity of artistic genius and the purposiveness of nature. What had at first been denigrated as mere artificial technical order is now rethought in terms of the artistic symbolism of a spontaneous technique of nature. This technique becomes valued as a way of appreciating unexpected design in nature:

> The reflective judgment thus works with given appearances so as to bring them under empirical concepts of determinate natural things not schematically, but *technically*, not just mechanically, like a tool controlled by the understanding and the senses, but *artistically*, according to the universal but at the same time undefined principle of a purposive, systematic ordering of nature.[23]

The technical and the artistic are here explored purely theoretically in the context of the metaphor of a technique of nature. Unfortunately, Kant did not apply these speculations about the spontaneity of technique in the body of the *Critique of Judgment*. Thus, as we saw in chapter 4, Kant failed to integrate the theory of artistic technique with his account of the workings of the aesthetic imagination.

However, from the theoretical standpoint of Kant's aesthetic of nature it is important to note that technical or artistic order is a specifically *human* sense of order. In the *Critique of Pure Reason* the idea of a discursive intellect applicable to any sentient creature—whether its intuition be "like or unlike ours" (*CR*,B148)—needed to be defined negatively in relation to a *divine*, architectonic order of reason. But in the third *Critique* the analysis of aesthetic judgment reveals how in man sense and reason are related through feeling. A reflective harmony of the human faculties allows Kant to suggest a more positive, if only regulative, sense of order. The idea of an artistic ordering of nature anticipates Goethe's poetic vision of nature. However, it can also be interpreted as preparing the ground for an aesthetic of history and Dilthey's ordering of the human studies.

In his lecture course on philosophical systems, which Dilthey is known to have given at least since 1898, he declared that Kant ". . . raises himself to the highest point in the *Critique of Judgment*. He conceives nature and freedom together under the concept of an immanent teleology of a wholly new kind. In this critically reflected concept, all the threads of knowledge and ethical commands, of reality and value are encompassed."[24] Although Dilthey gives no more specific reason for praising the third *Critique*, we can see that the concept of immanent teleology would be of particular interest to Dilthey, because it makes possible a nonconstructionist sense of order. Here Kant does not impose order or purposiveness from above as in his theory of epigenesis.[25] He establishes instead a countertendency of adapting universals to particulars and tracing the interrelations of parts and wholes. Thus in the case of symbolic knowledge as it was just discussed, the judgment first finds an intuitive analogue for a universal and then redefines the universal in the light of reflection on this intuition. This constitutes a clear case of the interdependence of particulars and universals and a model for the principle of specification, whereby a generic concept adjusts itself to the concrete instances to be encompassed by it.

Early in his career, on the occasion of his *Antrittsvorlesung* at Basel (1867), Dilthey had expressed the hope of finding in Goethe's intuition of a technique of nature the basis for a comparative study of man (*GS*,V,23f.), while avoiding the metaphysical excesses to which the intuition had led Schelling in his *Naturphilosophie*. Because he felt that the Romantics possessed valuable insights which could be reformulated in nonmetaphysical terms, Dilthey was able to take up Otto Liebmann's call "Zurück zu Kant" (1865), while at the same time stressing the importance of

---

[24] "Diltheys Kant-Darstellung," p. 51.
[25] See above, pp. 182–83.

the Romantic period: "Philosophy should return to Kant via Hegel, Schelling, and Fichte, without, however, silently passing over these [later] thinkers, who were able to enunciate the mystery of the world so successfully" (*GS*,V,13). In 1867 Dilthey could not yet have known that Kant himself had developed the idea of a technique of nature in the *First Introduction*, but he already saw that the appropriate framework for a more general application of the idea lay in the *Critique of Judgment*. In general, this work seems to be the most suitable point through which Dilthey could return to Kant from the Romantics. Although not Kant's most revolutionary work, it is in many ways the most forward-looking in dealing with some of the implications of the critical philosophy to be developed in the following century. Thus it not only suggests the idealism of the Romantics, but also the way it could be re-evaluated through Dilthey's own theory of history.

Kant's Aesthetic Judgment and Dilthey's Historical Judgment

It is the theoretical role aesthetics comes to have for philosophy that makes the *Critique of Judgment* epochal in nature. The differences between Dilthey's and Kant's particular aesthetic views become less significant in light of the fact that Kant had justified intersubjective agreement in areas (like taste) where conceptual demonstration cannot assure such agreement. Surely it is less important that Kant had retained a restricted concept of feeling than that he endowed it with new value for the problem of the communicability of sense between people. It is precisely the ability to bring transcendental considerations to bear on subjective experience that is of relevance to Dilthey's attempt to relate comparative psychology to the problem of historical understanding.

The limits placed on the constructionist outlook of discursive reason by reflective judgment are of the kind that

236

Dilthey noted throughout his search for a methodology of the *Geisteswissenschaften* and for a descriptive and analytic psychology in particular. Thus, when Kant speaks of the possibility of psychological accounts of the aesthetic experience, he strikingly anticipates Dilthey's call for description to replace the explanative hypotheses which are all too often impossible to test. In the *First Introduction* Kant notes that "psychological explanations are in a wretched state compared with physical ones, that hypothetically there is no end to them and given three different explanations a fourth, equally persuasive one can easily be conceived. . . . To make psychological observations, as Burke did in his treatise on the beautiful and the sublime, thus to assemble material for the systematic connection of empirical rules in the future without aiming to understand them, is probably the sole true duty of empirical psychology . . ." (p. 42).

In the *Metaphysical Foundations of Natural Science* (1786), Kant had already expressed doubts about the ability of psychology to provide more than a "natural description (*Naturbeschreibung*) of the soul."[26] However, by 1790 he seemed to acknowledge the value of such descriptions for epistemological considerations. Moreover, if we look at the "Critique of Teleological Judgment," we find Kant suggesting that a descriptive method is necessary on the transcendental level as well. It became clear to Kant, in considering the role of teleology in organic life, that the principle of mechanical causation does not suffice. Although mechanical explanation can be applied indefinitely—even to organisms—it will, given the limits of the human understanding, always leave something unaccounted for. We must, therefore, appeal to a principle of final causality as well. The relation of the principle of mechanical determinism and that of purposive activity is not explicable, for the two principles mark out irreconcilable approaches to reality. Since

[26] Kant, *Werke in Zehn Bänden*, 8, 16.

"one method of explanation excludes the other" (*CJ*,260), their interrelation is only understandable (*verständlich*) by means of a descriptive discussion (*Erörterung*) or exposition (*Exposition*) for the reflective judgment (*CJ*,261f.). Here the problematic in Kant's dualism of the theoretical and the practical is fully faced, for it is recognized that the two approaches to reality cannot be synthesized. All that can be done is to provide for a transcendental exposition of a territory of experience intermediate to the two *realms* of the determination of nature and the determination of freedom (*CJ*,13). This territory of aesthetic experience can be described in terms of an inner subjective purposiveness which is not itself subject to explanation. Interestingly enough, Kant not only appeals to a kind of descriptive reconciliation of the mechanical and teleological on purely transcendental grounds, but he also treats the concept of comparison as inherent in reflective judgment.

Because Dilthey did not sufficiently develop his ideas about comparative method and explore its relation to reflective experience, his own reliance on comparison is still criticized as morphological. The essay "Ueber vergleichende Psychologie" ends with a long exposition of how biology had successfully developed a comparative method. However, the text breaks off with the explicit warning that when applied to the *Geisteswissenschaften*, the method would have to be transformed. Although Dilthey never stated exactly how this was to be done, he would most likely have followed a Kantian rather than a biological model of comparison. We can best dispel misunderstandings about the biological influence on Dilthey's method of comparison by referring to the *First Introduction* where Kant directly relates comparison and reflection: "To *reflect* (or to deliberate) is to compare and combine given representations either with other representations or with one's cognitive powers, with respect to a concept which is thereby made possible" (p. 16). He then goes on to show how through comparison we aim to "detect *generically harmonious* forms" and that our search for them is grounded in a transcendental working principle which the reflective judgment prescribes to itself, i.e. the presupposition that "nature has observed in its empirical laws a certain economy, proportional to our judgment. . . ."[27]

By taking Kant's definition of comparison as a mode of reflective judgment and relating it to the experiential context of psychology, we can see how Dilthey's concept of reflective experience could become the basis for a comparative psychology. The special task of comparative psychology is to develop methods for defining individuality, which is a central problem for historical understanding.

As Baeumler points out, Kant had rethought the notion of system in the *Critique of Judgment* to make it applicable, not merely to the totality of the universe, but also to "the individual in the form of the aesthetic person and the organism."[28] However, the idea of systematic unity had become fundamentally subjective through its aesthetic analogue of a harmony of the human faculties. A person who understands himself as a system of faculties may experience a feeling of purposiveness, but no definite purpose can define his individuality. Even when applied to the empirical problem of organic life in the "Critique of Teleological Judgment," the idea of purposiveness remains a heuristic maxim of investigation. We may, for example, look at organisms in light of the maxim that their general purpose is self-preservation. But if we wish to specify organic purposiveness in terms of individual organisms, we notice that it remains conceived formally (CJ,228f.). Every part of the organism can be defined as both a purpose and a means (CJ,222). But such reciprocity of ends still allows no definition of individuality.

In terms of Kant's concern with the system of the natural sciences it was enough to pursue reflectivity only to the ex-

[27] Kant, *First Introduction*, p. 18.

[28] Alfred Baeumler, *Das Irrationalitätsproblem in der Aesthetik und Logik des 18. Jahrhunderts*, p. 303.

tent of applying it to an account of individuation in the organic sphere. But if Dilthey was to do for the system of the human studies what Kant had done for the natural sciences, he would have to apply reflectivity more concretely.

By considering the problem of individuality, not in relation to organic nature but in relation to history, Dilthey was better able than Kant to cope with the individual as a concrete objective fact. Kant intentionally left his idea of system abstract so as to leave room for aesthetic freedom and organic reciprocity. Dilthey, on the other hand, sought a more positive sense of historical freedom and interdependence. By reformulating Kant's subjective notion of system into the objective concept of type, Dilthey could focus on a concrete core of individuality without, however, exhaustively determining it. His aim was thus to transfer a concrete poetic vision to history, not a formal aesthetic order to organic nature. A vague sense of a harmony of parts must give way to an apprehension of an individual as a point of impression on which a system converges.

Dilthey's concern with poetic concreteness manifests itself in the parts of "Ueber vergleichende Psychologie" published as "Beiträge zum Studium der Individualität." He there shows how the understanding of individuality through comparing and contrasting character types is dependent on the insights of artists and poets. "Art attempts to express what life is," writes Dilthey. "The entire process of the individuation of the human historical world comes to understanding in poetry long before science strives to know it. And the means for the presentation of uniformities, the recurrence of differences, gradations, and affinities is typical vision (*das typische Sehen*)" (*GS*,V,280).

The ability to present the general in the particular is the peculiar gift of an artist. He portrays something so that it becomes indicative of more than just itself, and primes us to see things in their concrete fullness. By endowing the individual with typicality, the particulars of experience gain a kind of normative quality that gives them an affinity to other particulars. This results from the *first* sense in which the concept of the typical is applied. Dilthey cites the example of how in watching a skater or a dancer, "the appropriateness of the movements is inseparably bound to their apprehension. . . . Thus for every aspect of human expression of life there arises a type of its appropriate execution. This designates a norm lying between the deviations on both sides. Thus a typical expression of life represents an entire class" (*GS*,V,279).

This sense of type stresses its representative nature in relation to other particulars of a class. The part-whole relation seems to be central here, while in a *second* sense of type discussed by Dilthey it is the particular-universal relation:

> when I stress those features of such a type which express a regularity within the entire group, or specify them in bold strokes as it were, I can then also designate that which has been rendered prominent as the type. In this case, the concept of type designates that which has been brought out as the common trait. Even then the type still preserves its intuitive nature [*GS*,V,279–80].

This second sense of type could be compared to what is often called a schema: a concrete embodiment of a universal. We can see that such a particular-universal relation easily leads to a *third*, morphological sense of type which is ordinarily associated with the comparative method. This produces an abstract typology where a series of mutually exclusive universals are set side by side. However, for Dilthey comparison involves a reflection on similarities as well as a discernment of differences, so had he developed the essay on comparative psychology further, he might have related the morphological sense of type to the first concrete sense through the intermediary schema.

The emphasis in the essay, incomplete as it is, is on the first, intuitively apprehended types, where a part is representative of a larger whole. In the *Poetik*, Dilthey had already noted how the poetic imagination intensifies and completes experience into the typical.[29] As he phrases it in the comparative psychology, poetry can "condense" (*verdichten*) experiences so that their concentrated significance is worth reflecting on (*GS*,V,280). It is interesting to note that Dilthey avoids the term "invention" when discussing the imagination, but uses the concept of condensation, which refers to a process of making more dense or concrete. This suggests that the conception of *dichten* (to poeticize) which is traditionally seen as a mode of *er-dichten* (to invent) could be reinterpreted as a mode of *ver-dichten* (to condense). With the process of creation no longer reduced to invention, the imaginative and the reflective can be brought together in the typical poetic embodiment. Human spontaneity is not just ideational, but must be traced in terms of its individual, concrete objectifications. Whereas Kant's reflective judgment allows an idea or a universal to be suggested by a particular, Dilthey's reflective experience allows us to see the general in the particular.

Dilthey's handling of creativity can indicate the way he would go beyond Kant in dealing with the problem of historical freedom. According to Dilthey, freedom is not to be reduced to a transcendental postulate or an idea of abstract reflection, but must be experienceable—immediately in *Erlebnis* as well as reflectively through the objectifications of the human spirit. In reflective experience freedom can be intuited as objectified, for there certain objects are not merely natural events, but can also be recognized as human or historical projects of freedom. This means that Kant's overall systematic reconciliation of nature and freedom can be understood more concretely in terms of how history and freedom intersect in human individuals. Thereby Dilthey's comparative psychology contained the potential for developing our concrete understanding of history as the embodiment of human freedom.

Reflective experience, as conceived by Dilthey, relates cultural objects to the context of our inner experience. Only

[29] See above, p. 112. There no intermediary type was seen.

through reflective experience does anything like a universal context in which cultural objectifications can be evaluated become possible. By thus enlarging the sphere of the psychic to refer to cultural values, Dilthey brings into question the Neo-Kantian assumption that cultural values are valid apart from human experience. Rickert sees cultural values as exerting a priori constraints on us whether we acknowledge them or not (constraints similar to those of Kant's practical reason), and it is through them that we are supposed to understand history. But Dilthey does not consider Kant's categorical imperatives sufficient for understanding history, any more than Kant considered his own categories of the discursive understanding sufficient for comprehending the systematization of scientific knowledge. For Dilthey, cultural values must be connected with, but not reduced to, subjective human experience, and all but the most basic values, like freedom and respect for life, are subject to ever changing enrichment.

Admittedly, Rickert's theory of culture is closer to the letter of Kant's views, for Kant still viewed history as a chronicle of facts which could only be meaningfully ordered by the hypothesis of a future goal—an external purpose or categorical end.[30] However, it is through Dilthey that we see in Kant a basis for a conception of history that is much more profound. The nonhypothetical concept of immanent subjective purposiveness that Kant had attributed to aesthetic experience and then related to the objective description of immanent purposiveness in organic life, can be applied to history as well. Just as it is possible to discover an internal order in aesthetic experience and in organisms without appealing to an external purpose, so it is possible to find meaning in history without positing a final goal or a rational system.

Because Dilthey sought meaning in history apart from a

[30] Kant, "Idee zu einer allgemeinen Geschichte in weltbürgerlicher Absicht," *Werke in Zehn Bänden*, 9, 48.

rational system, Raymond Aron indicates that the title "Critique of Historical Reason" is misleading as a clue to Dilthey's work. He claims that Dilthey was really concerned with an historical critique of reason.[31] To be sure, Dilthey could not always get beyond criticisms of past conceptions of reason, but surely his fundamental aim was to do more. However pretentious Aron may find the idea of a Critique of Historical Reason, that of an historical critique of reason is self-defeating as a program. One does not project the relativization of reason—nor could one accomplish this—by a mere appeal to the facts of history. Dilthey wished to apply Kant's critical method to the problem of historical understanding and to reject traditional metaphysical dogmas about history as Kant had rejected those about God and nature. Insofar as he did this, we can see that Dilthey's project undoubtedly paralleled that of the *Critique of Pure Reason*.

Yet we can agree with Aron that Dilthey's own title is misleading because it tends to obscure the necessary reconceptualization of reason when one transfers the problem of knowledge from nature to history. Thus, unlike Hegel whose claims about history are determinant like Kant's claims about nature in the *Critique of Pure Reason*, Dilthey's are more similar to those of the *Critique of Judgment*. Just as Kant reevaluated his architectonic of reason in terms of reflective judgment, so Dilthey would have to redefine the ideal of historical reason in light of aesthetic judgment and reflective experience. Given Dilthey's stress on nonimposed order and the relative unimportance of

---

[31] Raymond Aron, *La philosophie critique de l'histoire. Essai sur une allemande de l'histoire*, Paris: J. Vrin, 1950, p. 25. It seems that Aron finds Dilthey of interest only to the extent that he resembles Bergson, both in a supposed negative attitude toward reason and in his concern with special categories of life like duration. This can be seen from the following quote: "Le sens banal de la critique de la raison historique se trouve donc encadre entre la conception d'une critique historique et celle des categories de la vie" (p. 26).

hypothetical connectedness in the human studies, the concept of reason is less fitting than that of judgment in characterizing the nature of historical understanding.

An historical judgment grounded in reflective experience establishes nondeterminant claims about the historical world. With such a concept of historical judgment we acknowledge the limited role Dilthey assigned to laws and explanations in history and point instead to the applicability of the descriptive and analytic method developed in psychology. It thus becomes feasible to transfer the mediated, but noninferred sense of psychic structure to our awareness of historical order as well. An historical judgment being fundamentally reflective in nature allows the description of particular historical data to suggest their own typical structures.[32]

Viewing Dilthey's life-project as in effect a Critique of Historical Judgment, we can see how Kant's epistemological use of the imagination in the "Critique of Aesthetical Judgment" was carried further in Dilthey's use of the poetic imagination as a model for understanding history. The idea of an aesthetic of history suggests that we can relate what

[32] The contemporary import of our attempt to define historical judgment in terms of the Kantian conception of reflective judgment, would be to support Dray's thesis that the historian's judgment does not presuppose a "covering law" or "an antecedent general hypothetical." Conversely, when Dray points to the inadequacy of Patrick Gardiner's idea of historical judgment, he is in effect providing a critique of the assumption that judgments should always be determinant in nature: "Gardiner does introduce the notion of 'judgement'; but he cannot bring himself entirely to abandon the view that judgement of a particular case is disreputable without the logical *support* of covering empirical laws—laws which 'warrant' the explanation. If the historian does not use a precise 'rule,' then a vague one *must* be found; if no universal law is available, then a qualified one *must* have been assumed. The alternative which is too much to accept is that, in any ordinary sense of the word, the historian may use *no law at all*." See William Dray, *Laws and Explanations in History*, London: Oxford University Press, 1957, p. 57.

has been said about the poetic imagination and reflective experience to obtain a more full account of historical understanding. But the actual demonstration of this relation will require a more explicitly hermeneutic theory of understanding.

CHAPTER SIX

Hermeneutics and Historical Understanding

THE IDEA of historical judgment can serve as a covering term for a whole range of concepts used by Dilthey in his continuing efforts to liberate the methodology of the human studies from the explanative and constructionist ideals of the natural sciences. Whether it be the methods of description and comparison first proposed through aesthetic psychology, or those of interpretation and *Nacherleben* (re-experiencing) in his later, hermeneutic writings, all alike are keyed to the use of reflective judgment as a defining characteristic of Dilthey's approach to history and the human studies. In the psychological aesthetics, reflective judgment is to be seen primarily as a mode of evaluation based on description and appreciation. In Dilthey's more specifically historical writings, where the meaning of the described content becomes more important, judgment as evaluative goes over into judgment as interpretive.

This change of emphasis from value to meaning is marked by a turn to hermeneutics which led to refinements in his concepts of *Erlebnis* and *Verstehen*. In this chapter, the problem of *Verstehen* will be considered first as a continuation of our analysis of reflective experience and then in relation to Schleiermacher's program for a critical hermeneutics. But before turning to a more detailed discussion, it will be helpful to review briefly Dilthey's general position on the problem of intersubjectivity in historical understanding.

Dilthey's insistence on *Verstehen* as intuitive suggests Romantic inclinations leading away from Kantian criticism.

247

Yet his *Verstehen* theory can still be considered a legitimate extension of the critical program if intuitive understanding is no longer claimed for our understanding of nature.

Because his epistemology was primarily oriented to the natural sciences, Kant had dismissed intuitive understanding as an impossibility for man. A concrete intellectual intuition was for him a divine ideal which can be humanly appropriated only by means of an abstract aesthetic symbolism. He clearly would not have approved of the Romantic attempt to concretize his aesthetic symbolism of a technique of nature into a *Naturphilosophie*. It was Dilthey's hope, however, to show that the Romantics were right in claiming that some human form of intellectual intuition is possible, but wrong in thinking that nature could be so grasped. Nature is not a text to be interpreted for its concrete meaning, in the way human actions may be said to be comparable to historical documents or poetic expressions and analyzed for their significance. By focusing on history rather than nature, on the *Geisteswissenschaften* rather than the *Naturwissenschaften*, Dilthey found it possible to defend a mode of intuitive understanding.

The terms *Verstand* and *Verstehen* both translate as "understanding." However, Kant's transcendental investigation into *Verstand* leads to those conditions which make our knowledge of nature possible, whereas Dilthey's analysis of *Verstehen* appeals to the special conditions of the human studies which make historical knowledge possible. As Kant considered any unifying system of science to possess a mere subjective, though universal, validity, so Dilthey admits that the validity of any interpretation of culture is rooted in subjective experience. However, it must be recognized that in the former case subjective validity points to a final aesthetic abstraction beyond which Kant could not proceed; in the latter to the concrete poetic beginning already established by Dilthey's early writings. The integral vision which is merely a heuristic or reflective assumption for

Kant's scientist investigating nature, is at least partly an experiential given for Dilthey's historian studying the world of man—a difference related to Dilthey's conviction that we have a certain implicit understanding of psychohistorical reality, but not of nature.

That history is a human product assures the historian at least an initial understanding of his subject matter, which is not, of course, claimed as constituting intersubjective understanding. The very fact that individuals can contribute to history in their own ways, can make it harder for them to agree on the meaning of historical events. The advantage possessed by Dilthey's theory of the *Geisteswissenschaften* over Kant's theory of the *Naturwissenschaften* is counterbalanced by the realization that generally the problem of intersubjectivity is much more acute for Dilthey than for Kant. The latter's assumption of universally shared human faculties which function in terms of a priori principles proved to be untenable. In its place, we have seen Dilthey postulate the not altogether satisfactory theory that there exists a common fund of psychological properties which occur as fundamentally different configurations in each individual.[1] These qualities manifest themselves with varying degrees of intensity and indeed some may be only latent. Thus while there is no guarantee of some faculty which provides a uniform basis for understanding, there is the possibility that an individual may recognize or draw out in himself those qualities shared with others. In this sense, intersubjectivity is given a more concrete though less certain grounding, and understanding takes on more of the attributes of interpersonal communication.

This aspect of Dilthey's thought has led some to interpret him as meaning, for example, that only a person who is really religious will be able to fully understand a Luther. While such obvious affinities would certainly be considered an advantage, it is clear that a person not in any way no-

[1] See above, pp. 138-39.

ticeably pious may nevertheless develop a sense of what it would mean to be pious. According to Dilthey,

> . . . the individuality of the exegete and that of the author are not opposed to each other like two incomparable facts. Rather, both have been formed upon the substratum of a general human nature, and it is this which makes possible the communion of people with each other in speech. . . . Individual differences are not in the last analysis determined by qualitative differences between people, but rather through a difference in the degree of development of their psychic processes. Now inasmuch as the exegete tentatively transports his own sense of life into another historical milieu, he is able within that perspective, to strengthen and emphasize certain psychic processes in himself and to minimize others, thus making possible within himself a reconstruction of an alien form of life.[2]

In such passages, however, it might appear that the understanding of others is, at bottom, merely a form of self-understanding. Some critics maintain that when the historian, following Dilthey, "transports his own sense of life" or develops "certain psychic processes in himself," he is doing no more than expanding the scope of his present self or illuminating present psychic processes. The usual objection to Dilthey's theory has been that it is restorationist, calling for uncritical absorption into the past. Here we have the opposite charge that it is all-too-centered upon the historian's present. To be sure, the early writings, focused as they were on the psychological description of *Erlebnis*, are open to both forms of criticism. The *Ideen* had contained the premise that the description of our own inner experience provides the intuitive basis for the understanding of others. And in the comparative psychology, Dilthey still

[2] *GS*, V, 329–30. Cf. "The Rise of Hermeneutics," trans. Fredric Jameson, in *New Literary History: A Journal of Theory and Interpretation*, 3, no. 2, Winter 1972, 242–43.

claims that the historian's understanding will be important to the extent that he makes his inner life universal.

However, the concept of reflective experience introduced in relation to a comparative method requires us to recognize certain Kantian limits to the process of self-expansion and the need for interpretation, or indirect understanding. Reflective experience can be seen as completing the description of inner experience, but at the same time, insofar as it refers beyond inner experience, defining its limits. Thus it is from the comparative psychology onward that Dilthey gradually worked out a theory of *Verstehen* which strikes a better balance between self and others.

Also, once *Verstehen* is questioned for its validity, a mere psychological grounding of understanding becomes inadequate. Transcendental and psychological justifications for the possibility of intersubjectivity as such do not establish methodological criteria for testing the objectivity of specific cognitive claims about history. A critical examination of *Verstehen* would lead Dilthey to hermeneutics or the theory of interpretation as a more satisfactory framework.

Erlebnis and *Verstehen*

In the early writings, where Dilthey's main concern was to establish his descriptive, analytical method in contrast to traditional explanative approaches, he made no particular effort to discriminate between *Erlebnis* and *Verstehen*. In arguing for the totality of psychic life, the two terms were used almost interchangeably with reference to the direct apprehension of psychic connectedness. Dilthey spoke of *Verstehen* in general terms to designate both self-understanding obtained through *Erlebnis* as well as the understanding of others. Since it was assumed that we apply the insights of *Erlebnis* to our perception of others, the understanding of others was considered an extension of *Erlebnis*. In short, self-understanding was more fundamental than the understanding of others.

As discussed in the *Poetik*, *Erlebnis* was conceived in terms of the primacy of inner form.[3] Outer experience served to complete inner experience, just as in the third law of imaginative metamorphosis new components added to an image were absorbed in the process of completing the original image.[4] But in reflective experience, where the outer is not submerged in the inner, *Erlebnis* is expanded to contain an external reference, which by remaining identifiable as such, makes the specific contributions of understanding others more discernible.

Although in his essay on comparative psychology, Dilthey still appears to view understanding through the self-completion of *Erlebnis*, it now really involves a kind of self-transformation of *Erlebnis*. The understanding of others does not merely supplement the self-understanding obtained through *Erlebnis*, but has a deeper effect in disclosing new unexpected possibilities for *Erlebnis* itself. This is indirectly affirmed when Dilthey remarks on the limits of extending *Erlebnis* in aesthetic transposition. Some kind of sympathetic affinity or even empathy may be a great boon to the appreciation of a work of art, but it is inadequate for understanding its meaning. Indeed, Dilthey clearly recognizes that empathetic projection of the self into the other can become an obstacle to understanding. Our understanding of the dramatic characters on the stage, for example, will be hindered by reading our own concerns and motivations into them (*GS*,V,277). What he by contrast regards as "transposition" does not allow us to simply attribute our feelings to others or view the characters in great literature as interesting variations of ourselves. Instead, we must reconsider ourselves and our *Erlebnis* in them.[5]

---

[3] See above, pp. 147–48.   [4] See above, pp. 102, 108–9.

[5] Because H. P. Rickman mistranslates Dilthey's concept of *Nacherleben* as "empathy" (Cf. *GS*, VII, 136 and *Pattern and Meaning in History*, New York: Harper & Row, 1962, p. 79), many English readers have assumed that empathy plays an important role in Dilthey's theory of *Verstehen*. It will become clear from our analysis in chap. 8

The conception of understanding thus indicated in the comparative psychology is neither the mere self-completion previously described in the aesthetic psychology, nor yet the self-transcendence involved in the concepts of objective expression and intentionality to be discussed in the following chapter. Because both the earlier and the later possibilities are also implicit in reflective experience, certain tensions are created between the descriptive and comparative psychologies.

With the introduction of reflectivity in comparative psychology, understanding is made more indirect. It can no longer be conceived merely as an extension of *Erlebnis* but as gained through conscious reflection on the expressions of others. Moreover, the very notion of reflective experience

---

that *Nacherleben* is a mode of re-experiencing which involves interpretation and is quite different from empathy (*Einfühlen*), a term that Dilthey uses very infrequently. Nagel's account of *Verstehen* as "empathic identification" represents the usual stereotype that *Verstehen* is purely intuitive, nonrational (See above, Introduction n. 4). By contrast, in Abel's account of *Verstehen*, "we 'understand' a given human action if we can apply to it a generalization based upon personal experience." Theodore Abel, "The Operation Called *Verstehen*," in *Readings in the Philosophy of Science*, ed. Herbert Feigl and May Brodbeck, New York: Appleton-Century-Crofts, 1953, p. 680. The kind of generalization that Abel has in mind is derived from "self-evident" experiential connections such as, "I hate him because he attacks me" (see p. 684). It is assumed that to "understand" someone else's aggressive behavior in response to an attack, I must attribute hatred to him as well. From Dilthey's perspective this would not provide an understanding of the meaning of the aggressive behavior at all, but merely a motive explanation for it. Such explanations are avoided by Dilthey, not just because they stereotype human behavior, but because they are mostly untestable hypotheses. Dilthey, on the other hand, would expect understanding to draw out the concrete meaning of y's aggressive behavior through placing it and the attack by x that triggered it in a context where it is possible to examine the basis for x and y interacting in the first place. This reference to a context, whether interpreted psychohistorically or socio-culturally, shows that understanding is not an immediate act, but an indirect and reflective process.

253

seems to put the immediate evidence of descriptive psychology in jeopardy. For can I really claim with any assurance to directly understand myself and my *Erlebnis* if I always find new possibilities for myself embodied in others?

Dilthey included the comparative method in psychology because he assumed that the psychological understanding of individuality was only possible relative to a whole range of character types. The typology was to be first delineated through a consideration of artistic objectifications insofar as they articulate fundamental modes of insight into human nature. But if psychology is assigned the task of comparing and reflecting on the typical vision of artists, it may become too wide in scope to be effective. Thus while reflective experience serves to relate psychology and historical understanding, it also raises the question whether reflectivity can be fully dealt with in the domain of the psychological.

Perhaps some considerations such as these kept Dilthey from pursuing his methodological reflections through psychology proper. But the fact that Dilthey failed to complete his treatise in comparative psychology need not betoken a crisis involving his psychological ideas alone, for the epistemological issues which were to be examined in the proposed second volume of the *Einleitung* also disappear temporarily from his writings. From 1896 through 1905 Dilthey was exploring in other contexts some of the possibilities he had raised through his notions of reflective experience and comparative method. In general, the decade following the comparative psychology was, as Hodges puts it, "a period of philosophical incubation."[6]

Dilthey turned to the historical study of important figures and periods in the development of German culture and philosophy.[7] The most important of these studies is "Die Jugendgeschichte Hegels," which was read at the Prussian

[6] Hodges, *The Philosophy of Wilhelm Dilthey*, p. 239.
[7] See *GS*, III and IV.

Academy in 1905 and then published as one of its *Abhand-lungen* (*GS*,IV,1–187). Based on intensive research of the *Hegelnachlass* in Berlin, it gave the first careful analysis of Hegel's so-called theological writings and opened up a new dimension in Hegel scholarship. The religious, ethical, and political reflections found in these early writings were, as Dilthey said, "still unconstrained by the force of the dialectical method" (*GS*,IV,3). The theoretical consequences of his re-evaluation of Hegel will be seen in Dilthey's last work on the *Geisteswissenschaften* (see chapter 8). Of greater immediate interest is the fact that Dilthey revived his youthful concern with Schleiermacher's hermeneutics and in 1900 published a general summary of his own work on the history of hermeneutics. Although this essay, entitled "Die Entstehung der Hermeneutik" ("The Rise of Hermeneutics"),[8] has been described as "little more than an historical retrospect," it is important because it provides at the same time a sketch for a more systematic approach to hermeneutics.

Verstehen and Interpretation

The understanding of nature had already been denied in the *Ideen*, but in "Die Entstehung der Hermeneutik" even the possibility of direct self-understanding through *Erlebnis* is put into question: "To understand nature—*interpretatio naturae*—is a metaphorical expression. But the apprehension of our own states is also inappropriately called understanding. To be sure, I say: 'I do not understand how I could have acted that way. I no longer understand myself.' With that I mean to say that an expression of mine, now part of the external world, stands over against me as alien . . ." (*GS*,V,318).

In the hermeneutic context, understanding is regarded as interpretation and is now explicitly restricted to the ob-

[8] See *GS*, V, 317–18. The essay was first published in a *Festschrift* for Christoph Sigwart.

jectifications of man. Dilthey asserts that I can only understand myself from without, just as I must understand others. This claim does not, however, justify Ludwig Landgrebe's existential exposition of Dilthey according to which the interpretation of others is necessary for the apprehension of any and all the possibilities of my own existence.[9] From Dilthey's hermeneutical perspective, the process of understanding is not so much one of disclosing to me my own possibilities, as of excluding certain possibilities. By standing over against certain acts or expressions of mine, I can contrast the potential inherent in *Erlebnis* with the actual choices I have been forced to make by my circumstances. I then reflect on myself by interpreting myself as an historical entity, both different from what I might have been and from what others are. Self-understanding is thus not directly fed into *Erlebnis*, but requires that I regard myself as a text to be interpreted. As a mode of hermeneutic understanding, it concentrates on the delimitation of possibilities and involves all the circuitousness of the comparative method.

Dilthey seems to attribute *Erlebnis* with an immediate sense which nevertheless needs to be explicated. There is of course a difference between those vague anticipations implicit in our lived experience and explicit imaginative expectations. The understanding of imaginative objectifications of possibilities become essential if *Erlebnis* is to go over into self-understanding. But while *Verstehen* makes its own distinct contribution, it nevertheless presupposes *Erlebnis*. Having limited comparative psychology in its ability to account for understanding, it is still possible to insist on the importance of the psychological description of *Erlebnis*. The relocation of the comparative method from psychology to hermeneutics can thus be seen as a move to protect what is fundamental about descriptive psychology.

The fact that *Verstehen* is essential for the articulation of

[9] Landgrebe, "Wilhelm Diltheys Theorie der Geisteswissenschaften," p. 328.

the meaning of our life does not prevent us from continuing to consider *Erlebnis* as the psychological source of all human significance. If we differentiate between subjective *potentiality* and objective *possibility*, then *Erlebnis* can be viewed as providing the potential significance which *Verstehen* articulates into definite and exclusive possibilities.

Landgrebe overlooks the potential of *Erlebnis* because he assumes it to be passive and without relation to the totality of life until reflection sets in.[10] Such a misreading of Dilthey could have been suggested by the distinction between inner and reflective experience. It would have been ironic had Dilthey, in seeking to overcome the Neo-Kantian dualism between the inner and outer, created a new one between *Erlebnis* as passive and understanding as active. Dilthey had repeatedly emphasized that *all* of psychic life is active, and there is no evidence to assume that he was abandoning this fundamental tenet. In point of fact, it was as modes of activity that Dilthey differentiated *Erlebnis* and *Verstehen*. *Erlebnis* already involves an active sense of totality, and what was said about the possibility of nonhypothetical mediation in reflective experience represents a refinement of the elementary modes of mediation implicit in inner experience. Perhaps Dilthey discontinued the discussion of reflective experience per se to avoid giving the false impression that either *Erlebnis* or inner experience lack their own reflective potential.

When Dilthey again takes up the question of the role of reflection and typologies in his final writings, he uses less psychological terms like *Selbstbesinnung* (self-reflection), *geschichtliche Selbstbesinnung* (historical reflection), and *Besinnung über das Leben* (reflection about life) (see *GS*,VIII,7,79,175,188). No longer distinguishing reflection simply as a type of experience, he analyzes it more in relation to *expressions of experience*. But the concept of expression, inserted between *Erlebnis* on the one hand and *Verstehen* on the other, does not act as a complete substitute

[10] Ibid., pp. 268f.

for that of reflective experience. Rather, expression and reflection should be regarded as complementary, for in effect
the hermeneutic concept of the expression of experience is
the objective counterpart to the psychological concept of reflective experience. Both serve a mediating role between inner and outer, self and other. Whereas reflective experience
incorporates objective reference into inner experience, expression makes inner experience public. We can regard reflective experience as providing something like a transcendental justification for intersubjectivity, while Dilthey's turn
to hermeneutics involves the search for objective methods
that can confirm intersubjectivity through a critical interpretation of human expressions. The main purpose of theoretical hermeneutics, he asserts is ". . . to preserve the general validity of interpretation against the inroads of
romantic caprice and skeptical subjectivity, and to give a
theoretical justification for such validity, upon which all the
certainty of historical knowledge is founded."[11]

Having discounted a natural, and even a psychological,
account of understanding, Dilthey now treats it as an interpretive activity which slowly developed from a special art
into a methodologically self-conscious and critical discipline
(*Wissenschaft*). It is made clear in the opening section of
"Die Entstehung der Hermeneutik" that understanding can
only attain "a controllable degree of objectivity" if it deals
with the kind of ". . . human expression that has been fixed,
so that we can repeatedly return to it" (*GS*,V,319). What
Dilthey considers to be an artistically sound understanding
of lasting expressions, he calls exegesis (*Auslegung*) or interpretation. "In this sense," Dilthey continues, "there is also
an art of exegesis whose objects are statues or paintings,
and Friedrich August Wolf already called for an archeological hermeneutic and critique" (*GS*,V,319). Properly,
hermeneutics must focus on linguistic expressions, for
". . . only in language does the inner life of man find its full,

[11] *GS*, V, 331 and "The Rise of Hermeneutics," trans. Jameson,
p. 244.

exhaustive, and objectively understandable expression" (*GS*,V,319). Thus exegesis is fundamentally rooted in *philology* which Dilthey characterizes as a personal kind of skill or virtuosity. Yet even an art as such becomes less and less personal, thereby producing general rules. These rules developed by different schools will often conflict, and it is the task of hermeneutical theory (*die hermeneutische Wissenschaft*) to find the means for dealing with such controversies (*GS*,V,320). Hence hermeneutics is defined as the theory of the art of interpreting texts; its ultimate goal is to analyze the starting point for any possible rules of understanding.

It is with these guidelines that Dilthey turns to a study of the gradual development of hermeneutics. His interest in the history of hermeneutics stems from his early work on Schleiermacher. In 1860, Dilthey had written a prize essay on the problem: "Verhältnis der Hermeneutik Schleiermachers zur Geschichte der Auslegung in Philosophie und Theologie." There Dilthey had been concerned to show how the rise of Protestantism necessitated a theory of Biblical exegesis. Once the authority of the Church in interpreting scripture was questioned, the problem of how an individual Christian is to understand the meaning of the Bible and how different possible readings might be reconciled became more pressing than ever. Dilthey's *Preisschrift* dealt with many theories of Biblical interpretation starting with that of Flacius. Although in "Die Entstehung der Hermeneutik," Dilthey goes back further to examine the rules of exegesis of the Greeks and the early Christian Fathers, he repeats his original assertion that hermeneutics as a theory did not originate until Flacius wrote his *Clavis* in 1567 (*GS*,V,324; *GS*,XIV,597). Flacius was able to solve some of the problems of religious expression by combining traditional rhetorical rules about the intentions of writers with certain insights into the nature of the Protestant religious experience. Thus he stressed the importance of resolving ambiguities in a Biblical passage by appealing to the

259

total Biblical context as well as to the particular textual context in which it stands. Dilthey points out, however, that an ahistorical, dogmatic conception of the Bible still lingers here. Flacius sets analogous passages from different books side by side to reenforce each other, thereby ignoring the different times at which these books were written.

Dilthey then traces some of the subtle advances in hermeneutics from the sixteenth century to Schleiermacher's time. Of particular interest is the importance attached to Semler who, like Michaelis, was led by English scholars to question overly logical and dogmatic methods of interpretation. Characterizing Semler as a predecessor of the great Christian Bauer, Dilthey points out that he

> ... demolished the unity of the New Testament canon, established the requirement that each individual book be understood in terms of its own local context, reunited them once again into that new unity which was implicit in the living and historical conception of an initial struggle in the church between Judaizing Christians and those following a more liberal dispensation, and then, in his propaedeutic to theological hermeneutics, peremptorily derived hermeneutics as a whole from two basic elements: interpretation based on linguistic usage and on historical circumstances.[12]

Out of this, the grammatico-historical school was founded. Although Dilthey recognized that this school had made invaluable contributions to the development of hermeneutics, he was often critical of its restricted sense of history. With its characteristic eighteenth-century emphasis on geographical determinants, history and human expressions are too readily interpreted through their external conditions. Such an empirically construed context may be less remote from the texts to be analyzed than a doctrinal or systematic context, but it is still inadequate.

[12] *GS*, V, 326 and Jameson, p. 239.

Out of the aesthetic and historical modes of awareness of the Romantics, there developed a new philological art of interpretation based on a sense of the original process of literary creation. It is now held that we must be able to unfold the moments of the genesis of a work if we are to appreciate it as a coherent whole. The concept of the inner form of a human objectification received its most radical formulation at this stage; the form of a work must be primarily understood from within, for the content prescribes its own form.

The techniques of this new mode of interpretation were worked out in the joint project of Friedrich Schlegel and Schleiermacher to provide the first comprehensive translation of Plato's dialogues into German. In addition to reconstructing the original order of the dialogues and determining which dialogues were genuine, they hoped to be able to define the unity between the character of Plato's thought and the artistic form of his works. Schlegel had originally conceived the project and brought to it greater philological skill than Schleiermacher, but Dilthey credits the latter with making the more important theoretical contributions to the development of hermeneutics.

In an earlier essay, Dilthey had shown that Schlegel's conception of a dialogue as a self-sufficient work of art proved less fruitful than Schleiermacher's notion that every dialogue carries out previous suggestions and prepares for later possibilities. Each dialogue, as Schleiermacher conceives it, becomes a microcosm, reflecting the Platonic corpus in a special way. Not only did Schleiermacher develop a better sense of the overall unity that characterizes Plato's thought, but from this larger perspective he was able to arrive at a more accurate chronology than Schlegel (*GS*,IV,365f.).

Dilthey ends his essay on the rise of hermeneutics by reviewing Schleiermacher's contributions to its theoretical foundation. "An effective hermeneutics," he writes, "could only develop in a mind where a virtuoso practice of philological interpretation was united with a genuine capacity for philosophical thought. Such a one was Schleiermacher."[13] He explicitly approached the interpretation of written works as the systematic working out of more general processes of understanding in ordinary life. Yet at the same time he saw that the rules for such interpretation cannot be fully formulated apart from a conception of artistic creativity.[14] Reflection on these rules shows that the different aspects of interpretation, whether of a logico-grammatical nature or of a psychological nature, cannot be separated from each other.

These methodological principles together with Schleiermacher's important formulation of the hermeneutic circle serve as the basis for Dilthey's own hermeneutics. A brief analysis of Schleiermacher's program will bring out some of the underlying considerations in Dilthey's approach to hermeneutics.

Schleiermacher and Critical Hermeneutics

In discussing Schleiermacher's contribution to religion, Dilthey calls him the "Kant of theology" (*GS*,XIV,535), because he used the "transcendental perspective" in defining both the grounds and limits of religious knowledge. Schleiermacher's advances in hermeneutics were in large part due to his also having applied the transcendental approach to the problems of interpretation. Going behind the particular rules of religious and literary exegesis to an analysis of interpretation in general, Schleiermacher addressed himself to the question, How is the understanding of human and divine expressions possible? More specifi-

[13] *GS*, V, 326 and Jameson, p. 240.

[14] Some of the implications of this will be drawn in chap. 8 where we show that although understanding as such is concerned with a work as a finished creation, rather than with the creative process, it may finally go over into *Nacherleben* whereby it becomes a kind of re-creative activity.

cally, how can we derive the possibility of valid interpretation and critically define its limits in terms of objective criteria?[15] Indeed, Schleiermacher's writings on hermeneutics reveal noticeable affinities with Kant's *Critique of Judgment*. It can even be said that Schleiermacher's hermeneutic circle reformulates a subjective Kantian dialectic between determinant and reflective judgment into a schema which has an objective core or focal point.

For Schleiermacher, the interpretation of a text must proceed, not only in terms of the concepts and propositions asserted, but also in terms of the organization or composition of the work. Thus Schleiermacher distinguishes (1) a *grammatical* part of hermeneutics which studies how a work is constructed from general ideas and common linguistic usage, and (2) a *psychological* part which looks for the peculiar combinations that characterize the work as a whole. The first, grammatical part has as its ideal a work of *classical* correctness, one whose language conforms to common forms and usages. Such language is economical in obtaining its effects, or as Schleiermacher says, "productive" in communicating effectively. The ideal of the second, psychological part is a work which is *original*, i.e. displays the particular "combinations" which define the uniqueness of an author. Although the grammatical and the psychological parts of hermeneutics have to be distinguished, their ideals are not to be considered mutually exclusive. The classical ideal, according to which an author must submit to common standards, and the psychological ideal of originality, according to which an author should remain true to himself, are merely relative. "Only the identity of both [ideals] is absolute" according to Schleiermacher and this he defines as the ideal of "the genial or archetypal."[16] A genius is one whose originality does not stand in the way of his effectiveness. He can produce an original effect through the use of

[15] See Dilthey's discussion of Schleiermacher, *GS*, V, 327.
[16] Friedrich Schleiermacher, *Werke*, Vol. 4, Leipzig: Verlag Felix Meiner, 1911, pp. 142, 143.

common language. Schleiermacher's conception of the genial anticipates Dilthey's effort to understand individuality in terms of a base of general, shared properties. An individual work is not to be defined by special qualities, but by the peculiar combination of common qualities. When Dilthey speaks of Schleiermacher's *Methodenlehre* he stresses that the interdependence of production and combination also applies to the nature of thought itself. Referring to Schleiermacher's distinction between productive methods of thought seeking generalizations and combinatory methods aiming at systematic order, Dilthey writes:

> Schleiermacher's axiom is that the differences among the methods of *production*, namely, induction and deduction, and those among the methods of *combination*, namely, the architectonic and heuristic procedures, do not designate separate methods. Production and combination, induction and deduction, architectonic and heuristic procedures are always interwoven in the solution of each scientific task insofar as one brings to full consciousness the conditions of one's approach and executes it artfully. We always know the whole only in the part and the part only through the whole. [GS,XIV,519, italics added]

Classically, thought has been conceived as either inductive or deductive. In both cases particulars are referred to a universal, thereby giving experience a general applicability. Thus induction and deduction are *productive* modes of thought. On the other hand, the methods whereby we *combine* thoughts, heuristically or architectonically, are rooted in the part-whole relation. To apprehend a thought heuristically is to consider its relation to other thoughts, for example, as part of the overall nexus of a person's outlook on life. Here again, we find that Schleiermacher's idea of combination allows us to focus on individuality. Whereas the heuristic approach tends to find affinities, the architectonic approach seeks contrasts whereby individuality can be defined. The architectonic aspiration for order and delimitation clearly indicates that the methods of combination can themselves be productive in unifying our experience.

Insofar as productive and combinatory methods tend to merge, the heuristic and architectonic approaches of combination seem to take in the inductive and deductive approaches of production. Thus for Schleiermacher the *abstract* problem of production, i.e. the construction of universal concepts, leads to the more important task of finding a *concrete* systematic order between parts and wholes.

The architectonic approach proceeds from the whole to its parts. This may seem like a deductive procedure, but to define a part would require an adequate classification based on induction. Because all architectonic connections are comparative, determinant judgment does not suffice for their articulation. Architectonic combination is thus always dependent on the heuristic approach which can provide an apprehension of the whole from a given part. That this move from part to whole is not simply a mode of induction is implied by Schleiermacher's use of the term "divination." To divine the whole from the perspective of a part is like Kant's symbolic knowledge. It has affinities with reflective judgment because it locates order from within, but is more specific in focusing on some crucial and indispensable part for intuiting the nature of the whole. Divination is more concrete than reflective judgment in that the unifying idea is embodied in the work itself rather than discovered by analogy.

For the result of heuristic divination to be objective, it must in turn be judged in relation to the architectonic. If this were merely a case of reversing the direction of Kant's thought and proceeding from reflective judgment to determinant judgment, an architectonic synthesis would be the final result. However, for hermeneutics the architectonic is not considered an end in itself. It is more appropriately viewed as a means for orienting understanding by providing a framework for comparing different interpretations.

The constructionist order of Kant's architectonic of reason can thus be transformed into a comparative system of critical interpretation. Just as genial literary production is expected to be archetypal, so the con-geniality involved in divinatory understanding must be able to meet the fundamental demands of critical judgment.

The architectonic aspect of interpretation could be said to justify Schleiermacher's famous dictum that the aim of hermeneutics is to understand an author better than he understood himself. The inspiration for this idea may well have come from the *Critique of Pure Reason* (A314–B370), where Kant expresses the conviction that his transcendental approach to metaphysical questions allowed him to more critically determine what Plato intended to accomplish with his doctrine of the Forms: "I need only remark that it is by no means unusual, upon comparing the thoughts which an author has expressed in regard to his subject, whether in ordinary conversation or in writing, to find that we understand him better than he had understood himself. As he has not sufficiently determined his concept, he has sometimes spoken, or even thought, in opposition to his own intention."[17] Kant is here supposing that an author may not fully understand his own intentions. A confused conceptual framework may lead an author like Plato to intend two things that are contradictory. It then becomes a matter of critical judgment which intention is more fundamental.[18]

[17] Bollnow has also noted the occurrence of the idea of understanding an author better than he can understand himself in Fichte's *Ueber die Bestimmung des Gelehrten* (1794), but Martin Redeker has further pointed to its occurrence in a letter of Herder concerning the study of theology dated the same year as the *Critique of Pure Reason*, which could indicate a more general origin. See Redeker's introduction to *GS*, XIV, liv.

[18] E. D. Hirsch, in a recent work on interpretation theory insists that the validity of a textual interpretation presupposes the standard of the author's intention and that this may not be questioned. He considers Kant's phrasing in the above quote to be ". . . inexact, for it was not Plato's meaning that Kant understood better than Plato, but rather

A similar conception of critical interpretation leads Schleiermacher to state that it must not merely serve to remove sources of misunderstanding. Hermeneutics must have more than the negative goal of overcoming obstacles in the way of regaining the original intention of the author. It must also allow for the more productive critique of a work whereby the particular intentions of the author can be refined, either by uncovering what fundamentally underlies them or by going beyond them.

Hermeneutics and History

Although Dilthey adopts Schleiermacher's general program as outlined, he dispenses with many of his elaborate formulations which abound with dialectically conceived oppositions and Romantic metaphors for their synthesis. Whereas Schleiermacher had relied on an overall architectonic order, Dilthey relied on history to provide the framework for interpretation. According to Dilthey, Schleiermacher failed to take properly into account the important respects in which historical perspective can contribute to the hermeneutic task of understanding an author better than he understood himself.

Instead, Schleiermacher's heuristic method of explicating and clarifying the intentions of an author had appealed to a doctrine of a *Keimentschluss* (seminal decision of an author). This organic image of a seed (*Keim*) from which a work grows, not only serves as a suggestive clue for *interpreting* the unity of a work, but is also used as a psychologi-

---

the subject matter that Plato was attempting to analyze." (Hirsch, *Validity in Interpretation*, New Haven: Yale University Press, 1967, p. 20.) To be sure, it is a reflection about the subject matter alone that can serve as the means of improving on an author. But this may then disclose that the author is guilty of shifts in his own intentions if the very concepts in terms of which these intentions could have any intelligibility for him were ambiguous enough to allow for self-contradiction.

cal core idea to actually *explain* the overall character of the work. For Dilthey, of course, this explanative aspect must be replaced by the more suitable approach of his descriptive psychology. And in rejecting the *Keimentschluss*, Dilthey points to it as symptomatic of how Schleiermacher's theory is compromised by Romantic preconceptions about an organic identity of spirit and nature. He suggests in fact that Schleiermacher's conception of the hermeneutic circle is somewhat comparable to that developed by Friedrich Ast out of the philosophy of identity.

Ast, a student of Schelling, had previously formulated the idea of a hermeneutic circle according to which we cannot understand a work except through its component parts while we cannot understand these parts without an original sense of the whole. Using the genetic schematism of the philosophy of identity, Ast noted three stages in creativity which can become the basis for describing the circular process of interpretive recreation. Dilthey first quotes Ast: "The beginning of all formation is unity, formation itself is plurality (opposition of elements), the completion of formation involves the penetration of unity and plurality, i.e. totality" (*GS*,XIV,658). He then elaborates as follows: "This process is repeated in reconstructive understanding. At first it encompasses the whole in a premonition or presentiment (*Ahnung*) until it raises the whole to a conscious unity informed by knowledge of particularity. Herewith the circle implicit in the concept of interpretation is solved insofar as the individual components can only be understood from the whole and vice versa . . ." (*GS*,XIV,659).

What in the constructionist approach of Ast seemed like a finite working out of a vague idea, becomes more like an infinite process of approximation in Schleiermacher. For Ast the whole is already prefigured at the start of interpretation, but Schleiermacher takes a less direct approach. Instead of beginning with an unconscious presentiment of the whole which is then consciously articulated, Dilthey remarks how Schleiermacher would gropingly (*tastend*) apprehend a whole from a hurried reading and then inaugurate the real process of interpretation (*GS*,V,330).

Schleiermacher's *Keimentschluss* is not an abstract projection of the whole, but rather a specific core content from which the overall form of the author's thought can be gradually unfolded. Nevertheless, Dilthey criticizes Schleiermacher for ultimately producing just as closed a sense of unity as Ast (*GS*,XIV,783)—the sole difference being that it need not be restricted to the scope of an individual work, but may be extended to encompass the corpus of an individual's works. Only if the notion of a central *Keimentschluss* is rid of its deterministic claims and reconceived aesthetically as a mere focal point, can the hermeneutic approach be applied to the problem of understanding the overall order of the historical world from a perspective within that world.

In the *Preisschrift*, Dilthey had concluded that both Ast's *Ahnung* and Schleiermacher's *Keimentschluss* should be reduced to the status of a "shiftable" hypothesis or schema (*GS*,XIV,708,781). Thus while characterizing the methodological contribution of the Romantic approach to hermeneutics, Dilthey nevertheless found it necessary to summarize its significance in his own language: "Since induction is always requisite for the deductive process, the architectonic search for antitheses by means of grounds of division does not begin with the concept of the world, i.e. an overall order . . . *but* begins in the middle, hypothetically: Provisional assumptions arise from the freedom of the imagination" (*GS*,XIV,519).

Reconceived as both provisional and relative, the *Keimentschluss* cannot of itself produce an understanding of the whole, but merely focuses a temporary understanding which needs to be refined. The very idea of a hermeneutic circle refutes the Cartesian faith in a fixed, self-evident starting point. It is impossible to determine where the circle begins or ends. In 1860, Dilthey indicated that any attempt to delimit the circle of understanding is hypothetical.

However, with reference to what has been shown in chapter 5, it would be better to define such a delimitation as reflective. For when Dilthey, as we have seen through his psychological writings, all but banishes hypotheses from the human studies, the purely imaginative nature of the focal point of the hermeneutic circle becomes even more noticeable. Such a point of crystallization allows interpretation to be reflective without being determinant and critical without being constructionist.

Dilthey's conception of the poetic imagination has already been characterized as articulating what is central or typical about a subject. We have discussed, for example, Dilthey's description of how an artist creates a portrait from a focal point of impression. He finds some point in a face especially impressive and articulates his vision around it. To properly understand this portrait, a spectator must modify his normal apprehension in order to recreate this point on which all other traits have been made to converge (GS,V,282). This conception of shifting one's focal point can now be applied to the hermeneutic circle of interpreting literary documents, or for that matter, to an historical hermeneutic in general.

Only by so rendering Schleiermacher's conception of the hermeneutic circle more flexible is it possible to obtain a proper perspective on the role of divination in historical understanding. In a series of addenda to "Die Entstehung der Hermeneutik," Dilthey is willing to speak of a "divinatory aspect of interpretation" in Schleiermacher's sense (GS,V,332). Yet Dilthey shows that it is not merely rooted in the geniality of the interpreter, or in his congeniality with the author, but in his familiarity with the subject matter as well. Divinatory skill may be important for the success of an interpretation, but it possesses no intrinsic validity for Dilthey. To the extent that divination appeals to *Erlebnis* it can never be totally wrong in the way an inductive hypothesis may be, but it is corrigible. Dilthey stresses the need for a comparative method, not just to confirm what

270

has been intuited, but also to correct and deepen it. "The comparative method allows me finally to understand each work, yes, each single sentence, more deeply than at first" (*GS*,V,334).

The primary framework for understanding troublesome propositions is the entire text, but this may still leave some of them ambiguous. It then becomes necessary to consider the work itself as part of a corpus, as part of a certain school of thought, or even as part of a genre. The aim of hermeneutics is thus to reduce potential meanings of a text to the one that was historically possible. It must ultimately turn into a comparative discipline, i.e. only indirectly can we approach an adequate understanding.

Whereas Schleiermacher attributed the ability to understand an author better than he understood himself to the unconscious nature of creativity, Dilthey finds it equally important to stress the fact that the critical understanding of a work presupposes the introduction of historical perspectives denied the author. There is no need to assume that the unity which defines the individuality of a work was inherent in its initial conception. What requires us, Dilthey asks in the *Preisschrift*, "to regard this unity as productive, as the seed (*Keim*) of the whole, rather than as the result of a formative process deriving from many points? . . . the unity could just as readily be *effected* by something that is added from without and thus able to connect already homogeneous parts, as by an original productive impulse of the whole" (*GS*,XIV,781). Unity as obtained through something-added-from-without may come relatively late in the course of the creative process or even in the interpretive process.

The unity that individuates cannot be understood as a closed synthetic affair, but is open to constant reinterpretation. If this were not the case, then understanding would be primarily an act of divination. But what Dilthey stresses about the process of interpretation is that it neither can nor should be terminated. Individuality is always subject to redefinition, not only in terms of internal development, but

271

also through external perspectives. We have already noted how Dilthey's psychology established that individuality is only gradually acquired.[19] From the hermeneutic perspective it becomes possible to say that the true unity of a work or an individual's character can only begin to be defined through historical retrospect.

We can see that Dilthey's hermeneutics and his descriptive psychology worked to make the process of understanding move beyond Schleiermacher's too direct appeal to divination and psychological explanation. Yet how compatible his own psychology and hermeneutics are in founding the human studies will have to be determined in the following two chapters. In "Die Entstehung der Hermeneutik," Dilthey still appeals to the fundamental importance of his descriptive psychology, but for the first time remarks that hermeneutics is ". . . an essential component in the foundation of the human studies themselves."[20] The increasing importance of hermeneutics in his final writings must be accompanied by a re-evaluation of the role of psychology vis-à-vis the historical studies.

[19] See above, p. 139–40.
[20] GS, V, 331 and "The Rise of Hermeneutics," trans. Jameson, p. 244.

CHAPTER SEVEN

Phenomenology and the Re-evaluation of Psychology

UNDOUBTEDLY the single most important influence on Dilthey during the transitional decade of 1895 to 1905 was Husserl's *Logische Untersuchungen* (1900–1901). Dilthey's enthusiasm for this work stemmed from a conviction that it provided the logically precise tools which would enable him to both clarify and further develop his own descriptive psychology. It was as if an organon for his own task of laying the foundation of the *Geisteswissenschaften* had been worked out. With the aid of a better phenomenological terminology and more reflection about his intentions, Dilthey became hopeful of overcoming some of the misunderstandings created by the *Ideen*. Thus in contrast to the general opinion that Husserl convinced Dilthey to abandon his psychology,[1] Dilthey attempted once more to relate his descriptive psychology to epistemology and thereby complete the task he had set himself in the *Einleitung in die Geisteswissenschaften*.

Yet as revealed in "Der Aufbau der geschichtlichen Welt in den Geisteswissenschaften" ("The Formation of the Historical World in the Human Studies")[2] of 1910, it is hermeneutics rather than Husserlian phenomenology, which provides the controlling framework in Dilthey's matured theory of psychology and the human studies. Moving from

[1] See above, p. 11.

[2] This treatise, first published in the *Abhandlungen der preussischen Akademie der Wissenschaften*, contains Dilthey's most definitive account of the human studies. Reprinted in *GS*, VII, 79–188. Hereafter to be referred to as the *Aufbau*.

a phenomenologically inspired analysis of psychic structure to an investigation of the concrete structuring of *Erlebnis* and its expression, Dilthey developed the hermeneutic conception of objective expression as central to historical interpretation and the delimitation of the human studies.

Husserl and Dilthey: An Exchange of Views

Dilthey quickly recognized the importance of Husserl's work. In a paper delivered to the Prussian Academy in 1905, he acknowledges that his epistemological treatment of psychic structure ". . . is indebted to the epoch-making *Logische Untersuchungen* of Husserl" (*GS*,VII,14). However, a genuine respect for Dilthey's accomplishments was to come only late in Husserl's life. Turned away by Ebbinghaus's critique of the *Ideen*, Husserl did not read it until after he had written his *Logische Untersuchungen*. Apparently it was Dilthey who established the first contact by inviting Husserl to visit him in Berlin in 1905.[3] As Husserl recalled in a letter of 1929, this personal encounter, rather than any particular writings of Dilthey, provided the impulse for developing his own *Ideen zu einer reinen Phänomenologie*. The concrete working out of this multivolume project up to around 1925 led to what Husserl described as "an intimate kinship with Dilthey, although by essentially different methods."[4]

Husserl's most positive evaluation of Dilthey's contributions can be found in his lecture notes for a course on phenomenological psychology offered in 1925. The first three lectures are devoted almost exclusively to a detailed exposition of what he considered to be Dilthey's decisive redefinition of psychology as a *Geisteswissenschaft*. According to

[3] Herbert Spiegelberg, *The Phenomenological Movement: A Historical Introduction*, 2nd ed., vol. I, The Hague: Martinus Nijhoff, 1965, p. 122.

[4] Quoted in George Misch, *Lebensphilosophie und Phänomenologie*, p. 328.

Husserl, Dilthey almost singlehandedly demonstrated how experimental psychology with its atomistic approach could not do justice to the facts of psychic life. Much attention is given to Dilthey's *Ideen* which Husserl credits as ". . . the first attack on naturalistic psychology; a genial, even though not fully matured work, which surely will remain unforgotten in the history of psychology."[5] He now realizes that Ebbinghaus had so fiercely censured this work because "the times were not yet ready to accept such thoughts."[6] Yet, predictably, Dilthey is found lacking in the necessary analytical precision to defend his insights. Convinced that phenomenology alone could provide a proper theoretical foundation for Dilthey's descriptive method both in psychology and as applied more generally to the historical world, Husserl concludes that Dilthey's ". . . writings contain a genial preview and certain rudiments of phenomenology."[7]

Although Husserl's view does allow for a continuity between Dilthey's psychological and epistemological concerns, it mistakenly implies that Dilthey could not have developed his own theoretical framework apart from phenomenology. But to whatever extent Dilthey may have been indebted to some of Husserl's phenomenological insights, he employed them only so far as they contributed to his own theoretical ends. Whereas Husserl considered phenomenology as the epistemological ground for all the sciences—the *Naturwissenschaften* and the *Geisteswissenschaften*—Dilthey looked to phenomenological analysis only as a means towards an epistemological foundation for the human studies which would at the same time distinguish them from the natural sciences.

The diverging concerns of Dilthey and Husserl are most apparent in their differing attitudes towards history. This was revealed in an exchange between the two on the impli-

---

[5] Husserl, *Phänomenologische Psychologie*, p. 6.
[6] Ibid., p. 11.   [7] Ibid., p. 35.

cations of Dilthey's theory of the *Weltanschauungen*.[8] In an article, "Philosophie als strenge Wissenschaft" ("Philosophy as Rigorous Science"), published 1911 in the first volume of *Logos*, Husserl interprets Dilthey's *Weltanschauungslehre* as a misguided attempt to derive the nature of philosophy from an empirical study of history. For his part, Husserl claims that history can give no clues to the question of validity or to the absolute goals of science, whether natural or metaphysical. Moreover, he discerns a very dangerous trend towards historicism in Dilthey's assertion that "the formation of historical consciousness destroys . . . a belief in the universal validity of any of the philosophies that have undertaken to express in a compelling manner the coherence of the world by an ensemble of concepts."[9]

Husserl admits that philosophical *Weltanschauungen* are historically conditioned, but considers this no argument against the possibility of philosophy as a rigorous science. The situation is similar for the exact natural sciences. Their theories are continually being disputed and revised. "Does that mean that in view of this constant change in scientific views we would actually have no right to speak of sciences as objectively valid unities instead of merely as cultural formations? It is easy to see that historicism, if consistently carried through, carries over into extreme sceptical subjectivism."[10]

These remarks concerning the sceptical consequences of historicism are often assumed to sum up Husserl's estimate of Dilthey. However, in 1968 Walter Biemel published some of the correspondence between the two men which sheds a better light on how they regarded each other. In a letter to Husserl, Dilthey denied that he was either a historicist or a sceptic. While remarking that Husserl was correct in

---

[8] This theory will be discussed more fully in chap. 9.

[9] Quoted in Edmund Husserl, "Philosophy as Rigorous Science," trans. Quentin Lauer, *Phenomenology and the Crisis of Philosophy*, New York: Harper & Row, 1965, p. 124.

[10] Ibid., p. 125.

observing that the mere historical variation of scientific views does not at all refute the notion of absolute scientific truth, Dilthey points out that the argument of historical consciousness against the validity of metaphysical *Weltanschauungen* is based on theoretical grounds. "It is not historical empiricism," replies Dilthey, "but the development of historical consciousness, namely, a systematic investigation proceeding from analysis as practiced in the *Geisteswissenschaften*, which is supposed to demonstrate the impossibility of metaphysics."[11] Not the history of *Weltanschauungen* per se, but reflection on it, had led Dilthey to the judgment that it is theoretically impossible to synthesize all knowledge into one system. Thus, he had argued in the *Einleitung* that metaphysical attempts to systematize all our knowledge about nature and history do not just happen to be inadequate, but must necessarily stand in the way of a scientifically valid system of the *Geisteswissenschaften*. Dilthey therefore attacked metaphysics precisely to head off scepticism about science.

In a conciliatory letter, Husserl assured Dilthey that the polemics against historicism in "Philosophie als strenge Wissenschaft" were not directed at him. But this may not be altogether candid, because many of Husserl's critical comments in the section on historicism and *Weltanschauung* philosophy either explicitly or implicitly refer to Dilthey's aims and methods.[12] Nonetheless, Husserl is now content to

[11] Walter Biemel, "Briefwechsel Dilthey-Husserl," *Man and World*, I, no. 3, 1968, p. 437.

[12] In fairness to Husserl it should be said that on p. 127, fn. k of "Philosophy as Rigorous Science" he had already qualified his comments to the effect that Dilthey's overall position seems to be directed against historical scepticism, but that the analysis of *Weltanschauung* types does nothing to offer any specific arguments against it. However, in his letter to Dilthey, Husserl offered to immediately publish a note in *Logos* to further clear Dilthey from the possible charge of historical scepticism. Because Dilthey died within months after this correspondence, such a note was never published. See Biemel, "Briefwechsel Dilthey-Husserl," p. 446 fn. 20.

stress underlying agreement despite differences in approach. He acknowledges that Dilthey's analysis from the perspective of the *Geisteswissenschaften* had correctly refuted the kind of metaphysics which posits a thing-in-itself behind phenomena. Noting that this analysis overlaps to a great degree with phenomenological analysis, Husserl writes: "What we, coming from different studies, determined by different historical motives, and having passed through differing development, strive for, harmonizes and belongs together: on the one hand, phenomenological analysis of elements, and on the other, phenomenological analysis on a large scale as disclosed in your morphology and typology of great cultural formations." He even went so far as to suggest that "serious differences do not exist between us at all. I believe, that an extensive conversation could lead to full agreement."[13] What Husserl overlooked —or perhaps hoped to overcome—is Dilthey's insistence that the historical should not be reduced to the natural. Since Dilthey thought that the objectivity of the human studies and the natural sciences can only be preserved by keeping their methods and goals separate, he would have to be as distrustful of phenomenology as he had been of traditional metaphysics for attempting to find an underlying unity among all the sciences.

In the last years of his life, as Dilthey worked out his theory of the *Geisteswissenschaften*, he seemed to draw away from Husserl. Spiegelberg surmises that this was due to the appearance of "Philosophie als strenge Wissenschaft." But we will see that even before then there was a lessening of Husserl's influence which was connected with the continuing modification of Dilthey's thinking about the relation of psychology and history. Some of the reasons are indicated in his final "Entwürfe zur Kritik der historischen Vernunft" ("Sketches for a Critique of Historical Reason")[14] when he

---

[13] Biemel, "Briefwechsel Dilthey-Husserl," pp. 441, 438.
[14] See *GS*, VII, 191–291. Hereafter to be referred to as *Entwürfe*.

criticizes the "psychological scholasticism" of Franz Brentano, whose revival of the concept of intentionality had
exerted a considerable influence on Husserl's phenomenology. Brentano's so-called scholastic school of psychology,
Dilthey writes, ". . . creates abstract entities, such as attitude, object, and content from which it wants to compound life. The extreme case in this regard is Husserl"
(GS,VII,237). Antagonistic to any approach that abstracts
from the given continuities of life, Dilthey on another occasion referred to Husserl as "a true Plato, who first con-
ceptually fixes the things that become and flow, and then
adds the concept of flow."[15]

Yet, interestingly enough, during the period of Husserl's
greatest influence, when Dilthey stressed the affinity between their work, he himself focused on the more static
aspects of his structural psychology. Dilthey's sense of his
divergence from Husserl in his last years is linked to a re-
emphasis on movement and dynamic process in psychology
which occurs under the corrective influence of his matured
aesthetic and historical theories.

Psychic Structure and the Self-Transcendence of *Erlebnis*

From 1905 to 1909 Dilthey read three papers to the Prussian Academy on the foundation of the *Geisteswissenschaften*. They were preliminary studies which eventually
led to the publication of the *Aufbau*. In the first of these
studies entitled "Der psychische Strukturzusammenhang"
("Psychic Structure"), Dilthey refers to Husserl to reaffirm
his own thesis of the *Einleitung* that it is the task of descriptive psychology to provide *Vorbegriffen* (preconceptions) for a *Theorie des Wissens* (theory of knowledge)
(GS,VII,10). Obviously regarding Husserl's critique of psychology as on the whole inapplicable to his own work, Dilthey indicates that his previous descriptive analysis of the

[15] Quoted by Misch in the introduction to GS, V, cxii.

elementary logical operations immanent in *Erlebnis* is actually confirmed by Husserl's phenomenological account of the prediscursive operations of consciousness. He notes how his procedure, too, had always been to "go back to the structural relations contained in the psychic nexus, in opposition to the idealistic theory of reason grounded in a pure ego" (*GS*,VII,13). Husserl, as we know, would move away from the realism of his *Logische Untersuchungen* to become increasingly idealistic and ever more insistent upon the need for a transcendental ego. Whereas he came to find in prediscursive operations of consciousness the basis for a new conception of the a priori, Dilthey always saw them as a means of refuting epistemological appeals to a priori forms of intellect.

Yet the rigidity that Dilthey finally saw in Husserl's approach was already implicit in the *Logische Untersuchungen* and betrayed itself as well in Dilthey's own formulations in "Der psychische Strukturzusammenhang." He there distinguishes two kinds of relationships that can be asserted to exist in psychic life. The one is experienced, the other is inferred. "Regularities of the latter kind are established by psychology when it singles out certain processes from the nexus of psychic activities and inductively infers regularities from them. Association, reproduction, and apperception are such processes. The regularities so established consist of uniformities (*Gleichförmigkeiten*) which correspond to the laws of change in the sphere of external nature" (*GS*,VII,14–15).

Dilthey has given up his effort made in the *Poetik* to reformulate the laws of association descriptively. He now considers them as mere hypotheses which embody the explanative ideal of the experimentalists. Such explanative *uniformities* are contrasted to the kind of regularity (*Regelmässigkeit*) pertaining to *psychic structure*.

Uniformities are rules which are to be exhibited in changes; every change is thus a particular case which can be subordinated to a universal. Structure, on the other hand, constitutes an ordering (*Anordnung*) in which psychic phenomena are related by an inner connectedness; every such datum so connected is part of a structural nexus. Thus the regularity of structure consists in the relation of parts to a whole. Uniformities deal with the genetic connections according to which psychic changes are dependent on each other. Structure, on the other hand, is apprehended in developed psychic life as an inner connection. [*GS*,VII,15]

An example of such structure would be the way that feelings constitute a grouping which is experienced as distinct from representations on the one hand and desires on the other. This kind of grouping had also been discussed in the *Poetik* and *Ideen* and shows the basically structural character of his early descriptive psychology. However, structure was there conceived more loosely so as to be able to encompass change. The semi-conscious structure of the acquired psychic nexus was used to elucidate the way particular activities are regulated by our values, etc.[16] The structures described in the present study are, by contrast, strictly conscious and defiant of change. Dilthey is willing to call the structure of psychic life teleological only in the sense that it constitutes a cooperative outcome of relations constructed from relatively simple *Erlebnisse* (*GS*,VII,17).

Description is now apparently unable to cope with psychic processes and becomes instead a source of preliminary structural concepts for an epistemology of the human studies. If this is so, then only the explanative methods of the natural sciences can deal with psychic change. Dilthey seems here to be moving toward the dualistic consequences he had attributed to the Neo-Kantian position. Psychology would now have to be considered both a *Naturwissenschaft* and a *Geisteswissenschaft*, for Dilthey implies

16 See above, pp. 99–100.

that it is the task of an explanative psychology to infer how *Erlebnis* leads to our overall fund of knowledge, whereas the description of psychic structure implicit in *Erlebnis* can only provide the foundation for a special epistemology of the *Geisteswissenschaften*.

Although he had previously claimed that *Erlebnis* is an ultimate given and not in any sense an epiphenomenon, Dilthey now appears to allow for the possibility that something may exist behind it. Thus he writes, "our life consists in processes manifesting themselves to consciousness in time, and whatever might exist behind them is not itself experienceable and therefore is not necessary for the foundation of those disciplines which have their material in *Erlebnisse*" (*GS*,VII,27). This leaves an opening for a naturalistically conceived psychology to explain *Erlebnis* in terms of hypothetical elements, while at the same time denying its relevance to the foundation of the *Geisteswissenschaften*.

If Dilthey gives a bit more to the Neo-Kantian position, this is because the main concern in his paper is to isolate those factors in his psychology which are specifically relevant to the epistemological foundation of the human studies. This is in contrast to Husserl, who had appealed to *Erlebnis* as the purely subjective experience which can serve as a presuppositionless phenomenological foundation for all scientific knowledge, both natural and historical. Dilthey, by preserving *Erlebnis* as a psychological concept, leaves its status for a more inclusive epistemology unclear.

Yet it is important to consider Husserl's epistemological analysis of evidence, for it in effect confirms Dilthey's claims about the interdependence of inner and outer experience. Because most inner experiences, such as feelings, are perceived as localized in the body, they cannot, according to Husserl, be considered fulfilled or intuitively evident experiences. Psychologically, inner experiences are already interpreted in terms of a transcendent natural framework and therefore are no more intuitively evident than normal perceptual experiences.

Both thinkers replace the naive conception of inner experience (*innere Erfahrung*) with that of *Erlebnis*, and propose the description of *Erlebnis* as a propaedeutic to epistemology. But for Dilthey, *Erlebnis* is meant to define inner experience in terms of its natural relation to outer experience, while for Husserl, *Erlebnis* is defined phenomenologically as a mode of experience rendered intuitively evident by a special attitude: "The pure givenness of *Erlebnis* presupposes the pure phenomenological attitude which inhibits all transcendent positing."[17] This was later more explicitly defined as the phenomenological *epoché*.

According to Dilthey, however, the description of *Erlebnis* still "operates totally within the presuppositions of empirical consciousness" (*GS*,VII,12). The reality of external objects remains presupposed, but is not affirmed. As a consequence, the world is neither naturalistically posited, nor phenomenologically bracketed. Both *Erlebnis* and outer experience refer then to the world, the former qua concern of the *Geisteswissenschaften*, the latter qua object of the *Naturwissenschaften*.

Dilthey now claims that even the description of *Erlebnis* will involve an objective reference. In the study on psychic structure, he had already spoken of perception as referring to an object (*auf einen Gegenstand*), of feelings such as sorrow about an event (*über ein Ereignis*), and of strivings after a good (*nach einem Gute*). In "Der Strukturzusammenhang des Wissens" ("The Structural Nexus of Knowledge"), the second paper he read to the Academy in 1905, Dilthey makes a similar use of prepositions to designate more generally what *Erlebnis* is of (*von*) or about (*über*). In discussing the nature of *Innewerden*, i.e. what is possessed in *Erlebnis*, he extends his earlier account[18] to distinguish between act, content, and intentional reference. "A feeling," writes Dilthey, "exists insofar as it is felt, and it is

[17] Edmund Husserl, *Logische Untersuchungen*, vol. II, part 2, 4th ed., Tübingen: Max Niemeyer, 1968, p. 232.
[18] See above, p. 213.

the way it is felt: the consciousness of it and its nature, its being given and its reality are not separable. . . . Yet if I want to designate this as *Innewerden*, then it must be understood in such a way that the relations of the contents of sense to an object are there for me just as much as the act of feeling that characterizes the *Erlebnis*" (*GS*,VII,27). Insofar as an object is *erlebt* it is apprehended as it exists for me. It is interpreted in what Dilthey would later call its *Lebens-bezüge*—in its relations to my life. References to it are real, regardless of whether it can be confirmed to stand there over against me in the natural world (*GS*,VII,27,33). "The noise which a feverish person assigns to an object behind him constitutes an *Erlebnis* which is real in all its components, namely, the taking place of the sound and its reference to the object. The reality of the fact of consciousness will be unaffected even if it turns out that the assumption of an object behind the patient's bed is false" (*GS*,VII,26). Thus Dilthey distinguishes between the way an object is apprehended through *Erlebnis* and the way it is apprehended through sensuous intuition.

For the apprehension of objects as part of the natural world, Dilthey speaks of perception (*Wahrnehmung*) based on what is sensuously intuitable (*das sinnlich Anschau-liches*) (*GS*,VII,32f.). Because such intuitive perception is interpreted in Husserlian fashion as inherently perspectival, there can be no single all-encompassing intuition (*An-schauung*) which grasps an object (*GS*,VII,35). The intuitive object designates a transcendent task. "To solve this task and really grasp the intended object, apprehension is driven on to ever new acts of representation" (*GS*,VII,35). This mode of apprehension is always inadequate and involves an unfulfillable synthetic ideal.

Husserl had contrasted this kind of perception to the *Er-lebnis* of an object by claiming that the latter is fulfillable in terms of its meaning. Reflection on how an object is *erlebt* leads to the certainty of apprehending it as it is meant, i.e. qua content. In applying his analysis of the act, content, and object of consciousness to the study of *Erlebnis*, Husserl focuses on the first two aspects. According to the theory of the intentionality of consciousness, he may not of course abstract from the objective reference of an *Erlebnis*, but he does reduce it to an abstract horizon. Dilthey, however, uses the three-fold distinction to add to the concreteness of his descriptive program. What for Husserl becomes a mere implicit background is transformed into an explicit context by Dilthey relative to which it is impossible to isolate content simply as meant.

Erlebnis is less fulfilled than Husserl claims because of its inherent tendency to transcend itself. Dilthey illustrates the transcendent references in *Erlebnis* by analyzing his own experience of lying awake at night, worried about finishing his manuscript for a Critique of Historical Reason. "There we have a structural nexus of consciousness," he comments, "in which objective perception constitutes the foundation. . . . A representation of my manuscript is the apprehended basis of my *Erlebnis* . . ." (*GS*,VII,28). The process of reflecting on what the worry is about, leads to a distinction of the *Erlebnis* and its object, with the result that "the object immanent in *Erlebnis*" becomes "partially transcendent" (*GS*,VII,28). It is crucial, according to Dilthey, to understand "that this partial transcendence is grounded in the *Erlebnis* itself as well as in the relation in which apprehension stands to it" (*GS*,VII,28).

Thus Dilthey discloses that the object which is possessed in *Erlebnis* is to be recognized as still in some sense independent of it. However, Dilthey is here more concerned to use the object of *Erlebnis* as a clue to the analysis of psychic objectivity pertaining to the apprehension of psychic structure. He continues his account of his manuscript-*Erlebnis* by stating: "Because I notice the object, I bring the structural relations which are implicit in the state of feeling to distinct consciousness. . . . From the generally uneasy feeling about this object I distinguish that of my tiredness as its basis and that of the worry grounded in it concerning the completion of this manuscript . . . all of which leads me back to structurally related *Erlebnisse* of the past" (*GS*,VII,28).

The psyche is characterized by what Dilthey calls *ein Fortgezogenwerden* (a being-pulled-forward) which involves a tendency to go from what is directly *given* in *Erlebnis* to explicating what is *included* in it, i.e. its relations to other remembered *Erlebnisse*. Transcendence is thus interpreted temporally rather than spatially. "The sequence of temporality and the memory which comprehends it are the objective grounds for the fact that a consciousness of transcendence can arise from *Erlebnis*" (*GS*,VII,29). The passivity both within the movement of "a being-pulled-forward" and its result—a looking backwards to structurally more fundamental *Erlebnisse*—serves to confirm that Dilthey is here not concerned with the dynamism of psychic life. As he himself put it, he is not describing genetic relations between *Erlebnisse*, but only grounding-relations (*GS*,VII,44).

The way *Erlebnis* transcends itself points to the psychic nexus as its structural context. According to Dilthey, the apprehension of this nexus involves "an infinite task just as much as does the apprehension of outer objects. But it consists only in extracting that which is contained in *Erlebnis*" (*GS*,VII,32). Whereas external objects totally transcend the sense-contents out of which they are to be synthesized, psychic structure only partially transcends *Erlebnis*. Its objective articulation involves no hypothetical inference but merely the elementary logical operations of analysis and explication. It is in this context that Dilthey speaks of representing (analyzing) psychic acts as contents.

Yet Dilthey's notion that "psychic acts can be represented as contents" (*GS*,VII,33) should not be interpreted as allowing an act to be its own content. Dilthey agrees with Husserl that no psychic act can involve the subjective transparency which Brentano associated with the theory of the intentionality of consciousness. When Husserl adopted the concept of intentionality he explicitly disavowed the notion of a secondary consciousness of a psychic act as cotemporal with, and implicit in, the primary perception of an object.[19] Pierre Thévenaz nicely contrasts Husserl's position to that of Brentano by analyzing the experience of hearing a sound: "He [Brentano] showed that there was no means of hearing the sound without having the *implicit* consciousness of hearing (of oneself hearing). And Husserl tells us that there is no means of having consciousness of hearing without the sound being implicitly present."[20]

To forestall any charges of psychologism, Dilthey warns that those elementary logical operations that he had described in the *Ideen* must not be interpreted as given in *acts* of consciousness separate from *contents* of consciousness. Moreover, the process of reflecting on *Erlebnis* and isolating elements in it by means of elementary logical operations presupposes an *objective* reference. His previous claim about logical operations being inseparable from our experience could have been interpreted in Brentano's sense, but it is now elaborated as presupposing implicit objective relations among contents. Dilthey gives the following example to show how such elementary relations are apprehended:

> The actual connection of color qualities with extension entails that color cannot be represented apart from extension. To be sure, the apprehension of this fact presupposes acts of connection and separation, but the relations do not occur between acts, but between the contents contained in the state of affairs. The validity of the designated relations is independent of the acts of consciousness in which they are apprehended. [*GS*,VII,37]

A similar position is manifested in his account of discursive logical operations:

[19] Husserl, *Logische Untersuchungen*, vol. II, part 2, pp. 229ff.
[20] Pierre Thévenaz, *What is Phenomenology? and Other Essays*, ed. James Edie, Chicago: Quadrangle Books, 1962, p. 119.

> In a syllogism . . . a state of affairs is apprehended. No consciousness of the operations of thought which we execute accompanies this objective apprehension. Only contents and their relations are present to consciousness. . . . A demonstrable structural relation exists . . . only between the act and the content which constitutes the material for the determination of the object. [*GS*,VII,37]

Any psychologistic attempt to derive the elementary logical operations from our consciousness of psychic acts would be just as hypothetical as an attempt to arrive at traditional logical principles by means of an inductive examination of nature.

In one sense, the elementary logical operations can be considered as the peculiar transcendental condition of objectivity in *Erlebnis*, just as the discursive logical operations constitute the transcendental condition for any natural objectivity. But in another sense, the elementary logical operations form the basis for discursive logical operations as well, thereby also applying to the realm of intuitive perception. Thus it is in his section on logical operations that Dilthey comes closest to Husserl's univocal theory of science.

However, Dilthey still maintained that there must be separate epistemological foundations for the natural sciences and the human studies. We saw that in denying the fulfilled nature of *Erlebnis*, Dilthey had used Husserl's theory of intentionality to develop a conception of psychic objectivity which must be distinguished from natural objectivity. When Dilthey applies Husserl's theory of signification we will find that language is interpreted more contextually in order to make possible the description of psychic structures as distinct from natural objects.

From Description to Expression

Through his analysis of the intentional meaning of language, Husserl had minimized the representational role of language. Using this phenomenological analysis to clarify his own account of description, Dilthey explicitly paraphrases a passage from the *Logische Untersuchungen* (II, part 1,39): "The physical phenomenon of the linguistic expression and the relation of the same to a meant objectivity do not constitute a mere cotemporal aggregate, but an inner unity. It is characteristic that while we experience (*erleben*) the word-representation, we live, not in the representation of the word, but exclusively in the realization of its meaning, its significance" (*GS*,VII,40).

Language is basically a transparency such that we can immediately experience (*erleben*) its appropriateness to what is meant. Ordinarily, we do not compare words and objects because we directly intend the object by means of the word. The word is an indication rather than a reproduction of reality. Thus we can see why early in the essay on psychic structure, Dilthey had claimed that the description of the human or historical world in the *Geisteswissenschaften* "is not in any way a copy or transcript (*Abschrift*) of a reality beyond it" (*GS*,VII,3). Instead, psychohistorical descriptions may present more than the objectively apprehended content of *Erlebnis*. In what Dilthey calls "significative apprehension," linguistic description actually completes and comprehends the initially unfulfilled evidence of *Erlebnis*. "The simple statement about an *Erlebnis* that says, 'this suffering is unbearable,' already contains two determinations about its nature which transcend the single *Erlebnis* and as such stand before me independently. . . . these determinations can not be traced back to the *Erlebnis* by adequation. They tend to exhaust the *Erlebnis*, bring it to distinct consciousness and encompass it" (*GS*,VII,30–31).

Inasmuch as certain descriptions can fully exhaust an *Erlebnis* and even transcend it, their appropriateness can be accounted for in terms of the *Fortgezogenwerden* of *Erlebnis* itself. Because *Erlebnis* is characterized by a partial transcendence in referring to its psychic context, it itself calls for linguistic description whereby its relatedness to other experience can be explicated.

This effort to justify description in psychology as based on the self-transcendence of *Erlebnis* raises further questions about the adequacy of introspection. Introspection can no longer be derived from the self-givenness of acts of consciousness, for the latter must be understood in terms of the intentional structures of the contents of *Erlebnis*. Dilthey had already limited the scope of introspection in the *Ideen*, but if *Erlebnis* is now seen as always transcending itself, how is it possible for introspection to grasp it at all?

In a set of notes written for a revised *Poetik* there is an important fragment entitled "Strukturpsychologie" ("Structural Psychology") which shows how around 1907 or 1908 Dilthey's reflections on language led to serious doubts about the reliability of introspection and its linguistic expression. Taking certain personal experiences as his starting point, Dilthey raises some problems:

> I am grieved about the death of my nephew; in this experience I remain localized in space and oriented in the sequence of time. This I now make an object of observation through introspection (*Introspektion*). Can I base a science on this? If I want to express this observation in words then we must recall that these words belong to a linguistic usage which has been conditioned in many ways. Observation itself is determined by the questions which I pose. As soon as I ask myself or someone else whether the aesthetic impression of a mountain contains empathy, then it is there immediately. . . . [*GS*,VI,317–18]

Once I reflect on the possibility of empathy being involved in the original act, how can I be sure that I am not reading empathy into it? Also, there exist many borderline areas in psychic experience where different languages may lead us to make divisions or definitions in various ways, so that what we identify as grief may be as much an indication of linguistic usage and local custom as an intrinsic quality of the state observed. How can I rule out the retroactive effect of such relative linguistic means of classification on the act of introspection itself?

Although Dilthey had always denied that introspection could give the sort of absolute self-knowledge claimed by the intuitionists, he had still assumed that, except for its inability to grasp the playful or evanescent, it did provide undistorted access to the givens of psychic life. But insofar as introspection is now recognized to involve not only elementary logical operations but also retroactive or reflective determinations which may introduce new components into the original act, introspection itself must be considered an interpretive act. Moreover, even were the original act or state to be grasped in its purity, the description of it would still be subject to the external conditioning factors of linguistic usage.

The interpretive components which render introspection or absolute self-knowledge impossible are precisely what makes it possible for psychological descriptions to be useful for self-understanding in everyday life. However, there comes a point when these components become so conventionalized as to stand in the way of greater self-understanding. Although the feasibility of description was derived from the self-transcendence of *Erlebnis*, there is no assurance that the particular way an *Erlebnis* transcends itself is not arbitrarily induced. What is to prevent psychological description from becoming unnecessarily artificial?

Dilthey's questioning of introspection and linguistic usage can be restated in terms of the more general problem concerning "the localization of psychic processes in the context of overall psychic structure" (*GS*,VI,317). As previously noted, the description of psychic structure was meant to provide preconceptions and ground rules for relating *Erlebnisse*. The descriptive psychological concepts provide a general orientation as the basis for judging how any particular *Erlebnis* is to be located. Whether hate is purely a feeling or already contains something impulsive in it cannot, we admit, be determined by appealing to the general descriptive distinction between feeling and willing. But this does not mean that the distinction is to be negated since we could exercise what has been called "reflective judgment" in considering how it may have to be refined through an explication of the concrete givens of psychic life.

Dilthey points here to the need to move away from direct descriptions and classifications of feelings to less direct accounts indicating what they are about, what values they embody, etc. For a more firm delimitation of *Erlebnisse*, Dilthey concludes, ". . . only one other method can lead further." This is an indirect method or procedure which goes through "an intermediary," namely, the study of expressions. As critics of introspection, "Brentano and Husserl had already applied this method to some extent," but it must be carried further, especially with regard to expressions of *Erlebnis* as found in poetry and literature (*GS*,VI,318).

Literary expression can preserve the fluidity of *Erlebnis* in raising it to objectivity. The poet allows his *Erlebnis* to unfold until it finds its natural terminus in what Dilthey would later call its *Erlebnisausdruck* (expression of lived experience) (see chapter 8). In a collection of literary essays, *Das Erlebnis und die Dichtung*, Dilthey points out that through a sensitivity to the syntactical forms of language, a poet like Hölderlin can more appropriately express the inner movement of psychic life than is possible in the direct use of descriptive words like "sadness," "joy," and "desire" (*ED*,285). Thus although Dilthey complained about the abstractness of the descriptive terminology of psychology, he at the same time points to the poetic use of language as being able to preserve the dynamic aspects of life while objectively delineating its structural relations.

Dilthey still holds to the view of "Die Entstehung der Hermeneutik" that linguistic expressions are the most useful form of symbolic communication, but he emphasizes that they cannot be studied in isolation from other forms of human expression. The investigation of expressions proceeds through insight into all aspects of life: ". . . expression, understanding, structure, function, and conduct" (*GS*,VI,318). Whereas Husserl's account of linguistic expressions was based on their intentional meaning alone, Dilthey's aesthetic and historical concerns make him no less interested in what they betray about their context than in what they directly assert and indicate. The concept of expression must be broadened to include not only linguistic expressions, but also bodily gestures, physical actions, or any form in which life manifests itself in the sensuous world. They range from the personal or individual to the more encompassing kinds of objectifications like religions, laws, and political institutions (*GS*,VII,319–21). And insofar as past life endures in these expressions, they provide the data of historical knowledge. In history, then, we study expressions of life as they are linked together in their temporal and dynamic relationships (*GS*,VII,261).

Expression (*Ausdruck*) is thereby added as a fundamental, intermediary concept between *Erlebnis* and *Verstehen* in the human studies. In "Die Abgrenzung der Geisteswissenschaften" ("Delimitation of the Human Studies") of 1909,[21] Dilthey states that the human studies are "all based on *Erleben*, the expressions of *Erlebnisse* and the understanding of these expressions" (*GS*,VII,71). The *Aufbau*, which was published the following year, elaborates this hermeneutical approach to the *Geisteswissenschaften*. It is through the hermeneutic interpretation of expressions of life that the general tasks of the *Geisteswissenschaften* are to be conceived:

> Even the psychophysical unit, man, knows himself through the same mutual relationship of lived experience and understanding; . . . but, when he tries to hold fast and grasp his states of mind by turning his attention upon himself, then the narrow limits of such an introspective method of self-knowledge show themselves;

[21] This is the third of the preliminary papers on the foundation of the *Geisteswissenschaften* Dilthey delivered to the Prussian Academy.

only his actions, his formulated expressions of life and
the effects of these on others, teach man about himself.
Thus, he comes to know himself only by the circuitous
route of understanding. . . . Briefly, it is through the
process of understanding that life gains illumination
about its depths, and yet we understand ourselves and
others only by putting what we have actually experienced into every kind of expression of our own and
others' lives. So mankind becomes the subject matter
of the human studies only because the relation between
experience, expression, and understanding exists.[22]

The Re-evaluation of Psychology

Although Dilthey had made it clear that the investigation
of expressions was meant to further the understanding of
psychic processes, it seems to have militated against his
plan to further develop his structural psychology. Generally, in his late writings, the status of psychology is made
ambiguous at best, and its contributions to historical knowledge appear to be minimized or even excluded. Thus, in the
Aufbau, where Dilthey characterizes understanding in the
human studies as moving from the outer (sensuous) to the
inner (meaning) side of expressions, he pointedly rejects
the "common error" of identifying ". . . our knowledge of
this inner side with the course of psychic life, that is, with
psychology."[23] Dilthey recognizes that historical understanding of Roman law obviously does not require psychological knowledge, but is achieved by going back to a spiritual product with its own structure (*GS*,VII,85). Similarly
the task of literary understanding is described relative to
an expression separable from psychic processes:

Before me lies the work of a poet. It consists of letters,
composed by type-setters and printed by machines.

[22] *GS*, VII, 86–87; here I have used the translation of Rickman, *Pattern and Meaning in History*, p. 71, but in a slightly altered form.
[23] *GS*, VII, 84; Rickman, p. 69.

But poetics and the history of literature deal only with the relation of this pattern of words to that which is expressed by these words. It is here decisive that what is expressed are not the inner processes in the poet, but a structure created in these processes yet separable from them. . . . Here a context of spirit or meaning is realized which is manifested in the world of the senses. . . . [GS,VII,85]

There is an obvious element of self-criticism here, for earlier in the *Poetik*, Dilthey had unwisely claimed that a spectator understands a work to the extent that he reproduces the creative process of the artist (*GS*,VI,191,194). Most commentators on Dilthey's aesthetics—René Wellek, Michael Scherer, Müller-Vollmer, to name a few—interpret this as evidence of Dilthey's rejection of his earlier psychological writings. Wellek, in his critical analysis of Dilthey's poetics, laments the tragic turn of events which made Dilthey realize at the end of his life that his entire psychological approach to literature had to be abandoned.[24] Assessing the situation more positively, Müller-Vollmer argues that Dilthey's main poetic insights were finally purified of contemporary psychological errors. In other words, it had merely taken Dilthey some time to properly separate psychological analysis from what Müller-Vollmer considers to be his underlying "ontological analysis" of literature.[25]

To be sure, Dilthey's turn to hermeneutics represents a fundamental maturation of his thought. But it should not be overdramatized as signaling either the tragic or happy denouement of his psychological program. As we shall see,

[24] "Wilhelm Dilthey's Poetics and Literary Theory," pp. 126–27.
[25] Müller-Vollmer, *Towards a Phenomenological Theory of Literature*, p. 188. It is far from obvious, however, that Dilthey ever did or would conceive of a pure "ontological basis of literary art." Müller-Vollmer's inspiration for his interpretation appears to be the phrase, "The Poet's Understanding of Reality," given in an outline for a proposed revision of the *Poetik*. See *GS*, VI, 308.

psychological considerations remain evident in the *Weltan-schauungslehre*; and despite his insistence on the imperson-ality of art and its understanding, the aesthetic psychology still has much to contribute. For the moment, it should be noted that the passage in the *Aufbau* from which the above quote was taken also contains a remark that the object of lit-erary understanding is "at first" (*zunächst*) completely dis-tinct from psychic processes. The significance of this quali-fication will become more evident in the next chapter after we have explored the specific nature of Dilthey's re-evalua-tion of the role of psychology in the *Geisteswissenschaften*.

Too much has been made of the fact that in "Die Abgren-zung der Geisteswissenschaften" psychology is not even mentioned as one of the human studies. If we look carefully at the highly qualified language of the introduction to this paper we can see that the hermeneutic approach is pre-sented there as an attempt to arrive at certain common cate-gories in terms of which both the *Geisteswissenschaften* and the *Kulturwissenschaften* could be defined.[26] Because Dil-they's concern was to find some general points of agreement with the Neo-Kantians, it is not surprising he would leave unmentioned the one discipline over which they most sharply differed. The disciplines Dilthey referred to in "Die Abgrenzung der Geisteswissenschaften" were given merely as examples of human studies; there is nothing to indicate that the listing was meant to be definitive. Thus the omis-sion of psychology reflects more a choice to suspend polem-ics than a decision to exclude psychology from the *Geistes-wissenschaften*.

[26] *GS*, VII, 70: "Ohne in die Ansichten polemisch einzugehen, die in diesen Debatten einander gegenüberstanden, lege ich einige Be-trachtungen vor, welche denselben Fragen gewidmet sind. Ich beginne mit der Frage, wie den Naturwissenschaften gegenüber eine andere Klasse von Wissenschaften abgegrenzt werden könne, mag man nun für sie den Ausdruck 'Geisteswissenschaften' oder 'Kulturwissen-schaften' wählen."

This is not to say that Dilthey was not in any way reconsidering the status of psychology. A glance at two earlier drafts for this paper will help to indicate the real course of his thinking. In the first draft Dilthey starts with the same partial list of *Geisteswissenschaften,* but he appends the observation that as a matter of fact psychology can be considered to be related to them. "When psychology stands in a relation to these *Geisteswissenschaften* whereby on the one hand it grounds (*begründet*) them and on the other hand it makes use of their data, then this should at first be taken merely as a fact, and the question whether it is one of the *Geisteswissenschaften* remains open" (*GS,*VII,304). This suggests that Dilthey was entertaining the possibility raised by his essay "Der psychische Strukturzusammenhang," that if the description of psychic structure serves mainly as a prelude to an epistemology of the *Geisteswissenschaften,* then qua its scientific contribution psychology should perhaps be classified simply as a *Naturwissenschaft.* Yet whatever the final classification, it will in any case continue to perform significant tasks relative to the human studies in general.

In the second draft, we see Dilthey considering on what basis psychology may be placed among the human studies. He points out that a definitive concept of the *Geisteswissenschaften* will only become possible as we make progress in finding general agreement about the individual disciplines to be included. In the meantime, the presence of *Erlebnis* and *Verstehen* would serve as a working criterion to distinguish the human studies from the natural sciences. The process of comparing *Erlebnis* and *Verstehen* to refine our knowledge of the human world goes through expression. But expressions can only provide an indirect unity for such knowledge, and any final unity will have to come through a demonstration of the thesis (*Satz*) that ". . . *Erlebnisse* themselves can ultimately provide a structural context comprehending both *Erlebnis* and *Verstehen*. . . . Not only can the nature of the *Geisteswissenschaften* be definitively established by this thesis, but also their scope can thereby be widened and their articulation determined" (*GS*,VII,312–13). It is, of course, psychology which must define the nature of this nexus of *Erlebnisse*. Thus ". . . if this thesis can be demonstrated, it will make possible a descriptive and analytic psychology, which will complete the class of the *Geisteswissenschaften* and give them systematic unity" (*GS*,VII,313).

These ideas do not appear in the third draft read before the Academy, but they are assumed and occasionally made explicit in Dilthey's remarks on the final aims of historical understanding in the *Aufbau*. There psychology once again reappears among the *Geisteswissenschaften* listed: "history, political economy, law, political science, the studies of religion, of literature and poetry, of the visual arts and music, of philosophical *Weltanschauungen* and systems, and *finally psychology*" (*GS*,VII,79; italics added). Although Dilthey no longer claims that psychology is the first of the *Geisteswissenshaften*, we can expect, in the light of the above suggestion, that it will complete the *Geisteswissenschaften* and "give them systematic unity."

It should also be mentioned that in the *Aufbau*, Dilthey makes use of both conceptions of psychic structure that had appeared in his previous writings: the stable conscious structures described in "Der psychische Strukturzusammenhang" as providing preconceptions for a theory of knowledge, as well as the dynamic, but not fully conscious, acquired psychic nexus of the early descriptive psychology. Not only does he explicitly refer us back to the lecture "Dichterische Einbildungskraft und Wahnsinn" (1886) and to other works where the concept of the acquired nexus was developed, but he also summarizes how this nexus is possessed by us and how it regulates our conscious acts (see *GS*,VII,80 fn.2). The recurrence in the *Aufbau* of the most central concept of his psychology indicates that although Dilthey might have contemplated modifications in his original program for a descriptive psychology, he viewed it as still useful in dealing with change and process.

The Hermeneutic Approach to the *Geisteswissenschaften*

In the *Aufbau*, the grounding of the *Geisteswissenschaften* is seen as involving three main tasks: (1) to describe the *logical* operations presupposed, (2) to clarify the *methods* used and their interrelations, and (3) to define their *epistemological* limits. By more clearly distinguishing among these three tasks than he had before and treating them in sequential order, Dilthey brings together in a matured statement the results of his psychological and hermeneutic approaches to the *Geisteswissenschaften*.

The opening section—which is largely based on the hermeneutically oriented drafts of "Die Abgrenzung der Geisteswissenschaften"—begins with a discussion of the distinction between the physical and psychical. This distinction, however, is justified on purely logical grounds. Dilthey admits that the concept of the psyche is an abstraction, but no more so than the idea of a physical object. "Both concepts can only be applied if we remain conscious that they are abstracted from the reality of mankind—they do not designate full realities, but are nevertheless legitimately formed abstractions" (*GS*,VII,81).

In his rather cursory remarks on psychology, the concept of the acquired psychic nexus is given a kind of transcendental justification which allows it to become at least a logical subject underlying descriptions of change in the human studies: "I do not know what would be objectionable about separating this nexus of *Erlebnisse* within the course of life by means of abstraction and making this psychological concept the logical subject of propositions (*Urteilen*) and theoretical considerations. The formation of this concept is justified by the fact that what is selected by it as a logical subject makes possible the propositions and theories necessary in the *Geisteswissenschaften*" (*GS*,VII,80–81). Although the psyche is not to be conceived as an entity directly given in experience, or discoverable through introspection, it remains logically indispensable as a way of organizing our *Erlebnisse*.

The logical foundations of the *Geisteswissenschaften* are further discussed in a more systematic section entitled "Objective Apprehension." This was also the title of the first part of the essay "Der Strukturzusammenhang des Wissens," and Dilthey elaborates on the account of logical operations given there. But it should be noted that in the essay of 1905, Dilthey first contrasted the *Erlebnis*-apprehension characteristic of the *Geisteswissenschaften* with the intuitive perception of the *Naturwissenschaften* before going on to analyze the elementary and discursive logical operations. In this section of the *Aufbau*, however, the question of the peculiarities of *Erlebnis*-apprehension is bracketed, as it were, and only the nature of logical operations is dealt with. While the earlier procedure might have implied a logical distinction between the natural sciences and the human studies, Dilthey now explicitly concludes that ". . . the same forms and . . . functions of thought enable us to make connections in the *Naturwissenschaften* and the *Geisteswissenschaften*." From this common logical foundation, ". . . there then arise specific methods in applying these forms and functions due to the peculiar conditions and tasks of the *Geisteswissenschaften*" (*GS*,VII,121).

Dilthey clearly recognizes that the concepts of the physical and the psychical can at best create certain logical parallels between the *Naturwissenschaften* and the *Geisteswissenschaften*. But because the *Naturwissenschaften* also deal with the psyche, and the *Geisteswissenschaften* with the physical, the parallel provides no criterion for delineating the two sets of disciplines. Thus he proceeds by claiming that the hermeneutic method of the human studies provides a more fruitful way of approaching an epistemological contrast with the natural sciences. It is not until the sec-

300

tion on methodological problems that Dilthey contrasts the *Erlebnis*-apprehension of the psychic nexus from the intuitive apprehension of physical objects (*GS*,VII,139f.).

It seems then that the role of the psychological will have to be re-examined at every level of investigation. Dilthey specifically states that his previous definitions of psychic structure and the psychic life-unity (*psychische Lebenseinheit*) are to be operative in his hermeneutical analysis of the methodology of the human studies (*GS*,VII,131). But this only shows that certain descriptive psychological *concepts* of the *Ideen* have logical implications for the *Geisteswissenschaften*. It entails nothing about the specific methodological contributions of psychology as one of the human studies.

The preparatory studies of 1905 had focused on the psychological description of static structures. By now discriminating more explicitly between logical and methodological problems, Dilthey can avoid the implication that because logically the concept of psychic structure is static, that therefore methodologically, such structures must be understood or described in static terms as well. In the historical context of the human studies, psychic change need not be accounted for in terms of the naturalistic methods of experimental psychology. Indeed Dilthey claims that the process of understanding conceived in terms of the hermeneutic circle is peculiarly suited to deal with the dynamism of historical life and its subsystems.

The hermeneutic method defines its subject matter through a series of mutually dependent perspectives: "Understanding presupposes *Erlebnis*, and this lived experience first turns into experience of life when understanding moves from the narrowness and subjectivity of *Erlebnis* into the region of totalities and generalities. Furthermore, the perfect understanding of the individual person presupposes systematic knowledge while the latter is dependent on the dynamic apprehension of the individual living unity" (*GS*,VII,131).

In the *Einleitung*, Dilthey had distinguished between the

301

Naturwissenschaften as displaying a constructionist order
and the *Geisteswissenschaften* as a looser cumulative system.[27] Although his effort to provide a descriptive psychological foundation might have been compatible with the initial cumulative ideal of the *Geisteswissenschaften*, the
circularity involved in Dilthey's later hermeneutic conception makes it impossible to regard descriptive psychology
or any other discipline as the first of the human studies.
Since from the hermeneutic perspective all the human
studies are interpretive and mutually dependent, none can
assume the primary role once assigned to psychology. Connected with this is the realization that the principle of
mutual dependence applies not only to interdisciplinary cooperation in the system of the human studies, but also to the
interdependence of the particular methods contributing to
hermeneutic interpretation. In this light the descriptive
method itself can no longer be construed as foundational.

Here again, it should be made clear that this is not to be
viewed as a particular argument against description—or by
extension, a further criticism of psychology as the discipline
with which it was most identified—but rather as an indication of (1) the recognition, earlier noted, that description
itself already involves interpretation and (2) the increased
awareness of the significance of analysis and comparison in
historical understanding. In point of fact, we may well
argue that it is precisely by discriminating among the descriptive, analytic, and comparative methods of his psychology, and by then drawing out the potential of the latter
two, that Dilthey could demonstrate the applicability to the
Geisteswissenschaften of the insights and procedures of his
psychological writings.

In defining the methodological task, Dilthey reasserts his
view that the *Geisteswissenschaften* are as much concerned
with individuality and concrete processes as with generalizing theory and abstract structure. Therefore he states that,

[27] See above, p. 71, for the meaning of the term *Aufbau*.

302

like psychology, all the human studies will have to be predominantly descriptive and analytic. Here, it is worthy of note that in referring back to the *Ideen*, Dilthey specifically cites only those of his discussions devoted to analytic procedures. This implies that, methodologically, psychology has most to contribute to the analysis and articulation of the concrete continua given in the human studies.

In fact, the *Individualpsychologie* that Dilthey refers to in a later section of the *Aufbau* involves much more analysis than previously thought, and is inseparable from the comparative method. We may then anticipate that psychology's contributions to the epistemological task of the *Geisteswissenschaften* will be associated with the comparative procedures necessary for delineating the categories through which understanding grasps individuals. With the hermeneutic circle to be completed in the apprehension of the life-unity of the individual, interpretation is always pulled back to the problem of individuality—the problem that Dilthey had earlier broached as he sought to develop a comparative psychology which would complete his descriptive and analytic psychology. In chapter 6, we suggested that Dilthey dropped his comparative psychology in order to better defend his claims for descriptive psychology, and that his ideas on reflective experience and judgment were taken up in his hermeneutic theory. If psychology is now to be characterized as the discipline that completes the system of the *Geisteswissenschaften*, the description must give way to the comparative method which is an integral aspect of interpretation. No longer able to claim that description is methodologically autonomous, Dilthey is forced to reinterpret his original program for descriptive psychology in terms of logical investigations. Thus we have seen how the description of psychic structure is preserved as a mere propaedeutic to the logical task of the *Aufbau*.

Also, with description no longer identified as the primary method of the human studies, Dilthey's earlier distinction between the *Geisteswissenschaften* as descriptive and the

Naturwissenschaften as explanatory is much weakened. However, against the formal sort of dichotomies implied by Windelband, Dilthey had already argued that the two sets of disciplines need not be distinguished according to any sharp division of method. Description and explanation can occur in both the *Naturwissenschaften* and the *Geisteswissenschaften*, but their scope and task will differ. In the final analysis, only an epistemological grounding for the *Geisteswissenschaften* can delimit them. Having denied that any particular method or discipline can be considered foundational, the epistemological delimitation occurs with reference to a conception of a historical world common to all the human studies.

CHAPTER EIGHT

Interpretation in the Historical World

As HE MOVES to the central portion of the *Aufbau*, Dilthey explicitly states that he is resuming the task of the *Einleitung* (1883). In the first volume of that work, as Dilthey reminds us, the grounding of the human studies had already been conceived in terms of a Critique of Historical Reason. Recalling how historical and psychological considerations had led him to deal with the whole person to obtain a proper epistemological orientation, he now turns to the complexities of the historical world, where a full cooperation of human functions is manifested (*GS*,VII,117). Through an analysis of the formation of the historical world Dilthey explicates the system of the human studies and finally arrives at an epistemological delimitation of the *Geisteswissenschaften* and the *Naturwissenschaften*.

Dilthey makes use of Hegel's concept of objective spirit in the *Aufbau* to define the historical world and to further demonstrate that his theory of interpretation is not psychologistic. While Husserl's concept of intentionality of consciousness had served to clarify psychic objectivity, the Hegelian term points to the objective communal basis of historical understanding. At the same time, Dilthey still sees the ultimate task of interpretation as the understanding of individuality. The concept of objective spirit provides the epistemological background for a projected *Individualpsychologie* (psychology of the individual) and the hermeneutic concept of *Nacherleben* (re-experiencing). These themes are raised in the *Aufbau* and developed in the *Entwürfe* which were to also make up his projected Critique of Historical Reason.

305

Objective Spirit and the Historical Subject

In his general discussion of the human studies, Dilthey had denied that they dealt with objects (*Objekten*) different in kind from those of the natural sciences.[1] Yet in indicating that a mere methodological distinction is not enough, he now claims that there is a difference in the subject matter of history due to an exclusive attention to the significance of its data. "The peculiar domain of history is to be sure external; yet the tones that form a musical composition, the court room in which justice is pronounced . . . derive only their material (*Material*) from nature; . . . the human studies deal solely with the meaning these facts have received through the efficacy (*Wirken*) of spirit" (*GS*,VII,118).

Because Dilthey defines the peculiarity of subject matter, not materially, but in terms of an embodied meaning, no ontological dualism between nature and history need be seen here. The Neo-Kantian criticism of the *Naturwissenschaft-Geisteswissenschaft* distinction can still be avoided if it is acknowledged that there exists a difference between subject matter (*Sache*) and material (*Material*). Dilthey continues to affirm that history receives its material from nature, but once its objects have been methodologically interpreted as the embodiment of spirit, they must be distinguished (*sachlich unterscheidet*) as constituting the subject matter of historical knowledge (*GS*,VII,118). Therefore, in concluding his account of the methodological task, Dilthey writes of the human studies:

> Their range is identical with that of understanding, and understanding has the objectifications of life consistently as its object. Thus the range of the human studies is determined by the objectification of life in the external world. The human spirit can only understand what it has created. Nature, the object (*Gegenstand*) of the natural sciences, embraces the reality which has

[1] See above, p. 222.

arisen independently of the efficacy (*Wirken*) of spirit. Everything on which man has actively impressed his stamp forms the object (*Gegenstand*) of the human studies.[2]

The distinction between nature and the objectifications of life in the external world can be justified on epistemological grounds without appealing to any speculative metaphysics. Man knows abstractly that he is a part of nature, but he can intuitively understand his participation in the transformation of nature as it is objectified and preserved in the products of his activity and understanding. To designate the realm in which the human spirit is embodied, Dilthey adopts the Hegelian term "objective spirit" (*objektiver Geist*). In it, as Dilthey writes elsewhere, ". . . the past is a permanently enduring present for us" (*GS*,VII,208) so that the concept designates the subject matter of history.

The *Aufbau* was written after Dilthey had explored the philosophy of life of the young Hegel and had come to have a higher regard for his philosophy in general. While still objecting to Hegel's constructionist approach and to its emphasis on the rational will, Dilthey pays tribute to Hegel's seminal ideas for the conceptualization of history: "In the writing of history his influence lasts precisely . . . in the ordering of stages of spirit. And the time will come when his attempt to construct a system of concepts which can master the ceaseless stream of history can be valued and turned to use" (*GS*,VII,116).

For Hegel, objective spirit constitutes a specific stage in an ideal development beginning with subjective spirit and culminating in absolute spirit. To make the concept of objective spirit fruitful for historical understanding, Dilthey argued, it must be freed from its one-sided grounding in reason and from any metaphysical construction so that it can adequately represent the irrationality and finitude of

---

[2] *GS*, VII, 148; cf. Rickman's translation in *Pattern and Meaning in History*, p. 125.

human existence as well. In Dilthey's usage, "objective spirit" does not, therefore, posit any ideal communion of spirit, but designates the plurality of objectifications that can be empirically discovered through the study of history. It is a covering term for *all* modes of expression of human life as they manifest themselves in the external world: ". . . it encompasses language, mores, every kind or style of life just as much as family, society, state and law. Also what Hegel included in absolute spirit—art, religion, and philosophy— now falls under the concept of objective spirit. Spirit objectifies itself in, and is recognized through, the powerful forms of art, religion, and philosophy. Especially in them does the creative individual show himself a representative of communality at the same time" (*GS*,VII,150–51).

This turn to the concept of objective spirit signals a more explicit acknowledgment in Dilthey's writings that the idea of the subject remains a formal abstraction apart from a communal context. Dilthey had always seen that the individual must be understood in relation to his socio-historical context and that knowledge of cultural systems involves higher-order concepts which cannot be simply derived from psychology. Yet, he had still assumed that such concepts could be anticipated by psychology, and referred to them as second-order psychological concepts.[3] In Dilthey's final writings the higher-order concepts necessary to analyze objective spirit are regarded as categories with their own independent justification (*GS*,VII,251).

Whether the psychological concept of *Erlebnis* or the hermeneutic conception of *Verstehen* constitutes the better starting point for the human studies is no longer in question in the *Aufbau*. Instead, it focuses on objective spirit as the medium wherein they stand structurally related. "*Every single expression of life represents a common feature* in the realm of this objective spirit. Every word . . . every gesture . . . every work of art and every historical deed is intelligible because the people who express themselves through

[3] See above, p. 69–70.

them and those who understand them have something in common; the individual always experiences, thinks, and acts in a common sphere and only there does he understand" (*GS*,VII,146). With Dilthey's definition of objective spirit we can reformulate Hegel's thesis that spirit must know itself absolutely by saying that man knows himself historically only through the communality of objective spirit.

Further evidence of Dilthey's increased sense of affinity with Hegel can be found in the *Entwürfe* where he comments on the use of psychology by pragmatic historians. Dilthey had previously criticized pragmatic historians for reducing the significance of history to the level of psychological motives and personal interests.[4] But, in the *Einleitung*, Dilthey made it clear that his critique stemmed from a kind of middle position between Hegel and the pragmatic historian, for he was still hopeful of reconciling the latter's approach to history with Hegel's systematic interpretation of history. In the *Entwürfe* however, Dilthey attacks pragmatic history much more harshly, and with language reminiscent of Hegel's critique of historians who feel "obliged to trace the supposed secret motives that lie behind the open facts of the record."[5] Whereas Dilthey had previously thought the dangers of psychological investigation of the motives of historical figures could be overcome by being integrated into a larger framework, he now rejects such investigations altogether, for their unrealizable goals can only produce historical scepticism.

In a fragment dealing with the problem of historical scepticism, Dilthey declares that the pragmatic historian who seeks to account for an historical deed in terms of a private motive is aiming at something that cannot be adequately ascertained: ". . . an individual knows his own motives only in an uncertain way, and others have even less of an insight

[4] See above, p. 62.
[5] Hegel, *The Encyclopedia of the Philosophical Sciences*, trans. W. Wallace in *The Logic of Hegel*, London: Oxford University Press, 1965, p. 256.

into them. What personal interest, ambition, need for power, and vanity contribute to historically decisive deeds can only be established to a limited degree. Even letters or verbal utterances remain questionable" (GS,VII,259). Beyond the difficulty of defining the different possible motives and weighing their relative importance, there is also the problem of deception being practiced on oneself and others. This leads Dilthey to a discussion about the appropriateness of psychological *raffinement* in history. In this context, Dilthey writes disparagingly of the French, who ". . . especially like to prove their perspicacity, their superiority over things and people by attributing petty and selfish motives to great accomplishments. They are accustomed to this by their use of the pragmatic method which investigates the relation of motive, act, and effect, if they are not applying political theory or assessing military-political forces" (GS,VII,260). For the sake of the objectivity of history, Dilthey expresses a willingness to forego the kind of psychological subtlety for which French historians have been noted, and speaks of a duty to place certain limits on subjective speculation. Historical scepticism, Dilthey concludes ". . . can only be overcome if historical methods are not expected to ascertain motives. . . . and when psychological *raffinement* is replaced by the understanding of the spiritual products of man" (GS,VII,260).

Evidently, Dilthey is in basic agreement with Hegel that pragmatic historians appeal to atomistic psychology ". . . which looks away from the essential and permanent in human nature to fasten its glance on the casual and private features shown in isolated instincts and passions."[6] One might ask, however, whether Dilthey's criticism of psychological *raffinement* does not apply as well to his own earlier claims for the relevance of a less atomistic descriptive psychology to history. To answer this, we only need to point out that the fundamental reason for rejecting psychological *raffinement* is that it constitutes a mode of hypothetical ex-

[6] Hegel, *Encyclopedia*, 256.

planation. Since the descriptive psychology was meant to replace such explanation, the implied criticism might hold only to the extent that Dilthey still allowed for something like motive explanations. But, as discussed in the early psychology, motives would have to be described in terms of the overall pattern of an individual's behavior and of the relatively stable structures of his professed values and ends, before they could be used explanatively. Such conditions restrict the historian to a consideration of only those motives that make sense in relation to the objectively ascertainable meaning of their psychohistorical context. More generally, it had always been Dilthey's view that a historian should arrive at a critical judgment about his subjects by understanding their interaction with the given circumstances—not by positing hidden impulses that claim to explain their actions, but only serve to explain away the given intentions and their results. For Dilthey, understanding had always placed limits on explanation, and the only explicit change involved in Dilthey's remarks about pragmatic history is that of a more severe restriction on motive-explanations.[7]

[7] Nonetheless, Dilthey's critique of psychological *raffinement* is seen as a self-criticism by Howard Tuttle, who claims that motive explanations were central to Dilthey's early theory of history. See Howard Nelson Tuttle, *Wilhelm Dilthey's Philosophy of Historical Understanding: A Critical Analysis*, Leiden: E. J. Brill, 1969, p. 66. Tuttle bases his case on a single line from the 1875 essay "Ueber das Studium der Geschichte der Wissenschaften vom Menschen, der Gesellschaft und dem Staat." He quotes from a section entitled "Kausalität und Motivation" where in commenting on the study of man, Dilthey had written: "The course of acting by causes such as those presented to us in physical nature is here dissolved through the play of motives and purposes" (Tuttle, p. 68; GS, V, 63). However, in the original, the discussion of motives is immediately placed in proper perspective by an examination of higher-order causal relations of an impersonal nature: "Daher das theoretische Grundproblem dieses ganzen Erkenntnisgebietes die besondere Natur der ursächlichen Beziehungen ist, welche im Individuum zwischen seinen Motiven walten, in höherer Ordnung dann zwischen Individuen oder zwischen den

Yet, Dilthey's sharp criticism of motive-explanation suggests that understanding should not dwell on personal agencies and inner conditions. Although Dilthey makes it clear that he does not intend to let higher-order historical categories submerge the value of individuality, they do entail a shift away from the individual. This betrays not so much a reduction of the intrinsic importance of the individual, as it does a new feeling that the individual subject is not always the starting point of historical understanding. Dilthey still speaks of individual subjects as carriers (*Träger*) of historical life and as the crossing points (*Kreuzungspunkte*) of cultural systems (*GS*,VII,151,154). But now such systems are not to be primarily defined in terms of the cooperation of individuals; they are less expressive of personal ends and more steeped in the communal.[8] No longer are individuals the sole creators of the values and goods in the spiritual world. Instead, Dilthey speaks of individuals, communities, and cultural systems as the co-carriers of historical life (*GS*,VII,153). Each such carrier possesses its own inherent unity: "Like the individual, every cultural system, every community has its center (*Mittelpunkt*) within itself" (*GS*,VII,154).

What is really involved here is a changed conception of the nature of a subject. Or more accurately, it represents a clarification and explication of those earlier reflections which had led Dilthey to reject any epistemological ego. The concept of self, as described in Dilthey's psychology, is explicated out of consciousness, and individuality is accordingly defined through a psychic nexus that has been

---

zusammengesetzten Totalkräften in der Gesellschaft und der Geschichte." (*GS*, V, 63–64). The understanding of higher-order relations between individuals does not involve motive-explanation. Tuttle's impression of a potentially "startling" change in Dilthey's theory of history (p. 73) is due to the fact that he mistakenly equated understanding with motive-explanation.

[8] For a comparison with Dilthey's views in the *Einleitung*, see above pp. 57–59, 62–65.

acquired. In the introductory sections of the *Aufbau*, Dilthey has shown that it is only for logical reasons that we assume a psychological subject as given.

Once the ego qua logical subject is justified as an indispensable abstraction, it also becomes possible to speak of transpersonal subjects without reifying them (*GS*,VII,285). If the psyche is acknowledged to be primarily the logical carrier of consciousness, Dilthey sees no reason why individuals, communities and cultural systems cannot also be conceived as the logical carriers of objective spirit. There is then nothing inappropriate about using expressions like *Zeitgeist* and *Volksgeist* so long as one does not anthropomorphize them by substituting *Seele* (soul) for *Geist* (spirit). The soul of a people (*Volksseele*) connotes a collective mode of consciousness, but the spirit of a people (*Volksgeist*) posits no such thing. In the *Einleitung*, Dilthey had dismissed both the concept of *Volksseele* and of *Volksgeist*, but in the *Aufbau* Dilthey distinguished between the two in order to reject only the former.

Dilthey insists that these logical subjects are not to be understood as superempirical realities providing the basis for a metaphysical construction of the historical world. Specifically criticizing Hegel on this score, Dilthey indicates that his own use of the concept of objective spirit is meant to address a basically Kantian problem:

> Insofar as life in its totality . . . takes the place of Hegel's "Reason," the problem of how the science of history is possible arises. For Hegel this problem did not exist. His metaphysics . . . has left this problem behind. But, today, the task is the reverse—to recognize the actual historical expressions of life as the true foundation of historical knowledge and to find a method of answering the question how, on the basis of what is thus given, universally valid knowledge of the historical world is possible.[9]

[9] *GS*, VII, 151; *Pattern and Meaning in History*, trans. Rickman, p. 127.

The given totality of life makes it impossible to posit a simple rational end in terms of which history can be understood. For historical knowledge, objective spirit is to be articulated through what Dilthey calls *Wirkungszusammenhänge* (dynamic systems). The order to be found in human life must be located in a plurality of these complex systems of interaction and their products in which experience and understanding, the irrationality and historicity of life are manifested in their interrelation.

Dynamic Systems and Historical Explanation

As a way of structuring objective spirit in terms of the dynamic relations discernible in historical life, the concept of *Wirkungszusammenhang* (dynamic system) is to be considered central to the human studies. It covers all the possible logical co-carriers of objective spirit by defining them as systems in which certain functions are structurally related as they cooperate in the course of time.

Because every dynamic system develops on the basis of its function, structure, and regularity, it is possible to view history (*Geschichte*) as having various levels of strata (*Schichten*) which embody the structurally related development of the past. Therefore history need not be construed as a simple flow of events, nor have imposed upon it some ideal order or development. The meaning of history can only come through analysis of the dynamic systems that compose it. "Whereas no law of development is discernible in the concrete order of events, its analysis into particular homogeneous dynamic systems opens up the vista of sequences of states, innerly determined, presupposing each other, so that higher levels are built on lower levels, as it were, and in such a way as to lead to an increasing differentiation and integration" (*GS*,VII,169).

Thus, while there is no determinate historical law nor a final end by which to explain or predict the overall course of the world, Dilthey does not rule out the possibility of his-

torical explanation altogether. Within the structural framework of particular dynamic systems, we can still explain
historical genesis and change. Similarly, we can allow for
limited use of construction, so long as it clearly is not applied to overarching relations between the dynamic systems. What Dilthey says about higher levels being built
upon lower levels is to be applied as an analogy only within
discrete dynamic systems.

We saw in chapter 4 that Dilthey thought it possible to
establish lawfully determined sequences of literary style-
forms within certain contexts. Now we must consider
whether the determinism involved in a particular dynamic
system such as literature is a causal relation, or more generally, whether Dilthey is positing a special kind of historical
causality. If this were the case, it could be argued that Dilthey is really making an ontological distinction rather than
the epistemological one insisted upon.

In defining the subject matter of the human studies as the
dynamic systems and their creations, Dilthey contrasts their
teleological character with the causal order of nature: "A
dynamic system (*Wirkungszusammenhang*) differs from
the causal system (*Kausalzusammenhang*) of nature in that
it produces values and realizes ends according to the structure of psychic life. . . . This I call the immanent teleological
character of spiritual dynamic systems, by which is meant
the nexus of functions grounded in their structure. Historical life is creative. It is constantly active in the production
of goods and values . . ." (*GS*,VII,153). The impression that
the immanent teleology of dynamic systems operates independently of nature is strengthened by a section in the
Entwürfe where Dilthey points to the importance for the
Geisteswissenschaften of special categories not derivable
from the *Naturwissenschaften*. "There is no natural causality in the historical world," he asserts, "for cause (*Ursache*)
in this sense entails that it produces effects according to the
necessity of laws: history *knows* only about relations of
doing (*Wirken*) and suffering, action, and reaction"

315

(*GS*,VII,197, italics added). Here Dilthey starts by presenting what would appear to be a metaphysical claim, but it turns out to have merely an epistemological justification. No case is made for the inherent impossibility of linking natural causes to human events. If this were Dilthey's intention, he would be denying his own assertion in the *Aufbau* that "we are ourselves nature, and nature works in us, unconsciously, in dark impulses . . ." (*GS*,VII,80). Rather, it is the direct significance of natural causality for historical understanding that is being questioned, for he goes on to declare that no matter how much the natural sciences may refine categories like causality, "all these conceptual products of natural scientific knowledge are irrelevant to the *Geisteswissenschaften*" (*GS*,VII,197).

Yet, because Dilthey does elsewhere discuss causes (*Ursachen*) in relation to historical change, he is often assumed to be employing the concept of *Wirken* as a causal category peculiar to the *Geisteswissenschaften* (See *GS*,VII, 120,158,165,270). Thus Hodges remarks, ". . . to call the historical object a *Wirkungszusammenhang* is to call it a causal system. Why then *Wirkungszusammenhang* and not simply *Kausalzusammenhang*? Because Dilthey wishes to remind us that historical causality differs specifically from the mechanical causality which rules in nature."[10]

However, when Dilthey speaks of historical causes, it is in the context of describing what the historian works with as his data. It is far from evident that he is thereby positing a special kind of historical causality operative in the dynamic system itself. The concrete causal nexus that the historian establishes through his research is arrived at by the inductive and synthetic methods generally associated with the natural sciences (*GS*,VII,158). It is not until this causal nexus is analyzed into the meaning relations of a dynamic system that it becomes part of a specifically historical explanation of change. "When we seek the complex of causes

[10] Hodges, *The Philosophy of Wilhelm Dilthey*, p. 268.

(*Ursachen*) to account for German literature moving away from its Enlightenment phase, then we distinguish groups of causes, estimate their relative weight, and at some point delimit the infinite causal nexus (*ursächlichen Konnex*) in accordance with the meaning of its moments and in relation to our ends. Thus we articulate a dynamic system (*Wirkungszusammenhang*) in order to explain (*erklären*) the changes in question" (*GS*,VII,158). In dynamic systems a causal nexus is redefined in relation to a meaning framework, so that it is misleading to interpret the concept of *Wirkungszusammenhang* as a causal category. Dynamic systems can encompass causal relations, but are not conceived in terms of them. The concept of *Wirkung* merely connotes a certain efficacy displayed in systems of interaction and their results.

The concept of *Wirkungszusammenhang* is intended then not to introduce a special historical causality, but to reduce the relevance of the concept of cause as such. Dilthey's claim that the proper categorial understanding of history "knows" nothing of natural causes (*GS*,VII,197), need not entail the stronger affirmation that historical events are to be divorced from natural causes. Here it is important to consider the relation of dynamic systems to purposive systems which we have already described as both teleological and causal.

Peter Krausser points out that in the "Uebersicht meines Systems" (1896–1897), Dilthey used the concept of *Wirkungszusammenhang* to replace that of *Zweckzusammenhang* (purposive system) as defined in his psychology, and that he gave the former preference from then on.[11] In point of fact, the word *Zweckzusammenhang* often occurs after 1897, while *Wirkungszusammenhang* is very seldom used until the *Aufbau* of 1910. In the meantime Dilthey inter-

---

[11] Peter Krausser, *Kritik der endlichen Vernunft: Diltheys Revolution der allgemeinen Wissenschafts- und Handlungstheorie*. Frankfurt am Main: Suhrkamp, 1968, p. 164.

mixes the terminology of *Zweck* (purpose) and *Wirkung* (efficacy) to produce terms like *Zweckwirken* (effectiveness) (*GS*,VII,17). Dynamic systems are described as having an "immanent teleological character" in that they produce values and ends (*GS*,VII,153). Whereas in the context of purposive systems immanent teleology was defined negatively as purposiveness without a purpose (see chapters 3 and 5), in the more neutral context of a dynamic system, it can be defined positively as directed or meaningful efficacy. Because the concept of dynamic systems is given from the perspective of the generalizing concept of objective spirit, it is of a higher order than the concept of purposive system and does not necessarily replace it.

The *Aufbau* was written very much as a continuation of his previous work, and Dilthey rather unrealistically assumes that the reader has retained a thorough knowledge of the way he had worked out his concepts, procedures, and general approach in formulating his psychological and aesthetic theories. In the *Ideen*, he had indicated that the explanative hypotheses of experimental psychology were to be ultimately integrated into his descriptive psychology. That is, the teleological structure of the psyche can serve as the framework for naturalistically conceived causal explanations of particular processes (*GS*,V,176). If purposive systems can be reconciled with natural causality, then the more neutrally defined dynamic systems should also be compatible with it.

However, Dilthey stresses that causal relations are not important in themselves. It is only by conceptualizing causal relations in terms of dynamic systems that we can understand the particular meaning of an event or movement as part of an historical world. According to Dilthey, a strictly causal account of history does not allow one to distinguish one epoch from another, or even to delineate radical transformations like revolutions. "For as such, all changes are causally connected with each other in the same way. Causally, the grounding of the German Reich and the

318

French Revolution are not demarcated from what happened before and after in the corresponding spheres" (*GS*,VII,270). A revolution is characterized, after all, by the fact that a movement ". . . pierces the given lawful order and extends itself over wide domains according to its inherent power" (*GS*,VII,270). Thus, the more smooth and uninterrupted the causal nexus that the historian establishes in his narrative, the harder it is to isolate meaningful moments within it or to recognize their broader significance in the interrelated dynamic systems of history. Certain great transformations like the Reformation and the French Revolution draw upon and affect a whole tradition of accumulated ideas and related cultural systems. "The fact that ideas come to fruition in such transformations," Dilthey writes, "allows them to be so encompassing in their efficacy (*wirken*), as to extend wherever related interests are dormant. Their significance is not exhausted by their factual consequences within the domain of interests from which they were initiated" (*GS*,VII,270).

As an historian of culture, Dilthey is keen to establish the influence of ideas on political life, without, however, claiming that there is a direct causal relation between them and definite political and institutional changes.[12] The efficacy of ideas gives them a certain explanative power, but not in the causal sense. In his essay, "Auffassung und Analyse des Menschen im 15. und 16. Jahrhundert" ("Conception and Analysis of Man in the 15th and 16th Centuries"), Dilthey writes: "Surely as little as the ideas of the French Enlightenment *produced* the French Revolution, did Luther's and Zwingli's sermons and writings bring about the Peasant Wars and the Baptismal Insurrections." Nonetheless, in describing the role of the Reformers, Dilthey illustrates how their thought helps to account for or "explain," as we might

[12] We have focused on Dilthey's work as an historian of culture because it best illuminates his theory of history. But the theoretical writings also recognize the importance of power relations, material conditions, etc.

say, the peculiar force and direction of the events of the time:
". . . new ideas imparted a higher right to the movement
and indicated a direction to it. . . . countless attacks on the
established law were effected by appealing to such guiding
ideas. The Reformation can neither be simply made responsible nor simply absolved for all the violent acts which were
perpetrated in its name, and the morbid convulsions that
followed in its wake" (GS,II,71). Dilthey's account of the
Reformation has been credited as an anticipation of the
Weberian thesis that the Protestant work ethic was indispensable for the rise of modern capitalism. To be sure, Dilthey does discuss the ascetic aspects of Protestantism in
order to make sense of capitalism, yet, unlike Weber, he
would not expect the legitimacy of such an interpretation
to be confirmed or denied by testing it through causal explanations. Rather, we see indications in Dilthey's writings
that understanding the efficacy displayed in historical dynamic systems engenders its own, noncausal mode of
"explanation."

The possibility of sui generis historical explanations has
subsequently been argued for by William Dray and W. B.
Gallie, among others, in opposition to Hempel's covering-
law model for historical explanation as derived from the
natural sciences. According to Gallie, for example, a genetic
explanation provides a necessary condition for an historical
event. As such, it is a perfectly complete explanation of its
kind and need not be supplemented with a causal explanation supplying a sufficient condition. In fact, Gallie argues
that a necessary condition of an event E, if genetically prior
to it, cannot be further explicated as a sufficient condition
of E. The possibility of also finding a covering-law explanation of event E is not ruled out, but is considered an independent question:

Suppose a historian is asked to explain how a certain
statement came to be made, or deliberate action to be
taken, or coherent policy pursued. It would be perfect-

ly natural to say that he has explained, e.g. the statement, when he has discovered or inferred the kind of question—or comment or threat or taunt—that evoked it. But in offering this kind of explanation the historian would not necessarily be claiming, and indeed is not likely to be claiming, that some ideally clever person could have predicted the making of the statement given the occurrence of the question; his claim would more naturally be taken to mean that but for the question's having been put—or but for some other of a disjunction of describable conditions—the statement would remain unintelligible in the sense of lacking an appropriate historical context. The predictive explanation in this case, although it would support the same conclusion, would be a further and quite different inference or explanation, of a different logical pattern, and resting upon partially different evidence.[13]

Dilthey, too, would have set no a priori limit on the feasibility of Hempel's program. Covering-law explanations may well be found for any *aspect* of an historical narrative; but they would be largely irrelevant for an historical understanding of the narrative in its totality. If we wish to explain in terms of causal relations, then Dilthey requires us to focus *within* the particular cultural and social systems as they center upon themselves. The urge for such explanations leads the more systematic human studies—such as economics, law, political and social theory—to isolate or abstract certain dynamic systems from the historical sphere which they presuppose. But for historical knowledge these particular systems must continue to be considered in their interrelations. It is only through understanding and its correlate of noncausal "explanation" that we grasp the com-

[13] W. B. Gallie, "Explanation in History and the Genetic Sciences," *Theories of History: Readings in Classical and Contemporary Sources*, ed. Patrick Gardiner, New York: Free Press, 1959, p. 387.

plex historical dynamisms involved and the meaning of the whole and its parts.

The *Aufbau* is especially concerned with broad, dynamic systems such as cultural movements, revolutions, generations, and epochs which must be described in the context of either national or world history. How the understanding of these larger historical systems is to be related to the interpretation of individuals and particular works is more explicitly dealt with in "Das Verstehen anderer Personen und ihrer Lebensäusserungen" ("The Understanding of Others and Their Expressions of Life") (*GS*,VII,205–227).

Types of Understanding and the Possibility of *Nacherleben*

Written in conjunction with the *Aufbau*, "Das Verstehen anderer Personen" is one of the essays in the *Entwürfe* which were to form the second part of the Critique of Historical Reason. In it Dilthey both summarizes and refines his hermeneutic analysis of expression and historical understanding. And most importantly, he develops the suggestion in the *Aufbau* that understanding is incomplete until it arrives at the apprehension of human individuality. The objective expressions discussed in the hermeneutic writings are now treated as forms of communication and analyzed in terms of how much they disclose about human life. The essay thus begins by distinguishing the expressions or utterances of life into three classes, according to the kind and extent of understanding they produce.

The *first* class of expressions consists of concepts, propositions, and larger thought-structures (*Denkgebilde*) which constitute our systematic knowledge. As such they are abstracted from the experience in which they occurred. ". . . they have a common fundamental character in their conformity to logical norms. They retain their identity, therefore, independently of the position in which they occur in the context of thought. A proposition asserts the validity of a thought-content independently of the varied situations in which it occurs, the difference of time and of people involved" (*GS*,VII,205). Language is the medium of communication and it functions here as Husserl indicated, i.e. by fully effacing itself for the sake of an ideal intersubjective meaning. Anything such expressions reveal about the subject uttering them is deemed irrelevant. Thus such linguistic expressions raise no fundamental problems for hermeneutics.

Actions, which form the *second* class of expressions, do not arise from any intention to communicate, but to achieve some end. However, it is possible for us to grasp their meaning ". . . because of the relation in which it [the action] stands to a purpose, the latter is contained in it. The relation of the action to the mind which it thus expresses is regular and so we can make assumptions about it."[14] For instance, we know what certain tools used by a workman are intended to do, and thereby we can infer what he wants to do without his asserting anything. All of a man's deeds are charged with a kind of conventional meaning by which he unwittingly reveals what his practical concerns are. And yet Dilthey cautions that no matter how accurately we may understand a person on this basis, we only touch a small part of him. A man's practical interests may have been imposed on him by his responsibility as head of a household or by his having accepted a certain profession; they do not necessarily reveal anything about his character or the whole content of his life. In this way practical, no less than theoretical, interests are abstracted from the individuality of a human being. As an agent, man need be no more than a *persona*.

For the *third* class of expression, Dilthey uses the term *Erlebnisausdruck* (expression of lived experience). Dilthey does not make clear what it consists of, but we know from other parts of the text that facial expressions and gestures,

[14] *GS*, VII, 206; *Pattern and Meaning in History*, trans. Rickman, p. 117.

artistic and reflective writings can be considered *Erlebnis-ausdrücke*. Since the first two classes are obviously identified with the theoretical and the practical, this class of expressions is most often assumed to arise from emotive or imaginative experience. But it is precisely the distinguishing feature of an *Erlebnisausdruck* that it expresses the *fullness* of lived experience; there is no identification with a particularized aspect of life as in the other two classes of expressions. "The situation is entirely different with the *Erlebnisausdruck*," Dilthey writes. "A special relation exists between it, the life from which it arises and the understanding that it produces" (*GS*,VII,206). The expression of *Erlebnis* can disclose more of the psychic nexus than any introspection because ". . . it rises from depths which consciousness cannot illuminate" (*GS*,VII,206).

This means that the understanding can only partially determine the relation between such an expression and what is expressed. "It cannot be judged as either true or false, but as sincere or insincere. For here dissimulation, lies, and deception sever the relation between the expression and that which is expressed" (*GS*,VII,206). It is clear that of all expressions, *Erlebnisausdrücke* can reveal most about human life, and thereby pose the greatest problems of understanding.

Turning then to the discussion of the way in which expressions can be understood, Dilthey discriminates a higher from an elementary mode of understanding. By elementary understanding he refers to the understanding of a single life-expression in any of the three classes of expression. Here we apprehend the immediate unity of expression and what is expressed (i.e. its meaning). Dilthey compares this unity to the intimate relation of an emotion and a gesture. "That fright and gesture are not juxtaposed, but one, is based on [the] basic relation of expression to spirit."[15] Even

[15] *GS*, VII, 206. Dilthey warns, however, against submerging the expression in the meaning. We should not interpret the gesture as a mere sign of fright which can be dispensed with once it is apprehended. If it were ignored then there would be no room for

the apprehension of a gesture as meaning fright presupposes our orientation with reference to objective spirit, which is the medium that makes all communication possible. "From this world of objective spirit the self receives nourishment from childhood on. It is the medium in which the understanding of other persons and their objectifications of life takes place. For everything wherein spirit has objectified itself contains something held in common by the 'I' and the 'Thou' (*ein dem Ich und dem Du Gemeinsames*)" (*GS*,VII,208).

Because individuals are immersed in objective spirit, the mutual understanding of language, action, and gesture need not be considered inferential. In its elementary forms, then, understanding requires no conscious inference to determine the relation between a life-expression and its meaning, but it does require reasoning by analogy as suggested by the regular relations contained in common experience. Thus a series of words indicates a proposition, a facial expression manifests joy or sorrow, an act embodies a certain purpose.

In all of these forms the expression is presented as part of a common context and is not yet related to its particular context. The elementary understanding of a proposition really concerns itself only with its accepted common meaning and what is explicitly asserted by it. It does not, as such, delve into the possible implications or presuppositions of the proposition, nor does it deal with the problem of *Kundgabe*, i.e. what an expression betrays about its user.

The transition to higher understanding takes place when we come upon uncertainties in meaning raised by ambiguities, inconsistencies, the possibility of contradiction or de-

---

special kinds of fright. It is important to attend to the physical nuances through which common feelings are expressed. Dilthey's theory of objective spirit or ideal subjects thus stops short of Husserl's idealism according to which the words by which we express an ideal meaning become transparent, as it were. To be sure, our interest is normally focused on the meaning, but never to the extent that the word in its sensuous manifestation is lost sight of.

ception, and so on. With the unity of expression and what is expressed no longer certain, the need for the inferential modes of higher understanding arises. To clarify the meaning of an expression we must test its implications by relating it to other expressions. But higher understanding need not merely set itself the task of correcting or clarifying a given meaning. It may also involve the more positive function of deepening our understanding of an already meaningful objectification. This requires that we more consciously relate expressions to a structural whole by determining how single expressions enrich each other to define a unity. This understanding is especially important in comprehending an *Erlebnisausdruck* and Dilthey illustrates this process through the understanding of artistic expressions. In a work of art, experience is expressed as a self-contained whole, and as previously noted, Dilthey viewed the artist as able to unfold his *Erlebnis* and objectively delineate its structural relations in an *Erlebnisausdruck*. Moreover, in discussing the problem of understanding *Erlebnisausdrücke*, Dilthey had pointed to great works of art as special cases in which the problem of deception is overcome:

> No truly great work of art can . . . aim to display a spiritual content misleading about its author. Indeed it is not intended to say anything about an author. Authentic in itself (*Wahrhaftig in sich*), it stands there fixed, visible, and lasting, thereby making hermeneutic understanding possible. Thus there arises a sphere between knowledge and deed in which life is disclosed in depths not discernible by observation, reflection and theory. [*GS*,VII,207]

It should be noted that even with regard to the expressions of *Erlebnisse*, understanding can be impersonal. This indicates that through its expressions, an *Erlebnis* is able to transcend itself so that what is expressed does not necessarily reveal anything psychological. Instead, the human significance of what is expressed must first be understood

in the elementary forms of objective spirit and then referred to higher forms dealing with the structural relations
and unity of the work itself. With reference to the latter,
Dilthey writes that

> . . . if we want understanding to yield the greatest pos-
> sible result for our knowledge of the spiritual world,
> it is most important that we affirm the validity of this
> form of knowledge in its autonomy. A drama is per-
> formed. . . . the literary spectator can live entirely un-
> der the spell of what happens on the stage. His under-
> standing is then directed on the context of the plot, the
> characters of the protagonists, the integration of mo-
> ments which determine a change of fate. Only then will
> he enjoy the full reality of the portrayed slice of life.
> . . . Such understanding of spiritual creations is con-
> trolled solely by the relation of expressions and the
> spiritual reality expressed in them. [GS,VII,211–12]

Yet despite this insistence on the impersonal meaning-struc-
ture of the work, Dilthey also indicates that a further development of understanding would deal with the question of
the creative process of the author. Thus he continues in the
same passage, "Not until the spectator notices how what he
just accepted as a piece of reality arose artfully and according to a plan in the mind of the poet, does . . . [he] go over
into understanding in which the relation between a creation
and its creator is dominant" (GS,VII,212).

All the modes of higher understanding we have so far
discussed involve an explication of the relation between an
expression and the meaning expressed. However, there is
also another mode of higher understanding which proceeds
from the expression qua product back to the processes producing it (*vom Erwirkten zu Wirkendem*). These productive processes illustrate the kind of efficacy Dilthey described
earlier in relation to dynamic systems, and it is here made
clear that this efficacy is to be conceived, not in terms of
causal explanation, but qua understanding of creativity.

The highest task of understanding is to retrospectively articulate the specific dynamic context in which an *Erlebnisausdruck* originated. Yet when Dilthey seeks to interpret the nature of creativity he speaks of the need for *Nacherleben* (re-experiencing). The terms *Nacherleben* and *Verstehen* are often used side by side in Dilthey's final writings. Both involve the finding of an inner meaning of an external objectification. But the *er-leben* root of *Nacherleben* indicates that this term is not strictly synonymous with understanding, for *Nacherleben* reintroduces the forward movement of *Erleben* that *Verstehen* had reversed.

"Understanding," Dilthey declares, "is in itself an operation running inverse to the course of production" (*GS*,VII,214). Such is Dilthey's rendering of the Kierkegaardian maxim that we live forward and understand backwards. Whereas life and experience move on into the future, our attempts to understand them lead back into the historical past. Unless the movement of *Verstehen* back to the origin or conditions of production is transformed into a concern with the context which provided the productive process its meaning, understanding will fall into an infinite regress. Origins as such cannot provide meaning; they, in effect, take away the meaning that the phenomenon possesses by deriving it as a mere effect of something else.

To avoid being degraded into a hypothetical reproductive activity, *Verstehen* must go over into *Nacherleben*. Although *Verstehen* presupposes a retrogressive movement, Dilthey makes it clear that a "fully sympathetic reliving requires that comprehension (*Verständnis*) proceed forward with the order of the events themselves" (*GS*,VII,214). Thus to be complete, interpretation must go full circle and incorporate both *Verstehen* and *Nacherleben*.

Although Dilthey writes that "*Nacherleben* is the creation in the direction of production . . ." (*GS*,VII,214), it does not reproduce the actual process of creation. We neither start with the particular state of mind of the author, nor do we necessarily end where the author ended. "A lyric poem makes possible a *Nacherleben* of an *Erlebnis*-complex in a temporal sequence: not of the real *Erlebnisse* which inspired the poet, but those that he places in the mouth of an ideal person on the basis of his own" (*GS*,VII,214). *Nacherleben* is a creative understanding which may go beyond the original. Its task is to understand a text as an unfolding continuity whereby the fragments of life that an author selects are articulated into a unified theme. The creativity of *Nacherleben* is specifically what makes it possible to understand an author better than he understood himself. According to Dilthey, the truth contained in this paradoxical saying of Schleiermacher is "capable of a psychological grounding" (*GS*,VII,217). He asserts that *Nacherleben* will not be given a "psychological explanation," although it is possible to relate it to psychological states like empathy.[16]

Thus *after* critical reflection on aesthetic questions has been independently initiated, the understanding of psychological processes can come into its own. This is also the underlying assumption in Dilthey's discussion of literary criticism in the *Aufbau*:

> The structure of a drama consists in a peculiar relation of material, poetic mood, motif, plot, and means of representation. Each of these moments fulfills a function in the structure of the work. And these functions are interconnected by an inner law of poetry. Thus the object which poetics or the history of literature deals with *at first* (*zunächst*) is completely distinct from psychic processes in the poet or his readers. [*GS*,VII, 85, italics added]

[16] *GS*, VII, 215: "Worin besteht nun aber dies Nacherleben? Der Vorgang interessiert uns *hier* nur in seiner Leistung; eine psychologische *Erklärung* desselben soll nicht gegeben werden. So erörtern wir auch nicht das Verhältnis dieses Begriffes zu dem des Mitfühlens und dem der *Einfühlung*, obwohl der Zusammenhang derselben darin deutlich ist, dass das Mitfühlen die Energie des Nacherlebens verstärkt" (Italics added).

Because the important qualifier *at first* has been overlooked or ignored, this passage has been interpreted as excluding psychological considerations from literary understanding. But it is now clear that Dilthey denied the relevance of psychological insights into creativity only for an immediate understanding of a work. Psychological observations about the genius of Goethe (to take an example close to Dilthey's heart), or any introspective remarks found in Goethe's *Dichtung und Wahrheit*, can deepen our understanding of his *Faust*.

Having analyzed the complex functions of hermeneutics, not only in terms of the various types of expression to be interpreted, but also in terms of the different possible levels of understanding, we can estimate the proper extent to which literary and historical interpretation should be impersonal. Dilthey stresses the importance of isolating the text from its author in order to give an initial characterization of the subject matter of poetics and history. By so doing, we can avoid the pragmatic historians' too ready recourse to motive explanation. Only after we have gained a higher understanding into the objective structures of a work—and affirmed the validity and autonomy of such knowledge—will consideration of the relation between the creation and its creator be truly fruitful. Only then can we claim that focusing on the psychological processes will enrich our understanding of both the creativity and enduring creations of life.

Any psychological clues about understanding would have to focus on the relation between *Verstehen* and *Nacherleben* and how the objective framework of the former tends to go over into the specific perspective of the latter. This is at least part of Dilthey's argument in the *Aufbau* that from the concept of objective spirit we must move to a principle of human individuation. "When the individual is apprehended through *Verstehen* on the basis and by means of the universally human, this gives rise to a *Nacherleben* of the inner connections which lead from the universally human

330

to its individual expressions. This process is grasped in reflection (*Reflexion*), and an *Individualpsychologie* projects the theory which grounds the possibility of individuation" (*GS*,VII,151).

It is clear then that the epistemological perspective of objective spirit leaves room for considerations of individual creativity and that the completion of historical understanding presupposes knowledge of psychic life (*GS*,VII,211). *Individualpsychologie* involves a reflective principle of systematic import for the *Geisteswissenschaften* because the individual is never exhaustively defined by the other systematic human studies. It is not the whole person, but only some of his processes that are involved in the cultural systems or communities in which he participates (*GS*,VII,167). The individual can in a certain sense transcend and survey them all.

> Understanding always has something individual as its object. . . . In the world of spirit, the individual is an object of intrinsic value, and indeed he is the only such value we can establish with certainty. . . . The secret of the person draws us for its own sake, into ever new and more profound attempts at understanding. Such understanding discloses the realm of individuals which encompasses man and his creations. Here lies the most characteristic accomplishment of the human studies. The objective spirit and the power of the individual together determine the spiritual world. History rests on the understanding of these two. [*GS*,VII,212–13]

History and psychology, as distinguished from the more homogeneous and methodologically refined systematic human studies, converge to complete the system of the human studies.

The suggestion that *Individualpsychologie* should be conceived in relation to reflection ties in with our earlier attempt in chapter 5 to clarify the comparative psychology in terms of the concept of reflective experience. The continuity be-

331

tween psychology, reflection, and interpretation will become more evident in the context of Dilthey's final aesthetic views as discussed in the following chapter. There, too, a reconsideration of the psychology of the imagination will help to further illuminate the process of *Nacherleben*.

The Theory of the *Geisteswissenschaften:* Status and Commentary

Before turning to the late aesthetic writings, it might be useful to briefly review some features of Dilthey's work discussed so far with several comments on the status of his theory of human studies. Although Dilthey sought to provide a special grounding for the *Geisteswissenschaften*, it must be recognized that his definition of them was still in some ways dependent on his conception of the *Naturwissenschaften*.

Indeed, whether they be hostile or friendly to his aims, most commentators believe Dilthey's theory of the human studies to be compromised by an unquestioning acceptance of the natural sciences as he found them in the late nineteenth century. On one end of the spectrum there are those philosophers of science who attack Dilthey for failing to recognize and explore the full potential of the methodology of the natural sciences. Had he done so, he would have seen that his distinction was unnecessary. At most, Dilthey described differences between the natural sciences and the human studies which reflected a mere contingent disparity in the stages of their development.

At the other extreme, phenomenologists have criticized Dilthey for retaining naturalistic ideals of objectivity. Dilthey's distinction between the *Geisteswissenschaften* and *Naturwissenschaften* is recognized to constitute an important step towards an understanding of man and history, but it does not go far enough in establishing the fundamental priority of the *Geisteswissenschaften*. Hans-Georg Gadamer, for example, claims that Dilthey's concern with methodology reveals him to be, unconsciously at least, still too much influenced by the natural scientists. Thus he bypassed the opportunity to challenge the status of the *Naturwissenschaften* from the perspective of the *Geisteswissenschaften*.

Peter Krausser's recent book, *Kritik der endlichen Vernunft* (*Critique of Finite Reason*), is of unusual interest because it questions the common assumption that Dilthey accepted the natural sciences at face value. Krausser attempts a general re-interpretation by claiming that Dilthey's work furthered the *Naturwissenschaften* as well as the *Geisteswissenschaften*. Thus instead of considering how much Dilthey borrowed from the natural sciences, and weighing this as being either too much or too little, he shows how much Dilthey actually contributed to the theory of the natural sciences. Krausser agrees that Dilthey's methodology is related to that of the natural sciences, but he does not consider this a flaw. Dilthey may not have directly challenged the natural sciences from the standpoint of the *Geisteswissenschaften*, but his insights into the hermeneutic historical method allowed him to anticipate a modern cybernetic theory of scientific investigation which was to revolutionize the natural sciences. Dilthey's hermeneutic theory, according to which the meaning of a textual passage must be interpreted through the interplay of its details and in light of some sense of its context, points to the operations of what Krausser calls "Finite Reason" in the modern cybernetic theory of knowledge. The hermeneutic circle is thus taken as the prototype of the modern cybernetic theory of knowledge as a self-corrective information system.

Krausser's thesis is based mainly on excerpts from the "Breslauer Ausarbeitung" of the *Einleitung in die Geisteswissenschaften*. This draft for the second volume of the *Einleitung* stems from the year 1880 when Dilthey was teaching at Breslau and demonstrates his involvement with the natural sciences as well as the human studies. Of especial interest to Krausser are those sections where Dilthey displayed his exact knowledge of physiology and described the cycle of psychic life (*Kreislauf des psychischen Lebens*) in terms of the centripetal and centrifugal functions of the nervous system. The dynamic structure of this psychophysical system is, according to Krausser, the naturalistic counterpart to the concept of the hermeneutic circle.[17]

By reformulating Dilthey's description of both the psychophysical life cycle and the hermeneutic circle into cybernetic language of input and output, feedback and adaptation, Krausser hopes to establish a terminology common to the *Naturwissenschaften* and the *Geisteswissenschaften*. Dilthey's hermeneutic method is interpreted to be a general method for testing and correcting hypotheses and is asserted to apply not only to the human studies, but also to the natural sciences. Dilthey is thereby credited with providing the basis for a new unity of the sciences.

We have interpreted Dilthey's life-long project as an effort to *complement* Kant's *Critique of Pure Reason*. Krausser, however, thinks that Dilthey revealed the greater ambition to challenge Kant's epistemology of the natural sciences when he called for a new critique of reason in a journal entry of 1859. He claims that Dilthey sought to replace Kant's transcendental epistemology and its a priori categories with a comprehensive empirical epistemology, and points to the fact that Dilthey discusses all the sciences together in the Breslau draft. He notes with approval Dilthey's remarks that science and philosophy are alike in never being presuppositionless and that our presuppositions must be constantly clarified and adapted to our experience. But Dilthey, at that point, is only giving a post-Kantian expression to some commonplace views reflecting his general empirical approach to philosophical problems. Whatever similarities he found between the natural sciences and the human studies, he always insisted that they required separate epistemological frameworks. His actual sketches for the Critique of Historical Reason were clearly meant to

[17] Krausser, *Kritik der endlichen Vernunft*, pp. 97, 178.

provide a foundation just for the *Geisteswissenschaften*, not also for the *Naturwissenschaften*. Dilthey challenges the *Critique of Pure Reason* only so far as necessary to make room for his theory of the human studies. While he does explicitly deny Kant's conception of time as phenomenal and affirms its reality, he questions Kant's concept of space only to the extent that certain of the relations asserted between it and time stand in the way of the development of psychological knowledge. As for his more general reconsiderations of Kant's epistemology, they continue, in effect, the process of rethinking begun by Kant himself in the *Critique of Judgment*.

One reason why Krausser overrides the distinction of the *Naturwissenschaften* and the *Geisteswissenschaften* is that he also rejects any underlying epistemological division between hypothetical and nonhypothetical knowledge. His unorthodox claim, that according to Dilthey all knowledge is hypothetical and thus in principle part of a relative cybernetic information system, can only be accounted for by his decision to regard the early writings of Dilthey as an index to the more mature works. This is dangerous because in his earliest discussions of the hermeneutic circle, Dilthey's primary concern was the rather negative one of ridding the *Geisteswissenschaften* of metaphysical speculation. In his *Preisschrift* of 1860 Dilthey attacked the hermeneutic system of Friedrich Ast for its Schelling-based mysticism, and in this context he pointed to Ast's notion of the anticipation (*Ahnung*) of the overall meaning of a text as a metaphysical concept which was to be deflated to the status of a scientific hypothesis. These early polemical remarks about Ast lead Krausser to assume that hypotheses are fundamental to Dilthey's hermeneutics. However, in terms of his developed theory of the human studies we have seen that hypotheses can only play a peripheral role in the hermeneutic situation. Interpretation is concerned to integrate parts into a whole, while the ultimate task of a hypothesis is to subsume particulars to universals.

What Dilthey means by "divination" in interpretation is a nonhypothetical sense of how the meaning of a whole can be given through some part of itself. To the extent that divination appeals to *Erlebnis* it is noninferential and can never be totally wrong in the way that a hypothesis may be. However, the process of articulating the meaning of the whole in terms of typical parts can never produce the kind of certainty of a well-supported hypothetical generalization. No amount of stress on the fact that both textual interpretation and scientific hypotheses are self-correcting should allow this difference to be glossed over.

Despite Krausser's questionable theses, his work serves to emphasize that Dilthey allowed the *Naturwissenschaften* and the *Geisteswissenschaften* to have much in common without thereby accepting the ideals of the natural sciences, or uncritically borrowing from them. All too often it has been assumed that in any contact between the two sets of disciplines, the lines of influence point in only one direction: from the natural sciences to the human studies. Even those who most stridently proclaim the primacy of the human studies betray this attitude when they would have Dilthey excise all terminology and methods associated with the natural sciences—as if to maintain any relations with the natural sciences were equivalent to being dominated by them. In point of fact, as Dilthey gradually became surer of the independent procedures and contributions of the human studies and clarified his views about what fundamentally distinguished them from the *Naturwissenschaften*, he was freed from the necessity of emphasizing differences. We thus see less of those contrasting definitions whereby a thinker still allows an opposed position to set the conceptual guidelines for his own views. In the early writings, Dilthey insisted on the uniqueness of the descriptive method. But his definition was largely dependent on a contrast with what he took to be the causal, hypothetical explanations of natural science. Here the fact that he held dated beliefs about the methodology of the natural sciences does compromise his distinction and leaves it open to the criticism that it is not fundamental—nor even necessary. However, by the time he wrote the *Aufbau*, the epistemological delimitation of the human studies was fundamentally determined by his conception of the historical world in the hermeneutic framework. Thus the validity of his definition of the human studies was no longer as dependent on the adequacy of his conception of the natural sciences.

Although to say that Dilthey sought a new unity for all the sciences on the basis of the hermeneutic method is to claim too much, it *is* true that Dilthey never divorced the human studies from the natural studies and that their delimitation is not ultimately keyed to a methodological distinction. Among the three tasks involved in grounding the human studies, the logical and the methodological lead to the third, epistemological task which completes the delimitation. We have seen Dilthey ready to admit that the same logical operations may be shared, and while the hermeneutic method itself remains a distinct feature of the human studies, he also allowed a carefully defined and limited role for the methods identified with the natural sciences.

On many of these methodological issues Dilthey's position is comparable to that of Ernst Cassirer (1874–1945). As a Neo-Kantian, Cassirer uses the expression *Kulturwissenschaften* in place of *Geisteswissenschaften*; however, as a member of the Marburg school, he explicitly rejects the idiographic and absolute value perspective of the Baden school.[18] Like Dilthey, he avoids the sharp division that Windelband and Rickert created between the natural and the cultural sciences, and his concept of *contextual explanation* is much closer to Dilthey's concept of understanding human products by studying their structural contexts. Nevertheless, he differs from Dilthey by placing his theory of culture in the framework of a philosophy of symbolic forms, thus stressing the continuity of natural science and cultural

[18]These criticisms are made in the context of a discussion of the concept of style and will therefore be reserved for chap. 10.

science. Form or structure is conceived more abstractly than structure had been conceived by Dilthey. Cassirer finds form a purely relational concept which can also be applied to the natural sciences by means of mathematics. Thus in twentieth-century physics we witness both causal laws and mathematical structural theory. Traditional causal laws of particles need to be supplemented by probabilistic hypotheses and symbolic representations of waves.

Taking advantage of the advances made in the natural sciences due to the rise of field theory and relativity, Cassirer could more easily reconcile explanation in the natural sciences and the human studies. He brings to our attention that the laws used to account for the behavior of physical phenomena need not constitute causal explanations. Once the indeterminacy of the location of particles in a field is recognized, the crude model of linear, causal explanation gives way to a more inclusive one of functional or contextual explanation. Thus the distinction between explanation and contextual analysis no longer defines a distinction between the natural sciences and the human studies, but can be made within each set of disciplines.

In his *Zur Logik der Kulturwissenschaften* (1942), Cassirer indicates that hermeneutic understanding provides "the real supporting base" (*die eigentliche tragende Grundschicht*) for the cultural sciences:

> Before we can write a cultural history and before we can construct any representation of the causal connections of its individual phenomena, we must have an overall view of the *achievements* of language, art, and religion. It is not enough that we have them before us as mere raw material. It is necessary that we penetrate their *sense* (*Sinn*); we must understand what they have to say to us. This understanding possesses its own method of interpretation or explication (*Deutung*) —an autonomous, most difficult, and complex "hermeneutic."

338

Yet this hermeneutic provides only a rough, preliminary ordering of the products of culture; it serves as a kind of propaedeutic to the properly theoretical tasks of the cultural sciences: "When, as a result of this hermeneutic, the confusion begins to recede, when ever-clearer, specific, and basic forms (*Grundgestalten*) begin gradually to be distinguishable in the monuments of culture . . . a new and twofold task begins."[19]

Analysis of culture as *achievement* must go over into analysis of the *processes* that led to it and into the analysis of the basic forms qua *forms*. On the one hand, hermeneutics prepares for historical explanations of the cause and effect relations involved in cultural events. On the other hand, it must be defined through a functional analysis establishing the interrelations of different basic forms of culture. Ultimately this leads to a philosophy of symbolic forms which is deemed applicable to all fundamental human activities. Thus in Cassirer's comprehensive theory of the sciences, hermeneutic understanding is made a preliminary mode of explanation, that is, reduced to a form of contextual explanation.

With explanation no longer seen as essentially causal, it might seem justifiable to speak of contextual explanation in both the *Geisteswissenschaften* and the *Naturwissenschaften*. Yet when Dilthey himself explored the possible convergence of explanation and understanding (*GS*,V,334), it was within the framework of the *Geisteswissenschaften* only. Here explanation would have to adapt itself to the requirements of understanding. This suggests the sui generis mode of historical "explanation" discussed earlier, which clearly cannot be equated with a common mode of contextual explanation. Dilthey places an emphasis on understanding the full meaning of individual documents which is

---

[19] Cassirer, *Logic of the Humanities*, p. 173. Cf. *Zur Logik der Kulturwissenschaften*, Darmstadt: Wissenschaftliche Buchgesellschaft, 1961, p. 97.

never exhausted by the formalistic explanations of theory. If this is accepted, then it must be added that it is totally inadequate to consider hermeneutical understanding as merely a pretheoretical explanation, as an elementary understanding of cultural achievements independent of any theoretical concepts of cultural forms.

The view of hermeneutical understanding betrayed by Cassirer is close to Lucien Goldmann's use of the term *comprendre*. According to the latter, to understand a text is to have analyzed what is given. To explain a work is, then, to place it in a sociological or, if need be, a psychoanalytical framework.[20] Neither Cassirer nor Goldmann really answer the question of how the work of art in turn sheds light on its particular psychohistorical context. Because Dilthey was concerned with this above all else, his theory of hermeneutical understanding is comprehensive enough to encompass Goldmann's concepts of understanding and of contextual explanation. Dilthey's concept of understanding includes the interplay of those two narrower concepts in the part-whole relation of the hermeneutic circle.

Cassirer in his attempt to find the common bond between the natural sciences and the cultural sciences, claims that they agree in uniting the particular and the universal. The part-whole relation of the hermeneutic circle is subsumed to the particular-universal relation. For Dilthey, however, to explain in terms of the particular-universal relation leaves unresolved the problem of understanding the part-whole relation. Yet he does agree with Cassirer that explanation and understanding both relate particulars to a context. All empirical inquiry involves a circularity in which we strive to integrate knowledge of details into a larger framework and test the latter by the former. The feature which *is* common to the *Naturwissenschaften* and the *Geisteswissenschaften* he calls the *classificatory*, not the hermeneutic,

[20] Lucien Goldmann, *Pour une sociologie du roman*, Paris: Gallimard, 1964, pp. 353–54.

340

circle: "The formation of general methods by means of induction presupposes concepts; these are . . . subordinated to each other by means of classification and every classification of concepts first receives its definitive character from the entire conceptual system" (*GS*,VIII,160). The strict naturalist may deny this circle by claiming that the observation of particulars leads to the formulation of a universal concept, but there must have been some vague notion of a common nature which led him to consider a given group of particulars rather than another. According to Dilthey, only logico-mathematical thought can escape the "circle of classification"—supposedly because it deals with ideal constructs. For all the empirical sciences, classification is provisional in that we always anticipate more than is immediately given.

But classification itself takes on a different character as it applies to natural objects or to spiritual realities. In the *Naturwissenschaften* the classificatory circle is refined in terms of self-correcting hypotheses; only in the *Geisteswissenschaften* does it turn into the hermeneutic circle. "The former classifications do not possess [a sense] of coherence (*Zusammenhang*) or connected structure within experience, but can only fill it out hypothetically. In the latter, this coherence or totality is experienced dynamically, and the origin and separation of the main forms is apprehended by reliving or re-experiencing (*divinatorisches Nacherleben*)" (*GS*,VIII,157).

In the *Geisteswissenschaften* the process of classification begins with an original continuum which is given to experience. We possess a nondiscursive sense of how experiences fit together. Or, when confronted with a human expression we experience its overall sense without having to appeal to any hypothetical inference. Hypotheses can, to be sure, have a subordinate role in the *Geisteswissenschaften*, but only to the extent that we may want to fit in, and relate, isolated details of meaning. The *Naturwissenschaften*, on the other hand, do not start with a lived continuum, so that connections between purely physical states or atomic particles are merely hypothetical.

On the basis of this difference in the epistemological conditions of the *Wissenschaften*, we can uncover a division within classification as such. In the *Geisteswissenschaften*, where connectedness is primary, the rationale for classification must lie in articulating appropriate divisions. Thus we find that the hermeneutic circle converges on the typical parts of a whole. In the *Naturwissenschaften*, the main goal of classification would be that of overcoming any initial discontinuities and discovering similarities and hypothetical connections. Thus it is that natural description leads to inductive uniformities whereby ever more particulars can be subsumed under universal laws.

Whereas in the natural sciences the refined universal allows us to increase the number of particulars to which it applies, in the human studies the enlarged context of interpretation serves as a basis for a better understanding of the original material under consideration. New facts are used not merely to confirm or refine generalizations derived from old data, but to reconsider the meaning of these very data. Thus, as we widen our context to that of universal history and of mankind as a whole, interpretation does not move away from the problem of individuality. Rather we are led to compare and reflect on typical differences and thereby characterize the uniqueness or concrete meaning of a given event or life-complex. To so bring the richness and scope of the historical world to bear on the understanding of individual life is the ultimate hermeneutic task of the *Geisteswissenschaften*.

PART FOUR

Aesthetics and History

CHAPTER NINE

Weltanschauungslehre and the
Late Aesthetics

ALTHOUGH Dilthey maintained that the different tasks man sets for himself in the *Naturwissenschaften* and the *Geisteswissenschaften* call for separate epistemological groundings, he also acknowledged the importance of philosophical reflection on the fundamental categories of life as a whole. Thus, in "Das Wesen der Philosophie,"[1] Dilthey concluded that philosophy, in addition to establishing the foundations of knowledge, has ". . . the task of coming to terms with the incessant need for ultimate reflection on being, ground, value, purpose, and their interconnection in a *Weltanschauung.* . . ."[2]

Philosophers have traditionally sought to answer questions about the character and overall meaning of life through metaphysical systems. But convinced that the ensuing conflict of systems would eventually lead to scepticism, Dilthey proposed instead a theory of *Weltanschauungen.* The analysis and comparison of typical attitudes toward life expressed in religion, poetry, and metaphysics were meant to introduce a more productive theory of philosophical reflection. However, when taken by itself, the *Weltanschauungslehre* creates more problems than it solves and remains in many respects the least satisfactory part of Dilthey's philosophy. Only when related to developments in his late aes-

[1] Published in 1907 in *Die Kultur der Gegenwart*, ed. Paul Hinneberg, Leipzig: B. G. Teubner, 1907, Vol. I, 6, pp. 1–72. Reprinted in *GS*, V 339–416.

[2] *GS*, V, 416; *The Essence of Philosophy*, trans. Stephen A. Emery and William T. Emery, New York: AMS Press, 1969, p. 76. I have slightly altered the Emerys' translation.

thetics—particularly concerning the imaginative articulation of *Erlebnis*—can we see how the abstract classification of *Weltanschauung* types might be translated into a more fruitful hermeneutic interpretation of life.

The Types and Structures of *Weltanschauungen*

A *Weltanschauung* (world-view) as Dilthey conceived it, is an overall perspective on life which encompasses the way a person perceives the world, evaluates and responds to it. Through an historical investigation of metaphysical systems in comparison with some related forms in religion and art (*GS*,VIII,15), Dilthey was able to distinguish three recurrent types of *Weltanschauung: naturalism, subjective idealism*, and *objective idealism*. The basic attitudes expressed in these types are described to indicate the dominance of either the feeling, the willing, or the intellectual aspects of consciousness.

One *Weltanschauung* type, *naturalism*, is the view of life which expresses a primarily cognitive attitude toward the world. Man's realization that he is a part of nature and determined by its unalterable uniformities leads to a reliance on his senses and an acceptance of his passions, on the one hand, and to the goal of manipulating nature through his accumulated knowledge of it, on the other. A second type, *subjective idealism*, involves an active, moral attitude in which the subject projects ideals that transcend given reality. It opposes human freedom to natural determination and a priori categories of mind to sensation. In a third type, *objective idealism*, reality is neither to be manipulated scientifically, nor dominated by the assertion of moral will, but viewed as an object of appreciative contemplation. "In this contemplative attitude, our life of feeling, which at first experienced the richness of life, value, and happiness only personally, expands to a kind of universal sympathy" (*GS*,VIII,114). Accordingly, reality is felt to be the objective embodiment of ideal values and is appreciated as akin to ourselves. All dissonances of life are resolved by the sense of a universal harmony of things as parts of a whole.

Dilthey does not present his three *Weltanschauung* types in a developmental sequence nor does he offer any hierarchical scheme whereby their relative merits can be evaluated. The problem of understanding *Weltanschauungen* is also complicated by the fact that they are expressed in religion and poetry as well as philosophy, and that no type is restricted to one of these cultural systems.

If the three great *Weltanschauung* types could have been parceled out, with each assigned its own cultural domain, evaluative problems raised by Dilthey's *Weltanschauung* typology might perhaps have been avoided. For then the differences between the types could have been regarded as merely complementary expressions of incommensurable cultural systems. In fact it does seem natural to suppose that poetry is always some more or less developed form of objective idealism since this *Weltanschauung* type is based on a contemplative, aesthetic approach to reality in which the attitude of feeling is dominant. Similarly, religion might appear to be the proper home for subjective idealism and its concern with the transcendent. And finally, naturalism with its search for knowledge and its assumption of inductive uniformities would appear to be the most appropriate type for philosophy, which according to Dilthey attempts to raise a *Weltanschauung* to the conceptual level and thus assure its universality.

However, Dilthey not only finds all three *Weltanschauung* types expressed in traditional philosophy, but also offers impressive representatives for each type: Protagoras, Hume, and Hobbes for naturalism; Plato, Kant, and Fichte for subjective idealism; Parmenides, Spinoza, and Hegel for objective idealism. No special status is assigned to any type as expressed in philosophy. In religion there are fewer alternatives since naturalism can be eliminated as a fortiori irreligious. Dilthey is able to establish religious precedents for subjective idealism (theism) and objective idealism (pantheism) (GS,V,391), but there is no justification for the belief that of these two types, subjective idealism is favored in religious thought. Finally, in applying his *Weltanschauungslehre* to an analysis of literature, he enumerates several writers who represent naturalism (Stendhal and Balzac), objective idealism (Goethe) and subjective idealism (Corneille and Schiller): "Stendhal and Balzac see in life a web of illusions, passions, beauty and decay, aimlessly created in a dark impulse of nature herself. In this kind of life, the strength of egoism prevails. Goethe sees in life a creative force which unifies organic products, human development, as well as the regulations of society in a valuable whole. Corneille and Schiller see in it the stage for heroic deeds" (GS,VIII,93).

Because Dilthey finds the three *Weltanschauung* types in a single domain like philosophy they can be seen as more directly vying with each other. The history of metaphysics shows a continual conflict of systems. Although one type may gain ascendency it is not able to completely dispose of any other. Dilthey is unwilling to grant naturalism a greater philosophical cogency than the other two types, and he insists that any formulation of it will inevitably be refuted by one of the other *Weltanschauung* types. But just as surely will naturalism keep on springing back to life. The same can be said for the other two types. They possess the tenacity of fundamental character types which resist reconciliation.

Indeed, the way Dilthey describes the *Weltanschauungen* displayed in metaphysical systems, conceptual formulations appear little more than means of expressing personal attitudes or character.

The nature of these types of metaphysical systems is manifested quite clearly when one looks at the great metaphysical geniuses who have expressed the *personal attitude* towards life operative in them by con-

348

ceptual systems with claims of validity. The typical disposition towards life so expressed is identical with their *character*. . . . And although their systems are self-evidently conditioned by the concepts in which they appear, historically considered their concepts are merely means for the construction and proof of their *Weltanschauung*. [*GS*,VIII,98, italics added]

But he also states that *Weltanschauung* types cannot be psychologically deduced. One reason for this may be that a person's character cannot be fully articulated until he has explicitly formulated his *Weltanschauung*. Moreover, on Dilthey's general principles, character itself cannot simply be explained psychologically because it incorporates historically conditioned factors. Nevertheless, character ultimately remains a psychological concept, and Dilthey's willingness to identify character and *Weltanschauung* indicates that the *Weltanschauungslehre* could be reduced to psychological roots. This becomes most evident in his analysis of the structure of the *Weltanschauungen*.

Although "Das Wesen der Philosophie" (1907) refers to almost every aspect of Dilthey's philosophy, his psychological theories are presented only in that section where he introduces the *Weltanschauungslehre*. The views expressed there reflect the static analysis of "Der psychische Strukturzusammenhang" of 1905 (see chapter 7), and Dilthey again distinguishes the experienced regularities of psychic structure from the inductive uniformities of psychic change (*GS*,V,372). As might be expected, he stresses only the former as background for discussing the formation of the *Weltanschauungen*.

The structural analysis of experience helps to delineate three features common to all *Weltanschauungen: Weltbild* (world-picture), *Lebenswürdigung* (evaluation of life) and ideals of *Lebensführung* (conduct of life). In Dilthey's essay "Die Typen der Weltanschauung und ihre Ausbildung in den metaphysischen Systemen" ("The Types of

World View and Their Development in Metaphysical Systems"),[3] These three features are described as strata constructively derived from each other.

> A *Weltanschauung* is determined in its structure by a psychic lawfulness (*Gesetzlichkeit*) according to which the apprehension of reality constitutes the basis (*Unterlage*) for the evaluation of states and objects in terms of pleasure and pain, satisfaction and dissatisfaction, approval and disapproval. This estimate of life is in turn the fundamental stratum for the determinations of the will. Our behavior regularly goes through these three levels of consciousness and the peculiar nature of psychic life asserts itself in the fact that in each case the lower stratum preserves itself. . . .
> [*GS*,VIII,82–83]

Such psychological explanation of hierarchical strata stands in sharp contrast to the description of psychic dynamism found in Dilthey's earlier account of the poetic imagination. In the *Poetik*, a poetic image (*Bild*) was not just the basis for arousing feelings, but was in turn metamorphosed by them. Each act was considered as an intersection of different attitudes. Even though we could call a certain act a perceptual act, it already involved the cooperation of feeling and willing. Thus it was acknowledged that a state of feeling presupposes some mode of sensation, but hypothetical claims to the effect that feelings can be derived from sensations were denied.

In the psychology of the *Weltanschauungslehre*, however, our cognitive representation of the world (*Weltbild*) serves as the foundation of our evaluation of life (*Lebenswürdigung*) without receiving any retroactive influence

[3] This was the essay that led to the Dilthey-Husserl exchange discussed in chap. 7. Published in *Weltanschauung, Philosophie und Religion*, ed. Max Frischeisen-Köhler, Berlin: Reichl, 1911, pp. 3–51. Reprinted in *GS*, VIII, 75–118.

from it. Dilthey claims that the structure of a *Weltanschauung* "... is in each case a totality in which on the foundation (*Grundlage*) of a perception of the world or a 'world-picture' (*Weltbild*), questions about the meaning and sense of the world are decided. From the latter in turn ... the supreme principles of the conduct of life (*Grundsätze für die Lebensführung*) are derived (*abgeleitet*)" (*GS*,VIII,82). In such a constructionist analysis, differences among *Weltanschauung* types can be reduced to differences at the elementary level of *Weltbilder*. What was first distinguished in terms of relative emphases on either the cognitive, evaluative, or volitional aspects of a psychic whole is transformed into an opposition between cognitive *Weltbilder*.

Because Dilthey provides no criteria for evaluating *Weltanschauung* types, he seems to be left with irresolvable contradictions. Moreover, the very possibility of finding such criteria is undercut when he locates the origin of *Weltanschauungen* in a more basic level of *Lebensstimmungen* (moods of life).[4] A *Lebensstimmung* underlies all the strata of a *Weltanschauung*. Dilthey refers to optimism and pessimism as the most comprehensive life moods, but indicates that they must be specified in terms of their individual nuances. In explaining the development of individual *Weltanschauungen*, such essentially subjective moods only seem to account for arbitrary variations of a fixed common structure rather than for meaningful continuities between the different types. Certainly, Dilthey's statement that "particular *Lebensstimmungen* dominate in different individuals according to their peculiarities" (*GS*,VIII,81), implies that *Weltanschauungen* are psychologically conditioned in the most relativistic manner.

[4] *GS*, VIII, 82. In the William Kluback and Martin Weinbaum translation of "Die Typen der Weltanschauung," *Lebensstimmung* is misleadingly rendered as "universal attitude." See "The Types of World Views and Their Unfoldment within the Metaphysical Sys-

While Dilthey gives the impression of exacerbating the problem of relativism in his analysis of metaphysical *Weltanschauungen*, his aesthetic writings better indicate how he might deal with the problem. For example, mood as an ordinary psychological concept is subjective and arbitrary, but in his aesthetic psychology Dilthey had shown how a mood can be objectively articulated through the poetic imagination (see chapter 4).

As Dilthey's aesthetic views matured, he became increasingly concerned with meaning in art and the initial value-orientation of his aesthetics is transferred as it were to his *Weltanschauungslehre*. The *Weltanschauungen* are relativistic precisely because they express irreducible human values. But this relativism which recognizes that no one absolute, all-inclusive perspective on life is possible—that any perspective must be partial and evaluative—does not entail relativism with respect to natural and historical knowledge. In chapters 7 and 8 we have already seen that Dilthey's work does not necessarily entail a logical or epistemological relativism. By tracing some themes of the *Weltanschauungslehre* within the hermeneutic framework of the late aesthetics, we may also indicate possibilities for developing a more unified approach to understanding the meaning of historical life.

A comparison of *Weltbilder* will only lead to fixed cognitive differences if one forgets that Dilthey's structural analysis serves a mere preliminary function. Static divisions of the classificatory circle must be dynamically reconceived in terms of the hermeneutic circle.

An unfinished essay of 1911 (the same year that "Die Typen der Weltanschauung" was published) does indeed confirm that a structural analysis of *Weltanschauungen* is not meant to deny dynamic interaction in psychic life as

---

tems," in *Dilthey's Philosophy of Existence*, New York: Bookman Associates, 1957, p. 24. *Stimmung* is thereby confused with other terms used by Dilthey to refer to attitude, namely, *Stellung* and *Verhalten*.

such.[5] For Dilthey writes that "every impression contains, together with an image, a determination of the life of feeling and impulse. We are never given solely inner life nor solely external world. They always exist together, not merely side by side, but in a dynamical interaction: only the development of intellectual products dissolves this nexus" (*GS*,VIII,16). Thus Dilthey concludes that the *Weltbilder* from which we have derived typological *Weltanschauung* differences are mere abstractions (*GS*,VIII,19).

When the analysis of *Weltanschauungen* is placed back in the concrete contexts of historical life, we see that it is possible for our *Lebenswürdigung* (evaluation of life) to exert a retroactive influence on our *Weltbild*. The interdependence of functions that Dilthey had already established for the psychic system can also exist in a *Weltanschauung* when it is related to our actual *Erlebnis* of life. This, however, is demonstrable only for religious and poetic forms of *Weltanschauungen*, not for their metaphysical formulations.

The religious *Weltanschauung* has its source in an *Erlebnis* of the unseen, supernatural forces in life. Dilthey develops what Schleiermacher had characterized as a religious sense of ultimate dependence into a more general religious *Erlebnis* of the invisible (*das Unsichtbare*). For a religious person, ". . . the great *Erlebnis* of an unconditioned, infinite objective value, to which all others are subordinated . . . determines his entire objective apprehension [of reality] and his overall projected ends . . ." (*GS*,V,390). The religious *Erlebnis* can lead to a fundamental reorientation of attitudes toward life, whereby a shift in our ultimate values and goals will in turn alter our underlying perception of reality.

Whereas religion brought us in the presence of invisible

[5] "Das geschichtliche Bewusstsein und die Weltanschauungen," *GS*, VIII, 3–71. For date, see Ulrich Herrmann, *Bibliographie Wilhelm Dilthey*, ed. Leonhard Froese and Georg Ruckriem, Weinheim: Julius Beltz, 1969, p. 100.

influences on life, the arts—including poetry—tend to focus on visible relations given in life. Not only our particular situation, but life itself is shown as a presence in a poetic *Weltanschauung*. "The poet is a seer who intuits the sense of life" (*GS*,V,394). Here, too, our *Weltbild* does not serve as the immutable base for our evaluative and volitional attitudes of life. The poet's *Erlebnis* suspends the practical considerations that normally constrain the apprehension of reality. This allows him to see a general meaning embodied in a particular situation. In a dramatic motif, for example, ". . . a life-relation is apprehended in its significance. In such a motif there is an active inner impulse which can adapt characters, processes, and deeds to each other in such a way that this general trait may be seen to exist in the nature of things . . ." (*GS*,V,394).

Metaphysics strives for stability and universality in its *Weltanschauungen*. The metaphysical formulation of a *Weltanschauung* must be disassociated from any religious mystery and invocation of invisible forces and may be viewed as an effort to give a conceptual order to the vision of the poet. The metaphysician above all seeks to prove that his systematized *Weltanschauung* is universally valid. This is a purely abstract ideal common to all metaphysics and there is no *Erlebnis* which can provide a concrete core or context for such a system, since no experience can justify claims for absolute necessity.

Dilthey's analysis of traditional philosophical *Weltanschauung* types does not move beyond his general constructionist schema built on the *Lebensstimmungen*, because metaphysics lacks the experiential, dynamic base found in the spheres of religion and poetry. As such, the *Weltanschauungslehre* really stands as the final argument in his life-long critique of metaphysical systems. Any heuristic use of the *Weltanschauung* types would require a nonmetaphysical conception of philosophy grounded in experience.

None of the *Weltanschauung* types discerned in *metaphysics* can do justice to the richness of life indicated in history and poetry.[6] Dilthey notes that "the effect of the various sides of life on the poet is too strong, his sensibility for its nuances too great, for a delimited type of *Weltanschauung* to be able to satisfy him . . ." (*GS*,V,397). A poet constantly reformulates his outlook on life and will not be restricted to one type of *Weltanschauung*. The same is true of Plato. Dilthey calls him both a subjective idealist and an objective idealist, and considers him sui generis as a philosopher-poet. Similarly, Dilthey points to "modern philosophers of life" who explore an "intermediate zone" between traditional philosophy and literature: "Their eyes remain focused on the riddle of life, but they despair of solving it by a universally valid metaphysics, on the basis of a theory of a world-order. Life is to be interpreted in terms of itself —that is the great thought which connects these philosophers of life with our experience of the world and poetry."[7] It is in poetry that life is most directly viewed in terms of itself. The objectivity expected of the metaphysical *Weltanschauung* is already foreshadowed in the poetic *Weltanschauung* which Dilthey describes as "impartial, universal, and insatiable in incorporating all reality. Its intuitive apprehension of nature and of the ultimate interconnection of things is always for the sake of penetrating deeply into the significance of life, and this very significance gives freedom and vitality to its ideals."[8] The claim for the impartiality of a poetic *Weltanschauung* reflects the underlying tendency in Dilthey's late writings to draw upon the more

[6] Dilthey does not align himself with any of the three *Weltanschauung* types, nor does he, as Rand has suggested, propose a fourth historical *Weltanschauung* type. See Calvin G. Rand, "Two Meanings of Historicism in the Writings of Dilthey, Troeltsch and Meinecke," *The Journal of the History of Ideas*, 25, 1964, 513. When Dilthey does speak of a historical *Weltanschauung*, he is only presenting the problematic of the *Weltanschauung* theory, not its solution. See above, pp. 3, 9n.

[7] *GS*, V, 370–71. I have slightly altered the Emerys' translation of *Essence of Philosophy*, p. 31.

[8] *GS*, V, 396; Emery and Emery, p. 57.

impersonal meaning-potential of his psychological aesthetics. This is made possible by placing his psychological conception of *Erlebnis* in a hermeneutic framework. We can move beyond the intuitive morphology of Dilthey's *Weltanschauungslehre* through his account of the imaginative metamorphosis of *Erlebnis*.

The Imagination and the Disinterestedness of *Erlebnis*

What role Dilthey's early psychology of the imagination should be assigned in the late hermeneutic approach to history and aesthetics is not evident at first hand. Dilthey's "Uebersicht der Poetik" ("Synopsis of the Poetics") drawn up in 1907 and 1908 indicates that the old *Poetik* was to be "reworked according to structural psychology" (*GS*,VI, 310). Since we have seen that psychic structure can be reconceived as resisting all transformation, the laws of imaginative metamorphosis might not have remained central had Dilthey actually revised the *Poetik*.

Moreover, when Dilthey discusses the psychological considerations underlying the *Weltanschauungslehre* in "Das Wesen der Philosophie" he refers to the imaginative processes merely in relation to the possibility of providing genetic explanations of human productivity. Thus, after using the psychological laws of association and reproduction as examples of inductive uniformities arrived at on the model of the explanative natural sciences, Dilthey goes on to link the processes of imaginative metamorphosis to them as well: "The peculiar formative processes by which perceptions are metamorphosed into imaginative representations contain a part of the explanative ground for myth, saga, legend, and artistic creation" (*GS*,V,372). If imaginative metamorphosis is now related to naturalistic explanation, it would seem that the psychology of the poetic imagination can no longer be claimed as a source of understanding in the human studies.

In our earlier account of the imagination, we have already noted that Dilthey's search for a psychic or inner causality had led him to formulate the dynamism of the poetic imagination in terms of quasi-explanative "laws" of exclusion, intensification, and completion (see chapter 2). Having subsequently rejected any such claims for inner causality in the *Geisteswissenschaften*, Dilthey could well have developed a more explicitly naturalistic interpretation of these laws as inductive hypotheses.

However, among the three laws of imaginative metamorphosis only the first two may be so reconceived. The laws of exclusion and intensification, it will be recalled, referred to partial aspects of consciousness: the interest of feeling and the attentiveness of will. If the descriptions of how certain components of an image are excluded and others intensified now become explicated in terms of specific conditions of interest and attention, they could be considered as explanative laws.

On the other hand, the third law of completion referred to the overall structure of the psyche and thereby defies such reformulation into a strict explanative law. In relating it to Dilthey's discussion of the point of impression, we saw that this law does not necessarily complete the process of image-formation in the sense of going beyond the ordinary processes of perceptual apprehension. It can also be interpreted to constitute the comprehensive framework presupposed by the more ordinary first two laws of exclusion and intensification. For this reason completion was considered the most crucial aspect of metamorphosis and was characterized as a principle of understanding. It is therefore significant that Dilthey's final, albeit fragmentary, suggestions for further development of the psychology of the imagination focus on the nature of completion.

When Dilthey revised the essay "Goethe und die dichterische Phantasie" for the second and third editions of *Das Erlebnis und die Dichtung*, he continued to speak of the metamorphosis of the imagination as a process—sometimes unconscious, sometimes deliberate—whereby images are transformed and articulated into typical products: "Aspects of images are excluded, others intensified, and intuitions are completed (*ergänzt*) by memory" (*ED*,116). To the extent that imaginative metamorphosis is still assumed to articulate the typical significance of an intuition, it cannot be reduced to a purely naturalistic process. The process of completion at least contributes to *Verstehen*, to our understanding of the meaning of a work. But the phrase "completed by memory" marks an important change in emphasis. The completion of images can take on a more objective character by being ascribed to memory rather than to the acquired psychic nexus as such.

In the *Poetik*, the memory by itself was considered to be too restrictive a condition for the imagination, so that images had to be related to the overall context of the acquired psychic nexus to be completed in a meaningful sense. However, the late writings on historical understanding suggest that memory need not be reduced to a process of reviving stored images whose meaning derives from the acquired psychic nexus. We can reinterpret memory in light of Dilthey's tendency to rely less on the mediating function of the acquired psychic nexus and more on such concepts as reflective experience and *Erlebnis* to obtain a direct meaning relation between the self and the world. If *Erlebnis* according to Dilthey's intentional interpretation has an inherent tendency to refer beyond itself, then memory is important to provide it with an objective orientation in reality. Memory is not just a subjective process to be explained by the acquired psychic nexus. It can also be understood as an activity which directly gives a transcendent meaning reference to an *Erlebnis*.

In *Das Erlebnis und die Dichtung*, the completion of images is still placed within the overall context of the acquired psychic nexus (*ED*,117). However, by specifically relating it to memory, Dilthey indicates that imaginative metamorphosis would be discussed less in terms of subjec-

358

tive images and psychic structures and more in terms of the objective meaning-relations of *Erlebnis*. This shift to a more objective conception of imagination is also suggested in the "Uebersicht der Poetik." It is clear from this outline that *Erlebnis* was to play a central role in the new *Poetik* and that the whole discussion of the poetic imagination was to be rooted in a new concept, that of *Erlebnisphantasie* (experiential imagination). The first section of the revised *Poetik* was to give an account of *Erlebnis* and its spheres. The second section was to be devoted to the imagination. For the third chapter of this section, Dilthey lists three headings (*GS*,VI,310) in terms of which the poetic imagination was to be analyzed:

1. *Erlebnisphantasie* (Experiential Imagination)
   a. Expression of *Erlebnis*
   b. Incorporation of *Erlebnisausdrücken* in Representational Poetry
2. *Dichterische Phantasiebilder* (Poetic Images)
3. *Sprachphantasie* (Linguistic Imagination)

Although the term *Erlebnisphantasie* is left undefined in the "Uebersicht der Poetik" we shall interpret it in terms of the self-transcendence of *Erlebnis*. The poet's *Erlebnis* is to be understood through its literary expressions (*Erlebnisausdrücke*) and these in turn can be analyzed in terms of poetic images (*dichterische Phantasiebilder*). The fact that poetic images were to be discussed after the *Erlebnisphantasie* indicates that they are products, not elements, of imaginative metamorphosis. Their locus is not psychological, but literary, and as such they have a life of their own; thus we avoid the danger of assigning images (*Bilder*) the kind of private status which Sartre has criticized as the outcome of a pervasive illusion of immanence. Both the concept of *Weltbild* and that of a *dichterisches Phantasiebild* connote a public pictorial structure, but in Dilthey's formulation they always betrayed their private origin. In any case, it is better to move away from the mentalistic language of images to an intentional, reflective analysis of *Erlebnis* and imagination.

In the *Poetik*, the poetic imagination was already assigned a principle of meaning, but its metamorphosis was described in terms of the personal *Erlebnis* of the poet and his evaluative activities. Now in the hermeneutic context, the interpretation of the imagination must proceed from its objectified meaning in the *Erlebnisausdruck*. In addition, we know from Dilthey's cryptic comments in the "Uebersicht der Poetik" that his analysis of the imagination was to make use of a more impersonal conception of *Erlebnis* itself. The disinterestedness that Kant had defined as an aesthetic freedom from interest necessary for judging a work of art is now claimed by Dilthey for the *Erlebnisphantasie* of the artist himself. "Disinterestedness is not merely a property of the [aesthetically contemplated] impression, but also of the *Erlebnis* of the creator. Thus Kant stands corrected. The liberation of the process of the imagination from the occasional or the so-called favorable moment (*von der Gelegenheit*) betokens its liberation from the personal" (*GS*,VI,317).

When Dilthey viewed aesthetics as an evaluative activity, he thought Kant was not justified in denying the inherent interest involved in aesthetic judgments.[9] But now Kant is criticized for having explored disinterestedness only in connection with the spectator, not the creator. In the context of *Das Erlebnis und die Dichtung* we can see how this disinterestedness applies to the *Erlebnisphantasie* of the poet. There Dilthey emphasizes that *Erlebnis* can come to incorporate the most impersonal characteristics and yet be lived through. The poet lives in the realm of the "experiences of the human world" (*Erfahrungen der Menschenwelt*) according to Dilthey. "No matter how far these experiences may be removed from his own sphere of interest or how distant in the past, they are a part of himself" (*ED*,118). The poet cannot help but see reality in terms of the way it has been interpreted in the traditions and forms of his art. His imagina-

[9] See above, pp. 122–23.

tion is already related to the world as it has been envisioned by other poets: ". . . life-relations (*Lebensbezüge*) dominate the poetic imagination. . . . Spontaneous, unnoticeable processes operate everywhere here. They constantly influence the color and form of the world in which the poet lives. Here is the point where the relation of *Erlebnis* and imagination in the poet first discloses itself. The poetic world is already there, before the conception of a work occurs to the poet through some event and before he writes down his first lines" (*ED*,118). The access to this historical, poetic world comes through *Nacherleben* (re-experiencing) as defined in the hermeneutical writings. We must therefore develop an interpretation of the poet's *Erlebnisphantasie* not only in terms of the structure of the acquired psychic nexus as described in the psychological aesthetics, but also in relation to the impersonal hermeneutic framework in which *Nacherleben* is the highest mode of historical understanding.

Earlier, we stated that *Nacherleben* is a mode of re-experiencing which is to be understood as a re-creation (*Nachbildung*) of an expressed meaning, rather than as a psychologistically conceived re-production (*Abbildung*). The creative understanding involved in *Nacherleben* is a function of the historian's imagination. Dilthey describes the "triumph of *Nacherleben*" in terms of imaginative completion: ". . . the fragments of a historical process are so completed that we think we have a continuous whole before us."[10] Similarly, the poet presents to us a life-situation as a meaningful whole. His work can itself be defined in terms of *Nacherleben*. As depicted in "Das Wesen der Philosophie" the poet creates a disinterested poetic image through his imaginative ability to re-experience some human event. "The representation of an event in poetry is the illusory appearance of a reality, re-experienced (*nacherlebt*) and of-

---

[10] *GS*, VII, 215; "The Understanding of Other Persons and Their Life-Expressions," trans. J. J. Kuehl in *Theories of History*, ed. by Gardiner, pp. 220–21.

fered for re-experiencing, set apart from the specific context of the actual and from the relations of our will and interest to it."[11]

For the task of historical understanding, the productive and spontaneous potential of the imagination is perhaps less important than its interpretive potential. Thus the poetic imagination is to be valued not only for the meaning it articulates, but also for the meanings re-created and interpreted in *Nacherleben*. Defined as a function of higher understanding, *Nacherleben* allows the interpreter to move from an impersonally conceived text to the person creating it. Conceived now in the context of the poet's *Erlebnisphantasie*, it also discloses that however personal the articulative imaginative process, its content is largely impersonal. What becomes a "part of" the poet's *Erlebnis* is not now, as in the *Poetik*, assumed to be describable in psychological terms. This point is perhaps best made in an appendix to "Das Verstehen anderer Personen" which deals with musical understanding.

There Dilthey claims that the role of the psychology of the imagination is not to ". . . define a psychological relation between psychic states and a representation of the same in the imagination" (*GS*,VII,222), but to articulate their interdependence and their objective unity. Having already brought out the inseparability of the historical and the psychological in the main essay, Dilthey shows its implications for the special problem of defining the source of the creativity of the composer: "What is at work psychologically in the composer can proceed either from music to *Erlebnis* or from *Erlebnis* to music or both reciprocally. . . . The composition alone can fully express the dynamic relations which existed in the depths of his soul. That is the very value of the music: it is an expression which makes objective what was active in the psyche of the artist" (*GS*,VII,222–23).

The unity of *Erlebnis* and *Ausdruck* is so intimate that

[11] *GS*, V, 392–93; Emery and Emery, p. 53.

one cannot hold up a psychological description of the artist's *Erlebnis* as the prototype for the final articulation of his
work. Again referring to music, Dilthey writes: "There is
no duality of *Erlebnis* and music, no double world, no
transference from one to the other. Genius involves simply
living in the sphere of tones, as if it alone existed; a forget-
ting of all fate and suffering by being absorbed in this tonal
world and yet so that all of the former is included in the
latter" (*GS*,VII,222). There is no simple way of demarcat-
ing the composer's *Erlebnis* from its expression because his
Erlebnis is already musical. Generally, an artist tends to experience reality by means of the conventions of the art in
which he has become steeped, so that his imagination is as
much a fact of objective spirit as of his particular individuality. In this way the psychological and the historical are
already linked in the aesthetic imagination.

It is the impersonality of artistic *Erlebnis* that makes it
possible to speak of works of art as providing an understanding of life. But this only gives a partial justification for
those who treat the history of art as a kind of illustrated history of *Weltanschauungen*. In "Die Typen der Weltanschauung," Dilthey cautions that world views are not to be
merely read into art works, but must be found in their inner
form. We should not expect to find them expressed in all
works of art, for Dilthey claims that as such artistic creation
has nothing to do with the production of a *Weltanschauung*
(*GS*,VIII,91). Only because the arts developed under the
tutelage of religion ". . . has there come about a secondary
relation between the works of art and *Weltanschauungen*"
(*GS*,VIII,91). Since sculptors, painters and composers dealt
with religious themes, certain general attitudes worked
themselves into the very styles or inner forms they have
created.

Of all the arts literature alone stands in ". . . a special relationship to *Weltanschauung*. For its medium . . . , language, allows it to provide lyrical expression, and epic or
dramatic presentation of everything that can be seen, heard

or *erlebt*" (*GS*,VIII,92). Although the visual arts were capable of embodying the *Weltanschauung* of the Renaissance, Dilthey feels that only literature uses a medium rich enough to do justice to the more complex *Weltanschauungen* of modern man. In fact, only the *poetic* impulse can contribute positively to the production of *Weltanschauungen*. The poet articulates his vision of reality through the meaning of words and thereby poetic images can embody a *Weltbild* necessary for a *Weltanschauung*.

This is in keeping with Dilthey's general emphasis on literature and the poetic imagination in his aesthetic writings. But the "Uebersicht der Poetik" shows that *Erlebnisphantasie* is to be explicated not only in terms of poetic imagery but also in terms of *Sprachphantasie* (linguistic imagination). Dilthey's late works reveal a greater interest in the aural qualities of language which ultimately led to speculation on the significance of the musical imagination.

Sprachphantasie and Musical Moods

Upon analysis, poetic imagery and *Sprachphantasie* disclose two different aspects of language. Poetic imagery illustrates the intentional use of language discussed in chapter 7. But, as Dilthey points out in *Das Erlebnis und die Dichtung*, language is not just a transparent medium referring beyond itself. In addition to being a vehicle for the articulation of meaning, its aural qualities possess their own inherent values which are exploited in *Sprachphantasie*: ". . . the sensuous beauty of poetry as found in rhythm, rhyme, and linguistic melody constitute a special realm of effects which are separable from what is meant by the words" (*ED*,120).

This passage is somewhat reminiscent of the discussion in the *Poetik* of the second and third spheres of feeling in referring to the pleasurable effects of art (see chapter 3). But now the aural aspects of language contribute more than an aesthetic pleasure, and they can be said to possess a musical import or sense as distinct from a verbal meaning. While the verbal meaning of language serves to present the visible aspects of reality, its rhythmic and melodic aspects can express the sense of what Dilthey calls the musical life of feeling and mood.

The aural and visual aspects of language are perhaps most perfectly balanced in Goethe's poetry. "The *Sprachphantasie* of Goethe which developed from the impulse and gift to express *Erlebnis* is connected with an impressive imagination in the sphere of the visual appearance of things" (*ED*,121). Here *Sprachphantasie* and *Erlebnisphantasie* produce poetic images capable of expressing a *Weltanschauung*. By contrast to Goethe for whom the musical aspects of language are still subsumed to the presentation of a vision of the world, Hölderlin, Tieck, and Novalis have explored the fuller potential of *Sprachphantasie* in light of contemporary developments in instrumental music. They produced a "new kind of lyrical poetry" that "expresses an abundance of feeling, the objectless power of mood which rises from inner life, as well as the endless melody of a psychic activity which derives from indefinite horizons only to dissolve there again" (*ED*,284). Hölderlin's poetry cannot express a *Weltanschauung*, yet like music it can evoke the moods underlying *Weltanschauungen*.

Because Dilthey made only a few comments about the idea of *Sprachphantasie*, they will be related to his discussions about the musical imagination. Despite the unsettling vagueness of these discussions they have significant implications for Dilthey's philosophy of life. A poetic *Weltanschauung* fashioned by the *Erlebnisphantasie* of a Goethe leaves certain reflective concerns not adequately dealt with. These are the kind of ultimate evaluative questions about the nature of life and death once prominent in the religious *Weltanschauung*, but also suggested by the musical imagination of a Beethoven in his late quartets. Whereas Dilthey had spoken of Goethe's poetic vision as in some sense anticipating the philosophical intuition of objective idealism, the invisible horizon evoked by Hölderlin's musical poetry seems to refer back in Romantic fashion to a religious sense of reality.

As early as 1853, in a letter to his father, Dilthey referred to a bond between music and religion, when he wrote, "Luther and Schleiermacher, our two greatest theologians, realized that music is the closest sister of religion and that listening to music, when this is true music, is a religious act."[12] It is interesting to note that the revival of his enthusiasm for music late in his life coincides with a return to certain religious questions.

During the last decade of his life Dilthey produced a series of studies on the relation between religion, poetry and music which were to be integrated into a comprehensive work entitled *Studien zur Geschichte des deutschen Geistes* (*Studies Toward the History of German Spirit*). Some of these essays have been published posthumously in *Von deutscher Dichtung und Musik* (*Of German Literature and Music*). In this work Dilthey contends that the different genres of German literature will be derived, not from the essence of poetry, but from their ". . . relation to other achievements of culture, such as religion, myth, ethos and custom. . . ." One such genre is the pagan hymn, which Dilthey calls a ". . . *Gesamtkunstwerk* (total work of art) in the realm of expression. . . . The same grand emotion expresses itself simultaneously in poetry, music, and rhythmic movement. A multitude filled with a common feeling moves rhythmically in procession or dance, and a choral song expresses what moves it" (*DDM*,44-45). This primitive but nonbiological context for poetry and music is recognized as the communal background for the more personal religious poetry and music of Christian times. "Liberated from rhythmic movement, the choral hymn attained its highest transfiguration in medieval hymns and Protestant cantatas" (*DDM*,45).

[12] In *Der junge Dilthey*, p. 9.

So seriously does Dilthey take the musical nature of the religious *Erlebnis* that he sees the supreme embodiment of Protestant consciousness not in Luther's writings, but in J. S. Bach's music. "The core of Lutheran religiosity is the inner conflict in the soul of the individual person. The motets and cantatas of Bach constitute the highest expression that this Lutheran congregational consciousness has ever found" (*DDM*,217). Dilthey's extended discussion of some of the human moods to be found in Bach's music and how these are given a religious orientation, does perhaps provide some justification for Bollnow's claim that his concept of *Lebensstimmungen* (life moods) is Heideggerian.[13] Although we saw no reason to assign anything but a subjective status to the life moods discussed in the *Weltanschauungslehre*,[14] in *Von deutscher Dichtung und Musik* Dilthey does allow music to express religious feeling in an ". . . objective mood that expands, as it were, into the infinite" (*DDM*,221). More specifically, Dilthey describes how melancholy moods discernible in Bach's music give a sense of ". . . sinking into boundless depths, the struggling of a powerful nature with the abyss . . ." (*DDM*,211). The concern with the invisible that characterizes the religious *Weltanschauung* seems to obtain a more objective sense in the musical context. Thus the fact of death, which as a theological concept looms larger than life, can become part of the religious *Erlebnis* of the living through Bach's *Passions*.

Nevertheless, Dilthey asks himself in the *Entwürfe* whether his philosophy of life could really do justice to the awareness of death that overshadows every moment in the life of a deeply religious thinker like Calvin. In his efforts to more explicitly relate the religious *Erlebnis* to his concept of life, Dilthey introduces themes that were developed by existentalist writers. His account of the religious *Erlebnis* and its unflinching confrontation with life is written in language which anticipates that of Heidegger's *Being and Time*:

[13] Bollnow, *Dilthey: Eine Einführung in seine Philosophie*, pp. 8ff.
[14] See above, p. 351.

The more resolutely a person lives in his own essence and has liberated himself from worldly drives and social entanglements, the more he is frightened by the shallowness in each of us. He feels more lonely and separated from others. This alienation he would like to overcome. . . . The decisive thing is always that in the religious genius there be no evasion, no yielding to the superficiality of being caught up in life (*Dahinleben*), nor to the everyday forgetfulness of past and future. There may be no flight of the imagination for him, and no satisfaction through the secular application of his powers, the latter also being a mode of the forgetfulness of death and of the salvation of the soul. [*GS*,VII,266]

The religious person can point up the shallowness and evasions of the secular person only if he himself does not flee from this world to another. The reference to the invisible contained in the religious *Erlebnis* must be shown to be rooted in life as one of its moments. For Dilthey, the religious *Erlebnis* of death, which has traditionally been understood to involve a reference to a beyond, is to be interpreted as an awareness of the dark depths within. Death is not to be viewed as transcending life, but as a way of estimating its value. Heidegger recognizes this insight in Dilthey (*BT*,494), and refers to his own analysis of death as similarly "this-worldly" (*diesseitig*) (*BT*,292). But whereas for Heidegger an ". . . existential interpretation of death takes precedence over any . . . ontology of life," (*BT*,291) Dilthey preserves life as his fundamental category by interpreting death as the inherent corruptibility of life itself. It is in this sense that Dilthey recurrently utters the phrase about understanding life out of itself. "Not a dream of something transcendent . . . is what we find in the religious genius. Rather, life itself experienced in its nature as true and hard, being peculiarly composed throughout of suffer-

368

ing and happiness, points to something that penetrates it from without, but stems from its own depths . . . " (*GS*,VII,266).

Moments are recognized when something that wells up from within life seems to impinge from without. Here the principle of completion, initially used to relate the inner and the outer when images and *Erlebnisse* are metamorphosed in the context of the acquired psychic nexus, is applied to life itself. Whereas images and *Erlebnisse* have been re-interpreted so that they can refer beyond the psychic nexus, life cannot be related to anything outside itself, so that any apparent addition from without must be interpreted as a completion from within. Such statements in rejection of the inner-outer dualism were to become even more characteristic of Heidegger's antipsychologistic philosophy.

It is in fact Heidegger's distrust of psychological accounts of dying that leads him to insist that death cannot be understood from the perspective of life. Rightly, he does not want to reduce the existential concept of death (*Tod*) to the experience of dying (*das Erleben des Ablebens*).[15] However, Dilthey's claim to understand death as inherent in life (*Leben*) is not at all based on a special, marginal kind of *Erlebnis*, but on a general interpretation of *Erlebnisse* and moods. When Heidegger criticizes the concept of life he supposes it to be either biological or psychological. According to Dilthey, on the other hand, it is primarily a historical concept. Yet the difference between Dilthey and Heidegger is not just terminological. Dilthey's philosophy of life involves a conception of history and objective spirit which differs from Heidegger's in that it posits a continuity with the subject.

Although Dilthey did see objective moods expressed in music, his conception of moods remains fundamentally sub-

---

[15] Martin Heidegger, *Sein und Zeit*, 11th ed., Tübingen: Neomarius, 1967, p. 247.

jective. At best, Dilthey's discussion of musical moods might be said to open up the double meaning of *Stimmung* as both *mood* and *being in tune*—subjective and objective. By contrast, Heidegger articulates an underlying sense of mood as a mode of *attunement with* the world. According to Heidegger's existential analysis of mood, "it comes neither from 'outside' nor from 'inside,' but arises out of Being-in-the-world, as a way of such Being" (*BT*,176). By replacing the concept of *Leben* (life) with that of *Dasein* (existence), Heidegger could develop a perspective fundamentally unconcerned about the inner-outer distinction which Dilthey constantly felt obliged to refine. Instead of claiming that reflective experience is neither inner experience nor outer experience, we have affirmed it to be both. Similarly, objective spirit has been used to interpret external facts as expressing something inner. Heidegger avoids the necessity of such paradoxical formulations with his ecstatic or projective account of *Dasein*. *Da-sein* is understood literally as "being-there" so that human existence can be interpreted as a being-there-in-the-world. What we would normally describe as a person's state of mind is rendered by Heidegger as his *Befindlichkeit*, i.e. the situation in which he finds himself (*BT*,172, especially fn. 2). Thus before all else, man's existential state is referred to the historical world and its established traditions. Dilthey's focus on psychology may be the source of paradox in his theory of history, but, as we shall see in the following chapter, Heidegger's more orthodox idea of the primacy of tradition brings with it its own problems.

Heidegger's analysis of *Stimmung* and *Befindlichkeit* develops ideas about man's relation to the historical world which Dilthey had already explored, not in his discussion of moods, but in his account of the impersonal nature of the poetic *Erlebnis*. But when we consider Heidegger's general critique of aesthetics we see that according to him it is precisely such an appeal to *Erlebnis* which spells the death of poetry.

Heidegger's Critique of Dilthey's Aesthetics

Heidegger complains that modern aesthetics has lost access to the traditional sense of beauty as "radiance" and has reduced it to a mere optical phenomenon. "For aesthetics art is *representation* of the beautiful in the sense of the pleasing. . . ."[16] This mediated representation offers no access to the truth and is valued merely for its conduciveness to enjoyment and relaxation. Heidegger sees here a compartmentalization of philosophy into logic and aesthetics, truth and value, knowledge and feeling, which makes it impossible to deal with the central ontological problem of Being.

The notion of *aisthesis* must be related back to the more active essence of *poesis* or making. If art is to be an important source of philosophical insight, it must be defined as a poetic "projection" (*Entwurf*) or "setting-itself-into-work" of *truth*. Thus Heidegger doubts ". . . whether the essence of poetry, and this means at the same time the essence of projection (*des Entwurfs*), can be adequately thought from the angle of imagination."[17] Even when the imagination is not explained by the subjective peculiarities of the artist, but described with reference to a disinterested mode of *Erlebnis*, Heidegger still assumes it to be a mere psychological faculty. Accordingly, the possibilities anticipated by the imagination are always reducible to psychological potentialities of *Erlebnis*. From Heidegger's standpoint, the imagination conceives the "merely possible" (*BT*,183) and cannot account for the way art projects truth.

In *Being and Time*, Heidegger characterizes projection more explicitly by relating it to a primordial sense of pos-

---

[16] Martin Heidegger, *An Introduction to Metaphysics*, trans. Ralph Manheim, Garden City, N.Y.: Doubleday Anchor, 1961, p. 111.

[17] Martin Heidegger, "The Origin of the Work of Art," trans. by Albert Hofstadter in *Philosophies of Art and Beauty*, ed. Albert Hofstadter and Richard Kuhns, New York: Modern Library, 1964, p. 694.

sibility, or what he calls the *existentiale* of Being-possible. Art has an ontological significance for Heidegger and cannot be defined in terms of an imagination which can understand only ontical possibilities i.e. things or situations *"not yet* actual" or not *"at any time* necessary" (*BT*,183). What the psychological subject anticipates through his imagination as a mere ontical possibility, "is on a lower level than actuality and necessity. On the other hand, possibility as an *existentiale* is the most primordial and ultimate positive way in which *Dasein* is characterized ontologically" (*BT*,183). Death is of course the existential possibility which is more than a mere possibility. Death is not an empty future possibility but the ground of an ontological conception of human history. Possibility as an *existentiale* is not then a vague conception, but a mode of Being which strangely "proves to be totally indeterminate and at the same time highly determinate."[18] What is logically indeterminate, may according to Heidegger be ontologically or historically determinate.[19]

It is interesting to note that in *Being and Time*, Heidegger describes his "existential-temporal analytic of Dasein" as a "radicalization" of Dilthey's historical analysis of man (*BT*,449–55). He is primarily critical of the aesthetic tendencies in Dilthey's analysis and finds Dilthey's friend, Count Yorck von Wartenburg, to have a better instinct for the essence of what is historical. With obvious agreement, he quotes Count Yorck's warning to Dilthey that the aesthetic tendencies of the comparative method in the human studies would obscure his true insights into history:

> Comparison is always aesthetic, and always adheres to the pattern of things. Windelband assigns [weist . . . zu] patterns to history. Your concept of the type is an entirely inward one. Here it is a matter of characteristics,

[18] Heidegger, *Introduction to Metaphysics*, p. 66.

[19] In chapter 10, we will explore Dilthey's suggestions about categories of historical life which are both determinate and indeterminate.

not of patterns. For Windelband, history is a series of pictures, of individual patterns—an aesthetic demand. To the natural scientist, there remains, beside his science, as a kind of human tranquillizer, only aesthetic enjoyment. But your conception of history is that of a nexus of forces, of unities of force, to which the category of "pattern" is to be applicable only by a kind of transference. [*BT*,451]

According to Heidegger, Count Yorck was right to point out the danger of a mere ocular appreciation of patterns in history. It is questionable, however, whether aesthetics necessarily reduces the significance of either art or history to a passive contemplation of merely pictorial possibilities. For such results Dilthey himself sometimes used the adjective "aesthetic" in a pejorative sense.

Although Dilthey makes no attempt to reduce the essence of art to a poetic projection of ontological truth, we have already referred to the fact that he too emphasizes the more active poetic aspects of all the arts. He locates this poetic quality in its ability to heighten *Erlebnis*, a concept which is used not just psychologically, as Heidegger fears, but also hermeneutically. The interpreter's experience of an artistic object need not internalize it. Dilthey's hermeneutic approach respects the independence of the work of art and gives the otherwise rather subjective and form-oriented history of aesthetics, an objective, meaning-oriented direction. On the whole then we can conceive of aesthetics and the comparative method not simply as ocular and contemplative, but as reflective and interpretive. If Kant's active play of the aesthetic imagination had already indicated fundamental reflective possibilities, then certainly Dilthey's *Erlebnisphantasie* can be said to be productive of concrete reflective insight into the meaning of life as actually lived.

His criticisms notwithstanding, Heidegger characterizes *Being and Time* as "resolved to foster the spirit of Count Yorck in the service of Dilthey's work" (*BT*,455). Thus Heidegger finds that Diltheyan concepts like understanding and hermeneutic circularity can be useful—but only when divorced from the aesthetic perspective which had enabled Dilthey to develop them as fruitful modes of articulating and analyzing the meaning of life.

Like Dilthey, Heidegger defines his approach as analytic, and expresses doubts about the logical concept of synthesis. For Dilthey, a synthetic logic is a redundancy in the *Geistes-wissenschaften* since phenomena are there given as part of a continuum. On the other hand, Heidegger considers logical synthesis as a superficial manifestation of a more fundamental act of synthesis, which can only be disclosed by means of the existential analytic. Heidegger does not accept Dilthey's psychohistorical standpoint whereby connectedness is given in experience. Instead, he considers synthesis to be made possible by a fundamental act of interpreting something *as* something, i.e. where one thing is made to point to some other thing beyond itself through a situational involvement. The copula "is," which relates in mere external fashion, must thus be grounded in the bond of the existential-hermeneutical "as" (*BT*,201). The reason that synthesis can be explicated by means of an existential analytic is that *Dasein* possesses the fundamental possibility of interpreting itself *as* Being-in-the-world.

In Dilthey, the hermeneutic concept of interpretation is used primarily to understand others by means of their expressions or objectifications; consequently self-understanding is not possible unless *Erlebnis* is placed in a social context. For Heidegger it is not enough to give interpretation a public, ontical framework. His Interpretation carries an ontological sense which overrides any initial self-other distinction. On the other hand, he defines Interpretation as the most fundamental means of coping with the structure of *Dasein*—its so-called fore-structure which makes it always anticipatory of something in the future, namely, its individuating death. As an historical Being, *Dasein* is characterized by a forehaving, i.e. a foresight about ultimate meanings

374

which first make it possible for a present *Erlebnis* to be meaningful.

Just as Heidegger rendered the notion of understanding more fundamental than immediate *Erlebnis*, so he radicalized the sense of the hermeneutic circle we have discussed in Schleiermacher and Dilthey. If for the latter the hermeneutic circle is necessary to arrive at reflective or critical judgments which go beyond the limited number of determinant judgments based on an elementary understanding, then for Heidegger the hermeneutic circle first makes such determinant judgments possible. Interpretation is necessarily circular in that it already presupposes some kind of understanding—what Heidegger assumes, however, is not an ontical intuition of the whole which constantly needs revision,[20] but an ontological pre-understanding. The hermeneutic circle thus creates the bond between the fore-having of *Dasein* and its Being-in-the-world which then authenticates any predicative synthesis. "This circle of understanding is not an orbit in which any random kind of knowledge may move; it is the expression of the existential *fore-structure* of *Dasein* itself. It is not to be reduced to the level of a vicious circle, or even of a circle which is merely tolerated. In the circle is hidden a positive possibility of the most primordial kind of knowing" (*BT*,195).

In another section of *Being and Time* entitled "Reality as an Ontological Problem," Heidegger takes cognizance of Dilthey's epistemological theory that "the Real gets experienced in impulse and will, and that Reality is resistance . . ." (*BT*,252). But claiming that Dilthey overlooked its ontological meaning, he argues that "the experiencing of resistance —that is, the discovery of what is resistant to one's endeavors—is possible ontologically only by reason of the disclosedness of the world" (*BT*,253). Resistance could not be experienced *as* resistance unless *Dasein* already presupposed a world in which it had its Being.

---

[20] For this Diltheyan conception see above, pp. 268–71.

However, Dilthey had himself spoken of the difference between resistance and its meaning as limitation. Because he did not distinguish between an ontical and ontological sense of "world," he formulated his conception in terms of the paradox that the consciousness of the external world is both given and mediate. This means that Dilthey includes in his account certain states in which impulses are nonintentional and therefore need not presuppose a beyond, but neither does he presuppose any notion of a self. Rather we have seen how self and world develop as correlates.

For Heidegger, on the other hand, our sense of self is defined not ontically in relation to the world in which we live, but through the anticipation of death, i.e. nothingness (*BT*,308f.). The finitude of *Dasein* is thus temporal and is not conceived as a limit relative to anything else. Accordingly, no basis for a sense of resistance is provided. Nor is it at all clear whether a sense of resistance is really possible for *Dasein* relative to life itself. Can *Dasein*, which has been defined as already beyond itself (Being-there), and ecstatically involved in the world, feel resistance? Surely, the experience of resistance includes not only a sense of the world, but also a sense of self in turn able to resist this world.

Inadequate provision is made in the concept of *Dasein* for the retrograde movement of self-consciousness. To the extent that *Dasein's* being-outside of itself is conceived ecstatically, transcendence fails to offer any ground for reflection and critical thought. In Dilthey's philosophy, by contrast, we have an awareness of an outside which carries with it a consciousness of being incomplete. Our sense of life and world, although conceived ontically, leads to reflection on the limitations of the self.

Anthropological Reflection and the Categories of Life

According to Dilthey, *Besinnung über das Leben* (reflection about life) is concerned with those aspects of life that cannot be assigned a definite historical meaning, but none-theless are not to be reduced or elevated, as the case may be, to having a transcendent significance only. We have already seen indications of Dilthey's increasing use of the musical imagination to deal with themes normally considered to involve metaphysical or religious speculation.

Whereas literature, especially drama, can be seen as a measure of man's historical understanding, music is the means whereby Dilthey reflects on life in general. Vocal music takes certain poetic lines as its starting point and to that extent it can be assigned a definite objective reference. The case is different for instrumental music. "In instrumental music there is no determinate object, but an infinite, i.e. indeterminate one. This is given only in life itself, however. Thus in its highest forms, instrumental music has life itself as its object" (*DDM*,224).

Like vocal music, instrumental music expresses *Erlebnis*, but it always lacks the specific meaning of an expression (*Ausdruck*) (*DDM*,221). Dilthey indicates that it really provides a more general impression (*Eindruck*) of *Erlebnis* and life. Here interpretation which concerns itself with meaning (*Bedeutung*) reaches its ultimate framework. Meaning is hermeneutically defined as a relationship that parts have to a whole. Since life is for Dilthey the encompassing whole in relation to which everything must be understood and behind which we cannot go, it cannot strictly speaking have meaning; it can at most make sense. *Besinnung* (reflection) produces a *Sinn des Lebens* (sense of life) rather than a *Bedeutung des Lebens* (meaning of life).[21]

In a discussion of his categories, Dilthey compared life to a melody which does not mean anything outside itself

[21] In "Das Wesen der Philosophie," Dilthey still interchanges the phrases *Sinn des Lebens* and *Bedeutung des Lebens* (*GS*, VII, 221). However, in his final manuscripts he makes the distinction self-consciously. See *GS*, VII, 74, 235, 287, and the following quote from 265: "Es besteht also hier ein Verhältnis der Teile zum Ganzen, in

(*GS*,VII,234). Thus we can claim to appreciate the sense of life without being able to explicate its meaning. The most appropriate way to characterize life would be to consider its implications—not as implying things that go beyond it, but as bringing things together. This is suggested by Dilthey's insertion of the terms "explication" and "implication" in the following musical analogue about the life-relations of *Erlebnisse*: "*Erlebnisse* are related to each other as motifs manifest themselves in an andante of a symphony. They are developed (explication) and what has been developed is then recapitulated or taken together (implication)" (*GS*,VI,316).

To understand Dilthey's use of explication and implication here we must consider the root *plicare* (to fold). Whereas explication folds out or opens up, implication folds in or draws together. Life not only explicates its motifs historically as they unfold their *meaning* in time, but also implicates, or draws in, those overtones which otherwise might be dissipated in a transcendent realm. Thus the dim horizon of death that may appear to derive from a beyond must be shown to implicate life itself and induce reflection on its value.

Earlier we saw Dilthey discuss this in terms of the religious genius, but such fundamental evaluations inform activity in all spheres of life. And while few may reflect on life in general (on the overall sense of life), every man, according to Dilthey, is led to reflection on the course of his own life. "Such self-reflection (*Selbstbesinnung*)," he writes, "though it may be limited in extent, is frequently made by every individual. It is always present and expresses itself in ever new forms. It is present in the verses of Solon as well as in the reflections of the Stoic philosophers, in the meditations of the saints and in the philosophy of life of modern times. It alone makes historical insight possible" (*GS*,VII,200–201).[22]

---

welchem die Teile vom Ganzen *Bedeutung* und das Ganze von den Teilen *Sinn* erhalten. . . ." (Italics added).

[22] In this discussion of self-reflection and in that which follows about

Autobiography is the literary expression of an individual's self-reflection. It illustrates how reflection attains an evaluative sense of life before definition of its historical meaning in biography. When Dilthey spoke of life as a melody which does not mean anything outside itself, he was referring to the concept of life in the impersonal sense. However, it can also be said that as aware of its mortality, each individual life-unit (*Lebenseinheit*) ultimately draws in upon itself and recognizes its own limits. No matter how much the individual needs to be understood in terms of his communal and historical context, his own *Erlebnisse* and deeds possess an inner coherence. These relations cannot, however, be articulated into a definite meaning framework as long as his life history is still incomplete. In biography we have such a finished framework whereby the meaning of a past life can be historically defined, but autobiography must appeal to reflection (*Besinnung*) to hold together in an indeterminate sense of life (*Sinn des Lebens*) this accumulation of meaningful experience that would otherwise become dispersed (*GS*,VII,247).

While the autobiographer thus sets forth a self-drawn framework for interpreting the stages of his life, Dilthey stresses that the reflective process involves the recognition of relations that have already been partially worked out by life itself. Even before consciously undertaking his task, the autobiographer ". . . has, in his memory, singled out and accentuated the moments which he experienced as meaningful; others he has allowed to sink into forgetfulness. The future has corrected his illusions about the meaning of certain moments. Thus, the first problem of grasping and presenting historical connections is already half solved by life" (*GS*,VII,200).

Autobiography possessed a peculiar fascination for Dilthey because "the one who understands the course of life is the same as the one who produced it . . ." (*GS*,VII,200). By contrast, biography is of course derivative. In giving a

---

autobiography, compare the quotations from *GS*, VII, 200–201 with Rickman's translations in *Pattern and Meaning in History*, pp. 86–87.

more determinate account of an individual life, it requires a comparative perspective and a much more specific understanding of historical conditions. Autobiography involves reflection on how the self is implicated by life, which biography then explicates by articulating objective spirit in terms of an individual life-history (see chapter 8).

What we have discussed as reflection on life and self-reflection is more generally designated by Dilthey as "anthropological reflection" (*anthropologische Besinnung*). In German, "anthropology" and "psychology" can be used interchangeably, and Dilthey applied both terms to his descriptive psychology. However, it is clear that Dilthey is here referring to man's life rather than to his psyche. Described as lying "at the root where the *Erlebnis* and *Verstehen* of the poet, the artist, the religious person and the philosopher come together" (*GS*,VII,266), anthropological reflection is the hermeneutic analogue to the reflective experience of the comparative psychology (see chapter 5). But, whereas reflective experience pointed beyond Dilthey's descriptive psychology to history, anthropological reflection provides the framework for both historical understanding and a new *Individualpsychologie*. In a section of the *Entwürfe* entitled "*Erlebnis* and Autobiography" Dilthey claims that self-reflection "alone makes historical insight possible. The power and breadth of our own lives and the energy with which we reflect on them are the groundwork of historical vision" (*GS*,VII,201).

The fundamental relation that Dilthey establishes between self-reflection in autobiography and historical interpretation can be seen more generally as one between anthropological reflection and a Critique of Historical Judgment. In so doing, we shall conceive of Dilthey's categories of life as reflective concepts which provide a sense-framework for historical understanding.

In sketching the guidelines of a categorial analysis appropriate for the *Geisteswissenschaften*, Dilthey claims that "Life is to be understood in its peculiar essence through categories which are foreign to the knowledge of nature. What is decisive here is that these categories are not applied to life in an a priori fashion as from without, but that they lie implicit in the essence of life itself" (*GS*,VII,232). Given the dynamism of historical life, the categories cannot be delimited as in Kant's *Critique of Pure Reason*. Their number must be left indeterminate, and none can be subordinated to any other (*GS*,VII,201). In light of a hermeneutic approach to the *Geisteswissenschaften*, these categories do not provide the ground for determinant judgments, but are designed to order the understanding of life from a reflective standpoint. We shall first consider the categories of value, purpose, and meaning as concepts for reflection on life in general and then in the next chapter examine time and other categories which are more specifically applicable to understanding the historical nature of life.

H. P. Rickman justifiably labels meaning as Dilthey's master category. But he interprets all the other categories in terms of meaning, so that purpose and value are defined as different ways in which things are considered meaningful.[23] The effect of this is to render meaning the common denominator of the other categories—a result hardly in keeping with the hermeneutic principle of mutual interdependence.

In discussing the relation among purpose, value, and meaning in his theoretical writings, Dilthey stresses the category of meaning, because through it alone is it possible to achieve an integral anthropological vision. One of his main objections to applying the category of purpose from psychic to historical life is that it tends to reduce the complexity of life by subsuming everything to one overarching end. The category of value is more appropriately applied since it encourages the appreciation of multiplicity in life. Yet by this very token, the value category gives a too dispersed view of reality. Through evaluation we may enjoy the richness of experience but lose any sense of unity. The

---

[23] See Rickman's introduction to chap. 3 of *Pattern and Meaning in History*, pp. 96f.

variety of life can only be held together by a nexus of meaning.

The distinguishing feature of Dilthey's reflective approach to the categories lies in their being linked to the dimensions of time. This is exhibited in a musical analogy through which the special importance of the category of meaning is suggested.

> From the perspective of values, life appears as an infinite manifold of positive and negative values of existence (*Daseinswerten*). It is like a chaos of harmonies and dissonances. Each of these values is a tonal pattern or chord that fills a *present* moment, but these chords have no musical relationship to each other. The category of purpose or good which apprehends life from the perspective directed towards the *future*, presupposes the category of value. From it too the totality of life cannot be constructed. For the relations of purposes to each other are restricted to those of possibility, choice, and subordination. Only the category of meaning overcomes the mere juxtaposition and the mere subordination of the parts of life. [*GS*,VII,202]

The category of meaning is crucial because it can do justice to a temporal continuum. Whereas the categories of value and purpose were said to focus on the present and the future respectively, Dilthey relates the category of meaning to our memory of the past: "When we look back in memory, we apprehend the nexus of elapsed phases of the course of life through the category of meaning" (*GS*,VII,201).

Dilthey does not tell us why he restricts values to that which is presently apprehended. Perhaps it is to signify their immediate nature. If immediacy of felt apprehension is accepted as the hallmark of values we can easily understand why it should be hard to mediate between them. Each moment of life can be enjoyed for its own relative value. Values can only be coordinated like a series of present moments in the flow of time.

That ends should be related to the future dimension and to some extent be removed from temporal development as such is understandable. But to claim that the category of meaning pertains especially to the past requires some justification. Certainly, Dilthey's assertion that when we look back in memory we apprehend the meaning of our past actions (*GS*,VII,201), does not suffice to orient the category of meaning towards the past. Rickman could easily argue that plans are also meaningful. If the past is nevertheless the most meaningful dimension of time, this must derive from the fact that the process of understanding meaning involves a regressive movement. But we have shown how understanding can go over into a forward, future-oriented movement as well.

It is because Dilthey defines the meaning relationship as essentially a part-whole relation that the past becomes so important for his philosophy of life. The past is the only mode of time that can be concretely apprehended as a whole made up of related parts. The integration of part and whole receives a peculiar significance for a theory of life and history because it can overcome the limitations of spatial coordination and rational subordination that characterize the natural sciences and metaphysical systems respectively. The part-whole relation is central to all dynamic systems in the human studies, and need not be considered a merely heuristic or regulative organic category once it is recognized to derive its initial evidence from our *Erlebnis* of the past.

Although Dilthey's theoretical interest in history has been misunderstood by many to be restricted to the past, he neither wishes, nor thinks it possible, to isolate the past from the less determinate dimensions of time. Indeed, the present and the future must be related to the past and thereby understood as meaningful. Thus the category of meaning can come to encompass all three modes of temporality as long as the past is granted primacy.

Dilthey's account of the past as a part-whole complex

should not be misinterpreted to demarcate a closed whole. The scope of the past is constantly being enlarged. But there is a more important sense in which the past is open to reinterpretation if we acknowledge Dilthey's claim that "what we set as a goal for the future, conditions the determination of the meaning of the past" (GS,VII,233). To demonstrate this would require a concept of the present which truly mediates between past and future. But for a more thorough examination of Dilthey's category of time, we must move from the abstract musical symbolism of his philosophy of life to concrete historical understanding of life. Relative to the problem of making more specific judgments about meaning in history, time is an experienced continuum which must be structurally delimited in terms of interpretive categories.

CHAPTER TEN

Style and the Conceptual
Articulation of Historical Life

A. C. BRADLEY once described poetry and life as "parallel developments which nowhere meet." This image allows him to maintain that poetry is not *in* or *of* the world and still agree that "we understand one by help of the other, and even, in a sense, care for one because of the other. . . ."[1] Thus he points to an "underground" connection between poetry and life which we have seen explored in Dilthey's philosophy of life. But the reflective judgment relating poetry and life needs to be specified for the sake of interpretation and critical judgment in an aesthetic of history.

The category of meaning, while one of the fundamental concepts for reflection on life itself, also allows us to move from the indeterminacy of anthropological reflection to the more determinate level of historical understanding. In addition to the evaluative categories of life, Dilthey suggests what might be called interpretive categories more appropriate for articulating the dynamic systems of historical life. These categories are never worked out in Dilthey's writings but may be characterized as determinate-indeterminate in nature. We will first develop Dilthey's notion of the determinate-indeterminate in terms of his category of time and then apply the results to the concept of style, which is of special interest because it can reveal the mutual implications of aesthetics and history.

One task of an aesthetic of history will be to refine the

[1] A. C. Bradley, "Poetry for Poetry's Sake," in *A Modern Book of Esthetics*, ed. Melvin Rader, 3rd ed., New York: Holt, Rinehart and Winston, 1960, p. 311.

vague sense of a life-style given in anthropological reflection into the articulate style of historically locatable works
of art. Anthropological reflection discloses some of the
structural conditions of the *Welt-anschauungen* analyzed
in the previous chapter, just as geometry establishes some
of the formal conditions for ordering our perceptions of objects or *Objekt-anschauungen*. Aesthetically, this analogy
can be elaborated to show that anthropological reflection
contributes to the search for meaning in the literary arts
what the laws of perspective contributed to the delineation
of beauty in the visual arts. And from a critical perspective,
we discover that the transcendental significance which Kant
attributed to geometry relative to an aesthetic of nature and
the intuition of space, can similarly be assigned to anthropological reflection vis-à-vis an aesthetic of history and the
intuition of time.

Time and the Presence of *Erlebnis*

Dilthey's categorial analysis of our intuition of time seems
to bear the influence of Bergson, although the latter is not
mentioned in this context.[2] Like Bergson, Dilthey emphasizes the immeasurable qualitativeness of time, which he
says "is not merely a line which could be conceived to consist of equivalent parts, a system of [formal] relations, of
diachrony, synchrony, and duration (*Dauer*). If we think
of time while abstracting from what fills it, the parts are
equivalent. In this continuum even the smallest part is
linear, a sequence. No part can be said to 'be' " (*GS*,VII,72).
Once time is conceived of as an abstract mathematical line
which can be extended ad indefinitum, it becomes inappropriate to stop at any point. Bergson had vehemently attacked the practicing scientist who tracks the mobility of

[2] There seems to be no explicit mention of Bergson's name in Dilthey's writings until 1911 when he published "Die Typen der Weltanschauung." See *GS*, VIII, 107, 111. Misch quotes another reference
to Bergson, but unfortunately assigns no date to it. *GS*, V, cvi.

time by the points through which a moving object has passed. But precisely because it is so obviously inappropriate, Dilthey does not seem to share Bergson's concern. Such geometrization of time does not represent a philosophical problem for Dilthey. It is merely a hypothetical expedient.

In point of fact, Dilthey shows greater suspicion of those who conceive of time simply as a restless function or a constant flow. If time is to be reflected on, we cannot simply characterize it as a flux where no part can be said to be. Although the parts of time lack the fixed beings of points, this does not entail that time as such possesses no structured being at all.

In opposition to Kant's conception of time as an empty, a priori form which has only a phenomenal status, Dilthey agrees with Bergson that time is a real manifestation of life. Yet, his conception of how time is experienced differs. Instead of accepting the unstructured plenitude of Bergson's intuition of duration, he links time to his category of *Erlebnis*.

Dilthey contrasts the usual dynamic account of a temporal sequence which discharges itself (*ein Ablauf*) to the more concrete temporality of a progression which advances (*ein Vorrücken*). Instead of interpreting time as a flux where all nows disappear, he suggests that its restlessness can be used to augment the scope of the present. Only by conceiving of time as an onward movement does an *Erlebnis* of it become possible. "Concrete time consists . . . in the indefatigable progression of the present (*der Gegenwart*) in which what is present (*das Gegenwärtige*) immediately becomes past and what is future becomes present. The present is a moment of time being filled with reality. It is an *Erlebnis* in contrast to the memory of it or . . . the expectation of one in the future" (*GS*,VII,72). The last claim about the *Erlebnis* of the present needs some explication, for on the next page Dilthey admits that because the present never is, what is present can really never be experienceable (*niemals erfahrbar*). This suggests that we can have an

387

Erlebnis of the present, but no *Erfahrung* of its content as presented. Although it may be legitimate to distinguish between time as dynamic and its content as static, we should not, however, conclude that the former is as such *erlebbar*. Indeed, in another account of the category of time Dilthey also asserts "that the flow of time is not *erlebbar* in the strict sense" (*GS*,VII,195). When time is construed as an *Ablauf* (discharge), the present is not experienced, but lived. Thus Dilthey claims that "we always live in the present which entails the constant corruptibility of our life" (*GS*,VII,72). To distinguish the *Erlebnis* of the present as part of the *Vorrücken* (advancement) of time we will call it a "presence." In fact, it is this *Erlebnis* of a temporal presence that allows us to preserve the present *as lived* in terms of what was presented as its content.

In contrast to life which is a flow of ephemeral moments, *Erlebnis* is inherently structural.[3] By interpreting life through the category of *Erlebnis* it seems possible to forestall the dualism between an intuition of time and discursive knowledge about it. Although Dilthey was critical of Fichte's *Wissenschaftslehre*, he recognized the importance

[3] Once we recognize that *Erlebnis* constitutes the structural presence of experience, it becomes apparent how misleading it is for Sauerland to describe Dilthey's *Erlebnisse* as "self-enclosed units" possessing an immediate distinctness, like points. (See Karol Sauerland, *Diltheys Erlebnisbegriff: Entstehung, Glanzzeit und Verkümmerung eines literaturhistorischen Begriffs*, Berlin: Walter de Gruyter, 1972, pp. 29, 97, 138, 142, 164.) For Dilthey, not even the present may be conceived as a point in time, and the presence of *Erlebnis* is so far from being an immediate self-enclosed unity that it bears within it direct relations to the past. To the extent that Dilthey wants to be able to distinguish one *Erlebnis* from others for descriptive purposes, he does so by assigning it a specific function in relation to our life as a whole: "Im Haushalt meines Lebens ist es ein für sich loslösbares, weil es strukturell zu einer Leistung in diesem Haushalt gegliedert ist. . . . Erlebnis bezeichnet einen Teil des Lebensverlaufs. . . . er [der Teil] enthält schon Vergangenheit und Zukunft in sich in dem Bewusstsein von Gegenwart . . ." (*GS*, VI, 314). Thus the very attempt to isolate *Erlebnis* shows it to be a part of a larger whole.

of its program to overcome the prejudice that concepts are static and necessarily distort what is dynamic. But instead of rendering concepts dialectically dynamic, Dilthey chose to focus on ways in which concepts can point to aspects of life that are already structured. More than anything, *Erlebnis* serves this function. It is truly temporal and yet it constitutes a dynamic structural unity which allows the momentary value of the *present* to become a meaningful *presence*:

> The qualitatively determinate reality which constitutes *Erlebnis* is structural. To be sure, it flows in time and is experienced as sequential; [but the concrete] temporal relations in it can be apprehended. That which is past in this structural sequence, but nevertheless is preserved as a force in the present, receives thereby a peculiar character of presence (*Präsenz*). Although it constitutes a flow, *Erlebnis* is a dynamic unity, and this not only objectively, but in our consciousness. [*GS*,VI,315]

Erlebnis, when interpreted as a presence, is able to structure life without fixing it. Dilthey is not really denying the fact that while life presents us with constant change, knowledge requires some stability. He is in his own way trying to cope with this tension. In the *Ideen*, Dilthey had gone so far as to speak of antinomies which arise, not just, as Kant had pointed out, when we transcend experience, but when we think about experience itself (*GS*,V,175f.). As soon as we attempt to explain totalities as they are experienced, we run into antinomies. This had suggested that we must therefore limit ourselves to a description of such totalities and only explain changes of individual parts (see chapter 3).

In the late writings, Dilthey deals with the problem differently by indicating the possibility of conceptualizing historical life in terms of the notion of the "determinate-indeterminate" (*bestimmt-unbestimmt*). One use of it appears in the context of describing the process of understanding language (*GS*,VII,220). What is given in an utterance is a series of words, each of which possesses a range of indeterminacy of meaning within certain determinate bounds. There is a variability of meaning in relation to the several dictionary definitions of a word; and an ambiguity of possible syntactical relations. The meaning will be delimited at least to some extent by understanding the individual words as parts of a whole established by the actual structure of a sentence.

Interpretation will always contend with some indefinite sense-context while further defining the understood core of meaning. Thus any category relevant to the interpretation of history must be contextual in nature and yet capable of locating a focal point or articulating a continuum. The category of *Erlebnis* understood as a temporal presence has both these traits. It reveals how the determinacy of past experience continues to assert its force as a source of the reality of the present, while the indefiniteness of the future keeps open the possibilities in relation to which the significance of *Erlebnis* will change and makes its presence indeterminate and subject to reinterpretation.

Through the presence of *Erlebnis*, the meaning of the past can be extended to the other modes of time without being interpreted deterministically. Such a conception of the past in relation to the present allows us to see that Dilthey's concept of *Wesen* (essence) retains the Hegelian idea of *Wesen ist was gewesen ist* (essence is that which has been) without implying a determinant definition. Thus when he characterizes the essence of philosophy through the study of its history, its past functions provide philosophy a general rationale, instead of some specific reason, for being. Dilthey reminds us of borderline areas between philosophy, religion and art which make it impossible to define any one of these fields exclusively. Philosophy itself is a dynamic system which has its own focal point, but no clear horizon. Its *Wesen* is to be a central human function.

Wesen as Dilthey uses it, has a certain neutral sense. It

can be applied to anything which displays an inner character or significance. In a section on the categories of life, Dilthey lists it as a category related to that of development (*GS*,VII,244). He uses the concept *Wesen* in ways analogous to the psychological concept of the acquired psychic nexus. *Wesen* articulates our sense of individuality, not just of individual life as described psychologically, but of any historical dynamic system. *Wesen* does not connote something innate, but what must be achieved through development.

Applied to the individual qua historical being, the concept of *Wesen* helps to preserve some of the qualities, such as a sense of freedom, that a descriptive psychology had made prominent. Although hardly sufficient to define anything as positive as the psychologically conceived *Erlebnis* of freedom, it does at least disclose a certain element of self-selection within the possibilities of development which can neutralize deterministic claims. Dilthey states that the nature (*Wesen*) of man is *bestimmt-Unbestimmbares*, that is, something determinate but nondeterminable, enduring but not fixed. "Implicit in this is that any change incorporating influences from without on the centralized context of life is at the same time determined by this life itself" (*GS*,VII, 244). Extreme changes imposed on man are at the same time opportunities for inner development. Individuals are bounded, not just spatially, but by what Dilthey calls self-drawn or inner bounds:

> Everything is held together by an inner force and inner bounds which manifest themselves in the definiteness of the individual and the consequent duration of his acquired psychic nexus. In all this the same inner nature (*Wesen*) is active (*wirksam*). . . . We find everywhere a limitation on what is possible. Yet we have the freedom to choose alternatives, and accordingly the wonderful feeling of being able to progress and realize

391

new possibilities of our own existence (*Dasein*). Such a relation in the course of life, determined from within ... I call "development." [*GS*,VII,244–45]

This more loosely construed sense of inner definition can be related to the way Dilthey describes the objective apprehension of development in a musical experience. The development of a symphonic movement has a certain rightness that is not, however, anything that could have been determined by the first set of notes. Here Dilthey contrasts the determinate idea of necessity (*Notwendigkeit*) with an indeterminate sense of *Sosein-Müssen* (having-to-be-thus).

> Note follows upon note and aligns itself according to the laws of our tonal system; but within this there lies an infinity of possibilities. . . . An earlier bar [of a melody] conditions a subsequent one, but at the same time the first bar of a rising melody, in a work of Handel, for instance, is grounded in the last. Likewise, the descending line strives towards a point of rest, is conditioned by it and conditions it in turn. Everywhere free possibilities. Nowhere in all this conditioning is there any necessity. . . . The having-to-be-thus (*Sosein-Müssen*) is not necessity, but is the realization of an aesthetic value. [*GS*,VII,221]

The outcome of a musical composition cannot be predicted and yet we have a feeling once it has ended that this is the way it should have ended. There is a must (*Müssen*) involved here, which alludes to a sense of appropriateness, or of what is fitting.

The sense of *Sosein-Müssen* is an indeterminate impression created by the work that some value has been realized. It is not explicit enough to express a specific meaning. This kind of evaluative response is frequently experienced through instrumental music and most evident in the impression or sense of life connected with anthropological reflection. Thus the self-reflection of the autobiographer involves a feeling of rightness or appropriateness about the overall development of his life, which might be called a sense of a life-style.

Earlier, we found Dilthey criticizing naturalistic artists for presenting mere impressions without focusing them on some dynamic point. Only the articulation of some focal point can provide works of art with a stylistic unity. Such a "point of impression" allows representational art to reorganize our vision in terms of what is typical (see chapter 2). Having now related the idea of an impression to reflection on life, the vague sense of rightness that either a work of art or a life-style can provide on the evaluative level must also be articulated in terms of stylistic meaning on the level of interpretation.

Although Dilthey never developed his concept of style beyond his discussion in *Die drei Epochen*, we shall attempt to refashion it more historically in light of our analysis of determinate-indeterminate categories. For the remainder of this concluding chapter we shall be recalling points developed throughout the preceding chapters as they bear on the problem of style. The concept of style in art history and criticism can thereby typify our interpretation of Dilthey's approach to aesthetics and history.

In the psychological aesthetics, poetry was interpreted as the imaginative metamorphosis of poetic *Erlebnis* which articulates the structure of the acquired psychic nexus. This psychic nexus provided the sense context for understanding the meaning relations of the poet's *Erlebnis*. Thus it was that the acquired psychic nexus served as a model for Dilthey's interpretation of style as the inner form that individuates a work of art. Style or inner form develops from the content of the work and is a pervasive structure that provides unity even when the outer form of the work is relatively complex. Whereas strict formal unity demands a coherence of composition, stylistic unity may encompass conflicting traits.

In discussing Dilthey's theory of inner form, it was

393

pointed out that there is a built-in reference to outer form, in the same way that the psyche is inseparable from its historical context (see chapter 4). Although the *Poetik* explicated inner form psychologically in terms of the experience of the artist, this experience was referred, not to any ready-made concept of the artist's ego, but to his acquired psychic nexus as developed through time and encompassing historical influences. Such influences were especially recognized in Dilthey's discussions of technique and style-forms.

The subsequent hermeneutic development of Dilthey's thought allowed for a more direct reflective relation to the historical dimension. We have already shown that Dilthey approached the stylistic unity of works of art from two perspectives: for the spectator it lies in a point of impression; for the creator it involves the articulation of his *Erlebnis*. A concept of style formulated in light of Dilthey's late aesthetic and historical theory must take into account the more impersonal meaning relations established for *Erlebnisphantasie* and will interpret stylistic unity more from the standpoint of the critic in specifying its historical context and meaning framework.

Whenever art historians have used style to conceptualize art history, they have assumed some principle of periodization. Since there are no natural divisions in history, the delineation of a relevant historical context for art presupposes reflective judgment relating part to whole. A period is not simply discovered, but requires interpretation to be delimited. This will become particularly clear when dealing with histories of style, where the use of certain polarities like Classical-Baroque has obscured other less significant styles of the time.

A reflective sense of temporal continuity is crucial for historical understanding. However, if such understanding is to provide the basis for specific historical judgments, then we must articulate ideal temporal divisions or structures as contexts for interpretation. In Dilthey's historical writings, dynamic systems were exemplified not only by cultural systems but also by relatively self-sufficient structures such as a *Zeitgeist*. Dilthey found it useful to characterize the works of Lessing relative to the *Zeitgeist* or spirit of the German Enlightenment. Yet, it is difficult to specify to what extent a *Zeitgeist* can illuminate the style of a work such as *Nathan der Weise*.

A *Zeitgeist* seems to function like the idea of a *Sinn des Lebens* in that it provides an indeterminate sense-context for reflection about the meaning of works. It allows us to speak only in the most general terms of how a work is "implicated" by its times, how it "reflects" a certain "life-style." Moreover, if we consider all the arts of a period to partake of the spirit of a time, we stand in danger of becoming insensitive to the peculiarities of the individual arts. This would seem to reduce the richness of the creative arts to the poverty of the schemas used by traditional historians of style.

To be sure, there exist certain periods like the seventeenth century which most experts agree to have manifested a remarkable degree of affinity among the several arts. But is it necessary for those who are interested in the historical correlation of different arts to assume that stylistic unity must be explained through a monolithically conceived *Zeitgeist*? All that can be expected from Dilthey's concept of *Zeitgeist* is a loose sense of coherence. Meyer Schapiro rightly observes that the unity of the Baroque "is not necessarily organic"; and that "it may be likened also, perhaps, to that of a machine with limited freedom of motion. . . ." He also notes that there are many periods when we do not find the arts to be unified at all. "We look in vain in England for a style of painting that corresponds to Elizabethan poetry and drama. . . ."[4]

To account for the fact that different arts have their own conditions which determine how closely they can reflect their historical milieu, Dilthey acknowledged that an

[4] Meyer Schapiro, "Style," in *Aesthetics Today*, ed. Morris Philipson, Cleveland: Meridian Books, 1961, p. 92.

epochal stage of a cultural system can be antithetical to the spirit of its age. Dilthey did not always distinguish between an epoch (*Epoche*), an age (*Zeitalter*), and the spirit of an age (*Zeitgeist*), but it is important to underscore the possibility of their distinction if the concept of style is to be given a more adequate historical delineation. We will distinguish epoch and *Zeitgeist*, not in order to refer style to one or the other, but to relate it to both—one determinate, the other indeterminate.

The most neutral term to designate a historical period is the word *Zeitalter* which means "age." One can speak of the Napoleonic age without making any claims about a *Zeitgeist*, for Napoleon's rise to power entails no fundamental change in the spirit of the times. However, when Dilthey wrote about the Reformation as both a *Zeitalter* and *Epoche*, he was among other things, referring to a specific, historical *Zeitgeist*. Because an age like the Reformation can be defined in terms of a pervasive spirit, it may also be described as an epoch. So understood, the concept of epoch marks a relatively sharp cut in time—a time span characterized by a "life-style" discontinuous from others. In this context, the word *epochē* meaning "cessation" or "fixed point," seems appropriate to bear in mind. However, this sense of epoch can be absorbed and replaced by the concept of *Zeitgeist* to make room for another, more technical sense of the term.

If we go back to the Greek verb *epechein* in the sense of "to pause," or "to hold back," and extend the meaning of its derivative noun *epochē*, it may be read to denote a stage or phase in the continuing development of a given dynamic system. This second, metaphorically extended sense of epoch will be used henceforth and applied to particular cultural systems. Whereas the three epochs or stages of modern aesthetic theory discussed in chapter 2 fall within clearly distinguishable ages, sometimes an epoch of a particular cultural system like music reflects a certain *Geist* (e.g. the Baroque) without falling within the *Zeitalter* (seventeenth century) that it is usually thought to characterize. Thus Dilthey recognized that Bach represented the Baroque epoch of music in an age when in other spheres Enlightenment ideas were already common enough to constitute the spirit of the times. "Music has its own movement according to which the religious style, which stemmed from the highest power of the Christian *Erlebnis*, attained its climax in Bach and Handel at the same time in which the Enlightenment was already the dominant direction in Germany" (*GS*,VII,185).

Music possesses its special conventions and may be considered as a dynamic system which develops according to laws of its own (*GS*,VII,185). This would explain how a certain stage of musical development in the eighteenth century can be more germane to the expression of the religious ideals of Pietism, which Dilthey described as a holdover of the old in the German Enlightenment, than to the dominant secular ideals of the Enlightenment as such.

The *Zeitgeist* of the Enlightenment is no more than a general direction common to a set of dynamic systems. "It is not a unity (*Einheit*) which could be expressed in terms of a fundamental thought, but rather a coherence (*Zusammenhang*) amongst the tendencies of life which establishes itself in the course of life" (*GS*,VII,185). Whereas epochs are phases within the development of a dynamic system, a *Zeitgeist* is itself a dynamic system.

Because a *Zeitgeist* is the most complex of dynamic systems, it cannot monolithically determine everything that it encompasses. In the *Poetik* of 1887, Dilthey asserted that a *Zeitgeist* depends on individual genius for its articulation (*GS*,VI,230). Accordingly, the life and work of Lessing was interpreted to actively embody a sense of the German Enlightenment, thereby providing it a real unity not previously existent. But in the *Aufbau* of 1910, Dilthey claimed that it is especially the great figures of an age who are determined by the *Zeitgeist* (*GS*,VII,186). Thereby he suggested that a *Zeitgeist* can be operative prior to its articulation by individuals. Despite a seemingly new emphasis on the tendency of a *Zeitgeist* to consolidate the status quo and to thwart individual contributions productive of change, it can be argued that Dilthey here developed a more pluralistic conception of *Zeitgeist* which contains cross-currents within it. For example, Pietism was claimed to persist as a counter-movement to the Enlightenment even though Dilthey saw the stamp of the new *Zeitgeist* in the increasing indifference of the Pietists towards traditional church forms and a greater stress on tolerance (*GS*,VII,183).

A *Zeitgeist* is at once overpowering and ephemeral, absolute and relative. "As it arose from the insufficiency of an earlier [*Zeitgeist*] so it carries within itself the limits, tensions and suffering which prepare for the future" (*GS*,VII, 186–87). In that a *Zeitgeist* is to a large extent a reaction, it can be seen to differ from other dynamic systems by having no clearly definable center. Accordingly, Dilthey is unable to treat it purely hermeneutically as a structural framework for understanding individual historical phenomena, and he resorts to vague language concerning the general "efficacy" of a *Zeitgeist* on the arts. By contrast he ascribes laws of epochal development to individual dynamic systems of culture. An example of this is the lawful sequence of literary style-forms discussed in chapter 4.

Although Dilthey does not so argue, it is reasonable to think that a *Zeitgeist* provides a sense framework which implicates the artist and his work, but can only be explicated retrospectively in terms of a theory of epochal development. Whereas a *Zeitgeist* represents an indeterminate but encompassing division, an epoch constitutes a determinate but partial phase within a larger continuum. From the art-historian's perspective an epoch can serve as a specific meaning framework by which he defines a style-form as an ideal structural unity.

The importance of discussing style as inner form was to make the uniqueness of the work a function of its meaning. Bennison Gray's claim that literary stylistics is based on the assumption of the full translatability of expressions would render the uniqueness of a style irrelevant to its meaning.[5] This has the effect of reducing style to a mere rhetorical ornament. Yet the individuating style of a work of art as distinguished from a style-form manifests itself in the concrete texture of the work as well as in its formal traits. An individual style does not merely represent an ideal quality but articulates concrete historical reality. The works of Shakespeare, Leonardo, and Dürer demonstrate, in Dilthey's words, "how remote an enduring style is from so-called idealization: exactly that which is most brittle, factual, and particular is used in the greatest of styles as a moment in the process of producing an impression of reality" (*GS*,VI,284). To insist on the historical facticity of style means that there will always be something indefinable about it. When the determinate meaning of an epochal style-form remains rooted in the indeterminate sense of a *Zeitgeist*, style becomes a determinate-indeterminate concept.

A determinate meaning may be reproduced and translated while an indeterminate sense always demands reinterpretation. But the significance of style as a determinate-indeterminate concept is that it embodies its own fragile perfection, thereby challenging repeated interpretation and limiting re-creation.

Perspectives on a Concept of Style

Style as a historical concept which is determinate-indeterminate in nature allows for cross-illumination between poetry and life, aesthetics and history. Yet the danger in relating art to its life-context is to read it as an index to something extrinsic to itself. Art then ceases to have an import of its own. The ideal attitude to take would be to follow the allusions of a work to its context only to the extent that they can be integrated back into the structure of the work itself. This will render its style meaningful in a world-

---

[5] Bennison Gray, "Stylistics: The End of a Tradition," *Journal of Aesthetics and Art Criticism*, 31, Summer 1973, 510–11.

ly sense without reducing it to a mere part of the world, or a copy thereof.

In many histories of art, discussions of style focus only on the intrinsic formal qualities of works of art. Accordingly, styles have been divorced from the general historical context and formulated schematically as solutions to a given set of aesthetic problems. In Heinrich Wölfflin's influential writings, for instance, the concept of style is abstracted from the Zeitgeist and deals only with epochal changes of forms in the visual arts. Certain optical schemata are claimed to impose themselves on all the art works of an epoch no matter what their content.

Wölfflin's studies had concentrated on the differences between the visual arts of the sixteenth and seventeenth centuries, but he considered the differences between the Classical and the Baroque to be based on more fundamental differences which recur throughout the development of the visual arts. Although reality can be seen in terms of two basic alternating optical sets, at any given time only one set will be open to the artist and consequently will limit the possibility of artistic representation for him. "Doubtless certain forms of beholding pre-exist as possibilities," Wölfflin writes, "whether and how they come to development depends on outward circumstances."[6] Factors such as national history are allowed to play a certain role in changes of style, but only in the sense of providing the initial conditions for a law of vision. Individual names can only be inserted into Wölfflin's art history after the appropriate optic set, nationality, and epoch have been determined.

In describing the fundamental schemata that determine a style, Wölfflin asserts that a painter can represent an object in terms of tactile outlines (linearly) or in terms of visual appearances (painterly); he can give a sense of depth by the use of distinct vertical planes or by gradual

[6] Heinrich Wölfflin, *Principles of Art History: The Problem of the Development of Style in Later Art* (1st German ed., 1915), trans. M. D. Hottinger, New York: Dover Publications, 1932, pp. 11, 230.

recession; he can confine the eye of the spectator within the closed form of the frame or lead him beyond it. A fourth alternative is established by choosing between the additive or integrative organization of motifs. Finally, Wölfflin speaks of the concepts of absolute clarity and relative clarity of the subject. He claims that the first term in each of these pairs of concepts is realized in the Classical style of the sixteenth century and the second in the Baroque style of the following century.[7]

Wölfflin places the greatest emphasis on the first polarity and often simply refers to Classical art as linear and Baroque art as painterly. Nevertheless, he stops short of proposing the kind of systematic connection whereby tactile outlines would entail a closed form or any of the other attributes of linear representation. Speaking of the set of attributes that constitute the linear and painterly styles respectively, Wölfflin acknowledges that "Although they clearly run in one direction, they are still not derived from one principle. . . . It is possible that still other categories could be set up—I could not discover them—and those given here are not so closely related that they could not be imagined in a partly different combination. For all that, to a certain extent they involve each other. . . ."[8]

Insofar as Wölfflin's categories focused on five definite senses of visual form—contour, perspective, frame, organization, and precision—he was right to warn that they could not be derived from any single principle. It would have been better had he refrained from using one kind of form—that of contour or outline—as the basis for labeling the two basic styles as such. What is to be claimed for the categories pertaining to a given style is no more than a kind of family resemblance.

In an early essay, Erwin Panofsky argued that these categories reflect a limited number of artistic problems which "can be ultimately derived from one basic antithesis: dif-

[7] Ibid., pp. 14–16.   [8] Ibid., p. 227.

ferentiation *vs.* continuity."[9] But to derive these different senses of form from one a priori antithesis is impossible. Even if it could be done, Panofsky would be at a loss to explain why, for instance in impressionistic art, a painterly effect cannot be neatly correlated with an integrative manner of composition.[10]

Whereas Panofsky went too far in his derivation of Wölfflin's formal analysis of styles, Cassirer's *Zur Logik der Kulturwissenschaften* provides what is perhaps its most reasonable theoretical defense. Cassirer's analysis of style is especially interesting because it is related to some of the more general theoretical questions concerning the *Geisteswissenschaften* we have dealt with in the conclusion of chapter 8. By taking into account the accomplishments of Wölfflin and Burckhardt in the study of art and cultural

[9] Erwin Panofsky, *Meaning in the Visual Arts*, Garden City, N.Y.: Doubleday, 1955, p. 21.

[10] Yet if we are willing to distinguish between artistic technique and aesthetic effect the affinity of Wölfflin's "painterly" categories can still be defended. There need be no embarrassment about the fact that the Impressionists composed additively—both in terms of dabs of color and motifs—if we can at the same time discern a continuity in the effect on the spectator. The important thing then is not to appeal to an a priori ground to explain away additive composition, but to observe how the latter could be reconciled with a fused aesthetic effect. It is necessary to recognize that the Impressionists expected the spectator to keep a strict distance from the canvas.

It would be unwise to argue for a general separation of technical means and aesthetic effects. The Impressionists were led to this separation by certain pseudo-scientific pretensions. To use Diltheyan terminology, their naturalism led them to think of the aesthetic effect as an illusion and blinded them to a more sane aesthetic which apprehends the aesthetic effect in and through the medium itself. Yet the Impressionists were important historically in counteracting the view that the medium is a mere support. At least they saw the dab of color as something in itself and as something for the artist (if not the spectator) to focus on. However, the full scope of the medium could not be acknowledged until the representational ideal of art came to be questioned.

history, Cassirer saw that the Neo-Kantians of the Baden school had a deficient understanding of history and culture.

Rickert had claimed that the concepts of the cultural sciences can be related to value-concepts. But Cassirer finds that a more exacting examination of the concrete state of affairs in the cultural sciences discloses a "radical difference" between style-concepts and value-concepts: "What style concepts present is not an ought, but simply an 'is'—even though this 'is' is not concerned with physical things but with the persistence of 'forms.' " Thus according to Cassirer, Wölfflin's theory of style forms is not to be conceived deterministically. Style is merely a descriptive, not a normative concept: "When Wölfflin speaks of 'classic' and 'baroque,' these two concepts have for him merely a descriptive, not an aesthetically qualitative, or normative, significance. Connotations of the excellent or paradigmatic are by no means attributed to the concept of the 'classic.' . . . Instead, Wölfflin sees in both styles merely divergent solutions to a specific problem, each of which is equally justified aesthetically."[11]

Style as a descriptive concept of culture must according to Cassirer be contrasted with the nomothetic concepts of the natural sciences on the one hand, and with the idiographic concepts used in history on the other. Seemingly accepting Windelband's characterization of historical inquiry as idiographic, Cassirer nevertheless rejects his attempt to define this as the method of the cultural sciences as such. The cultural sciences are not merely concerned with an account of particular human phenomena, but seek to discover certain general forms that relate these phenomena to each other. Like Dilthey, Cassirer assumes that description goes hand in hand with some sense of what is typical. However, he goes beyond Dilthey by allowing the description of a particular to pass over into the description of a general form.

[11] Ernst Cassirer, *Logic of the Humanities*, pp. 126–28.

By locating an intermediary domain between the nomothetic and the idiographic, Cassirer claims that the natural and cultural sciences agree in uniting the particular and the universal. The difference is that in the natural sciences the particular is *subordinated* to the universal, while in the cultural sciences the particular is merely *coordinated* with the universal.[12] The coordination of particulars and universals in the cultural sciences involves the establishment of persistent forms or what could be called "ideal types" which can illuminate the understanding of the given. Thus Burckhardt is praised for presenting a portrait of an ideal (universal) man of the Renaissance in his writings, although no empirical research has ever found such a (particular) man. Burckhardt's Renaissance man is not a norm to which actual figures can be subordinated, but it is an ideal in relation to which many of them can be coordinated. This ideal type is then only a composite individual, a device to unify the period, and no more should be expected of it.

Similarly, style for Cassirer is not a standard of perfection with which to judge actual phenomena, but a convention whereby to order them. It functions as a coordinating principle and refers to certain persistent forms discernible in the history of art. Styles do not, as in Wölfflin's deterministic theory, recur in accordance with some law of vision. Cassirer thus insists that no work can be fully painterly or linear in nature, but he finds the two polar concepts useful in their ability to structure art history without foreclosing any expressive possibilities inherent in art. The painterly and linear styles are merely two a priori forms that make expression possible. As expressive forms, they do not predict any specific goal for art which restricts the creativeness of individual artists, but project infinite tasks.

Cassirer's concept of style thus approaches, albeit formalistically, one function of style as the articulation of the typical. However, the typical need not merely be conceived as some ideal combination of qualities, and may be made more

12 Ibid., p. 137.

concrete. Dilthey's own method of writing history was to concentrate on some actual human being as typical of an epoch, and he complained that Burckhardt's *Civilization of the Renaissance* gives only background, no foreground (*GS*,XI,73). As was shown in chapter 1, coordination stands not only for a simple logical relationship, but also for a dynamic relationship. It involves a dynamic tension between the ideal and the real. The meaning of a historical epoch can be articulated by tracing the concrete ways in which the style of a great individual like Goethe can embody the sense of the whole, rather than by employing some ideal type which is a composite universal transcending the real components from which it was derived. Typicality is to be articulated within the empirical domain of history itself, not constructed synthetically.

A more strictly historical approach can avoid the dualistic formalism remaining in Cassirer's notion that Wölfflin's ideal styles are merely alternative, and equally valid, solutions to a problem. History leads us to question the underlying assumption that there exist only two basic solutions to a given problem in art. Apart from the obvious danger of automatically dismissing whatever may not be readily identifiable in terms of these two solutions, such a theory of style is only neutral about those artists who explicitly aim at one of them.[13] What is often regarded as the mere dissolution of one polarity for the sake of another, may in fact be

[13] Ackerman criticizes art historians like Wölfflin who describe works in terms of how much they anticipate a certain solution to a problem. Thus even without claiming that the Baroque paintings of Rembrandt constitute progress over the Classical works of Raphael, they cannot help but study only those artists in between who lead from the breakdown of the linear to the rise of the painterly. Those that do not make a contribution to this process are dismissed as insignificant. "The history of art has been fashioned into another version of the materialist success-story." James S. Ackerman, "A Theory of Style," *Aesthetic Inquiry: Essays on Art Criticism and the Philosophy of Art*, ed. Monroe C. Beardsley and Herbert M. Schueller, Belmont, Calif.: Dickenson Publishing Co., 1967, p. 58.

a genuinely creative style. In Wölfflin's epochal theory where the Classical provides a determinate framework of meaning, the Mannerist art of a Tintoretto is too easily relegated to decadent classical art. Mannerism will be better appreciated as a unique style through a concept of style which also takes into account the indeterminate sense-framework of a *Zeitgeist*. It is precisely the advantage of our determinate-indeterminate style concept that the meaning of Mannerist art can then be hermeneutically explicated relative to theories of the epochal development of style-forms. This last point deserves to be underscored, for a consideration of the indeterminate-historical aspects of style is meant to enrich, rather than to displace, the meaning defined through formal and structural analysis. Concepts like the Classical and Baroque need not function to restrict the meaning to be found in an individual work or style, so long as they are recognized as useful constructions in a phase of hermeneutic interpretation.

The call for a more historical concept of style does not therefore exclude the contributions of a modified formalism such as Cassirer's. Using Dilthey's definition of style as inner form for our point of departure, we have found that a concept of style remains important in articulating both historical and structural unity. However, it must be admitted that the historical approach to art can lead to the rejection of structuring principles altogether. R. G. Collingwood's work is a well-known case in point.

Collingwood is often compared with Dilthey because he too focused his philosophy on problems of aesthetics and history. Both stressed the importance of the individual in history and proposed what has been called a theory of reliving the past. Like Dilthey, Collingwood was concerned that the content and individuality of art expressions not be lost in formalistic abstractions, yet it is a significant symptom of their differences that in the extreme anti-formalism of the latter's expression theory the importance of a style concept is denied.

In the *Idea of History*, Collingwood claims that there is "... no history of artistic problems, as there is a history of scientific or philosophical problems."[14] Instead, the history of art is to be conceived as a series of individual achievements, defined as solutions not so much to problems of technique or form as to problems of expressing the content of experience.

> The artist's problem, so far as he is an artist, is not the problem of doing what his predecessor has done and going on to do something further which his predecessor failed to do. There is development in art, but no progress: for though in the technical processes of art one man learns from another ... the problem of art itself consists not in mastering these technical processes but in using them to express the artist's experience and give it reflective form, and consequently every fresh work of art is the solution of a fresh problem which arises not out of a previous work of art but out of the artist's unreflective experience. [p. 330]

In the theory of expression, the work is primarily related to the artist and his experience. The artist's activity is viewed as the imaginative expression of emotion leading to self-consciousness. But this is not yet a reflective activity and the imaginary world created in each work can be considered an isolated expression having no significant relation to any other. "Purely imaginary worlds cannot clash and need not agree," Collingwood asserts. "Each is a world to itself" (p. 246). As an individual solution to the problem of expressing unreflective experience, it seems the only rele-

[14] R. G. Collingwood, *The Idea of History*. New York: Oxford University Press, 1956, p. 314. Page numbers in the text following refer to this work.

vant questions concerning the work are whether it is true to itself (consistent) and true to its author (sincere).

Collingwood emphasizes the use of the imagination in both poetry and history to disclose possibilities which immediate experience does not offer. But his notion of the imagination is similar to that of the Kant-Schiller play theory where the aesthetic imagination only indirectly adds to knowledge by means of suggestion. Both novels and works of history are seen as products of "the *a priori* imagination." But while the artist remains at the purely imaginary level where the distinction between the real and the possible has not yet been made, the historian must be able to distinguish them. "As works of imagination, the historian's work and the novelist's do not differ. Where they do differ is that the historian's picture is meant to be true" (pp. 245–46).

We have shown, however, that the poetic imagination can make a more direct contribution to historical knowledge. Poetry may not be *true* in the way that a historical monograph is true by virtue of describing what happened according to the given historical data. Yet poetry is more than just *true to itself* in the way of inner consistency, or *true to its author* as a sincere expression. Instead, it articulates a historical *truth* by going beyond the given and still disclosing something about it. The poetic imagination so conceived does not lead to the kind of exaggerated contrast in Collingwood between an aesthetic pluralism and an historical monism. While denying any essential relation amongst artistic expressions, he claimed that "there is only one historical world, and everything in it must stand in some relation to everything else, even if that relation is only topographical and chronological" (p. 246).

The emotions expressed by the artist are always inseparable from a specific life-context, but according to Collingwood thoughts sustain themselves independently of their original context. Therefore only thoughts can be re-enacted to serve as historical evidence, and history is given a purely intellectualistic definition as the reliving of the thoughts of past individuals. Dilthey's notion of reliving the past in his *Verstehen* theory should not of course be conceived within this narrow idealistic interpretation of history. To limit the context of art to unreflective experience and raise thought to the fully reflective involves an unwarranted idealistic fiat. It is not surprising then that Collingwood was in a quandary about art history. Even his substitution of a history of artistic achievements for a history of artistic problems, can make no sense on the basis of his own premise that the artist does not, except rarely, offer us his thoughts. The very backbone of Collingwood's critical history, which is "evidence" allowing us to re-enact the past—as distinct from mere "testimony"—does not exist here (see p. 203). All we can do is to accept the artist's expression as testimony about the life of the emotions. Something is obviously wrong with a theory of art which is forced to consider the audience's aesthetic experience an act of faith about the artist's sincerity. The idea of historical evidence has been so rigidly defined by Collingwood as to be inapplicable to aesthetic experience. There is, in effect, no history, but a mere succession or chronicle of isolated artistic achievements. According to his own distinction of chronicle and history, change of itself does not constitute history. On this point, he is in agreement with Dilthey who also saw that only a condition that abides with what it conditions can be historically meaningful.

To divorce aesthetic experience from the historical process is to preclude any style-concept and to dismiss those dimensions of artistic expressions which are discernible only in their aesthetic and historical interrelation. There exist, for example, aspects of a work of art that fall in a certain tradition, betray a certain time, and can only be understood as (affirmative or negative) responses to previous artistic accomplishments. A concept of style can illuminate such relations and serve as a structuring principle in art history without losing sight of the content and individuality of artistic expressions with which Collingwood is rightly concerned. It was an abstract formalism, not the idea of style itself, that led historians of style, such as Wölfflin, so far afield as to conceive of an "history of art without names." But Collingwood's expression theory can well lead us to the opposite excess of art names without history.

What is missing in Collingwood's aesthetics is the recognition that something genuinely communal is betrayed in a work of art. Artistic styles, when viewed as a means of conceptualizing historical life, take into account not only what individuates a work of art in terms of its specific psychohistorical context, but also how the work is rooted in the common and tradition-oriented medium which Dilthey called "objective spirit."

Because Dilthey too spoke of the work of art as an expression of experience, he is often classified with Collingwood as an expression theorist. But he conceives an *Erlebnisausdruck* hermeneutically as an objectification in the historical world, and focuses on the meaning embodied in the expression rather than its "sincerity" in being true to the artist. What it expresses is more important than what it is an expression *of*. For Collingwood emotive expression defines the nature of art. Dilthey, on the other hand, did not even ascribe expressiveness to all the arts. In *Die drei Epochen*, Dilthey had listed the following three roots of artistic activity: the decorative impulse, the imitative impulse (which is dominant in much of visual art), and the expressive urge (especially dominant in music and dance) (*GS*,VI,277). Obviously, neither decoration, nor imitation, nor expression is adequate for defining the nature of artistic creation as such. An artistic expression presupposes the artist's *Erlebnis*, to be sure, but for hermeneutic, historical understanding it is as important to know what the work says about human experience in general as to look for what it discloses about the author's particular experience. Similarly, it is essential to point to common stylistic qualities of works of art before locating individuating differences.

Herman Nohl, a student of Dilthey, has attempted to explain these common stylistic aspects through the *Weltanschauungslehre*. Following Dilthey, his concept of style refers to the form as well as the content of a work of art, but his interpretation places more stress on style as an expressive quality. More specifically, styles are seen as expressions of typical attitudes toward life. Extending the *Weltanschauung* typology from poetry to other arts, Nohl correlates differences among the three types with fundamental stylistic differences in painting and music. Dilthey himself praised Nohl for seeking *Weltanschauungen* in the inner form of a work, while at the same time reaffirming his own position that, of all the arts, only poetry can contribute to the formation of *Weltanschauungen*.

According to Nohl, the dualistic tensions characteristic of subjective idealism are reflected in the form and content of Michelangelo's works. His paintings tend to oppose foreground figures and background, and depict grand or heroic themes to create a respectful distance between the work and the spectator. In contrast to the linear delineation used by subjective idealists, an objective idealist such as Raphael focuses on color to empathetically draw the spectator into the pictorial space. Objective idealists aim to integrate figures into their surroundings and commonly portray this harmonious relation in terms of idyls, dreams, etc. Naturalists neither overwhelm the spectator nor identify with him, but produce an indifferent distance which allows the observer to feel himself superior to the impression of reality that he receives. Whereas the subjective idealist portrays self-sufficient figures, and the objective idealist a sufficient totality, a naturalist like Manet makes us aware that he is giving us a mere fragment of reality.[15]

Nohl ultimately dismisses the naturalistic style for being inadequately expressive and reconceives it in terms of a subcategory of objective idealism.[16] By evaluating style exclusively in terms of its expressive qualities, he overlooks

[15] Cf. Herman Nohl, *Stil und Weltanschauung*, Jena: E. Diederichs, 1920, pp. 62f, p. 44.
[16] Ibid., p. 96.

411

the suggestiveness implicit in the impressionistic techniques of naturalism. Although Dilthey, too, had been critical of naturalists, he nevertheless found it possible to make Impressionism stylistically relevant through his theory of articulation.

Nohl has shown some interesting relations between style and *Weltanschauung*, but in his work the typology remains a classificatory device whereby artists are abstracted from their historical contexts. Moreover, since many works of art simply do not, and need not, express a *Weltanschauung* the typology has a limited usefulness for the analysis of style. Like other expression theorists, Nohl has difficulty in adequately understanding style because the relation between the author and his work has been considered a direct one. To be made applicable to style theories, the expressive relation must be qualified to account for the indirect expressiveness of style. In light of our earlier discussion of *Erlebnisausdrücke* as forms of communication, we can say that an author and his time are at best indirectly communicated in the style of a work.

From Panofsky's later iconographic perspective, style is that "content . . . which a work betrays but does not parade. It is the basic attitude of a nation, a period, a class, a religious or philosophical persuasion—all this unconsciously qualified by one personality, and condensed into one work."[17] In Arnold Hauser's sociological approach the mediated expressiveness of style becomes even more pronounced. According to him "a social outlook creates a style only when it cannot find expression directly." This he relates to the psychoanalytic theory of creative sublimation according to which poetic ambiguity "is above all, a result of a latent meaning prevented, for some reason or other, from expressing itself directly."[18]

The indirect expressiveness referred to by Panofsky and

[17] Panofsky, *Meaning in the Visual Arts*, p. 14.
[18] Arnold Hauser, *The Philosophy of Art History*, Cleveland: World Publishing Co., 1963, pp. 29, 102.

Hauser really represents a negative formulation of our characterization of style as articulating some context, whether it be the continuum of the acquired psychic nexus, the common medium of objective spirit, or a reflective sense of life. In relation to Dilthey's earlier aesthetics, where the acquired psychic nexus was the ultimate context for understanding creativity, the expressive process was deemed unnecessary for the articulation of style (see chapter 4). But with the work of the poet analyzed in terms of anthropological reflection, life itself becomes the direct context for literary understanding. In this enlarged framework, it is possible to see the poet as both *expressing* a personal attitude toward life and *articulating* a more impersonal *impression* of life. Music was thus described in the late writings not only as an expression of the artist's *Erlebnis* but also as providing an impression (*Eindruck*) of *Erlebnis* in general (*GS*,VII,222). Moreover, we can say that any art can give an impression of life, or a *Zeitgeist*.

From the perspective of expression, a work of art is expected to be determinate; from that of impression a work tends to be indeterminate. Only when the concept of articulation is made central to the idea of style can it be recognized as inherently determinate-indeterminate, allowing us to specify the meaning of expressions without abstracting from their sense-contexts. Thus from the hermeneutic viewpoint, the style of a work can be said (1) to encompass an impression or reflective sense of life and (2) to articulate this through the meaning of *Erlebnis*, of historical conditions, and of a *Weltanschauung*, if the latter is expressed.

Application in Critical Hermeneutics

The hermeneutic concept of style is contextual in nature, and in developing its historical dimensions, we have suggested how an epochal theory linked to the sense of a *Zeitgeist* can provide a meaning framework in relation to which style articulates a unity. But with style thus conceived in its historical life-context, it may be objected that interpretation will be restricted to mere contemplation or restoration of past meaning. The problems of style and art history lead us, therefore, to the recurrent question whether in emphasizing historical understanding we forego considerations of validity and critical analysis.

If the contextuality of style is taken seriously, then we must acknowledge that there *are* certain limits placed on the applicability of stylistic meaning from one historical epoch to another. It is essentially for this reason that Hans-Georg Gadamer discounts Dilthey's concept of style as providing a mere retrospective orientation for understanding art. Instead, he calls for a more "forward-looking" historical interpretation of the history of art which freely applies meaning to successive contemporary contexts. He thereby hopes to carry out an important task of hermeneutics claimed to be overlooked in the Schleiermacher-Dilthey school.

Referring to J. J. Rambach's *Institutiones hermeneuticae sacrae* of 1723, Gadamer reminds us that hermeneutics was divided into three branches: *subtilitas intelligendi* (understanding), *subtilitas explicandi* (interpretation), and *subtilitas applicandi* (application).[19] Schleiermacher's advance is admitted to lie in the inner unity fashioned between the first two aspects of hermeneutics, namely, understanding and interpretation. His conception of the hermeneutic circle recognized that the interpretation of the whole of a text presupposes understanding its parts, and the understanding of the parts some at least preliminary interpretation of the whole. But this insight, according to Gadamer, came at the price of ignoring the third hermeneutic task of applying understanding to new historical situations. It is the latter "historical" dimension of interpretation that concerns Gadamer most.

To be sure, Schleiermacher's connection between under-

---

[19] Cf. Hans-Georg Gadamer, *Wahrheit und Methode*, pp. 290f.

standing and interpretation can be achieved ahistorically through the mere comparison of parts and wholes. We have seen, however, that Dilthey was explicitly aware of the importance of historical consciousness for interpretation aimed at understanding an author better than he understood himself. Nevertheless, Gadamer dismisses Dilthey's historical perspective, on the assumption that the latter's *Verstehen* theory reduces historical consciousness to the infinite expansion of self-understanding. Thus Gadamer carries Heidegger's critique a step further by charging that Dilthey's theories only enable him to contemplate the past aesthetically as another mode of the present. "The foundation of history in a psychology of understanding, as it appeared to Dilthey, places the historian in an ideal contemporaneity with his object which we have called aesthetic. . . ."[20]

The illusion of contemporaneity is identified with Dilthey's reliance on the comparative method. If, as Gadamer appears to assume, comparison is made possible only by conceiving phenomena in direct juxtaposition, then a comparative procedure would require that the work and its interpreter be made contemporaneous by transporting one or the other out of its context. However, this is more reminiscent of Collingwood, in whose idealistic theory of history critical re-enactment presupposed the isolability of thoughts. Dilthey's comparative method does not contradict his basic contextual approach if its affinity with the Kantian analysis of reflective comparison and aesthetic judgment is recognized (see chapter 5). Comparison as we have understood it involves indirect analogies between different contexts.

Thus we, too, can characterize Dilthey's approach to history as "aesthetic," but in contrast to Gadamer, precisely to stress its inherent contextuality. In our earlier account of reflective experience we saw that comparison becomes a means of self-delimitation as well as self-expansion. Similarly, the comparative method is part of the hermeneutic

[20] Ibid., p. 218.

process of delimiting significance. The concept of style limits the degree to which the meaning of a work can be translated. This entails that it cannot be indiscriminately applied as relevant to other historical situations.

Gadamer, on the other hand, asserts that philological and literary hermeneutics have much to learn from theological and juristic hermeneutics where the main issue has always been to determine how a dogma or a law, and the traditions they have instituted, bear on a present situation: "here understanding always already involves application."[21] If hermeneutics must always involve the historical application (*Anwendung*) of meaning to subsequent contexts, and especially the present, then it would be premature to characterize any style apart from its relevance to all other ages. The effect of Gadamer's Heideggerian theory of history is to absorb the stylistic meaning of a work of art in the traditional meaning that accrues through successive applications.

In his attack on Gadamer's hermeneutics, E. D. Hirsch argues that to stress application is harmful because it erodes the meaning of a historical document for the sake of its subsequent significance. By emphasizing how the significance of a work changes with the times through which it endures, Gadamer loses the determinate meaning of the work itself and thereby the basis for valid interpretation. "Validity requires a norm—a meaning that is stable and determinate no matter how broad its range of implication and application," he writes. "A stable and determinate meaning requires an author's determining will. . . ."[22] For Hirsch, then, valid interpretation is possible only if critics will recognize the notion of the author's intention. He hopes to bolster what he considers to be the fundamentally sound thrust of Dilthey's theory of understanding by reinterpreting intention in Husserlian terms. The author's intended meaning is not to be construed psychologistically, for inten-

[21] Ibid., p. 292.
[22] E. D. Hirsch, *Validity in Interpretation*, New Haven: Yale University Press, 1967, p. 126.

416

tion has nothing to do with what went on in the psyche of the creator before or during the act of recording his ideas on paper. Instead, it refers to an ideal object intended by the very words written down. The intended meaning is not contained in any "actual contents of consciousness," but transcends them to include certain unconscious, but nevertheless willed, implications.[23] Here implications are not allowed to be loosely related to the explicitly asserted meaning, but must somehow be circumscribed by a willed type. This entails that criticism cannot really add to the meaning of a work—all of its meaning must already have been vaguely intended by the author. Critics can only find new significance in it, i.e. new ways of applying its previously determined meaning to changing times and places.

Upon analysis, we see that Hirsch's "attempt to ground some of Dilthey's hermeneutic principles in Husserl's epistemology and Saussure's linguistics"[24] ignores Dilthey's own methodological ground rules which do not permit the validity of interpretation to depend on the reproduction of the meaning intended by an author. To expect that would be to invite historical scepticism. Moreover, a principle of the "determinacy of implications" as Hirsch calls it, goes against the very ideal of Dilthey's hermeneutics to understand an author better than he understood himself. If the full meaning of his work is circumscribed by his intention then the most profound aspect of Dilthey's approach to historical understanding is lost, namely, the ability to circle in on the individuality of a work by means of its historical context. Dilthey's hermeneutics not only explicates what is there, but also discerns how historical factors are implicated. To describe this kind of structure in the work is to go beyond what was willed by the author. Because the work stands between the author and his times, its style has already been characterized as determinate-indeterminate. The meaning of a work of art cannot be strictly divorced

---

[23] Ibid., pp. 38, 49.   [24] Ibid., p. 242 fn.

from a sense of its original historical context nor from its present significance. Therefore, it is a mistake to think that we can first fix its meaning and then determine its historical significance as a mere application.

Although Hirsch sees himself as irrevocably opposed to Gadamer, he shares with the latter the assumption that there exists a binding claim that the work has on us. For Hirsch it is the claim of the author's intention, for Gadamer it is the more general efficacy of the tradition of the work itself. Hirsch regards the concept of tradition as too unstable, but in fact it is quite conservative the way Gadamer uses it, that is, any new interpretation of a work's significance must be tested by the meaning previously assigned to it. Such an interpretation cannot be totally discontinuous with past interpretations if it is itself to become part of the traditional meaning. This confrontation of the present and the tradition could have been developed into a true dialectic were it not for an unfortunate conception of applicative hermeneutics. Application is used as a *Dienstform* (service form) where the particular is subordinated to the universal. Just as a present-day court takes the validity of an established law for granted and decides only on its applicability to particular circumstances, so understanding for Gadamer does not really question the traditional meaning. The emphasis in Gadamer is not on criticism of the tradition, but on the authority it exerts on us in the present. The traditional meaning is taken as a norm merely to be applied to new situations, and this is about the extent to which Gadamer is willing to be forward-looking.

The backward movement of understanding in Dilthey, which Gadamer condemns as restorationist in character, is really meant to ensure a critical hermeneutical approach. Congeniality is important to Dilthey only insofar as it prevents the interpreter from making arbitrary, external criticisms based on misunderstandings. First, the demands of elementary understanding must be satisfied, that is, the norms embodied in the subject matter must be described

418

and explicated. But Dilthey was never naive enough to think that description does not also involve norms introduced by the describer. The ideal would be to have these additional norms not merely externally appended to the former, but developed out of them. Then there would exist no norm for understanding which could not itself be subject to re-evaluation, no universal which could not be reconsidered from the perspective of particulars. The traditional meaning of a work is a function of all subsequently accepted applications of its significance. By contrast, its stylistic meaning remains distinct from such determinations of its relevance, although it must be tested by them. In the one case, an indeterminate, but overwhelming continuum of interpretations is produced which stifles any real critique; in the other, interpretation leaves room for criticism. Whereas the distinction between meaning and significance is a necessary condition for external criticism, our earlier discussion of the stylistic tension between meaning and sense suggests the possibility of internal criticism as well. For example, one of the advantages of a concept of style not exclusively defined by an epochal theory is that it provides an interpretive base for critical reflection on a *Zeitgeist*. The determinate meaning framework of an epoch, while being located in the indeterminate sense context of a *Zeitgeist*, can represent the latter and yet provide its own measure of articulative unity.

Opponents of the *Verstehen* theory, such as Richard McKeon, have expressed the fear that once ". . . you can account for a doctrine by the circumstances in which it originated, there is no need to analyze it or refute it."[25] Such suspicions might be legitimate if *Verstehen* were a mode of contextual explanation rather than contextual interpretation (see chapter 8). To interpret a position in terms of a particular context is often the prelude to more large-scale comparisons, and thus no guarantee that it will be accepted on its own terms. To be sure, it is usually from without that a

[25] Richard McKeon, *Thought, Action and Passion*, Chicago: University of Chicago Press, 1954, p. 213.

viewpoint first becomes criticized. Yet only by getting back into it can one adequately refute such a view with the confidence that one fully understands it.

We can use Dilthey's historical essay on aesthetics, *Die drei Epochen*, as a case in point. Although Dilthey related three different aesthetic theories to their respective philosophical contexts, the task of the essay was to make the methods and tools of past aesthetics available to present aestheticians and to test their scope. Such a determination of their present significance certainly involves analysis and questions of validity. Dilthey's attempt to understand a theory in terms of its context was not meant to deny it validity out of this context. In fact, the past methods of aesthetics retain their validity, but only if stripped of their metaphysical frameworks and if combined in the ways discussed in chapter 2. Neither the normative, theoretical, nor descriptive methods dominant in the three respective epochs may be discounted if aesthetics is to be a proper *Geisteswissenschaft*.

The interpretation of the meaning of these three methods should work together with a critique of their significance. This link between interpretation and criticism is overlooked by Hirsch who in his eagerness to ascertain validity in interpretation is willing to sacrifice the same quality in criticism. Accordingly, the interpreter is said to be constrained by the intentional meaning presented in the text, but the critic is permitted to pursue whatever strikes him as valuable or relevant. An unhealthy split between interpretation and criticism is produced by Hirsch's assertion "that verbal meaning is determinate, whereas significance and the possibilities of legitimate criticism are boundless. . . ."[26]

Although Kantian orthodoxy may overstress the limiting aspect of a critical perspective, it has been shown that reflective judgment makes it possible to revise the a priori limits of determinant judgment without arbitrarily canceling them. It is crucial to insist over against Hirsch that at

[26] Hirsch, *Validity in Interpretation*, p. 57.

least some indeterminate bounds for criticism be established. These bounds cannot derive from the concept of application; they only make sense if it is realized that criticism is a mode of interpretation that goes back to the very roots of evaluation in anthropological reflection. The concept of style, for example, has been used as a hermeneutic counterpart to the value-concept of *Sosein-Müssen*. One of the main tasks of hermeneutics, when applied to our understanding of literature and the other arts, is to transform a vague sense of rightness experienced while enjoying a work into a valid interpretation of its stylistic meaning. It is this kind of articulative process that makes it possible for evaluation to move beyond the level of appreciating values and to become critical.

Our reflections on style and the problem of the conceptual articulation of historical life re-enforce the importance of Dilthey's claim that history must be understood in terms of human concerns and values rather than through an uncritical application of the methods of the natural sciences. Historical order involves a human order which, as suggested in Kant's aesthetics, is universal if not objective in the naturalistic sense and necessary if not fully determinable. Dilthey's philosophy of the human studies provides no grounds for absolute standards of value other than life itself, but it does justify the possibility of logical and methodological coherence in reflecting on our experience of life as well as the possibility of validly interpreting its meaning.

Bibliography

Primary Sources

COLLECTED WORKS OF WILHELM DILTHEY

Gesammelte Schriften. 17 vols. 1914–1974. Vols. 1–12, Stuttgart: B. G. Teubner and Göttingen: Vandenhoeck & Ruprecht; Vols. 13–17, Göttingen: Vandenhoeck & Ruprecht.

Vol. I. *Einleitung in die Geisteswissenschaften: Versuch einer Grundlegung für das Studium der Gesellschaft und der Geschichte.* Edited by Bernard Groethuysen. 4th ed., 1959. First published in 1922.

Vol. II. *Weltanschauung und Analyse der Menschen seit Renaissance und Reformation.* Edited by Georg Misch. 6th ed., 1960. First published in 1914.

Vol. III. *Studien zur Geschichte des deutschen Geistes: Leibniz und sein Zeitalter. Friedrich der Grosse und die deutsche Aufklärung. Das achtzehnte Jahrhundert und die geschichtliche Welt.* Edited by Paul Ritter. 3rd ed., 1962. First published in 1921.

Vol. IV. *Die Jugendgeschichte Hegels und andere Abhandlungen zur Geschichte des deutschen Idealismus.* Edited by Herman Nohl. 2nd ed., 1959. First published in 1921.

Vol. V. *Die geistige Welt: Einleitung in die Philosophie des Lebens. Erste Hälfte: Abhandlungen zur Grundlegung der Geisteswissenschaften.* Edited by Georg Misch. 2nd ed., 1957. First published in 1924.

Vol. VI. *Die geistige Welt: Einleitung in die Philosophie des Lebens. Zweite Hälfte: Abhandlungen zur Poetik, Ethik und Pädagogik.* Edited by Georg Misch. 3rd ed., 1958. First published in 1924.

Vol. VII. *Der Aufbau der geschichtlichen Welt in den Geisteswissenschaften.* Edited by Bernard Groethuysen. 2nd ed., 1958. First published in 1927.

Vol. VIII. *Weltanschauungslehre: Abhandlungen zur Philosophie der Philosophie.* Edited by Bernard Groethuysen. 2nd ed., 1960. First published in 1931.

Vol. IX. *Pädagogik: Geschichte und Grundlinien des Systems.* Edited by Otto Friedrich Bollnow. 2nd ed., 1960. First published in 1934.

Vol. X. *System der Ethik.* Edited by Herman Nohl. 1st ed., 1958.

Vol. XI. *Vom Aufgang des geschichtlichen Bewusstseins: Jugendaufsätze und Erinnerungen.* Edited by Erich Weniger. 2nd ed., 1960. First published in 1936.

Vol. XII. *Zur preussischen Geschichte: Schleiermachers politische Gesinnung und Wirksamkeit. Die Reorganisatoren des preussischen Staates. Das allgemeine Landrecht.* Edited by Erich Weniger. 2nd ed., 1960. First published in 1936.

Vol. XIII. *Leben Schleiermachers. Erster Band: Auf Grund der 1. Auflage von 1870 und der Zusätze aus dem Nachlass.* Edited by Martin Redeker. 3rd ed., 1970.

Vol. XIV. *Leben Schleiermachers. Zweiter Band: Schleiermachers System als Philosophie und Theologie. Aus dem Nachlass.* Edited by Martin Redeker. 1st ed., 1966.

Vol. XV. *Zur Geistesgeschichte des 19. Jahrhunderts: Portraits und biographische Skizzen, Quellenstudien und Literatur-Berichte zur Theologie und Philosophie.* Edited by Ulrich Herrmann. 1st ed., 1970.

Vol. XVI. *Zur Geistesgeschichte des 19. Jahrhunderts: Aufsätze und Rezensionen aus Zeitungen und Zeitschriften 1859–1874.* Edited by Ulrich Herrmann. 1st ed., 1972.

Vol. XVII. *Zur Geistesgeschichte des 19. Jahrhunderts: Aus "Westermanns Monatsheften": Literaturbriefe, Berichte zur Kunstgeschichte, Verstreute Rezensionen 1867–1884.* Edited by Ulrich Herrmann, 1st ed., 1974.

OTHER EDITIONS AND WRITINGS OF WILHELM DILTHEY

Aus Schleiermachers Leben in Briefen, vols. 3 and 4. Edited by Wilhelm Dilthey. Berlin: G. Reimer, 1861, 1863.

"Briefe Wilhelm Diltheys an Bernhard und Luise Scholz 1859–1864." Edited by Sigrid von der Schulenburg. Sitzungsberichte der preussischen Akademie der Wissenschaften, phil.-histor. Kl., 1933.

Briefe Wilhelm Diltheys an Rudolf Haym, 1861–1873. Edited by Erich Weniger. Berlin, 1936.

"Der Briefwechsel Dilthey-Husserl." With introductory comments by Walter Biemel. *Man and World,* 1, no. 3, 1968, 428–46.

Briefwechsel zwischen Wilhelm Dilthey und dem Grafen Paul Yorck von Wartenburg, 1877–1897. Edited by Sigrid von der Schulenburg. Halle a.d.S.: Max Niemeyer, 1923.

Das Erlebnis und die Dichtung: Lessing, Goethe, Novalis, Hölderlin. 13th ed. Stuttgart: B. G. Teubner; Göttingen: Vandenhoeck & Ruprecht, 1957. First published in 1906.

Fragmente aus Wilhelm Diltheys Hegelwerk. Edited by Friedhelm Nicolin and Otto Pöggeler. Bonn: H. Bouvier, 1961.

Die grosse Phantasiedichtung und andere Studien zur vergleichenden Literaturgeschichte. Edited by Herman Nohl. Göttingen: Vandenhoeck & Ruprecht, 1954.

Grundriss der allgemeinen Geschichte der Philosophie. Edited and supplemented by Hans-Georg Gadamer. Frankfurt am Main: Klostermann, 1949.

Der junge Dilthey: Ein Lebensbild in Briefen und Tagebüchern, 1852–1870. Edited by Clara Misch, née Dilthey. 2nd ed. Stuttgart: B. G. Teubner; Göttingen: Vandenhoeck & Ruprecht, 1960. First published in 1933.

"Diltheys Kant-Darstellung in seiner letzten Vorlesung über das System der Philosophie." In Dietrich Bischoff, *Wilhelm Diltheys geschichtliche Lebensphilosophie.* Leipzig: B. C. Teubner, 1935.

Leben Schleiermachers, vol. 1. Edited by Hermann Mulert. 2nd ed. Berlin: W. de Gruyter, 1922. First published in 1867–1870.

Die Philosophie des Lebens: Eine Auswahl aus seinen Schriften, 1867–1910. Edited by Herman Nohl. Frankfurt am Main: Klostermann, 1946.

"Ueber die Einbildungskraft der Dichter." In *Zeitschrift für Völkerpsychologie*, X, 1878, pp. 42–104.

"Vier Briefe Wilhelm Diltheys an Erich Adickes: Winter, 1904–1905." *Deutsche Akademie der Wissenschaften zu Berlin, 1946–1956*. Berlin, 1956, pp. 429–84.

Von deutscher Dichtung und Musik: Aus den Studien zur Geschichte des deutschen Geistes. Edited by Herman Nohl and Georg Misch. 2nd ed. Stuttgart: B. G. Teubner; Göttingen: Vandenhoeck & Ruprecht, 1957. First published in 1932.

ENGLISH TRANSLATIONS OF DILTHEY'S WORKS

"The Dream." Translated by William Kluback. In *Wilhelm Dilthey's Philosophy of History*. New York: Columbia University Press, 1956, pp. 103–09. From *Gesammelte Schriften*, VIII, 220–26.

The Essence of Philosophy. Translated by Stephen A. Emery and William T. Emery. New York: AMS press, 1969. From *Gesammelte Schriften*, V, 339–416.

Pattern and Meaning in History: Thoughts on History and Society. Translator unacknowledged. Edited by H. P. Rickman. New York: Harper & Row, 1962. From *Gesammelte Schriften*, VII.

"The Rise of Hermeneutics." Translated by Fredric Jameson. *New Literary History: A Journal of Theory and Interpretation*, 3, no. 2, Winter 1972, pp. 229–44. From *Gesammelte Schriften*, V, 317–31.

"The Types of World Views and Their Unfoldment within the Metaphysical Systems." Translated by William Kluback and Martin Weinbaum. In *Dilthey's Philosophy of*

Existence. New York: Bookman Associates, 1957. From *Gesammelte Schriften,* VIII, 75–118.
"The Understanding of Other Persons and Their Life-Expressions." Translated by J. J. Kuehl. In *Theories of History: Readings in Classical and Contemporary Sources.* Edited by Patrick Gardiner. New York: Free Press, 1959, pp. 213–25. From *Gesammelte Schriften,* VII, 205–20.

FRENCH TRANSLATIONS OF DILTHEY'S WORKS

Introduction à l'étude des sciences humaines. Translated by L. Sauzin. Paris: Presses Universitaires de France, 1942.
Le monde de l'esprit. Translated by M. Remy. 2 vols. Paris: Aubier, 1947.
Theorie des conceptions du monde: Essay d'une philosophie de la philosophie. Translated by L. Sauzin. Paris: Presses Universitaires de France, 1946.

BIBLIOGRAPHIC WORKS ON DILTHEY

Diaz de Cerio, Francisco. "Bibliografia de W. Dilthey." *Pensamiento,* 24, Madrid, 1968, pp. 196–223.
Herrmann, Ulrich. *Bibliographie Wilhelm Dilthey.* Pädagogische Bibliographien. Reihe A. Band 1. Edited by Leonhard Froese and Georg Ruckriem. Weinheim: Julius Beltz, 1969.
———. "Zum Stand der Ausgabe der Gesammelten Schriften Wilhelm Diltheys." *Zeitschrift für Pädagogik.* XVI, 4, 1970, pp. 531-36.
Weniger, Erich. "Verzeichnis der Schriften Wilhelm Diltheys von den Anfängen bis zur Einleitung in die Geisteswissenschaften." In *Gesammelte Schriften,* XII, pp. 208–13.
Zeeck, Hans. "Im Druck erschienene Schriften von Wilhelm Dilthey." *Archiv für Geschichte der Philosophie,* 25, Berlin, 1912, 154–61.

Secondary Sources

BOOKS

Abrams, M. H. *The Mirror and the Lamp: Romantic Theory and the Critical Tradition.* New York: Norton & Co., 1958.

Aldrich, Virgil. *Philosophy of Art.* Englewood Cliffs: Prentice-Hall, 1963.

Allen, Robert J., ed. *Addison and Steele: Selections from the Tatler and the Spectator.* New York: Holt, Rinehart & Winston, 1966.

Antoni, C., *From History to Sociology: The Transition in German Historical Thinking.* Translated by Hayden V. White. Detroit: Wayne State University Press, 1959.

Apel, K. O. *Analytic Philosophy of Language and the "Geisteswissenschaften." Foundations of Language, Suppl. Series*, V. Dordrecht: Reidel, 1967.

Aron, Raymond. *La philosophie critique de l'histoire. Essai sur une theorie allemande de l'histoire.* Paris: J. Vrin, 1950.

Baeumler, Alfred. *Das Irrationalitätsproblem in der Aesthetik und Logik des 18. Jahrhunderts bis zur Kritik der Urteilskraft.* Darmstadt: Wissenschaftliche Buchgesellschaft, 1967.

Bergson, Henri. *Time and Free Will.* Translated by F. L. Pogson. New York: Harper Torchbooks, 1960.

Betti, Emilio. *Allgemeine Auslegungslehre als Methodik der Geisteswissenschaften.* Tübingen: J.C.B. Mohr, 1967.

Bischoff, Dietrich W. *Wilhelm Diltheys geschichtliche Lebensphilosophie.* Leipzig: B. G. Teubner, 1935.

Bollnow, Otto Friedrich. *Dilthey: Eine Einführung in seine Philosophie.* 2nd ed. Stuttgart: Kohlhammer, 1955.

Boring, Edwing G. *A History of Experimental Psychology.* 2nd ed. New York: Appleton-Century-Crofts, 1950.

Brentano, Franz. *Psychologie vom empirischen Standpunkt.* Leipzig: Duncker & Humblot, 1874.

Cassirer, Ernst. *Zur Logik der Kulturwissenschaften.* Darmstadt: Wissenschaftliche Buchgesellschaft, 1961.

Translated by Clarence Smith Howe, as *The Logic of the Humanities*. New Haven: Yale University Press, 1961.

———. *The Philosophy of Symbolic Forms*. Translated by Ralph Manheim. 3 vols. New Haven: Yale University Press, 1953.

Coleridge, Samuel T. *Biographia Literaria*, vol. 1. Edited by John Shawcross. London: Oxford University Press, 1958.

Collingwood, R. G. *Essays in the Philosophy of Art*. Edited by Alan Donagan. Bloomington: Indiana University Press, 1964.

———. *The Idea of History*. New York: Oxford University Press, 1956.

———. *The Principles of Art*. New York: Oxford University Press, 1958.

Danto, Arthur. *Analytical Philosophy of History*. Cambridge: At the University Press, 1968.

Dewey, John. *Art as Experience*. New York: Capricorn, 1958.

Diwald, Hellmut. *Wilhelm Dilthey: Erkenntnistheorie und Philosophie der Geschichte*. Göttingen: Musterschmidt, 1963.

Dray, William. *Laws and Explanations in History*. London: Oxford University Press, 1957.

———. *Philosophy of History*. Englewood Cliffs: Prentice-Hall, 1964.

Droysen, Johann Gustav. *Grundriss der Historik*. Edited by Erich Rothacker. Halle a.d.S.: Max Niemeyer, 1925.

Erxleben, Wolfgang. *Erlebnis, Verstehen und geschichtliche Wahrheit*. Berlin: Junker und Dünnhaupt, 1937.

Flory, Paul Marion. "The Principle of Teleology in the Philosophy of Wilhelm Dilthey." Ph.D. Dissertation, Cornell University, 1934.

Freud, Sigmund. *On Creativity and the Unconscious*. New York: Harper & Row, 1958.

Gadamer, Hans-Georg. *Wahrheit und Methode*. 2nd ed. Tübingen: J.C.B. Mohr, 1965.

Gallie, W. B. *Philosophy and the Historical Understanding*. New York: Schocken Books, 1964.

Glock, Carl Theodor. *Wilhelm Diltheys Grundlegung einer wissenschaftlichen Lebensphilosophie.* Berlin: Junker und Dünnhaupt, 1939.

Goldmann, Lucien. *Pour une sociologie du roman.* Paris: Gallimard, 1964.

Gorsen, Peter. *Zur Phänomenologie des Bewusstseinsstroms: Bergson, Dilthey, Husserl, Simmel und die lebensphilosophischen Antinomien.* Bonn: H. Bouvier, 1966.

Groeben, Margarete v.d. *Konstruktive Psychologie und Erlebnis: Studien zur Logik der Diltheyschen Kritik an der erklärenden Psychologie.* Stuttgart: Kohlhammer, 1934.

Habermas, Jürgen. *Knowledge and Human Interests.* Translated by Jeremy J. Shapiro. Boston: Beacon Press, 1971.

Hauser, Arnold. *The Philosophy of Art History.* Cleveland: World Publishing Co., 1963.

Hegel, Georg Wilhelm Friedrich. *Aesthetik.* Edited by Friedrich Bassenge. Mit einem Essay von Georg Lukacs. Frankfurt am Main: Europäische Verlagsanstalt GmbH, 1955.

———. *The Logic of Hegel.* Translated by W. Wallace, from *The Encyclopedia of the Philosophical Sciences.* London: Oxford University Press, 1965.

Heidegger, Martin. *Einführung in die Metaphysik.* 3rd ed. Tübingen: Max Niemeyer, 1966. Translated by Ralph Manheim, as *An Introduction to Metaphysics.* Garden City, N.Y.: Doubleday Anchor, 1961.

———. *Hölderlin und das Wesen der Dichtung.* München: Langen, 1937. Translated by Douglas Scott, as "Hölderlin and the Essence of Poetry." In *Existence and Being.* Chicago: Henry Regnery, 1949.

———. *Sein und Zeit.* 11th ed. Tübingen: Neomarius, 1967. Translated by John Macquarrie and Edward Robinson, as *Being and Time.* New York: Harper & Row, 1962.

Herrmann, Ulrich. *Die Pädagogik Wilhelm Diltheys: Ihr wissenschaftstheoretischer Ansatz in Diltheys Theorie der Geisteswissenschaften.* Göttingen: Vandenhoeck & Ruprecht, 1971.

Heynen, Walter. *Diltheys Psychologie des dichterischen Schaffens. Abhandlungen zur Philosophie und ihre Geschichte,* vol. 48. Edited by B. Erdmann. Halle a.d.S.: Max Niemeyer, 1916.

Hirsch, E. D. *Validity in Interpretation.* New Haven: Yale University Press, 1967.

Hodges, Herbert A. *The Philosophy of Wilhelm Dilthey.* London: Routledge & Kegan Paul, 1952.

——. *Wilhelm Dilthey: An Introduction.* 2nd ed. London: Routledge & Kegan Paul, 1949.

Hofstadter, Albert. *Truth and Art.* New York: Columbia University Press, 1965.

Hofstadter, Albert and Kuhns, Richard, eds. *Philosophies of Art and Beauty.* New York: Modern Library, 1964.

Hughes, H. Stuart. *Consciousness and Society: The Reorientation of European Social Thought 1890–1930.* New York: Alfred A. Knopf, 1958.

Hume, David. *An Inquiry Concerning Human Understanding.* Indianapolis: Bobbs-Merrill, 1955.

——. *A Treatise of Human Nature.* Oxford: Oxford University Press, 1968.

Hünermann, Peter. *Der Durchbruch geschichtlichen Denkens im 19. Jahrhundert.* Freiburg: Herder, 1967.

Husserl, Edmund. *Cartesianische Meditationen und Pariser Vorträge. Husserliana,* vol. I. Edited by S. Strasser. 2nd ed. The Hague: Martinus Nijhoff, 1963. Translated by Dorion Cairns, as *Cartesian Meditations: An Introduction to Phenomenology.* The Hague: Martinus Nijhoff, 1960.

——. *Ideen zu einer Phänomenologie und phänomenologischen Philosophie. Erstes Buch: Allgemeine Einführung in die reine Phänomenologie. Husserliana,* vol. III. Edited by Walter Biemel. The Hague: Martinus Nijhoff, 1950. Translated by W. R. Boyce Gibson, as *Ideas: General Introduction to Pure Phenomenology.* London: George Allen & Unwin Ltd., 1958.

——. *Logische Untersuchungen.* Vol. II, part 2. 4th ed. Tübingen: Max Niemeyer, 1968.

Husserl, Edmund. *Phänomenologische Psychologie. Husserliana*, vol. IX. 2nd ed. The Hague: Martinus Nijhoff, 1968.

Israel, Walter. "Die Dichtung und die Weltlichkeit des modernen Menschen. Eine Interpretation des Wesens der Dichtung bei Wilhelm Dilthey." Inaugural Dissertation, Freiburg im Bresgau, 1952.

James, William. *The Principles of Psychology*. Vol. I. New York: Dover Publications, 1950.

Jameson, Fredric. *Marxism and Form: Twentieth-Century Dialectical Theories of Literature*. Princeton: Princeton University Press, 1971.

Kamerbeek, J. Jr. *Allard Pierson (1831–1896) en Wilhelm Dilthey (1833–1911)*. Mededelingen der Koninklijke Nederlandse Akademie van Wetenschappen, Afd. Letterkunde, Deel 20, No. 2, Amsterdam: N.V. Noord-Hollandsche Uitgevers Maatschappij, 1957.

Kames, Henry Home. *Elements of Criticism*. New York: A. S. Barnes and Burr, 1859.

Kant, Immanuel. *Critique of Judgment*. Translated by J. H. Bernard. New York: Hafner Publishing Co., 1951. From *Kritik der Urteilskraft*.

———. *Critique of Pure Reason*. Translated by Norman Kemp Smith. New York: St. Martin's Press, 1961. From *Kritik der reinen Vernunft*.

———. *Erste Fassung der Einleitung in die Kritik der Urteilskraft. Werke in Zehn Bänden*, vol. 8. Edited by Wilhelm Weischedel. Darmstadt: Wissenschaftliche Buchgesellschaft, 1968.

———. *First Introduction to the Critique of Judgment*. Translated by James Haden. Indianapolis: Bobbs-Merrill, 1965. From *Erste Fassung der Einleitung . . .*

———. *Kritik der reinen Vernunft. Werke in Zehn Bänden*, vols. 3 and 4. Edited by Wilhelm Weischedel. Darmstadt: Wissenschaftliche Buchgesellschaft, 1968.

———. *Kritik der Urteilskraft. Werke in Zehn Bänden*, vol. 8. Edited by Wilhelm Weischedel. Darmstadt: Wissenschaftliche Buchgesellschaft, 1968.

————. *On History*. Edited by Lewis White Beck. Indianapolis: Bobbs-Merrill, 1963. From *Werke in Zehn Bänden*, vol. 9.

————. *Der Streit der Fakultäten*. *Werke in Zehn Bänden*, vol. 9. Edited by Wilhelm Weischedel. Darmstadt: Wissenschaftliche Buchgesellschaft, 1968.

Kluback, William. *Wilhelm Dilthey's Philosophy of History*. New York: Columbia University Press, 1956.

Krakauer, Hugo. *Diltheys Stellung zur theoretischen Philosophie Kants*. Breslau: Koebner'sche Verlagsbuchhandlung, 1913.

Krausser, Peter. *Kritik der endlichen Vernunft: Diltheys Revolution der allgemeinen Wissenschafts- und Handlungstheorie*. Frankfurt am Main: Suhrkamp, 1968.

Kremer-Marietti, Angêle. *Wilhelm Dilthey et l'anthropologie historique*. Paris: Editions Seghers, 1971.

Langer, Susanne K. *Feeling and Form*. New York: Charles Scribner's Sons, 1953.

Lehmann, Rudolf. *Poetik*. München: H. Beck, 1919.

Lessing, Gotthold E. *Laocoon. An Essay upon the Limits of Painting and Poetry*. Translated by Ellen Frothingham. Boston: Little, Brown, 1898.

Liebe, Annelise. "Die Aesthetik Wilhelm Diltheys." Dissertation. Halle a.d.S.: Bleicherode i. Harz, 1938.

Lieber, Hans-Joachim. "Die psychische Struktur. Untersuchungen zum Begriff einer Struktur des Seelenlebens bei Dilthey." Inaugural Dissertation, Universität Berlin, 1945.

Liebert, Arthur. *Wilhelm Dilthey: Eine Würdigung seines Werkes zum 100. Geburtstage des Philosophen*. Berlin: E. S. Mittler & Sohn, 1933.

Linschoten, Hans. *Op weg naar een fenomenologische psychologie*. Utrecht: Erven J. Bijleveld, 1959.

Löwith, Karl. *Heidegger: Denker in dürftiger Zeit*. 2nd ed. Göttingen: Vandenhoeck & Ruprecht, 1960.

Lukacs, Georg. *Die Zerstörung der Vernunft*. *Werke*, vol. IX. Berlin-Spandau: H. Luchterhand, 1962.

McKeon, Richard. *Thought, Action and Passion*. Chicago: University of Chicago Press, 1954.

Mandelbaum, Maurice. *The Problem of Historical Knowledge: An Answer to Relativism*. New York: Liveright Publishing Corp., 1938.

Mill, John Stuart. *A System of Logic*. Vol. 2. 7th ed. London: Longmans, Green, Reader, and Dryer, 1868.

Misch, Georg. *Lebensphilosophie und Phänomenologie: Eine Auseinandersetzung der Diltheyschen Richtung mit Heidegger und Husserl, Mit einem Nachwort zur 3. Auflage*. Darmstadt: Wissenschaftliche Buchgesellschaft, 1967.

————. *Vom Lebens- und Gedankenkreis Wilhelm Diltheys*. Frankfurt am Main: G. Schulte-Bulmke, 1947.

Morris, Wesley. *Toward a New Historicism*. Princeton: Princeton University Press, 1972.

Müller-Freienfels, Richard. *The Evolution of Modern Psychology*. Translated by W. Beran Wolfe. New Haven: Yale University Press, 1935.

Müller-Vollmer, Kurt. *Towards a Phenomenological Theory of Literature: A Study of Wilhelm Dilthey's* Poetik. The Hague: Mouton & Co., 1963.

Nagel, Ernest. *The Structure of Science: Problems in the Logic of Scientific Explanation*. New York: Harcourt, Brace & World, 1961.

Nicolai, Heinz and Schwinger, Reinhold. *Innere Form und dichterische Phantasie*. München: Beck, 1935.

Nietzsche, Friedrich. *The Birth of Tragedy*. Translated by Clifton P. Fadiman. In *The Philosophy of Nietzsche*. New York: Random House, 1927.

————. *The Will to Power*. Translated by Walter Kaufmann and R. J. Hollingdale. New York: Random House, 1967.

Nivelle, Armand. *Kunst- und Dichtungstheorien zwischen Aufklärung und Klassik*. Berlin: Walter de Gruyter, 1960.

Nohl, Herman. *Stil und Weltanschauung*. Jena: E. Diederichs, 1920. Reprint of two earlier essays: "Die Weltanschauungen der Malerei" (1908), and "Typische Kunststile in Dichtung und Musik" (1915).

Ortega y Gasset, José. *Concord and Liberty*. Translated by Helene Weyl. New York: Norton & Co., 1963.

Palmer, Richard E. *Hermeneutics: Interpretation Theory in Schleiermacher, Dilthey, Heidegger, and Gadamer*. Evanston: Northwestern University Press, 1969.

Panofsky, Erwin. *Meaning in the Visual Arts*. Garden City, N.Y.: Doubleday, 1955.

Petersen, Julius. *Die Wissenschaft von der Dichtung: System und Methodenlehre der Literaturwissenschaft*. 2nd ed. Berlin: Junker und Dünnhaupt, 1944.

Pöggeler, Otto. *Der Denkweg Martin Heideggers*. Pfullingen: Neske, 1963.

Rader, Melvin, ed. *A Modern Book of Esthetics*. 3rd ed. New York: Holt, Rinehart & Winston, 1965.

Radnitzky, Gerard. *Contemporary Schools of Metascience*. 2 vols. 2nd revised and enlarged ed. New York: Humanities Press, 1970.

Richards, I. A. *Principles of Literary Criticism*. New York: Harcourt, Brace and World, 1925.

———. *Science and Poetry*. Rev. ed. London, 1935.

Rickert, Heinrich. *Kulturwissenschaft und Naturwissenschaft*. 3rd ed. Tübingen: J.C.B. Mohr, 1915. Translated by George Reisman, as *Science and History, A Critique of Positivist Epistemology*. Princeton, N.J.: Van Nostrand Co., 1962.

Rickman, H. P. *Understanding and the Human Studies*. London: Heinemann Educational Books, 1967.

Riegl, Alois. *Gesammelte Aufsätze*. Ausburg-Wien: Dr. Benno Filser Verlag, 1929.

Rodi, Frithjof. *Morphologie und Hermeneutik: Zur Methode von Diltheys Aesthetik*. Stuttgart: Kohlhammer, 1969.

Rothacker, Erich. *Logik und Systematik der Geisteswissenschaften*. München: R. Oldenbourg, 1965. First published in 1927.

Ryle, Gilbert. *The Concept of Mind.* New York: Barnes & Noble, 1961.

Sartre, Jean-Paul. *The Psychology of Imagination.* New York: Citadel, 1961.

Sauerland, Karol. *Diltheys Erlebnisbegriff: Entstehung, Glanzzeit und Verkümmerung eines literaturhistorischen Begriffs.* Berlin: Walter de Gruyter, 1972.

Scheler, Max. *Vom Umsturz der Werte.* Vol. II. Leipzig: Der Neue Geist, 1923.

Scherer, Michael. "Wilhelm Dilthey und die Wissenschaft von der Dichtung." Inaugural Dissertation, Ludwig-Maximilians-Universität, München, 1950.

Schleiermacher, Friedrich. *Werke.* Leipzig: Felix Meiner, 1911.

Sjaardema, Hendrikus. "A Critical Examination of the Concept of Understanding in the Psychologies of Wilhelm Dilthey, Eduard Spranger, and Karl Jaspers." Ph.D. Dissertation, University of Southern California, 1939.

Spiegelberg, Herbert. *The Phenomenological Movement: A Historical Introduction.* Vol. I. 2nd ed. The Hague: Martinus Nijhoff, 1965.

Stein, Arthur. *Begriff des Verstehens bei Dilthey.* 2nd ed. Tübingen: J.C.B. Mohr, 1926.

Stover, Robert Capner. "An Introduction to Wilhelm Dilthey's Philosophy of Experience." Ph.D. Dissertation, Columbia University, 1954.

Suter, Jean-François. *Philosophie et histoire chez Wilhelm Dilthey.* Basel: Verlag für Recht und Gesellschaft, 1960.

Tartarkiewicz, Wladyslaw. *Nineteenth Century Philosophy.* Translated by Chester A. Kisiel. Belmont, California: Wadsworth Publishing Co., 1973.

Thévenaz, Pierre. *What is Phenomenology? and Other Essays.* Edited by James Edie. Chicago: Quadrangle Books, 1962.

Tumarkin, Anna. *Methoden der psychologischen Forschung.* Leipzig: B. G. Teubner, 1929.

Tuttle, Howard Nelson. *Wilhelm Dilthey's Philosophy of*

Historical Understanding: A Critical Analysis. Leiden: E. J. Brill, 1969.

Unger, Rudolf. *Literaturgeschichte als Problemgeschichte, zur Frage geisteshistorischer Synthese, mit besonderer Beziehung auf Wilhelm Dilthey.* Berlin: Junker und Dünnhaupt, 1924.

Wach, Joachim. *Die Typenlehre Trendelenburgs und ihr Einfluss auf Dilthey.* Tübingen: J.C.B. Mohr, 1926.

Walsh, W. H. *An Introduction to Philosophy of History.* London: Hutchinson & Co., 1955.

Walzel, Oskar. *Gehalt und Gestalt im Kunstwerk des Dichters.* Berlin: Akademische Verlagsgesellschaft Athenaion, c. 1923.

Wellek, René. *Concepts of Criticism.* New Haven: Yale University Press, 1963.

Wild, John. *The Radical Empiricism of William James.* Garden City, N.Y.: Anchor Books, 1970.

Wimsatt, W. K. *The Verbal Icon: Studies in the Meaning of Poetry.* New York: Noonday Press, 1954.

Winch, Peter. *The Idea of a Social Science and Its Relation to Philosophy.* New York: Humanities Press, 1967.

Wölfflin, Heinrich. *Principles of Art History: The Problem of the Development of Style in Later Art.* Translated by M. D. Hottinger. New York: Dover Publications, 1932.

Wright, Georg Henrik von. *Explanation and Understanding.* Ithaca: Cornell University Press, 1971.

Wundt, Wilhelm. *Völkerpsychologie: Eine Untersuchung der Entwicklungsgesetze von Sprache. Mythus und Sitte.* Vol. I, part 1. Leipzig: Wilhelm Engelmann, 1900.

Zech, Adolph. "Wilhelm Dilthey's Application of his 'Erlebnis' Theory to English Literature." Ph.D. Dissertation. Stanford University, 1937.

ARTICLES AND ESSAYS

Abel, Theodore. "The Operation Called *Verstehen.*" *Readings in the Philosophy of Science.* Edited by Herbert

Feigl and May Brodbeck. New York: Appleton-Century-Crofts, Inc., 1953, pp. 677–87.

Ackerman, James S. "A Theory of Style." *Aesthetic Inquiry: Essays on Art Criticism and the Philosophy of Art.* Edited by Monroe C. Beardsley and Herbert M. Schueller. Belmont, California: Dickenson Publishing Co., 1967.

Bergson, Henri. "Introduction to Metaphysics" (1903). In *The Creative Mind.* Translated by Mabelle L. Andison. New York: Philosophical Library, 1946.

Biemel, Walter. "Briefwechsel Dilthey-Husserl." *Man and World*, I, no. 3, 1968.

Bradley, A. C. "Poetry for Poetry's Sake." *A Modern Book of Esthetics.* Edited by Melvin Rader. 3rd ed. New York: Holt, Rinehart & Winston, 1960.

Danto, Arthur. "Causation and Basic Actions." *Inquiry*, XIII, 1970, 108–25.

Donoso, Anton, "Wilhelm Dilthey's Contribution to the Philosophy of History." *Philosophy Today*, XII, 1968, 151–63.

Ebbinghaus, H. "Ueber erklärende und beschreibende Psychologie." *Zeitschrift für Psychologie und Physiologie*, IX, 1895, 161–205.

Flach, Werner. "Die wissenschaftstheoretische Einschätzung der Selbstbiographie." *Archiv für Geschichte der Philosophie*, LII, 1970, pp. 172–86.

Fischer, Aloys. "Methoden zur experimentellen Untersuchung der elementaren Phantasieprozesse." *Zeitschrift für pädagogische Psychologie und experimentelle Pädagogik*, XII, 1911, 448–56.

Friess, Horace L. "Wilhelm Dilthey: A Review of his Collected Works as an Introduction to a Phase of Contemporary German Philosophy." *Journal of Philosophy*, XXVI, 1929, 5–25.

Gallie, W. B. "Explanation in History and the Genetic Sciences." *Theories of History: Readings in Classical and Contemporary Sources.* Edited by Patrick Gardiner. New York: Free Press, 1959, pp. 213–25.

Goebel, Julius. "Wilhelm Dilthey and the Science of Literary History." *The Journal of English and German Philology*, xxv, 1926, 145–56.

Gray, Bennison, "Stylistics: The End of a Tradition." *Journal of Aesthetics and Art Criticism*, xxxi, Summer 1973, 501–12.

Gutmann, James. "Wilhelm Dilthey: An Introduction." *Journal of Philosophy*, xliv, 1947, 609–12.

Heidegger, Martin. "Der Ursprung des Kunstwerkes." *Holzwege*. 4th ed. Frankfurt: Klostermann, 1963. Translated by Albert Hofstadter, as "The Origin of the Work of Art." In *Philosophies of Art and Beauty*. Edited by Albert Hofstadter and Richard Kuhns. New York: Modern Library, 1964.

Hesse, Mary. "In Defence of Objectivity." *Proceedings of the British Academy*, lviii, pp. 3–20.

Hodges, Herbert A. "Symposium on Phenomenology with Gilbert Ryle and H. B. Acton." *Proceedings of the Aristotelian Society*, Supplement to vol. xi, 1932.

Holborn, Hajo. "Wilhelm Dilthey and the Critique of Historical Reason." *The Journal of the History of Ideas*, xi, 1950, 93-118.

Horkheimer, Max. "The Relation between Psychology and Sociology in the Work of Wilhelm Dilthey." *Studies in Philosophy and Social Science*, viii, 3, 1939, 430–43.

Husserl, Edmund. "Philosophie als strenge Wissenschaft." *Logos*, 1, 1910–1911, 289–341. Translated by Quentin Lauer, as "Philosophy as Rigorous Science." In *Phenomenology and the Crisis of Philosophy*. New York: Harper & Row, 1965.

Isenberg, Arnold. "Critical Communication." *Aesthetics and Language*. Edited by William Elton. New York: Philosophical Library, 1959.

Janssens, Marcel. "Wilhelm Dilthey en de Oorsprong van de 'Geistesgeschichte' in de Duitse Literatuurwetenschap." *Revue belge de philologie et d'histoire*, xxxvii, 1959, 683–94.

Kamerbeek, J., Jr. "T. E. Hulme and German Philosophy: Dilthey and Scheler." *Comparative Literature*, XXI, 1969, 193–212.

Kolakowski, Leszek. "Historical Understanding and the Intelligibility of History." Translated from the French by Henry Beitscher. *TriQuarterly*, 1971, pp. 103–117.

Kornberg, Jacques. "Wilhelm Dilthey on the Self and History: Some Theoretical Roots of *Geistesgeschichte*." *Central European History*, V, 1972, 295–317.

Krausser, Peter. "Diltheys philosophische Anthropologie." *Journal of the History of Philosophy*, I, 1963, 211–21.

———. "Dilthey's Revolution in the Theory of the Structure of Scientific Inquiry and Rational Behavior." *The Review of Metaphysics*, XXII, 1968, 262–80.

Kuypers, K. "Mens en Geschiedenis bij Dilthey." *Algemeen Nederlands Tijdschrift voor Wijsbegeerte en Psychologie*, LIV, 1961–62, 61–75.

Landgrebe, Ludwig. "Wilhelm Diltheys Theorie der Geisteswissenschaften (Analyse ihrer Grundbegriffe)." *Jahrbuch für Philosophie und phänomenologische Forschung*, IX. Edited by Edmund Husserl. Halle a.d.S.: Max Niemeyer, 1928, 237–367.

Lieber, Hans-Joachim. "Geschichte und Gesellschaft im Denken Diltheys." *Kölner Zeitschrift für Soziologie und Sozialpsychologie*, XVII, 1965, 703–42.

Linge, David E. "Dilthey and Gadamer: Two Theories of Historical Understanding." *Journal of the American Academy of Religion*, XLI, December 1973, 536–53.

Marcuse, Herbert. "Das Problem der geschichtliche Wirklichkeit." *Die Gesellschaft*, VIII, no. 1, 1931, 350–67.

Masur, G. "Wilhelm Dilthey and the History of Ideas." *The Journal of the History of Ideas*, XIII, 1952, 94–107.

Meyer, Jurgen Bona. "Das Wesen der Einbildungskraft." *Zeitschrift für Völkerpsychologie und Sprachwissenschaft*, X, 1878, 26–40.

Pearce, Roy Harvey. "Historicism Once More." *Kenyon Review*, XX, 1958, 554–91.

Philipson, Morris. "Dilthey on Art." *Journal of Aesthetics and Art Criticism*, XVII, 1958, 72–76.

Rader, Melvin. "Art and History." *The Journal of Aesthetics and Art Criticism*, XXVI, Winter 1967, 157–68.

Rand, Calvin G. "Two Meanings of Historicism in the Writings of Dilthey, Troeltsch and Meinecke." *The Journal of the History of Ideas*, XXV, 1964, 503–18.

Ricoeur, Paul. "The Model of the Text: Meaningful Action Considered as a Text." *Social Research: An International Quarterly of the Social Sciences*, XXXVIII, Autumn 1971, 529–62.

Riedel, Manfred. "Wilhelm Dilthey und das Problem der Metaphysik," *Philosophisches Jahrbuch*, LXXVI, 2, 1968–69, 332–48.

Schapiro, Meyer. "Style." *Aesthetics Today*. Edited by Morris Philipson. Cleveland: Meridian Books, 1961.

Schmidt, Ferdinand. "Das Erlebnis und die Dichtung." *Preussische Jahrbücher*, CXXIII, Berlin, 1906, 201–19.

Taylor, Charles. "Interpretation and the Sciences of Man." *The Review of Metaphysics*, XXV, September 1971, 3–51.

Wellek, René. "Wilhelm Dilthey's Poetics and Literary Theory." *Wächter und Hüter, Festschrift für Hermann J. Weigand*. New Haven: Yale University Press, 1957, pp. 121–32.

Windelband, Wilhelm. "Geschichte und Naturwissenschaft." Reprinted in *Präludien*, vol. 2. Tübingen: J.C.B. Mohr, 1924.

Index

Abel, Theodore, 253n

Abrams, M. H., 160

acquired psychic nexus (*erworbener seelischer Zusammenhang*): active nature, 99, 100, 103, 104, 281, 298; articulation of, 156, 191–92, 194; breakdown in dream and insanity, 155–57; neither conscious nor unconscious, 99, 108, 281, 298; as controlling psychic structure, 98, 103, 109, 115, 168, 217, 281; as framework for explanation, 101; normative structure, 98, 100, 101, 108, 154; systematic intersection of inner and outer, 108–9

acts of consciousness: and contents, 283–84, 286–88; and objective reference, 283–88

Addison, Joseph, 85

aesthetic contemplation: criticized by Heidegger and Gadamer, 18, 371–74, 415; reflective potential, 19, 24, 229, 232–33, 373

aesthetic feeling: dependence on representation, 120; and interest, 122–23

aesthetic judgment, *see* reflective judgment, 232

aesthetic of history, 245; not contemplative, 19, 24, 25; and Kant's aesthetic of nature, 17; and Kant's artistic order of nature, 234–35; and the order of the human studies, 235; and reflection, 19, 24–26, 385–86.

See also anthropological reflection

aesthetic pleasure: in rational order, 83; and spheres of feeling, 118–19, 120–24

aesthetic point of impression, relation to stylistic unity, 114–15, 393

aesthetic principles: elementary and higher, 128–30; and spheres of feeling, 118–28; universal but partial, 128

aesthetics: central in development of Dilthey's thought, 15, 77; as evaluative, 9n, 360, 392; historical system of, 87; as meaning-oriented, 9n, 360, 373, 392; as a model human study, 15, 78; as reflective and interpretive, 373; three epochs, 82, 420

analysis: as focusing, 185–86, 201; relation to synthesis, 178, 184–85, 201; and typification, 23. *See also* articulation

analytic logic, and immanent form, 184–85, 191

anthropological reflection: and aesthetic of history, 385–86; and evaluation, 421; and our sense of life, 380, 392, 413; and reflective experience, 380

anthropology, relation to psychology, 55, 380

Aristotle, 197; Trendelenburg on, 47–48

Arnheim, Rudolf, 123

Aron, Raymond, 244

443

INDEX

causal relations, role in human
studies, 66, 98, 315–21. *See also*
explanation
causal system (*Kausalzusammen-*
hang), 315–16
classification, circle of: contrasted to hermeneutic circle,
340–42, 352; in human studies,
341–42; in natural sciences,
341–42
Clement of Alexandria, 47
Coleridge, Samuel Taylor, 16,
168–70
Collingwood, R. G.: artistic expressions not historically related, 407-8; and Dilthey, 15,
406, 409–10; expression theory,
407–10; history as the reliving
of thoughts, 408–9; history of
artistic problems, lacking, 407;
idealistic theory of history, 5,
409, 415
community, 64, 308; co-carrier
of historical life, 312; logical
subject of objective spirit, 313
comparative method, 206, 207; as
aesthetic, 372, 415; as morphological, 238, 241; and reflective
experience, 238–39, 415; and
understanding individuality,
254, 270–71
comparative psychology, 138,
250–53, 254, 256, 331; relation
to descriptive psychology, 206–
7, 221, 303; and understanding
history, 219–21, 236, 238; and
understanding individuality,
206, 239–40. *See also* "Ueber
vergleichende Psychologie"
Comte, Auguste, 4, 23, 37–38, 41,
62, 68
constructionism, *see* human studies
Copernicus, Nicolaus, 61
Corneille, Pierre, 348
creative process: artist's account
of, 79, 110, 150, 330; psychological analysis of, 89–90. *See also*
poetic imagination

Critique of Historical Judgment,
205, 245; relation to anthropological reflection, 380
Critique of Historical Reason,
7–8, 50–51, 322; relation to
Critique of Historical Judgment, 205, 244–45; and epistemology of the human studies, 17,
305; interdisciplinary nature of,
4; as Kantian, 21–22, 334–35;
and problem of critical standards, 3–4. *See also* "Entwürfe
zur Kritik der historischen
Vernunft"
Croce, Benedetto, 5
cultural sciences (*Kulturwissen-*
schaften): exclude psychology,
39; Neo-Kantian theory, contrasted to human studies, 39–44,
296. *See also* Cassirer; Rickert;
Windelband
cultural systems (*Kultursys-*
teme): relation to dynamic
systems, 321, 394–95; relation
to external organization of society, 63–68; logical subjects of
objective spirit, 313; as purposive systems, 63–68, 81; science and art contrasted, 79
cultural values, Rickert's theory
questioned, 41–42, 243, 403

Danto, Arthur, 5n, 6n
Dasein (existence), 370, 372, 374–
76
Descartes, René, 50, 269; axiomatic system, inadequate model
for human studies, 71; cogito
transformed by Kant, 173–74
description: of *Erlebnis*, 283,
289–90; completes *Erlebnis*,
289; and explanation, 251, 304,
389; and expression, 292; involves interpretation, 302;
methodological role in human
studies, 302, 304; of spheres of
feeling, 118–19, 124
descriptive psychology, 8; as proposed in *Einleitung*, 58–59, 90;

445

guished, 175–77, 179, 201; naturalistic meaning, 168; and synopsis, 171–72, 179, 183; as comprehensive totality, 176–77, 179, 191, 201

synthesis of the imagination: as productive, 182; as reproductive, 172–73, 182

synthetic disciplines, distrust of, 67

system of the human studies, *see* human studies

systems of modern aesthetics, one-sidedness of, 82

technique, *see* poetic technique

teleology, *see* purposiveness

theology, historical significance of, 47

Thévenaz, Pierre, 287

Tieck, Ludwig, 49, 156–57, 365

time: determinate-indeterminate category, 385; and *Erlebnis*, 387–89; as lived flux, 387–88; intuition of, 210–11, 386; and spatial analogies, 17

Tintoretto, 406

Trendelenburg, Friedrich Adolf, 46; influence on Dilthey, 47–48

Tumarkin, Anna, 136–37

Tuttle, Howard, 311–12n

type, as morphological, 241; as schema, 241; and the typical, 108, 112, 240–42, 393

"Typen der Weltanschauung und ihre Ausbildung in den metaphysischen Systemen, Die" ("The Types of World-View and Their Development in Metaphysical Systems"), 349–52, 363

typical, the: concreteness of, 112, 240–42, 405; and the imagination, 102, 108, 112, 158, 240–42

typology, abstractness of, 241, 254

"Ueber vergleichende Psychologie" ("Concerning Comparative Psychology"), 59, 206-7, 219–22, 238, 240

"Uebersicht der Poetik" ("Synopsis of the Poetics"), 356, 359–60, 364

understanding: author better, 266–67, 271, 329, 415; backward movement of, 328, 383, 418; circularity in, 174–75; distinct from contextual explanation, 337–39, 419; as definitive method of human studies, 80; discursive and intuitive, 6, 23, 57, 235, 247–48; divinatory, 265–66, 270–72, 336; elementary, 324–25, 327, 418; and empathy, 6n, 7, 252–53; and *Erlebnis*, 251, 256–57, 297; distinct from explanation, 80, 134–35, 215; higher, 325–28, 330; and interpretation, 255, 258; life out of itself, 368; musical, 362–63; and *Nacherleben*, 328–30, 361–62; of nature denied, 255; presupposes a sense of context, 174; proceeds from whole to parts, 135; replaces inner explanation, 134; self and others, 249, 250–51. *See also* hermeneutic circle, hermeneutics

Unger, Rudolf, 144

value: as a category of life, 381; cultural, 41; immanent in life, 41–42; and meaning, 247, 382, 385, 392, 421; of moments of life, 382; objective correlative of feeling, 119

Verstehen, see understanding

"Verstehen anderer Personen und ihrer Lebensäusserungen, Das" ("The Understanding of Others and Their Expressions of Life"), 322–31; on unity of *Erlebnis* and *Ausdruck*, 362–63

Volk (people, nation), explicated analytically, 162

Library of Congress Cataloging in Publication Data

Makkreel, Rudolf A   1939-
   Dilthey, philosopher of the human studies.

   Bibliography: p.
   Includes index.
   1. Dilthey, Wilhelm, 1833-1911.   I. Title.
B3216.D84M26   193   74-25620
ISBN 0-691-07200-0
ISBN 0-691-10032-2 (pbk.)